BEN LOVE

D1431869

NUMBER EIGHTEEN

KENNETH E. MONTAGUE SERIES

IN OIL AND BUSINESS HISTORY

Joseph A. Pratt, General Editor

BEN F. LOVE

BEN LOVE

MY LIFE IN TEXAS COMMERCE

foreword by JAMES A. BAKER, III

TEXAS A&M UNIVERSITY PRESS *College Station*

The paper used in this book meets the minimum
requirements of the American National Standard
for Permanence of Paper for Printed Library Materials,
z39.48-1984.
Binding materials have been chosen for durability.
∞

ISBN: 1-58544-489-8

Library of Congress Cataloging-in-Publication Data

Love, Benton F., 1924–
  Ben Love : my life in Texas Commerce / by Benton F. Love ; foreword by James A.
Baker, III. — 1st ed.
      p. cm.
  Includes bibliographical references and index.
    1. Love, Benton F., 1924–   2. Bankers—Texas—Biography.   3. Texas Commerce
Bancshares—History.   I. Title.
  HG2463.L68A3   2005
  332.1′092—dc22

                                                                    2005011568

CONTENTS

Foreword, by *James A. Baker, III* ix

1 Growing Up in Paris 1

2 Coming of Age during World War II 25

3 Growing Old over Europe 44

4 Back to the Real World 80

5 From Business to Banking 104

6 Downtown to Texas Commerce 117

7 Solidifying the Base, 1968–72 143

8 The Glory Years, 1972–84 168

9 A New Home for Texas Commerce 206

10 The Economic Downturn and Merging with Chemical Bank,
    1983–89 218

11 Striking a Balance: Investing in Politics and the Community 252

12 The Lessons of a Life 282

    Index 315

ACKNOWLEDGMENTS

This book would not have been written without Joe Pratt, Cullen Professor of History and Business at the University of Houston. He and Walter Buenger wrote the history of Texas Commerce Bancshares in the 1980s, and the resulting book (Walter L. Buenger and Joseph A. Pratt, *But Also Good Business: Texas Commerce Banks and the Financing of Houston and Texas, 1886–1986*, Texas A&M University Press, 1986) pleased us all. During that project, Joe said that my life would be instructive for young people going into business, a thought I initially dismissed. Then he encouraged one of his graduate students in the history department at the University of Houston, Lydia Osadchey, to begin to write my biography as the topic of her master's thesis. I agreed to be interviewed numerous times, and in the course of these sessions, Joe again took up the theme that my life story would be instructive for young people.

I finally gave in. With that, work began on a project that was increasingly to dominate my life. Several years into this labor, when family circumstances forced Lydia to lay down her work, Barbara Eaves picked it up, completed the research, and joined with Joe to help me draft and revise several versions of what had become my autobiography. If the book would not have been started without Joe Pratt, it would not have been finished without Barbara. She gained insight into the bank and an understanding of its place within the community during her twenty-three years as manager of employee communications at Texas Commerce. She was uniquely qualified for the job. She is a writer, she knew the bank, and she knew the players.

When the first draft was completed, Bruce LaBoon, managing partner of the Liddell Sapp Zivley & LaBoon law firm (now Locke Liddell & Sapp), and a man who, in the troubled days of the mid-1980s, traded a successful law practice for a bank executive salary, again gave (literally) the bank his professional skills. He carefully read the manuscript and offered invaluable advice and encouragement for which I am very grateful.

Jody Grant helped formulate our original merger policy; Walter Buenger helped write the centennial history of Texas Commerce. Both read the full manuscript and tactfully made suggestions that vastly improved the overall readability of the book. Photographer Joe Aker, who was Texas Commerce's virtual in-house photographer during the 1980s, not only opened his huge, well-organized files of negatives to us, but also converted the pictures we chose from his collection and others from our own scrapbooks into the format requested by Texas A&M University Press. Scores of other colleagues, customers, directors, business leaders, civic leaders, and friends spent countless hours answering questions, verifying dates, and digging up snapshots, for which I will be eternally grateful.

Finally, my boundless appreciation goes to my wife, Margaret, for a beyond-wifely, lifetime partnership that began when she learned to keep books at Gift-Raps and later positively entered into participating actively in the nightly social life of the wife of a bank CEO while mothering three children, Jeff, Jan, and Julie. Many times, it would have been easy for Margaret to say, "No more!" But she never did. She was a real trouper and she still is.

Ben F. Love

Ben Love represents everything that is good about America. He started life with little more than a bright, inquisitive mind, a healthy frame that eventually stretched to six feet four, and parents who cherished probity and education. Yet, through hard work, attention to detail, and unwavering optimism, he became an influential banker and a civic pillar who shaped his industry and his community like few others.

Ben epitomizes the men and women portrayed in Tom Brokaw's book, *The Greatest Generation.* Tempered by adversity during the Great Depression and World War II, motivated by the rewards our nation's system has to offer, Ben and countless other Americans of his era answered Franklin Roosevelt's challenge to make "a rendezvous with destiny." In his book, Brokaw referred to people just like Ben when he wrote, "The young Americans of this time constituted a generation birthmarked for greatness, a generation of Americans that would take its place in American history with the generations that had converted the North American wilderness into the United States and infused the new nation with self-determination embodied first in the Declaration of Independence and then in the Constitution and the Bill of Rights."

Brokaw's analysis squarely fits the story of Ben Love. Like so many of his era, Ben's life was shattered when the stock market crashed in 1929. His father's cotton brokerage business crumbled, as did his family's comfortable middle-class existence in North Texas. When Ben was eight years old, the Loves moved to a ramshackle family farmhouse in East Texas. His parents toiled long hours to scratch out a meager existence. But they wanted more for their son and were determined that he get a good education—even if this meant that his mother sell her engagement ring to buy the horse that carried him twelve miles round-trip to school in Paris, Texas. Ben's dedication to his books paid off when he won a college scholarship in debate.

Ben carried the Depression-era lessons he learned throughout his life. Existence is tenuous. Tough times are but another Black Friday away. Hard work can overcome hard knocks. A man's word should be as good as a government

---

* U.S. secretary of state, U.S. secretary of the treasury, and White House chief of staff for presidents Ronald Reagan and George H. W. Bush.

bond. Those lessons were reinforced during World War II, when he joined the Air Force during his sophomore year at the University of Texas. Smart and able, Ben was quickly promoted to a lead navigator for the Eighth Air Force, flying twenty-five combat missions over Hitler's Europe and earning eleven decorations. He saw firsthand the devastation of war. Friends died. He also gained the organizational skills that would serve him so well later in the private sector. Combat aboard a B-17 flying in one-thousand-bomber formations depended on precise planning. He did not forget that when he later entered the business world.

After the war, Ben returned to the University of Texas, worked hard, earned a bachelor's degree in business, and married his sweetheart, Margaret McKean. Now he was ready to take the next step—finding a place where more hard work would reward his pocketbook. As Ben writes, he "had become infatuated with Houston as a heady place of promise where, if you worked, you had some chance for material success. Houston was inclusive. There was energy here. Those businessmen were progressive and positive. They weren't jealous of each other." Houston was Emerald City for Ben.

Ben Love's business career in Houston is nothing short of remarkable. He started a successful company that revolutionized the packaging of gift wrapping paper. But the movers and shakers in Houston believed that the capable Ben Love could clear a higher bar. A sixteen-month stint as president of River Oaks Bank & Trust Company ended when he was forty-two, and Ben was named senior vice president of Texas National Bank of Commerce. In short order, he was promoted to president of Texas Commerce Bank, and by 1972, he was CEO of Texas Commerce Bancshares. Under his direction, the bank experienced rapid growth and expansion. During one stretch, the bank enjoyed sixty-five quarters of year-over-year earnings increases. During his administration, Texas Commerce grew from one bank to seventy-three member banks in twenty-eight Texas communities. Ben's account of those years of great changes in the state's banking industry is a fascinating read.

But, Ben's tale is more than the story of a banker—it is also the story of Houston. He prodded and nurtured the maturation of his city from an oil boomtown to a global hub of energy and commerce. In many ways, Ben extended the path laid out by a predecessor of his at the bank, Jesse Jones. Both seemed to understand intuitively Winston Churchill's observation that "the price of greatness is responsibility." Ben abided by Churchill's definition of greatness by helping build Houston. Look around the city and you will see the fruits of Ben's civic labor. His fund-raising efforts helped build the University of Texas M. D. Anderson Cancer Center. He played leadership roles in the construction of the city's light-rail line and in a new era of sports facilities. He helped bring top-notch people to his city, like Houston Grand Opera director David Gockley. Houston is a better place because Ben chose to live here.

My close friendship with Ben started in 1969, when he asked me to serve on the board of Texas Commerce Bank–Houston. At the time, I was a partner with the Andrews & Kurth law firm and not yet involved in politics. Partly because my father and grandfather had served in similar roles for precursor banks that eventually rolled into what everyone came to know simply as TCB, I agreed to his request. I also joined because I knew Ben Love was an innovative goal-setter who applied modern business principles to what, until then, had been a conservative world of banking.

Over the years, I developed a deep respect for Ben that went far beyond his professional abilities. This is a man who sticks by his friends. He is honest in his dealings. He possesses extraordinary drive and focus. When I was secretary of state, I believed that it was important for the United States to be respected by our allies and feared by our adversaries. I think Ben operated with this same principle in mind when he ran TCB. He was respected by his friends and feared by his adversaries.

In time, I came to appreciate another, more subtle, trait in Ben—an enduring quality that Brokaw says is common to those like him. Brokaw's observation focuses not on the accomplishments of those of the greatest generation, but on their unassuming response to them. "As they now reach the twilight of their adventurous and productive lives, they remain, for the most part, exceptionally modest," Brokaw writes. "They have so many stories to tell, stories that in many cases they have never told before, because in a deep sense they didn't think that what they were doing was that special, because everyone else was doing it, too."

In the twilight of his extraordinarily eventful life, Ben remains a truly modest man. His ego is no larger than the Depression-era farmhouse of his childhood. His humility is evidenced by the fact that Joseph A. Pratt, Cullen Professor of History and Business at the University of Houston, had to persuade him to write this autobiography. Ben doubted others would be interested in a life so similar to those of his contemporaries. In his mind's eye, Ben saw many of his tales as merely a collection of bedtime stories he told his children in order to teach them the merits of hard work. We are fortunate that

Ben heeded Professor Pratt's suggestion. Although Ben, modest as he is, may not acknowledge the importance of his stories, those who read his book will. Ben's story of hard work, ethical behavior, and dedication to family, business, and community is inspiring.

But this autobiography contains more than an interesting chronicle of an exemplary life. It offers lessons in leadership. Ben did what he thought was right, even when the choices were difficult. His tough decision on the merger of his bank, for example, provides a textbook lesson in leadership. It was not easy to give up control of the mammoth Texas Commerce Bank in 1987. But more important to Ben than where control of the bank rested was his commitment to protect the bank's shareholders, even when that meant merging TCB into an East Coast financial institution that had the wherewithal to weather the state's oil and real estate busts. At the same time, other Texas banks were failing because their leaders would not make the same tough choice. This type of decision making is a hallmark of leadership. Ben knew what to do, and he did it. By protecting his bank, he protected his city and his region. Throughout his life, he has shielded his country, his bank, and his community.

This compelling autobiography is the tale of a man as great as his city. The two grew up and prospered together. In the annals of Houston, he sits at the head table with the titans. Augustus Chapman Allen. John Kirby Allen. William Marsh Rice. Capt. James Addison Baker. Monroe Dunaway Anderson. Jesse Holman Jones. Ross Shaw Sterling. James Anderson Elkins Sr. Hugh Roy Cullen. Joseph Stephen Cullinan. Gus Sessions Wortham. George Herbert Walker Bush.

Benton Fooshee Love Jr.

I encourage people to read this autobiography, especially young Americans with aspirations of fashioning a "greatest generation" of their own. If they pay close attention, they will recognize that concepts like honor, responsibility, and perseverance are not simply lofty platitudes. Adherence to such virtues is a right way of life. Hopefully, future Americans will not face the same economic and global strife that tested Ben. But hard times and difficult decisions are unfortunately inevitable. The lessons from the story of Ben Love are remarkable, and they can serve us all.

BEN LOVE

I was born in 1924 in Vernon, Texas, a growing center of trade and commerce some two hundred miles northwest of Dallas. The 1920s were a time of optimism as an economic boom opened opportunities for more and more Americans. During my early childhood, my family seemed destined to lead a comfortable middle-class life. I do not remember the details about our life in Vernon or even about the promise of the 1920s, but I do remember how that promise evaporated with the Crash. I do remember how my mother and dad and I spent the decade of the Great Depression working hard to survive on my grandfather's small farm outside of Paris, Texas, and I do remember seeing my dad devastated by economic forces beyond his control. Those experiences have stayed with me my entire life, as did the values I learned while growing up poor during those hard times.

Both sides of my family had roots in the South; both had moved to Texas in search of opportunities. What I know about my father's father comes from family stories, a few old photographs and newspaper clippings, and his detailed Civil War military records that an Alabama attorney living in Washington, D.C., secured from the National Archives and mailed to me in 1992. I read my grandfather's military records at a time when I was most interested in understanding the impact of my military service in World War II on my own life. The parallels between our experiences some eighty years apart in two of the nation's major conflicts were of tremendous interest to me.

My paternal grandfather, Henry Benton Love, was born in 1839 and grew up near the small Alabama town of Athens on the outskirts of the larger city of Huntsville, a trading center just south of the Alabama-Tennessee border some one hundred miles west of Chattanooga.[1] His family had lived in the area for at least two generations. Unlike southern Alabama, with its large cotton plantations that used thousands of slaves, northern Alabama, where Henry Benton Love was raised, was in the "hill country," unsuitable for large-scale farming and, therefore, not dependent on slave labor. When the Civil War began, however, my twenty-one-year-old grandfather enlisted as a private in the Fourth Alabama Infantry, which became a part of the Army of Northern Virginia. His four years of service and the defeat of the Confederacy marked a turning point in his life.

Henry Benton Love saw heated action as an infantryman in thirty-three of the major battles of the war. His unit first marched to Harper's Ferry, Virginia, the site of a major Union arsenal. Slightly wounded at the First Battle of Manassas, he went on to fight at Chickamauga and Fredericksburg, where he suffered more serious injuries to his hands, face, and thigh from bombshell explosions. He was wounded a third time at the Battle of Spotsylvania Courthouse and engaged in action close to his grandfather's farm near Huntsville before taking part in the pivotal battle at Gettysburg, where his unit fought at Round Top.

He returned home after the war walking on a crutch. His fate is summarized in a note on the back of one of the few photos I still have of him: "When I got home, everything was burned. My sweetheart was waiting for me. We decided to go to Texas."

In the chaotic aftermath of the Civil War, he and his young wife, Louisa Fielding Love, made their way to northeast Texas, where they acquired a 154-acre farm outside of Hopewell, near the larger city of Paris, Texas, a farming center and the seat of Lamar County located about one hundred miles northeast of Dallas. There he settled down and began a new life.

After Louisa died in 1882, my grandfather married Mollie Fooshee of Paris in 1884. He had a total of twelve children from the two marriages. Large families were common among farmers in that day. Children were expected to help with the hard work of growing crops and livestock for food and raising cotton to bring in much-needed cash.

My father, Benton Fooshee Love, his father's tenth child, was born in 1887 and grew up on the farm near Hopewell. His mother died when he was only seven. A local newspaper article (undated, but probably from the late nineteenth century) about the family of H. B. Love includes a photograph of "the widower" and his twelve children. After reviewing my grandfather's service in the Civil War, the article concludes, "there is not a man in Lamar County who is held in greater esteem by his friends and neighbors." [2]

My father's life took an abrupt and difficult turn when Henry Benton Love became terminally ill. With his older half-brothers and half-sisters already living away from home in various towns in Texas and Oklahoma, my father, still in his early teens, became the "man of the house." He dropped out of

My father, Benton Fooshee Love Sr., before we moved to the farm in 1932 (Love family archives)

school and took care of the family, including one older sister and two younger ones. Their source of income was the farm. My father had grown up helping his father, and primary responsibility for the farm now passed to him. He met the challenge with a sense of duty and a well-developed work ethic that held the family together both before and after his father's death in 1912.

From the age of fourteen, my father, Benton Fooshee Love Sr., was an adult. He was a good farmer, particularly adept at raising and selling cotton. While still a young man, he had earned enough respect from the other farmers to be named Lamar County Cotton Weigher, a public position of considerable importance in a county so dependent on cotton.

In these years, he grew especially close to his youngest sister, Bess, and he provided her with a home until she married Oscar (O. K.) Allen, an engineer from Louisiana. Uncle Oscar met Bess while he was working on a project at Lake Gibbons, the lake near the Love farm that supplied Paris with its municipal water. After the project was completed, the Allens moved to Winnfield, Louisiana, finally freeing my father to leave the farm. An older

My mother, Nell Scott Love, about the time she married my father (Love family archives)

half-brother and half-sister had moved to Vernon, Texas, several hundred miles west of Paris, and my father relocated there to take a job buying cotton for Hyman Samuels Cotton Company, a Houston-based trading firm.

In June 1923, my father married my mother, Nell Scott, and they established their home in Vernon. She was one of nine children, born on a farm near Ladonia in Fannin County. While still in her forties, her mother died of diabetes in the days before insulin, and her father, William Scott, visited us only twice that I recall. The one time I especially remember was when I was about five or six. I had dug a hole at the base of our front porch steps to create a "lake" to collect water. When my grandfather—known in the family as "Poppa"—came out of the house, he stepped in the lake, fell hard, and broke his arm. My mother's sisters viewed me as one dangerous kid!

If my mother can be taken as representative of her side of the family, the Scotts were a determined lot with a passion for education. I do not know whether her ambition came from her mother or her father, and I do not know how much education her father had, but I do know that his three sons and six daughters revered him. My mother always had a total, complete dedication to her own education and to the American system of public education. Her dream was to teach in the Dallas school system, and she achieved that goal, teaching high school English there before her marriage. Quite unusual for her time and place, she also took supplemental summer college courses at Cornell University, Columbia University, and the University of Chicago. Her experiences at these well-established universities no doubt fueled her passion for the education of her only child, which was of prime importance to her. Many of my lasting memories of childhood are of her efforts to assure that I had the best opportunities available and that I took advantage of them.

My first eight years of life were in Vernon. My own memories of those years are rather limited but deeply engraved in my life's quest to excel. The town had about five thousand inhabitants in the 1920s, but because it was the county seat, the population swelled on Saturdays as Wilbarger County farmers came in to buy the goods and services they needed. Stores and banks lined the courthouse square, and the town had a well-developed school system where my mother taught second grade. We lived in a neat, one-story white house with a green manicured lawn and colorful flowers tended lovingly by my mother, with weekend help from Dad. Our yard regularly won awards as the "most beautiful" in Vernon. In these years, we even enjoyed the luxury of a family vacation, once driving all the way through Houston to the Gulf of Mexico at Galveston.

My dad bought cotton from farmers in West Texas and Oklahoma. In those days, cotton was king in Texas, just as timber had been—and oil would become—a dominant commodity that shaped the state economy. Cotton, which remained labor intensive until the coming of mechanized harvesting after the 1930s, was the central economic pursuit of hundreds of thousands of farmers in the region who grew, picked, and sold it as their cash crop. My dad and hundreds of men like him played a central role in connecting the regional cotton farmers with broader markets. The cotton they bought was shipped down through the Port of Houston to customers all over the world. In the process, cotton prices, crops, and markets influenced positively—or negatively—the health of diverse enterprises, from retailing to real estate, throughout Texas.

My dad's job required him to drive a lot, so his company supplied him with a shiny new Chevrolet each year. The car my parents owned was a plain black Model T Ford sedan, just like most of the cars on Vernon's uncrowded streets. My father, who had worked hard to secure a place for his family off the farm and in the middle class, must have felt justifiable pride in himself, and the new shiny company car no doubt was a symbol of his success.

★ THE GREAT DEPRESSION

After I turned seven, I knew something was happening that worried my parents frightfully. My mother no longer taught school; my father no longer bought cotton or went on long business trips. One day, he drove his shiny new Chevrolet to company headquarters in Houston, left it there, and re-turned to Vernon on a Greyhound bus. The company he worked for had—like so many—gone out of business, and my father no longer had a job. The Crash and the Great Depression that followed put 20 percent of this nation's able-bodied men out of work. They could find no jobs, and their families suf-fered accordingly.

The price of cotton dropped from twenty-nine cents a pound to six cents a pound in an eighteen-month period from 1932 through mid-1933, which was catastrophic for the Texas economy. The Port of Houston had been ex-porting from one million to more than two million bales of cotton each year through 1935, and this export volume plunged by more than half by 1940.[3] Such a destructive blow to the state's major industry fed a downward spiral in the economy as a whole. Retail stores in San Antonio went out of business, real estate values in Dallas plunged, and so it was throughout Texas. Gloom and doom were everywhere as I grew up during the Great Depression.

My father believed that he really understood the cotton business, so after the Hyman Samuels Cotton Company closed and he lost his job, he collected what money our family could scrape together and invested all of it in the cot-ton futures market, betting cotton prices would rise. But the price of cotton continued to plummet. Worse yet, the bank in Vernon where my parents had their remaining savings went under. In the days before the Federal Deposit Insurance Corporation, a bank's failure would wipe out its depositors. It was the final blow for our family.

The financial cost was tragic, but the human cost was even worse. I have never forgotten the stark reality of what happened to my father, even to this day. I was not old enough to talk with him about his thoughts, but I think the spirit was taken out of him. Life was never quite the same for him. A muscu-lar, handsome man, about six feet two and 210 pounds, he had developed the quiet assurance of a self-made man. He lost that, along with his job, his savings, and his upward mobility at the onset of the Great Depression.

Yet choices still had to be made; lives had to go on. Like many other people who felt the sting of hard times, Mom and Dad turned to family for help. Fortunately, we had family members willing and able to provide assistance.

My father's youngest sister, Bess, enjoyed good fortune despite the economic dislocations of the times. Her husband, O. K. Allen, had prospered, becoming wealthy finding and producing oil near Winnfield, Louisiana. In 1918, Uncle Oscar served as the assessor for Winn Parish. There he met an ambitious young politician named Huey Long and joined a small group of local men who supported Long's initial campaign for public office, his successful run for a seat on the Railroad Commission of Louisiana.

Long's strong personality, oratorical skills, and driving energy impressed Uncle Oscar, who, according to my dad, responded to Long's urgent request for campaign funds with a meaningful five-hundred-dollar contribution—large in that era—that allowed Long to buy a Model A Ford and continue to travel from town to town speaking to voters. The early bond between the two men grew stronger. As Long ascended to the governorship of Louisiana in 1928, Uncle Oscar was elected to the state senate as part of the Long slate. Governor Long then appointed Uncle Oscar to the Louisiana Highway Commission, where he helped initiate and engineer a massive highway construction program that built new bridges and replaced many impassable dirt roads with concrete highways. "Long-Allen" signs throughout Louisiana identified and marked this new highway construction and helped solidify Long's political support.

When Long was elected to the United States Senate in 1932, Uncle Oscar also won a landslide victory for the governorship. As a Long loyalist, Governor Allen was expected to look after political affairs in Baton Rouge while Senator Long moved onto the national stage in Washington.[4]

Uncle Oscar and Aunt Bess thus had done quite well in Louisiana, financially and politically, while our part of the family experienced economic disaster in Texas. However, they remembered her big brother's care in the years after her father's death, and they stepped forward at a crucial time to repay this kindness.

My father left one morning from Vernon on a Greyhound bus headed to Baton Rouge to visit his sister. My mother told me that the purpose of the trip was to ask Aunt Bess to lend him enough money to buy the now-abandoned 154-acre Love family farm near Paris. Mother explained to her young son that Dad did not have enough money left to pay the mortgage on our nice home in Vernon. The only thing left to do was to move to the family's old farm, which was for sale at the distressed price of twenty-eight hundred dollars.

My parents could not and did not try to shield me. We became a unit of three in dealing with the problems resulting from the nationwide economic collapse called the Great Depression. I matured rapidly, emotionally and mentally, if not physically. Thus, before I had turned eight, I had learned what seemed to me to be a fundamental truth: nothing in life is guaranteed. Devastating times can erupt suddenly and with scant advance warning, destroying the plans and dreams of even hardworking people. For me, the key lesson of the downward spiral that plunged the nation into the Great Depression was simple: economic insecurity was a fact of life.

Dad returned from Baton Rouge and told us that Uncle Oscar and Aunt Bess had agreed to buy the farm and allow us to live there. We would leave for Paris as soon as we could pack. Two days later, in the summer of 1932, we climbed into our tightly packed Model T and began our journey to a new life . . . slowly. Always a cautious driver, Dad began the long drive, ambling down the narrow highway at thirty miles per hour.

★ A CITY BOY MOVES TO THE COUNTRY

As we neared the farm, the concrete highway gave way to a dirt road marked by deep ruts. We were all excited, but my mother's excitement faded visibly when she looked beyond the two giant cedar trees, which had been there when my grandfather first arrived on the farm after the Civil War, and viewed the small, unpainted, dilapidated house surrounded by waist-high weeds and covered by a roof with visible holes and missing shingles. In fact, she began to cry. Maybe the contrast to the neat home she had loved and left in Vernon overwhelmed her.

My dad gazed silently at the rundown house and the nearby smokehouse that was falling down underneath a huge walnut tree. Sheets of galvanized metal were missing from the roof of the barn. The barnyard and pasture were empty because the farm had no cows, horses, or mules. The barren peach and pear orchard to the left of the house was overgrown with weeds. Everywhere were signs that the farm he had run as a young man had been deserted and neglected. At every turn, we saw evidence of how quickly and thoroughly nature can reclaim an abandoned house in the country.

But my eight-year-old spirits were high! Upon seeing a yellow-breasted field lark fly by, I excitedly grabbed my Daisy air rifle, filled it with BB pellets, whistled to my collie Tip, and ran after the bird. The open spaces in this new world seemed to present unparalleled possibilities for a "city boy" like me.

★ A HARD LIFE ON THE FARM

It quickly became clear just how much our life had changed. In Vernon, the three essentials—food, clothing, and shelter—had been so readily available that we took them for granted. When we moved to the farm, those three necessities seemed unattainable without monumental effort and extraordinary luck.

As for the first essential, the nearest grocery store was in Paris, six miles away. Mom and Dad had barely enough money to buy staples such as milk and flour and a little gasoline for the car. On our first day at the farm, Mother spotted a plot of ground near the old house that she suspected had once been a garden. She and Dad immediately cleared the weeds and brush from the plot and began to plant vegetables. Then Dad turned his energies to the peach and pear orchard while Mother wrote to the Agricultural and Mechanical College of Texas (now Texas A&M University) and asked for all of its publications about growing vegetables, melons, and fruits.

After the first year, we grew more vegetables and fruit than we could use, and so we congregated with other farm families on Saturdays at Market Square in Paris to sell our excess produce to the people living in town. But Great Depression hardships had also visited the shoppers. They were unrelenting in their quest for ever-lower prices, and the Market Square's cash-strapped farmers became Saturday prey for townspeople who walked from wagon to wagon bargaining for cheaper prices. It became a "take it or leave it" process, very harsh and very serious. Yet Saturday's struggles on Market Square provided an indispensable—albeit small—trickle of cash for us during the summers.

At other times, Mother bartered these crops for services like medical care from the kindhearted Dr. Goolsby and speech lessons for me from the ablest teacher in Paris, Miss Henrietta Bentley. My mother determined that speech lessons would help me overcome shyness, and whatever speaking ability I developed in life originated from her deal with Miss Bentley for my Saturday speech lessons during our first three years on the farm.

Mother also supplied most of the second essential, our clothing, with her vegetable money. She would buy bolts of material and make her dresses and most of my clothes on a Singer sewing machine she had brought from Vernon. So serious was my mother about my education that she insisted that I wear to Hopewell rural school clean starched shirts and short pants similar to those worn by students in the Highland Park classes she had taught in Dallas before her marriage. Though my fancy homemade outfits forced me to learn to stand up to schoolyard bullies clad in blue denim shirts and striped overalls, they were also part of Mother's larger plan to demonstrate that she had different ambitions for me than those of the other parents of farm boys who attended my two-room elementary school in Hopewell.

The third essential, shelter, was the most difficult to come by. My father soon found enough tin to repair the roof, but it seemed to leak more each time he patched it. When it rained hard, Mother put out empty syrup buckets to catch the water as it cascaded through our porous roof.

At first, we had a woodstove for cooking and heating; after two years we were able to buy a Florence-brand kerosene stove with far superior heat controls. Mother's baked goods began winning blue ribbons at the Lamar County Fair. But both stoves together could not keep our house warm during the frigid gales of a North Texas winter. It was not a question of insulation. The old house had none. It was a question of holes. The house had settled unevenly through the years, leaving gaps in the walls. The cold wind whistled in!

Like most farms in Texas, ours was without electricity in the early 1930s, so we did not have a radio or electric fans. Until President Roosevelt's Rural Electrification Administration extended service to the farm four years after we moved there, kerosene lamps provided our only light. Thus, from the fourth through the seventh grades, I studied after dark under their dim glow. For refrigeration, we relied on an uninsulated icebox. The twenty-five-pound block of ice delivered each week from Paris quickly melted in the summer heat.

Of course, there was no running water. Throughout my boyhood in Hopewell, our household water came from a cistern that was supplied entirely by rainwater that flowed into it through gutters off the roof of the house—that is, when we had rain. For hot water, we heated the cistern's cool water in a bucket on top of the woodstove and then poured the warm water into a round metal washtub that served as our bathtub inside at night and as Mother's laundry tub outside during the day.

During our second summer on the farm, it did not rain for two or three months. Our cistern ran so low that the bucket went all the way to the bottom, then came up only half full with dirty brown water. It was obvious that the cistern had not been cleaned out for years and, with the water so low, Dad decided that now would be a good time to remedy that situation. We had no idea what else besides muddy water might be at the bottom of that pit. Even animals and snakes could have fallen in!

At nine years old and by far the smallest member of the family, I was the logical candidate to climb into the bucket and be lowered to the bottom to clean out the cistern. The job was vital to the family's well-being, and I took it on with a sense of adventure mingled with pride. How many other nine-year-old boys had been lowered into a deep, dark hole perhaps filled with dead animals—maybe even live snakes—and where the only light that entered its five-foot diameter came from an opening twenty-five feet above?

Using a short-handled hoe and a spade, I filled the bucket with mud and shouted for Dad to pull it up to the surface. He poured out the mud and lowered the bucket back down to me, where I waited to do the same thing again. I remember the feel of the soft, cool muddy ooze on my bare feet and the strange echo in the bottom of the cistern as I yelled up to Mother and Dad.

When Dad pulled up the first bucket, I made the mistake of looking up and got a face full of slimy mud. Time and again, I was drenched by mud as my father pulled up bucket after bucket of slime from the bottom of the cistern.

At lunchtime I rode up in the bucket and emerged blinking in the bright sunlight, covered with mud from head to toe. Mother and Dad, who seemed not to recognize me for a moment, used a little of their precious clean water to wash off a bit of the mud before feeding me lunch topped off by my favorite dessert, brown caramel pie.

We finally finished late that afternoon. I was so tired I could barely stand, but the floor of the cistern was clean. If dead rats or cats had been there, I had shoveled them into the buckets with everything else. I felt wonderful. I had helped my dad do a job he could not do by himself. That was the first day of my life that I had performed sustained adult labor, and I felt the sense of achievement that comes from a hard day's work well done.

Even the best efforts of our three-member family could not, however, fix the many problems with our dilapidated house. During our third summer on the farm, my parents decided to find some way to build a new house, and again they turned to Aunt Bess and Uncle Oscar. Dad hoped to persuade them to lend us eight hundred dollars. Dressed in his best clothes, Dad drove our Model T Ford to Paris and boarded the Greyhound bus for the governor's mansion in Baton Rouge. In her customarily thorough manner, Mother had already solicited estimates from out-of-work carpenters who almost begged to be given the job. Grown men working as day laborers were happy to be paid a dollar a day—plus lunch—for toiling from sunup to sundown.

Because we had no telephone and telegrams were not delivered from Paris to our farm, we had to wait five long days to learn our fate. Finally, Dad stepped off the bus from Baton Rouge with a smile on his face and a bounce in his step. He also wore an expensive, handsome suit, compliments of Uncle Oscar, who had handed down some of his old suits. Dad happily gave Mother a check for eight hundred dollars. Thanks to the help of family, a new house was no longer just a dream.

Soon our sparkling new four-room, square home arose on the exact spot behind the two tall cedar trees where my grandfather had built his original farmhouse after the Civil War. My parents and I had shared the only bedroom in the old house; now I had my own room. The new house also had a bedroom for my parents, a kitchen with a small dining table attached to one wall, and a living room dominated by the Victrola we had brought from Vernon. Its cabinet was filled with nothing but Mother's precious opera records that featured such soloists as Lily Pons, Madame Ernestine Schumann-Heink, and Enrico Caruso.

The glory of the house was its newness. It even smelled new. The paint was clean and fresh. Mother papered the living room and their bedroom with cheerful flowers; she papered mine with rich brown and orange stripes. The colors contrasted starkly with the drabness of our previous surroundings. All three of us were elated. Since the 1930s, I have moved into several homes, including my current home in the upscale River Oaks section of Houston, but none has ever filled me with the same excitement as that new four-room square home in Hopewell.

As we struggled to secure food, clothing, and shelter, my father worked hard to grow cotton on much of our 154-acre farm. With only two mules and little equipment, this was a big job. I helped with the work, especially when it came time to pick the cotton. We also had the help of a hired hand named Charley Harris, who earned a dollar a day by assisting with the planting and harvesting of the crop. Itinerants, who picked most of the crop, were paid a set rate per hundred pounds of cotton picked. Our farm was by no means the smallest in the region; our hard work was by no means uncommon. People throughout Lamar County, Texas, and the South as a whole, struggled mightily to make money by raising cotton during the Great Depression. Before mechanization revolutionized cotton farming, this was literally a hard row to hoe. My father's days behind our mules were far more physically demanding than his earlier days behind the wheel of his company car. Indeed, our new life on the farm demanded adjustments from the entire Love family.

★ EDUCATION: THE TOP PRIORITY

Our move to Paris did not change Mother's primary focus—assuring that I had the best education possible under the circumstances in which we lived. Given her own background, she knew firsthand that a good education could broaden my horizons as well as my choices in life. Above all else, she believed that my escape from the poverty of the Great Depression depended on the quality of my education. She played an active role in finding the best available options for me in Hopewell and in Paris, but her "tough love" creed made it implicit that it was *my* job to study and be fully responsible for my results.

The fall after arriving on the farm, I entered the fourth grade at the Hopewell School. Each school day, I walked about a mile from our farm down a dirt road to the two-room structure. In one room, one teacher instructed about twenty students in the first through the fourth grades; in the other room, the principal taught twenty or so students in grades five through nine. No one expected a Hopewell farm child to "waste time" going to school beyond the ninth grade. After all, an education did not teach boys how to farm or girls how to keep house. The boys also reasoned that school was for children; freed from its demands, they could be doing "man's work," helping their fathers plow the fields.

My mother had different plans for me. Her passion proved to be contagious: early on I began to see myself as different. One day the principal asked each boy what he aspired to do when he grew up. The answers were all the same: "I hope to be a farmer like my old man." When it came my turn, I answered rather shyly that I wanted to be an inventor. At that, the class bully whirled around in a flash and snarled at me, "An inventor! I can eat anything you'll ever invent." At first, I was terribly embarrassed, but later I wondered if my classmate was scared of the world, scared to try anything new or different, and was trying to scare me so that I would be afraid to try to improve my future, too. Even as a nine-year-old new boy in school, I had begun to share Mother's belief that I was destined for a future that would take me far beyond Hopewell.

During my fourth and fifth grade years at Hopewell, I learned—often the hard way—about ignorance and bullies and limited horizons. However, my mother, with her motivating encouragement, planted the seeds of ambition in me. The desire to achieve more helped me overcome two trying years as the tall, skinny new boy from the city in a country school full of farm children.

A trip to see my relatives in Louisiana during my tenth summer encouraged those seeds to take root and grow. After two years of adjusting to the hard life on the farm, I received a letter from Aunt Bess in Baton Rouge inviting me to spend a week with my cousin Asa Benton Allen, who was then nine. The contrast between the luxury of the governor's mansion and our situation in Hopewell drove home to me the importance of education in expanding my options in life.

Uncle Oscar and Aunt Bess sent their chauffeur to Hopewell to pick me up in their personal Pierce-Arrow touring sedan. When that long, black, shiny, expensive car rolled into the farm's dusty driveway, I was so overwhelmed that I experienced severe qualms about climbing in and leaving my family behind. I had never before been outside of Texas. My rather solitary life on the farm had made me self-sufficient, but I now feared that I did not have the clothes and social graces required to mix with my cousin and his friends.

Would my meager knowledge of the world embarrass everyone if my aunt or uncle asked me a question? I knew how to pick cotton, clean a cistern, milk a cow—but I also knew the deep humiliation of being poor. Above all else, I knew that my life-on-the-farm experiences had not equipped me to feel at ease and confident with those I would doubtless meet in the Louisiana governor's mansion.

As my dad stowed his battered suitcase filled with my freshly washed clothes in the limousine's vast trunk, I thought I noted mist in his eyes, but before I had time to look again, we were off and I was absorbed in the adventure of a long car trip over unfamiliar terrain. I learned that the friendly chauffeur, Jim, was a Louisiana state trooper assigned to drive for the governor's family. As we crossed the Texas-Louisiana border, we were met by two uniformed motorcycle police officers who escorted us all the way to Baton Rouge, sounding their sirens whenever traffic slowed our speeding sedan.

In about two hours we arrived at the large, beautiful mansion, guarded by white columns and surrounded by an acre of manicured green grass and colorful flowers. Armed guards admitted us through the gates. We parked in a basement garage and took an elevator up to the living quarters. My bedroom was enormous; it seemed almost as big as our entire four-room farmhouse. I had never seen a room so white. The lace curtains were white; the carpet, which sank like quicksand beneath my feet, also was white; the bedspreads were white and looked luxuriously expensive. Bouquets of fresh flowers brightened the room, as did two colorful sofas and the scattering of plush upholstered chairs. If my room could be this grand, I wondered what the remainder of the mansion must be like.

As a pleasant young maid named Mary unpacked my suitcase, Aunt Bess burst into the room and hugged me hard, making me feel welcome. After talking briefly about my parents she excused herself and said she would see me that night at dinner. My cousin Asa soon arrived and told me about movies we could see, horses we could ride, and places we could go.

He mentioned that Mary would be back soon to bathe us before dinner, then continued: "Pop always wants all of us to be seated in the dining room when he arrives. He is constantly rushing around, but at dinner each night the family gets together and it is usually fun unless Huey Long phones from Washington." Well, I had a hard time listening to what he said after the words, "Mary will bathe us." I could not imagine being bathed by the maid! I had bathed myself even before we left Vernon for the farm. I shuddered, a sense of growing apprehension fed by my customary modesty and shyness. Yet, I feared that if I protested too vigorously, I might appear ignorant if being bathed by a maid was the custom for boys my age in a governor's mansion.

Before I could decide how to resist, however, Mary admonished us both to hurry and prepare for our baths so she would not be blamed if we were late for dinner. The next thing I knew, Mary had Asa and me in a battleship-sized bathtub, scrubbing our backs. Asa laughed at my red face and totally delighted in my discomfort. He seemed to enjoy introducing me to an affluent life where maids cleaned your room, others laundered your clothes, someone named Mary bathed and helped dress you, chefs cooked your food and butlers served it, secret service and militiamen guarded you, and chauffeurs drove—all in stark contrast to the self-sufficiency of my life on the farm.

Dinner was another adventure. A huge chandelier hung over a long dining table filled with beautiful place settings on a white linen cloth. Mother's careful coaching on table manners was quickly replaced by sheer panic. I forgot everything. I feared that I would be exposed as a country bumpkin, and I deeply yearned to open the door and run back to the farm.

During the next seven days, I witnessed how people lived when their decisions and actions were not controlled by poverty. I observed how the ultimate power—political power—affected millions of people, including those who wielded it. This was my first exposure to substantial wealth and to a family that was simultaneously revered and feared because of its political power. Every day brought new revelations of how the other half lived, and I gradually relaxed.

On one particularly memorable day, while Asa was taking his riding lessons, I explored the mansion and wandered into the huge pantry quarters. The butler welcomed me and offered me a Coca-Cola. I thought he was offering to drive me to a store, because I had never seen Coca-Cola anywhere except in a grocery store. I thought such a trip would be fun, but I worried about the cost. My mother had given me three nickels to spend on the trip, and if I bought a Coca-Cola for a nickel, I would have only ten cents left. As I pondered my dilemma, the butler opened a refrigerator that held more Coca-Colas than I had ever seen—even in a grocery store! I was dumbfounded. I tried to decide what to do. Perhaps the butler was selling the drinks as a sideline to supplement his income. If so, I was certain they must be really high priced, perhaps even beyond my fifteen cents. Unable to sort out such possibilities, I awkwardly declined, excused myself, and retreated to my room to think through the situation alone.

The next afternoon I walked back down to the kitchen area and opened the door that led to the butler's quarters. To my discomfort, he was there, and he again offered me a Coca-Cola. Before I could decline, he took one out, popped off the cap, and thrust the frigid bottle into my hand. Red-faced with confusion and consternation, and intent on not appearing to be a beggar, I looked up before I took a sip and asked how much I owed him. He answered that I owed him nothing and that I could have another cold drink any time

I wanted one. I knew that I must have missed something. Did he see me as a poor relative, unable to pay? My fierce pride overcame even my desire to preserve the three nickels in my pocket. I knew the price of a Coca-Cola, even though I had bought only three or four in my life, and I pulled a nickel from my pocket, handed it to the butler, and thanked him for the drink. He thanked me in a friendly but confused tone, and I realized I had much to learn about manners and money.

That week in Baton Rouge gave me my first glimpse of a totally different world from that I had known and to which—like Cinderella—I would return in seven days. What I saw in the governor's mansion was not a fairy tale. These were real people, my three cousins, my aunt, and my uncle. Mother had always impressed on me the value of making excellent grades, but the rewards for doing so had never been clear in my mind. Now they were. For the first time in my life, I had seen with my own eyes a world free from the insecurity and limitations that defined my world. During those seven days, I was never more certain of my shortcomings, but I returned home more determined to amend those shortcomings and make something of myself.

★ "MAKE YOUR WORD AS GOOD AS A GOVERNMENT BOND"

Before I entered the sixth grade, my mother made a move that dramatically changed my education and my life. Deciding that I was not receiving an adequate education at the Hopewell school, she engineered my transfer into the much larger and better school district in Paris.

Her first hurdle was convincing school officials that I could do the work at West Paris Elementary School. She drove the Model T to the school, which was six miles from our farm, and spent the day lobbying the principal and two of the sixth grade teachers. The principal sympathized with my mother, but the teachers raised numerous objections. They reminded Mother that she would have to pay fifteen dollars per semester tuition because I would be coming from another school district. They also warned her that I would probably be moved back a grade as no Hopewell student could hope to do grade-equivalent work at their elementary school. But Mother persisted, pointing out that, as a former teacher, she was certain that I would make top grades at West Paris Elementary. She won her argument, and several weeks later we received a letter informing us that I could attend the school in the fall.

That was half the battle. Now we had to find a way for me to make the twelve-mile round trip each day. I had walked to school in Hopewell, but Paris was simply too far away, especially in the winter when frequent storms plagued the region. We could not afford the gasoline to make the trip by car, and often the dirt roads between the farm and the school became so muddy that our Model T would get stuck anyway. Mother's solution was simple. She sold her engagement ring for fifty dollars, and Dad scouted the area for a dependable horse. He finally found a wholesale grocer in Paris willing to sell a red pony named Billy, complete with saddle and reins, for fifty dollars.

I rode Billy home that day, trailing behind our slow Model T in a long trip back to the farm. After some initial concerns about Billy's health, we determined that we could count on him. We were right. He reliably got me to school and back for the next two years. We were not always on time when it was sleeting or snowing hard, but my teachers considered the fact that I was doing my best, both on the road and in the classroom.

Our routine was always the same. I awoke at six o'clock, dressed, and ate a breakfast of scrambled eggs, ham or bacon, and biscuits. As I ate, Dad fed and saddled Billy. Then I gathered my books from underneath the Aladdin kerosene lamp on the table where I had studied the night before, put them in a canvas bag, and hurried to the barn. Mother walked with me, carrying my lunchbox in one hand and my thermos in the other. Dad put my books into one saddlebag and my lunch into the other, opened the barn gate to the pasture leading to the dirt road, and off Billy and I would go. The pleasant interlude of this morning ritual fortified me as I headed off to school. Looking back, I understand more clearly the love and encouragement embodied in my parents' concern for me each morning.

The six-mile ride also quickly became a routine. Billy and I passed out of our pasture, through a gap to Tigertown Road, across the Pine Creek Bridge, and to the edge of West Paris. From there, I led him to a small barn within walking distance of the school, where I unsaddled him and gave him water and hay. After school, we reversed the trip, often returning home near dusk.

However, this routine proved anything but routine when the weather turned cold or rainy or both. In 1936, the coldest winter in years blew through North Texas, blanketing the fields with snow and ice, but West Paris Elementary School was open every day, blizzard or no blizzard. Those who lived in the city had little trouble getting to school, but the roads to and from our house were terrible. When Dad protested that it was too cold for me to ride

Billy, Mother countered that she would wrap me with enough layers of clothes so that I would not freeze. When she took such a firm stand, Dad always complied.

And so, all through the winter of 1936, Billy and I regularly faced cold rain, sleet, and snow driven by howling winds throughout our daily twelve-mile round-trip trek. The sleet cut into my bare cheeks, and poor Billy walked with his head lowered close to the frozen, rutted dirt road. His hoofs often slipped on the glass-like surface, but he never fell. Such trips took much longer than usual, but my teachers did not scold me for being late; in fact, on many frigid mornings they seemed surprised when I appeared at all.

Billy and I also survived the Great Flood of 1937. After four days and nights of rain, the shallow creek in our pasture roared out of its banks like Niagara Falls, but even "Niagara Falls" did not prevent West Paris Elementary School from opening on Monday. As before, there was no doubt about whether I would ride Billy to school. If school was open, I would be there. Our major obstacle was the Pine Creek Bridge. The storm had swelled the creek so much that the bridge's wooden plank roadbed was completely submerged. Billy and I edged warily forward. As we advanced, the water churned up above Billy's belly, threatening to push us against the bridge's steel guardrail or, worse, over the rail into the swirling creek. Turning back was no option, so we moved forward, one step at a time, with no alternative but to make it over the bridge. We made it! And when Billy's hoofs finally hit land, we both shuddered in joyful relief.

My grades continued to be straight As, which pleased Mother and me. I guess my teachers were pleased, too, because near the end of my sixth grade year the principal called me into his office and told me that he and the West Paris teachers had chosen me to be president of the seventh grade class when school convened in the fall. I certainly had not anticipated such an honor!

The climax of graduation week at West Paris Elementary was the seventh grade play. Each year the class president was assigned the lead role. And each year parents, grandparents, uncles, aunts, cousins, friends, and classmates packed the spacious West Paris Auditorium for the major school event of the year.

My class chose to perform *The Stirring Life of William Penn*. We rehearsed for weeks. Nearly everyone in the seventh grade had a part, but the action revolved around William Penn (me), so I memorized not only my own lines, but the lines of everyone else. As the lead, I felt responsible for the play's success, and my classmates and teachers seemed happy that I accepted this responsibility.

The play was to be performed on the final Saturday night before graduation. On Friday, about midnight, a gentle rain began to fall. On Saturday morning, the heavens opened and unleashed a deluge that seemed intent on drowning everything on earth! By Saturday noon, Dad told Mother that the Tigertown Road was impassable for the six-mile trip into town. Our alternative was an eight-mile drive on the asphalt Sumner Road, but we lived two miles from the Sumner Road, and the flood had made the dirt road leading to it as impossible to drive as the Tigertown Road. However, two miles of mud was shorter than six miles of mud, so the choice was clear.

Now, Dad was born before the automobile was invented. He grew up with the automobile. Always visibly muscular and effortlessly coordinated, Dad could drive his old Model T through Hopewell's deep ruts and mud as smoothly as a golf pro could swing his two-iron on St. Andrew's windswept Old Course. But despite his experience, skill, and confidence, he told Mother at 5:00 p.m., two and one-half hours before curtain time, that even the two-mile dirt road to Sumner Road was impassable. He felt sure the play would be rescheduled due to the drenching rain. And he began to take off his gray tweed suit.

Mother became very, very quiet. I learned early in life that, when Mother became noticeably silent, there was much truth to the saying, "the quiet before the storm." Suddenly, she turned to Dad and declared, "Those people in Paris drive on concrete streets, Benton. They don't even know it is raining. The play will go on as planned, and it is our responsibility to get our son there. Everyone is depending on him. Our family's honor is at stake! We gave our word to Mr. O'Brien that he could depend on us, and our word must be as good as a government bond!"

Well, Dad knew the decision had been made. I had to be at the West Paris Auditorium before 7:30, and he had to get me there. He donned his old work clothes. Resigned, he told Mother that he would hitch Rough and Rowdy (our two mules) to the wagon, then chain our Model T to the wagon and try to pull the car the two miles through the mud to Sumner Road. Mother and I climbed into the Model T; Dad sat in the wagon, drenched to the skin, his prematurely gray hair limply hanging over his forehead. And slowly, our wagon-car procession began to move. I have always wondered what he was thinking at that moment as he held Rough and Rowdy firmly with the reins.

We arrived at Sumner Road at 7:00 P.M., just thirty minutes before curtain time. All three of us knew the teachers must be wild with anxiety about whether we would be there by 7:30 — or at all. Dad quickly pulled the chain from the car; Mother roared off toward school at thirty-five miles per hour, determined to get me there in time. Out of the rear window, I saw Dad standing in the rain waving to us.

When we arrived and breathlessly rushed in, at about 7:28, Mr. O'Brien hugged us both. I had never seen him emotional before. But that stormy night, he was emotional as he said, "I announced to the audience a moment ago that this terrible storm might delay you, but that I was sure you would arrive because you were dependable people." But the audience never knew about the family drama, starring my determined mother and my compliant father, that was still unfolding a scant two minutes before the first curtain went up.[5]

Throughout my childhood, Mother repeated the standard of honor, character, and responsible behavior she had learned from her father, William Scott. That standard was encapsulated in a single sentence, oft repeated: "Make your word as good as a government bond." For the rest of my life, this single experience of defying the weather and getting to the play on time influenced my actions, my acceptance of duty, and my determination to follow my Mother's and Dad's example by making my word "as good as a government bond."

★ LEARNING THE BASIC PRINCIPLES
OF LEADERSHIP AT PARIS HIGH SCHOOL

After seventh grade, I moved up to Paris High School, a change that required numerous adjustments. The high school was in downtown Paris and could not be reached by a quiet side street suitable for riding Billy. Nor was there a barn nearby. My transportation to school again became Mother's problem, and she attacked it with her characteristic blend of determination and activism. She learned that Texas law required Lamar County to run a school bus to surrounding rural areas that were without a four-year high school if a minimum of forty parents in those areas signed a petition demanding bus service to the "consolidated" high school (in Paris). Facing skepticism from many of the parents in Hopewell, she nonetheless set about the task of collecting signatures within that ten-mile radius. Driving from farm to farm at night after the chores were done, she finally convinced forty farmers to sign her petition. Her progressive action and her courage in the face of sometimes nasty opposition provided high school educations for many who otherwise would have been denied the opportunity.

In the fall of 1937, I began a new daily routine. Now instead of the six-mile horseback ride to school, I walked two miles to the store that served as the school bus stop en route to Paris High School. However, my school days remained much the same: I was on a mission to prove that I belonged, to justify my mother's confidence in me. Excellent grades continued to be the measure of my progress. I made a determined and successful effort to earn high marks as a symbol of my transition to high school and continuing quest for an education.

There were personal adjustments as well. PHS had about eleven hundred students, and I was not accustomed to so many people. Living isolated on the farm, I knew relatively few other students, and my natural reserve and shyness prevented me from making friends easily. I remained focused in the class, and at noon I would return to the school bus to eat the sandwiches Mother had prepared for my lunch.

In my sophomore year, I began to gain more confidence and standing with my classmates, in large part through participating in debate. The speech lessons my mother had bartered vegetables for with Miss Henrietta Bentley provided me with a foundation, but a redheaded history teacher named Katie Feeser steered me toward the debate contests that gave me the forum to improve my public speaking.

I discovered an aptitude and a passion for debate. My partner Sam McClure and I traveled as far as Dallas, Waco, and Tyler to tournaments where we more than held our own against teams from larger schools that boasted more highly developed debate programs. As we won debates, I lost some of my shyness and began to work harder to get to know my classmates. To my surprise, I was elected vice president of the PHS sophomore class. That was quite something for a boy who rode a bus to school each day and could not, therefore, participate in the town's teenage social events.

In my junior year, I devoted myself to study and debate, and Sam and I won most of our matches against other schools. One day, after hearing me speak to the local Rotary Club, the manager of the Paris radio station asked me to try out as an announcer. I passed the test and worked four hours a day that summer as an announcer at Paris's only radio station, KPLT ("Keep Paris Leading Texas"). Despite all this, and the fact that my grade average improved to more than ninety-seven, I was not elected an officer of my junior class. This disappointment caused me to pause and wonder if I had concentrated on grades and debate so much that I had forgotten to pay attention to the other kids. Looking back on this episode, I realize that I was already beginning to form attitudes about the basic principles of leadership. High school obviously is different from later life, but not totally so. You still have to care sincerely about those around you and pay attention to them. You must be cheerful when you say hello and call people by name, but you also have to excel at something so that people look at you and say "he can really do that well." Otherwise, you are nothing more than a backslapper and glad-hander. I started to understand this facet of leadership after my junior year, and I was quite pleased that at the end of my senior year my class of 319 students elected me its "permanent president."

My senior year was a blur of activities. With a 97.3 average, I ranked seventh in my class. Sam and I won every major debate tournament before the district meet, including a major tournament in North Dallas. There, in the finals judged by three men from Dallas, we defeated the eventual state champions in their home auditorium. At the end of the year, the faculty chose me as the "Best All-Around Boy," which was considered the school's highest honor. This award confirmed that I had experienced a successful senior year, one that filled Mother and Dad with pride and bolstered me with new confidence in myself. And I needed confidence, because we continued to struggle with financial limitations so severe that they called into question whether I could attend college.

Pride and confidence would not pay for college tuition. My radio announcing job and a sales job at Sears provided me with my first-ever spending money, but it was far short of the amount I needed for college. The valedictorian and salutatorian of PHS were assured two-year scholarships to Paris Junior College, but I did not rank first or second in my class. I realized that all of my hard work and awards would be small consolation if I could not attend college. Without more education, my career would probably be a full-time sales job at Sears. I placed my hopes on receiving a debate or academic scholarship, and Katie Feeser, my debate coach, and Charles "Preacher"

Dickey, my pastor at Central Presbyterian Church, took the initiative to seek a college scholarship for me. I had come to idolize Charles Dickey after attending his church for four years. In fact, I had confided to Mother, and later to Dr. Dickey, that I was considering departing from my long-held ambition of becoming a lawyer in order to become a Presbyterian minister.

On the final day of classes, Miss Feeser burst into my Latin class, unable to conceal her excitement. Proclaiming that "Dr. Dickey is on the phone, and he has some wonderful news," she grabbed my arm and practically dragged me to the principal's office. Dr. Dickey got straight to the point. He said: "Dr. Wear, the president of Trinity University, has just advised me that Trinity is offering you a debate scholarship, full tuition paid, and has an afternoon job arranged for you in Waxahachie's large department store, Cheeves Brothers, that should pay enough to handle the cost of room and board." To my embarrassment, tears started running down my cheeks. I was going to college! Through choked sobs, I mumbled, "Thank you, thank you, thank you, Dr. Dickey."

NOTES

1. The city of Huntsville, Alabama, subsequently developed strong historical ties to Huntsville, Texas, a city about fifty miles north of Houston. The families of several prominent twentieth-century Houstonians, notably Gus Wortham and Judge James Elkins, had roots in Huntsville, Alabama, before migrating to Huntsville, Texas, and then on to Houston.

2. "Captain Henry Benton Love," *Paris Morning News,* undated newspaper article.

3. Walter L. Buenger and Joseph A. Pratt, *But Also Good Business: Texas Commerce Banks and the Financing of Houston and Texas, 1886–1986* (College Station: Texas A&M University Press, 1986), 112.

4. T. Harry Williams, *Huey Long* (New York: Alfred A. Knopf, 1969).

5. Ben F. Love, *Once Upon a Time . . . Memories of Life on the Farm,* Love archives, Houston. This is a series of anecdotes about the lessons learned while growing up on the farm, including the one entitled, "Make Your Word As Good As a Government Bond." These stories were recounted in the 1950s by Ben F. Love to his children and then written down for the next generation. A number of these episodes are related in this chapter.

I was sixteen years old when I left home for college in the fall of 1941, a young wide-eyed boy heading out into the world in search of education and opportunity. Over the next four years, I was educated in wholly unexpected ways. In rapid order, the national tragedy of Pearl Harbor focused my attention onto the outside world; then the personal tragedy of the death of my father forced my mother and me off the farm. Finally, the realities of service in World War II rapidly matured me, requiring adult behavior in a military environment. In the four short years from the time I left the farm for Trinity University until the end of World War II, I came of age. Indeed, between my sixteenth and twenty-first birthdays, I grew old far beyond my years.

The first step on this journey from home to adulthood came in September 1941 with my first trip to Trinity University in Waxahachie. Mother sent me off with Dad's huge black leather suitcase packed with freshly laundered clothes and an empty, fabric-covered shipping box for my dirty clothes. Postage to mail my clothes home to Mother cost much less than having my clothes laundered in Waxahachie.·

I naturally decided to hitchhike rather than spend any of my meager savings for a bus ticket. Catching a ride from Paris to Dallas would be easy, and Waxahachie was only thirty miles south of Dallas. The hard part would be getting through Dallas and onto the right highway to Waxahachie. However, the trip went smoothly. My parents dropped me off in West Paris on the highway to Dallas early that morning, and I arrived at Brooks Boarding House across from Trinity University in Waxahachie that evening in time for supper.

There I settled into my new life as a college student. My clean and spacious room had several windows, suggesting that it had been a living room before the house was converted for boarders. I shared my room with Hugh Johnson, another freshman. Mr. and Mrs. Brooks lived on the first floor across the hall from us; three upperclassmen occupied smaller individual rooms upstairs.

Trinity was a four-year college, but it had only three hundred and fifty students, about a third of the number who had attended Paris High School during my years there, and so I had no difficulty in getting acquainted. Most of the students were from small towns. Few worked, as I did during the school year, but most were not from wealthy families. I sold clothes at Cheeves Brothers department store from 1:00 to 6:00 P.M. daily. The pay was modest but invaluable in covering my expenses.

As I settled into a routine of classes, work, study, and debate, I quickly gained confidence that I could handle my new situation. My grades were fine; my debate partner, Victor Aubrey, and I enjoyed complete success in our tournaments; and I was elected president of the freshman class. I liked Trinity.

However, the serenity of life at Trinity, and everywhere else, was severely jolted on December 7, 1941. On that quiet Sunday afternoon, my roommate and I were studying in our room when suddenly we were distracted by a loud commotion upstairs. We ran up and found the three upperclassmen standing frozen, absolutely transfixed, around a small radio. The announcer reported excitedly in a shrill voice that Japanese bombers had launched a surprise attack on Pearl Harbor, inflicting heavy casualties and severe damage to the U.S. Pacific fleet there. The atmosphere of the school changed instantly. Most freshmen were seventeen or eighteen years old, and we sensed that our lives were about to change.

★ MY LAST TRIPS HOME

Christmas brought a welcomed relief. Even during the worst times of the Depression, Christmas had been a special time of celebration in our family, and I looked forward to seeing my parents for the first time since September. After hitchhiking from Waxahachie to Paris, I caught my last ride to the fork in the road leading past the Hopewell Cemetery to the farm, then rapidly walked the last two miles home. It was after midnight when I pounded on the back door. Mother and Dad were as overjoyed to see me as I was to see them.

This was a Christmas to remember. Mom fed me as if I had been the victim of a famine. Dad took me hunting for our Christmas goose. We walked together to the blinds he had built with corn and sugarcane stalks and waited there through the crisp morning for the birds to descend through the fog and prepare to land in his winter wheat field. I recalled that on such occasions as a child I had yearned for him to talk to me. I would say to him, "Dad, talk to me." And he would say, "What about?" But now we talked in a conversational manner, man-to-man, as if Dad sensed that I was really maturing. This was the only time that I can recall that we really talked. He seemed to enjoy me, and I assuredly enjoyed being with him. This vacation proved to be a special time for the two of us.

At night, we listened to news of the progress of the war on our Atwater-Kent radio.[1] Japanese military forces were moving unchecked throughout Asia; Hitler had conquered vast portions of Europe with Germany's Blitzkrieg and was posing a dire threat to Great Britain; the United States was rapidly rebuilding a military force that had only 5 armed and fully manned divisions as compared to Hitler's 168. But even those doses of reality could not dispel the special joy of that holiday season. When Mother and Dad drove me back to my "hitchhiking spot" on the Paris-to-Dallas highway on January 2, 1942, all three of us were as happy as I could ever recall.

Back at school, I immediately began preparing for my first round of college final exams. About a week before finals, the university president, Dr. Wear, sent word for me to come to his office, and there began a whirl of events that dramatically altered my life. He told me that my father was seriously ill and that my Presbyterian pastor, Dr. Charles Dickey, was driving from Paris to rush me home to see him. Preacher Dickey, notorious for driving fast, drove as if he had to beat a deadline, which, indeed, he did. He was a gregarious man, but we talked little. It was dark when we arrived in Paris.

Preacher and I walked through the hospital corridor and quietly entered Dad's room. He was lying in bed, asleep, breathing deeply and laboriously. The doctor explained that my father had become very ill suddenly with nephritis, an inflammation of the kidneys, and could not last much longer. He encouraged me to talk to him when he roused.

I sat in a chair beside the bed and gently took his large, strong brown hand in mine. After a couple of hours, he opened his eyes and saw me. He smiled, said he was glad to see me, and murmured that he was sorry he had become sick. With a tremendous effort, in a stronger and more deliberate voice, Dad told me, "Benton, I believe I am dying. Take care of your mother." His eyes closed again, but the worried lines on his face relaxed. I held his hand all night. The next morning, at age fifty-four, he died.

We buried him on a cold January day in the Paris Evergreen Cemetery plot that Mother had bought that week. About one hundred people attended the service at the Central Presbyterian Church, including O. K. Allen Jr., the oldest child of my Aunt Bess and Uncle Oscar, who had driven to Paris from Baton Rouge. After the funeral, O. K. Jr. told Mother and me that we could continue to live on the farm, which his mother owned, as long as we wanted to. However, if we chose to move, Aunt Bess would sell the farm and the livestock. Mother and I knew that we could not run the farm without Dad, so we told him that we would be moving.

That was a hard day for both of us. Mother had no husband. I had no father. We had no money. We had no home. But we did have each other, and my mother had always been an optimist and resourceful woman. I resolved to be equally strong, remembering my dad's final request of me. Even at the age of seventeen, I knew that Mother and I would find a way to survive.

What I could not fully understand, at that juncture of my life, was the giant hole that had been ripped in the fabric of my life. The loss of my father before his time—certainly before I was mature enough to confront the loss—staggered me. For one brief Christmas holiday, Dad and I had begun the process of building an adult relationship, and now that process had ended abruptly. I would try to take care of my mother, but sobering financial challenges confronted us: How would we live? What about the war? How would I complete my college education? The death of a parent usually brings with it an extended period of mourning in which to come to grips with the loss. Indeed, as I watched my own children grow up without the benefit of my father's presence, the sorrow that I felt at age seventeen returned to me many times, deeper and more profound than ever. Even today, so many years after my father's burial, a visit to his grave produces a sense of loss, a sort of sadness for the boy I was in 1942, standing on that spot contemplating the past and my uncertain future.

In our time of need after my father's death, help again came from family, this time from my mother's younger sister Mackie and her husband Fred Tacquard. They invited us to live with them and their two daughters in Austin with no charge for room and board. Uncle Fred, who was principal of the Texas State School for the Blind, assured me that he would help me gain admission to the University of Texas for the last half of my freshman year. He even volunteered to lend me twenty-five dollars for tuition and help me find a job. Uncle Fred was a saint. His entire family—including daughters Eleanor and Jane, my contemporaries—always made us feel welcome.

Late on the afternoon of the funeral, Mother and I drove her rattletrap

Model T Ford out to the farm for one last look. I walked past the house to the barn and patted Daisy and Dot, two of the oldest cows. Then I continued, pausing at the pasture pool, where I used to swim, surrounded by the willow trees that shaded croaking frogs, perch, catfish, and water moccasins. Slowly resuming my walk out into the pasture, I spotted the four mules grazing in the far distance. I nostalgically waved goodbye to the old "hands," Rough and Rowdy—their black hair showing patches of gray after eight years of hard work plowing the fields—and then watched as the younger bay mules, Jake and Lena, cavorted as though time had passed them by.

Then I caught sight of Billy ambling across the pasture toward me. Like Rough and Rowdy, Billy looked older, his once-sleek coat of red hair now a dingy dull brown. But his affection shone as bright as when he carried me twelve miles to school over the rutted Tigertown Road. He nuzzled his warm gray nose in the palm of my hand, looking for a small ear of corn or a cube of sugar. An hour passed. The sun set. Silently and sadly, I said goodbye to the farm, although in memory I would never really say goodbye.

Mother and I then drove away from the place that had been our home for a decade. She drove to Austin and I hitchhiked back to Trinity to complete my finals. Afterward, I hitchhiked to Austin and enrolled at the University of Texas as a pre-law major.

★ THE UNIVERSITY OF TEXAS BEFORE I ENTERED THE WAR

The University of Texas had about eight thousand students at the time, and I was awed by its size. Uncle Fred had arranged a job for me at The Toggery, an upscale college men's clothing store on the street known as "The Drag" across from the campus. The store's owner, Jesse Rose, must have been more than a little skeptical when his new employee arrived. My clothes showed neither the quality nor the style of those sold at The Toggery. Indeed, I had much to learn about how to dress in the fashion then favored by the smartly attired collegiate young men who shopped there. Mr. Rose and his wife, who also worked at the store, were extraordinarily patient with me, and I gradually learned how to be an effective salesman. Aided by my salary and spurred by the discount Mr. Rose offered me, I improved my own attire enough to give me some credibility when I recommended upscale clothes for Toggery customers.

Many of our customers were reasonably well-off, if not wealthy. One of them, Oren Johnson, an undergraduate from Harlingen (and later the president of the State Bar of Texas), invited me to visit the Delta Kappa Epsilon (Deke) fraternity house. I knew nothing about fraternities, or UT's fraternity system, but he talked to me about it. I found that the Dekes at UT generally ranked high among the campus fraternities in scholastics and intramural athletic competition. Both were important to me. I was determined to make good grades. I also hoped to make use of a talent as a softball pitcher that I had developed by throwing balls against the barn on our farm in Paris. It was the one thing I could do well athletically. However, when I discovered how much it cost to join the fraternity, I had to explain the financial facts of my life to Oren. I simply could not afford to join. But he eventually arranged for these charges to be altered and paid in a way that I could afford, and I became a member.

The Dekes formed the core of my friends at the university before and after the war. My time in the fraternity was a unifying experience with a group of people different from any I had ever associated with. Plus I enjoyed playing intramural softball and basketball and living at the fraternity house.

That first semester at UT, I worked hard, both in class and at The Toggery, and I played hard with the Dekes. One proud accomplishment was being named the "UT All-Intramural Softball Pitcher." Saturday night beer busts relieved the stress of study while building lasting friendships. Serenading the Theta, Kappa, and Pi Phi sororities seemed as much a part of that fleeting moment in time as did the war's threat to upend the lives of those who merrily sang "A Band of Brothers Is DKE."

During the summer of 1942, I stayed with my mother in San Antonio. She had taken a job there with the U.S. Censorship Office and put her college studies in English to work reading volumes of letters leaving the country, censoring disclosures of information that might be valuable to our nation's enemies, and referring suspicious letters to the FBI. I worked as a salesman in the shoe department at Sears.

When I returned to UT in the fall of 1942, the war was on everyone's mind. By radio, newspaper, and *Time* magazine, students followed the course of the fierce fighting in Europe and the Pacific. The Allies' situation seemed desperate. We wanted to help out and held heated discussions about which was the best branch of service. Some became more serious in their coursework; others neglected their studies in anticipation of their departure from campus for military service. Despite my lifelong commitment to excellence in the classroom, I found myself increasingly disengaged from my studies. I still wince as I remember my mounting disinterest in academic pursuits when I began my second year of college.

I knew that on my eighteenth birthday, November 19, 1942, I would become eligible for the draft. I also knew that there were clear advantages in volunteering. I could choose my branch of service, for example. I quickly narrowed my choices to the Army Air Corps or the Navy submarine service. Both promised a high probability of combat, which a surging patriotic fervor made desirable. Both also paid a premium over standard military base pay to compensate for the higher risk, which was also desirable.

Decades later, I read an interesting account of the history of the Eighth Army Air Corps that put forward several key reasons why young men volunteered for combat flying duty.[2] I realized that I had felt every one of these reasons. I had grown up in an era when aviation was an exciting frontier with barnstorming shows and Lucky Lindy's solo flight across the Atlantic. I was drawn to the romance of flying and the prestige of wearing wings almost as much as to the significantly higher compensation offered by flight pay. But I also shared with many other volunteers the sense that we could play an important role in winning the war. This feeling was reinforced by the stirring reports of the Battle of Britain we heard on the radio during the early years of the war.

★ JOINING THE ARMY AIR CORPS

On the day I turned eighteen, I walked from my classroom to the Army Air Corps recruiting office and volunteered for service in the air cadet program, hoping to do my part as a pilot flying combat missions over Europe and the Pacific. I passed the physical in December 1942 and was accepted for active duty in February 1943.

Events then moved quickly. The moment the semester ended in January 1943, I was ready to go. Rather quickly, I was ordered to report to the White Plaza Hotel in San Antonio, where I joined several hundred other new recruits on a late evening in February. We had been instructed to bring few clothes since we would be issued uniforms immediately. That evening, many of us launched our Army Air Corps tours of duty by standing on a street behind the White Plaza Hotel, drinking Pearl and Jax beer from longneck bottles and speculating about what lay ahead.

After a restless night, we boarded a troop train crowded with guys eighteen to twenty years old—many from various colleges in Texas—and rumbled slowly northwest toward Sheppard Field in Wichita Falls, Texas. When we stepped off the train at about 10:00 P.M., the wind was blowing fiercely and the place was freezing. However, our welcoming committee, a group of tough, professional sergeants who obviously held in disdain this trainload of unlikely-looking officer candidate material, quickly warmed us up. We fell out and immediately commenced six weeks of intense physical training and discipline.

First, we marched to the mess hall where sardonic, sleepy privates slammed huge globs of food on our tin trays, perhaps three times as much food as anyone could possibly eat. When we tried to leave with food remaining on our trays, the sergeants ordered us back to the table, admonished us about wasting food, and commanded us not to leave until we had eaten every last morsel. It was a very effective way to deliver a basic message: we had entered a new world with a new set of rules and grizzled taskmasters eager to instill in us the discipline needed to transform us from college students to real soldiers.

The next morning we began a routine that we repeated every day for the next five weeks. We arose at 4:30 A.M., cleaned our shotgun barracks to immaculate perfection, and made our cot-like iron beds, tucking the linens tight enough to flip an inspection sergeant's quarter. Then we marched to breakfast. Afterward, we prepared for the obstacle course or any other demanding physical exertions deemed necessary to build discipline and respect for the military chain of command. One constant about winter in Wichita Falls was the freezing, driving wind that incessantly pelted our faces with stinging sand.

Beer was a sedative for the utter fatigue we felt at the end of each grueling day. But I also gained comfort from the guys in my barracks, including several close friends from the University of Texas. Tom Landry, who later gained fame as a professional football player and then as head coach of the Dallas Cowboys for twenty-nine years, lived in my barracks. He had joined the Dekes the year after I had, and as his big brother, I had been responsible for familiarizing him with the fraternity. Also there were Ralph Schnitzer Jr., from the prominent Schnitzer family of Houston; Hutch Bass, a close friend and UT basketball star who died of leukemia while an officer at Fort Worth National Bank after the war; and Jack Valenti, a University of Houston student who later became special assistant to President Lyndon Johnson, then chairman and CEO of the Motion Picture Association of America.

Such friends made life bearable both during and after training, and I missed them after I contracted the measles and was moved into quarantine in a makeshift barracks where, among other miseries, we were responsible for preparing our own meals. When I heard that we had received orders to ship out for flight training in a week, a kind doctor took pity on me and released me from sick bay somewhat prematurely so that I could stay with my friends during the next phase of our training.

In comparison to the hard, cold month at Sheppard Field, our next five months of training at East Central State College in Ada, Oklahoma, were downright enjoyable. The College Training Detachment (CTD) at Ada provided the type of environment pictured in the Army Air Corps recruiting brochures. We lived in college-style dormitories with two cadets to a room. We carried a prescribed classroom curriculum, learned to fly single-engine Piper Cubs and Aeroncas at Ada's Municipal Airfield, and maintained our physical conditioning through vigorous calisthenics and athletic competitions. The conduct of the instructors and officers was absolutely benevolent compared to that of the drill sergeants at Sheppard Field.

We spent off-duty weekends swimming, fishing, and drinking 3.2 beer on Saturday afternoons at a downtown Ada tavern called Pappa LaSalle's. The citizens of Ada made us feel at home when we ventured into town. In short, CTD was an oasis where we learned to fly—most of us had never been in a plane—while absorbing lessons from superiors who personified the phrase "an officer and a gentleman."

Our stay at Ada stretched from late March through August of 1943. During that time, we took almost four hundred classroom hours of coursework, including European history, basic writing, a healthy dose of physics, and refresher courses in math and geography. In addition, we had one hundred and twenty hours of preflight training, which included an introduction to radio, aerial map reading, meteorology, and basic navigation. All in all, it proved a stimulating summer, highlighted by my learning to fly. I recall vividly the thrill of putting a Piper Cub through every routine imaginable, from slow rolls to chandelles to stalls and more. I genuinely loved flying and found it as exciting as the words of the Army Air Corps's song, "Off we go, into the wild blue yonder."

During our months in Ada, we seemed far away from the war that was raging on the eastern front in Europe, in northern Africa, in the Pacific, and in the air over Western Europe, where the Eighth Air Force intensified its daylight bombings of industries vital to the German war effort. Photographs in my bulky Army Air Force album show us taking excursions in a car owned by a fellow cadet's new girlfriend from Ada. Clippings from the base newspaper record the outcome of various athletic contests—and announced the selection of first baseman Tom Landry and pitcher "B. Love" to the Air Crew All-Star softball team. The officer instructors also selected me as a "Wing Adjutant," one of the top student-officer posts. I interpreted this to mean that those above me thought that I had what it would take to succeed as a pilot and officer. These were pleasant, active days tinged with the keen anticipation all of us felt during our training to fly combat missions.

In my case, these memories included one deep disappointment. At the end of CTD in August 1943, we boarded a train for Lackland Air Force Base in San Antonio, where we were to be assigned for future training. There, to our dismay, we learned that the Army Air Corps had too many pilots. Of course, the rumor mill shifted into overtime as we awaited reassignment—the bomber command needed more gunners, not more pilots, and so on. Final word of our fate did not come for several weeks, and we mostly filled our time with acute apprehension and intense calisthenics. One memorable calisthenics instructor was Enos "Country" Slaughter, the St. Louis Cardinal baseball star whose career had been interrupted by the war. A physical specimen of astounding stamina, he seemed determined that each of us would leave Lackland as fit as he was. He pushed us hard in long-distance running, scaling twelve-foot obstacle walls, slithering through barbed-wire barriers, and setting records for push-ups and sit-ups.

Finally, official word replaced rumors. There was indeed a glut of pilots. Our class would be tested and placed for further training in one of four categories: pilot school, bombardier school, navigation school, and gunnery school. Only the first three assignments provided an opportunity to become an officer. Competition would be intense; most of us would wash out and be sent to gunnery school.

For several days, we took mechanical-aptitude tests, written math tests, and tests on a variety of other topics. As we waited for the results, a fear of failure gripped me so intensely that I remember it vividly more than sixty years later. When the results were announced, I won half a prize. I would be among the lucky ones who would be designated as an Army Air Corps cadet, but I would *not* be going to pilot school. However, on the basis of my high math scores, I *would* be assigned to navigation school at Ellington Field about fifteen miles south of Houston near the site that, two decades later, became the Manned Space Craft Center. This assignment proved to be two blessings in disguise: during my seven months there, I discovered an aptitude for navigation, and I discovered my future hometown.

★ NAVIGATORS' TRAINING IN HOUSTON

Ellington Field in September of 1943 was a bustling training center. The base had opened in 1917 and became one of the nation's largest aviation training facilities during World War I. It was placed on standby after the war and then closed down in 1927. In late 1940, as World War II intensified in Europe, Congress appropriated money to reopen the field. At the height of the war, the base had approximately five thousand personnel.

I was a member of Class 44-5 for Advanced Navigators, some one hundred and twenty young men drawn primarily from colleges across America. Perhaps nine hundred to one thousand Army Air Corps cadets began training at Ellington Field when I did, with that number roughly equally divided between navigators and bombardiers. Of course, calisthenics and marching drills continued, but we spent most of our time in classrooms, learning how to navigate airplanes to and from their targets.

Our classes focused on daytime navigation using instruments and pilotage (visual sightings) and nighttime celestial navigation using a sextant to shoot star positions based on the precise position of a star vis-à-vis the globe at any hour, minute, and second. By sighting stars at different angles, we learned that a navigator on an airplane traveling at 150 knots per hour could determine its precise position by the same method Columbus used on the *Santa Maria* in 1492 traveling a few knots per hour. Neither the science nor the equipment had changed dramatically in 450 years. Those sextants might not be sophisticated by today's standards, but an alert navigator could keep a plane on course by making accurate observations with swift and correct mathematical calculations in his head and with his now-primitive equipment centered on a drift meter.

The pressure was on to learn our lessons well. As we progressed, classroom theories were increasingly tested in the real world of flying. Six cadets would board a Lockheed Lodestar airplane an hour or so after being handed maps marked with six landfalls we were to hit before returning to Ellington Field. A "lead" cadet would be designated to navigate the pilots through each mission while the other cadets silently plotted the precise location where they thought the lead navigator had instructed the pilots to fly. Jet-black shades covering the windows ensured that no one could cheat by looking out and sighting landmarks below. The only exceptions to these "blackouts" were those few missions when the lesson involved pilotage.

The last hurdle of navigators' school was a flight that tested all of our skills. During this "square search mission," we had to navigate the Lodestar to a distant assigned position, with windows blacked out, using only compasses, drift meters, and other implements of the trade. I was designated to direct (i.e., navigate) the pilots from point to point. After about four hours of intense concentration, I told the pilot that we should be over our final destination. The shades were lifted, and to my profound relief, we were! I took tremendous pride in earning the top grade awarded on this final flight and in being named one of the seven honor officers from my class. Learning to navigate at Ellington Field produced more tension than learning to fly in Ada, but I took my work very seriously, understanding that I would need all of the knowledge I could accumulate to do my job well when I went to war.

My commission as a second lieutenant in the Army Air Corps is not all I took away from Ellington Field. During my seven months of training there, I also acquired a healthy respect for the city of Houston. The city's skyline impressed a young man not far removed from the farm. On my many bus trips into Houston on weekend passes, the first building to come into view was the thirty-four-story Gulf Building, then the tallest structure in the city. Twenty-five years later this same building housed the office I occupied as CEO of Texas Commerce Banks. Looking back, I can say that my love affair with the city that adopted me as its own first took hold on these weekend passes.

In 1940, Houston was a sprawling city of almost four hundred thousand. An extraordinary surge of growth in the 1920s and 1930s had doubled its population and made it the largest city in Texas. Our bus into town from Ellington passed through an industrial complex that lined the ship channel from Houston to the Gulf of Mexico, some forty miles southeast of the city. The giant oil refineries and petrochemical plants along the Houston Ship Channel were booming to meet the demands of war, supplying as much as 20 percent of the nation's refined petroleum products and an even larger percentage of its petrochemical products. In addition to numerous large factories that generated equipment needed by the petroleum industry, the city still benefited from its more traditional cotton and timber trade. Its port was among the fastest-growing in the nation.

Yet there was more. Houston had an optimism and energy you could almost feel. It had always been the home of aggressive entrepreneurs who pushed the city forward as they built their own enterprises. I was fortunate to meet some of these men during my Saturday afternoons at the USO Club, and their enthusiasm for their city's future proved contagious.

One of my closest friends at Ellington Field was Ralph Schnitzer Jr., who frequently invited me to spend the weekend with him at his parents' home in Houston, where his grandfather and uncle had founded the Magnolia Paper Company. His father, a Stanford graduate, was president of the company. Ralph's parents became not only my good friends and mentors, but his mother also became a dear friend of my mother. I greatly enjoyed the many Saturday nights when Ralph's mother would serve us wine with our dinner. When she would leave the room, Ralph's underage brother Kenneth (who later became one of the major developers in Houston and an important customer of Texas Commerce Bank) would grab one of the wine glasses and gulp as much as he could before she returned.

My interest in returning to the city after the war grew out of what I saw in Houston at that time and from conversations with businessmen who visited with the troops at the USO Club on weekends. I also benefited from numerous talks with Mr. Schnitzer and his business friend Bob Straus, owner of the Straus Frank Wholesale Appliance and Equipment Company. One day, they invited me to ride in the backseat as they toured the developing industrial sections along the Houston Ship Channel and on Clinton and Navigation streets. I heard them talk about the fortunes to be made there; they were excited about the future of the city I decided then that, if I survived the war, I would change my major at UT from pre-law to business. This would allow me to complete my college education more speedily and move to Houston to participate in the growth and opportunity they so exuberantly predicted for business.

My graduation ceremony from navigators' school on April 8, 1944, was a day of tremendous celebration. Mother traveled to Houston by bus from San Antonio to watch me receive my wings and my second lieutenant commission. The joyful mood of good friends from my training class and many

Cadet Benton F. Love with mother, Nell Scott Love (Love family archives)

members of their families was tempered by the realization that we had finished the last major segment of our training.

The war called. My orders sent me to the Army Air Corps base at Kearney, Nebraska. En route from Houston to Kearney, I stopped in Paris and spent a quiet, contemplative time at Dad's grave. I also visited Paris High School, where I talked to the principal, Thomas Justiss, and my favorite teachers. As I posed for a photograph in front of the case that displayed the debate trophies that Sam McClure and I had won, I felt grown up and distant from the things that had been so important to me less than two years earlier.

Momentous events were rocking the entrenched Germans on the European front at this time. D-Day exploded on June 6, 1944. The ultimate outcome of that invasion was in the balance as American, Canadian, and British troops fought heroically to break out from the areas near the Normandy beaches and begin their drive across France toward Germany. We knew we were bound for the skies over Europe, and we knew that the war there had entered a critical phase. Our training had come to an end at a time when our best efforts were critically needed in Europe to help the Allies secure victory.

In Kearney, the navigator's "tools of the trade" were issued to me on June 17, 1944. I was also assigned to my first crew—three other freshly minted second lieutenants: pilot Allen Barnhart, a sheep rancher from Lewiston, Montana; copilot Jack Hoskins, the son of a steel mill foreman from Hammond, Indiana; and bombardier Alex Wodje from Milwaukee, Wisconsin.

All that was left to do before we joined the Eighth Air Force in England was to train in B-17 bombers exactly like the ones we would fly in our combat missions over Europe. This came in May and June 1944 at Dyersburg, Tennessee. And what a plane it was! I fell in love with the B-17. The "Flying Fortress" was a stable craft with a one-hundred-foot wing, a seventy-five-foot fuselage, and a sleek profile. It could cruise at one hundred and fifty miles per hour and bomb from approximately thirty thousand feet.[3]

The navigator's position in the nose of the B-17 was to be my home during combat missions. The bombardier with his Norden Bombsite occupied a small space immediately in front of me in the plane's Plexiglas nose. In addition to our primary duties, the two of us also fired .50 caliber machine guns that defended our positions in the nose of the plane from attacks by enemy fighter planes. We clearly had much to learn individually and as a team.

Boeing had developed the B-17 in the 1930s as a sturdy, long-range bomber. Its four twelve-hundred-horsepower engines gave it sufficient power to fly at a maximum of 290 mph, although on our missions, flying tight formations, we generally maintained a steady 150 mph pace. The B-17 had a range of two thousand miles while carrying a typical five-thousand-pound bomb load. Its normal ten-person crew had up to thirteen .50 caliber machine guns mounted in locations that protected the plane against fighter attacks from all angles. When flown in the tight bombing formations mandatory on the daytime missions over Europe, the bomber formations could sustain—and mete out—withering fire from all directions.

The plane itself was immensely strong. It could withstand numerous hits from fighter planes and ground flak and continue on its mission. The aircraft often managed to return to base even after incurring battle damage as severe as the loss of three engines, gaping holes in the fuselage, or the loss of large sections of the vertical tail. What had been learned about the B-17 in combat during the early years of the war had been set down in a series of technical manuals that we studied diligently at Dyersburg.

★ OFF TO THE FRONT

With our training completed, we boarded a troopship and embarked from New Jersey for England on July 2, 1944. I felt a sense of adventure as I left the United States for the first time. Since leaving Paris, Texas, two years earlier, I had traveled to places and done things that I could not have imagined while growing up on the farm.

The eight-day trip across the Atlantic gave me time to think about the past and my future in the Eighth Air Force. Our ship, the *Kungsholm,* had been a luxury liner in the Swedish cruiser fleet before the war; it now carried about five thousand troops as a part of a convoy of perhaps thirty-five vessels. A few ships from the Navy, including at least one destroyer and several destroyer escorts, accompanied us as protection from the German submarines that preyed on Allied shipping in the North Atlantic. The constant dull thud of their depth charges and the tremendous spouts of water thrown up by their explosions fended off the ever-lurking German U-boats and reminded all on board that we had entered the war. Most of the men aboard the *Kungsholm* were infantrymen. No doubt they had heard about the fierce fighting of D-Day and knew that they were about to enter a bloody theater on the ground in Normandy, with constant deadly battles and miserable nights in foxholes.

Those of us in the Army Air Corps knew that we would face dangers as well, but we also knew that during those days when we were not under flak and fighter attack, we would enjoy vastly better conditions than the poor dogface infantrymen. When we returned from a bombing mission, we would have hot meals, a warm bed, and freedom from enemy fire until our next mission. What we could *not* yet fully fathom was what we would face *during* our missions. But we did know that we would be joining the Eighth Air Force, which had already earned a reputation as a dangerous assignment.

The Eighth had been created just after the bombing of Pearl Harbor and was activated in late January 1942 in Savannah, Georgia. Within months, a headquarters had been established in England, and a buildup of men and equipment began that ultimately would make the "Mighty Eighth" the largest air armada in the world. By war's end, one hundred and seventy thousand Americans had served in the air and another one hundred and eighty thousand on the ground with the Eighth, which at its peak size could put as many as one thousand bombers and one thousand fighters in the air for a single mission.

These missions were vital to the success of the Allied war effort in Europe, and those who flew them paid a heavy price. Until D-Day in June 1944, there had been heavy pressure to open a second front in Europe so that Allied ground troops could move from the west toward Germany as Soviet troops battled the Germans on the eastern front. The steady bombardment of Hitler's war-related industries by the Eighth Air Force and the Royal Air Force (RAF) not only paved the way for the invasion of Normandy by ground troops, but also forced the Germans to concentrate considerable resources on the defense of its industrial facilities and its cities against sustained air attacks by British and American bombers. In this sense, the Eighth Air Force had opened a second front long before D-Day.

The British and the Americans took different approaches to this bombing. In August 1942, the Eighth mounted its first daylight raids over Europe. The RAF had previously conducted only night raids as far inland as Berlin. Night raids reduced casualties, but paid a high price in bombing accuracy. Those in charge of the Eighth Air Force—Gen. Hap Arnold and others—believed strongly that daytime bombing would result in greater accuracy in damaging the industries that equipped the German war machine. However, after German fighters and flak inflicted near catastrophic damage and casualties during early raids, the top command had been forced to back away temporarily from this costly strategy while offering air support at a critical time in the North African campaign.

In early 1943, Gen. Ira Eaker and his Eighth Air Force staff journeyed to Casablanca to convince military leaders and Franklin Roosevelt and Winston Churchill of the need to resume daylight bombing in Europe. Churchill, who had originally argued that daylight bombing would inflict catastrophic losses, agreed to the resumption of such attacks after a highly regarded Eighth Air Force commander commented that Hitler could not withstand Allied "bombing around the clock." Under the agreement reached at Casablanca, British forces would continue bombing at night while American planes would bomb during the day, giving Germany the job of defending key targets against heavy air assaults twenty-four hours a day.

Everyone knew that the Eighth Air Force would absorb extremely heavy casualties, but we calculated that Germany would suffer greater damage. During its three-year involvement in the war, the Eighth endured the highest casualty rates of any branch of American forces. It lost more than fifty-three thousand men and nearly nine thousand aircraft; its combat crews endured a casualty rate of more than 31 percent. That statistic bears repeating: of the one hundred and seventy thousand air crew members who flew combat missions over Hitler's Europe, the Eighth Air Force suffered more than 53,000 casualties, with 26,000 (more than 15 percent) killed in action, and 28,000 more wounded and/or shot down and who survived as POWs.

Such extreme losses were accepted by the Allied high command as part of the price to be paid to cripple Germany's capacity to manufacture vital war supplies and take charge of the air over Europe. Our raids destroyed almost sixteen thousand enemy aircraft while pulverizing enemy targets with an estimated seven hundred thousand tons of bombs.[4] American factories could build replacement bombers much faster than German industry could produce new planes and the fuel to fly them. American farms and towns could produce more crews for these bombers, sending them to attack in wave after wave, despite very heavy losses.

I learned these statistics after the war. At the time, our best inkling of what lay ahead was the often-repeated "rule" that the average crew member of the Eighth Air Force completed fifteen missions before being shot down. Because twenty-five missions were then assigned as a full tour of duty, we knew that we were not about to enter friendly skies.

Such thoughts remained an abstraction, however, as we disembarked from the troopship at Liverpool and made our way by rail to the air base at Polebrook, East Anglia. This was one of about one hundred airfields used by the Eight Air Force in the British countryside northwest and southwest of London. Here, weather permitting, British and American bombers embarked on missions against strategic targets in Europe day and night. Here we would finally have the chance to put our training to use in combat.

NOTES

1. The Rural Electrification Administration brought electricity to the Love farm in 1936, the year after the new house was built.

2. Philip Kaplan and Rex Alan Smith, *One Last Look: A Sentimental Journey to the Eighth Air Force Heavy Bomber Bases of World War II in England* (New York: Abbeville Press, 1983).

3. The B-24, the other four-engine bomber in the Eighth Air Force, was built by Lockheed. It cruised at 180 mph and bombed at about twenty-five thousand feet. So it was speed versus altitude, advantage versus disadvantage.

4. Comparison of the numbered air forces World War II statistics courtesy of Maj. Gen. Lewis Lyle, commandant of 303rd Bomb Group, Eighth Air Force.

Chapter 3 GROWING OLD OVER EUROPE

The most intense period of my life began on July 10, 1944, when my crew arrived at the 351st Bomb Group, Polebrook, East Anglia, England. This was to be my home for the next eleven months, during which time I felt that I matured and aged by at least eleven years. It was to be the base from which I flew my twenty-five missions, bombing Hitler's military installations in Germany and German-occupied Europe.

As I walked into the shotgun barracks for the first time, I felt as green as I had on my first night at Sheppard Field more than a year before. Four of us entered the barracks together, and we were thankful that it seemed empty, thus giving us time to adjust to our new environment before the combat crews returned from their mission. After months of intensive training, we were on the threshold of flying our first combat missions. Our adrenaline was pumping.

Then, through the gloom, we saw a man sleeping on a bunk about halfway down the aisle. He woke up and greeted the latest replacement crew—us. We introduced ourselves, somewhat self-consciously in our first meeting with a man who had actually flown *real* missions. He was a navigator named Morrie, and he assured us, matter-of-factly, that the flak and fighters were not too bad. We sat and listened with rapt attention as he told us that he had flown fourteen missions. Earlier in the day, his plane had developed mechanical problems over the English Channel and he had to abort, thus explaining why he was not flying today's mission. He said he had only eleven missions left to fly and could hardly wait to get back home to Brooklyn and see his family.

That was a welcome and reassuring introduction to life at Polebrook. Morrie's reflections provided a measure of comfort to our untested crew as we pondered our upcoming experience in combat. But that was the last we saw of him. As he flew his fifteenth mission the very next morning, his B-17 was hit by flak over the target and blew up. Morrie's sudden death slapped us in the face with stark reality.

At Polebrook, although we would live in relative comfort compared to those in the infantry, the price we paid would be twenty-five extraordinarily intense and high-casualty days flying in B-17s under siege on bombing missions over the enemy's heavily fortified territory. During my eleven months at Polebrook, I led two lives—one on the ground that was relatively serene and one in the air that was extremely tense.

Life on the ground revolved around the barracks, target practice with our .45s on the firing range, softball games, and bicycle excursions into the surrounding countryside and small towns where we met the locals who gathered at pubs. We also enjoyed evening poker games in the officers' club near Frankie's Bar.

Initially, I lived in an open-bay barracks with about forty other officers. Our iron, cot-like beds, with thin mattresses and primitive springs, were lined up in rows on either side of an open center aisle dominated by two coal-burning stoves. At the foot of each bed was a wooden footlocker where we stored everything but our uniforms. Uniforms were hung on a rack behind the head of the bed. Such barracks were standard throughout the Eighth Air Force bases in the United Kingdom. They provided efficient housing for large numbers of servicemen. But forty combat airmen in a relatively confined open space had one drawback. We were regularly awakened by the screams of men whose courage had been proven amidst enemy flak and fighters, but whose sleep was disrupted with nightmares about their combat missions. After our first mission, we understood. Each of us, at one time or another, would awake drenched with sweat from a nightmare about our own B-17 being hit and violently exploding or spinning out of control on fire or ditching in the frigid English Channel, with the accompanying dismemberment or deaths of our crew members.

About a month after my arrival at Polebrook, perhaps accelerated by my having been accorded a rare "superior" rating by my final instructor at Dyersburg AAF base, I was promoted from my original crew to a three-officer lead crew. The honor was considerable. So was the responsibility. All planes in a squadron, or group, or wing, or division, or the entire Eighth Air Force, flew in assigned positions for each mission in tight formation and followed designated lead crew bombers. As a lead crew, we had to get things right!

TABLE 3.1: *The Organization of the Eighth Air Force*
Squadron = 12 B-17s
Group = 36 B-17s
Wing = 108 B-17s
Division = 324 B-17s
Eighth Air Force = 972 B-17s and B-24s

The "lead crew": Fred "Fritz" Ralph, bombardier; Ben Love, navigator; and Jim "Hoot" Gibbons, pilot. We flew eight lead missions together and formed friendships that were as close as the brothers I never had. (Love family archives)

My promotion to a lead crew came after my fifth mission. From then until my sixteenth mission in October, I flew with several different lead crews. But for a mission to Cologne on October 18, the 351st Bomb Group formed a new lead crew, consisting of pilot Jim "Hoot" Gibbons from Ukiah, California; bombardier Fred "Fritz" Ralph from Barre, Vermont; and me as navigator. We flew together as Lead Team for most of the remainder of my tour.

As members of a lead crew, we had the privilege of moving into a semi-private barracks. During my last eight months at Polebrook, Fred Ralph and I shared a comfortable twelve-by-sixteen-foot cubicle that was compact, cozy, and much quieter than the shotgun barracks. Life instantly improved. We slept better, for one thing. An enlisted man made our beds each morning, kept coal available for our small stove, and woke us up when we were scheduled to fly early-morning missions, real or practice.

On days off, we frequently flew practice missions. We had no orders to do this, but we knew that practice would inevitably improve our performance. We would pick our time of day and then Jim, Fred, and I would board an idle B-17, take off, and fly on a northwest heading toward the Isle of Man, where the seemingly indestructible Scares Rock jutted out of the ocean. We would fly practice bomb runs over and over, dropping dummy bombs on Scares Rock. From the splash, we could tell in seconds how close the bomb came to the rock. This was not play. Such practice improved our chances of hitting important German targets when we flew real missions.

We also enjoyed the countryside near the base. Soon after arriving at Polebrook, I took the base bus with my original copilot, Jack Hoskins, into Peterborough, a town some fourteen miles away. One evening, after drinking our fill of 'alf and 'alf mild and bitter beer, we bought two used bicycles on a lark. I did not know how to ride a bicycle, but that fourteen-mile, precarious, and hilarious trek back to the base was one great way to learn!

My bike quickly became a valued possession. I rode it often through the rolling green stream-filled countryside around Polebrook. This country filled my eyes and soul with the most beautiful scenery I had even seen, with undulating green vistas, breathtakingly clear streams, and quaint thatched-roof villages complete with local pubs

The British treated us well. One member of the Eighth Air Force later recalled a measure of tension between the brash American fliers and their hosts in England. Many of the British men had gone far overseas to fight the war while the Americans had traveled across the Atlantic to fight alongside the British in Africa and Europe. Some complained that the Yanks were "overpaid, overfed, oversexed and over here." The American servicemen responded, half in jest, that the "Britons are underpaid, undersexed and under Eisenhower." [1]

Despite complaints that our hosts occasionally took advantage of the Yanks by raising prices, the overwhelming majority of these steadfast Britons made us feel like welcome guests. I admired these stoic, stable, courageous, civilized people and genuinely liked them.

On nights off, when we knew we would not be flying the next day, we occasionally let off steam with boisterous, uninhibited behavior befitting young men on the loose in the world. We would bicycle into the neighboring village to drink the Brits' warm beer at a pub and play a game of darts with the locals. Such "nights on the town" often concluded at the Polebrook Officers' Club, where some of us inevitably sat down to play poker. One of my personal goals was to leave military service with a nest egg, and my winnings in these small-stakes poker games added about one thousand dollars to a bankroll that totaled roughly four thousand dollars when I was discharged.

Every sixty days or so, Eighth Air Force combat personnel received three-day passes for "Rest and Recreation," or "R & R." Typically, two or three friends would take their passes and catch the train from Peterborough to London, about ninety miles south of Polebrook.

Despite the ravages of war and continuous bombardments, London was a stimulating center of varied lifestyles and diverse activities. Theaters remained open, and I could choose from plays written by such famous names as Dame Edith Sitwell and George Orwell and performed by Laurence Olivier and John Gielgud. Although most London museums had stored their contents in bombproof basements for the duration, I still saw the Magna Carta, the Rosetta Stone, and first editions of Shakespeare and Chaucer. Once, while I was enjoying Johann Strauss's operetta *The Merry Widow,* a V-1 rocket hit nearby with a deafening explosion. I nearly jumped out of my seat, but no one else stirred. The performance continued, as if to proclaim the British disdain for Hitler's deadly, rocket-propelled bombings.

After one trip, I wrote to my mother that "I really had a good time seeing the sights, but I am not as impressed with the Old World as I thought I would be . . . the best thing I saw was a wax exhibit at Madame Tussauds. It was realistic in every detail of the world's past and present famous people." Clearly at the age of nineteen, I was becoming a bit more of a sophisticated man of the world. But I had a long way to go.

I lived in a world of young men, most eighteen to twenty-four years old, who were growing up fast in our new surroundings in England and in the skies over Europe. A shared sense of purpose and the unifying experience of danger and death cemented close friendships. I never had a brother; my Deke fraternity brothers at the University of Texas had become the closest friends I had ever had. But my "brothers in arms" at Polebrook were as important to me in that stressful point in my life as anyone outside my own family, before or since.[2] We depended on one another for our very lives. We comforted each other in times of trouble. Together we encountered death, often watching as it snatched friends and comrades, flying beside us, from the sky in a random process that forged even closer bonds among those who survived.

As we lived the reality of war, letters from home helped us keep in touch with the lives we had left behind. Decades later, I found that Mother had filled an album with every single one of the ninety-eight letters I had written to her from Polebrook. I cannot imagine the anxiety my then recently widowed mother must have felt about the fate of her only son.

The censors did not allow us to write any details about our missions, so I filled my V-mail correspondence with general discussions about plans for after the war and reassurances that I was doing fine. Although thoughts of life and death filled our minds, we wrote about the mundane events in our daily lives. I wrote, "I have always wanted to travel and see a few of the things I read about in history. And here came Uncle Sam on the spot and gave me a tour of the United States and then some." I wrote to her about the feelings of patriotism that fueled my passion to help my country defeat Hitler. Mother kept me supplied with Vitalis hair tonic and wrote about the aches and pains of relatives and the comings and goings of friends.

Her dispatches from that saner world reinforced my confidence that I would survive the war and return home to a real life. But for the duration of my tour of duty, my real life was not in Texas or even in the barracks at Polebrook. My real life was the time I spent in a B-17 Flying Fortress flying bombing missions over Europe. All the rest—the close friendships, the friendly pubs, poker at the Officers' Club, the excitement of exploring London— provided temporary respite from the mixture of duty, responsibility, and anxious determination that I felt each time I climbed into a B-17 to fly my next mission.

The general routine followed on the days of our missions has been depicted in numerous accounts of the history of the Eighth Air Force. A sergeant would wake Fred Ralph and me, usually between 02:30 and 04:30 hours. We would slog through the chill to the latrine (some twenty-five yards away), then eat a hearty breakfast of Spam, toast, and powdered eggs, knowing that it would be twelve to seventeen hours before we would eat again, after the completion of our mission.

Then it was on to Group Briefing. There, the 351st Bomb Group's base commander, Col. Robert Burns, pulled the curtains and unveiled the day's target on a huge map of Europe. The map included the carefully drawn route we were to follow to our designated target. The route was doglegged in order to dodge major flak installations (if possible) and mislead German fighters as to the location of our ultimate target. After a briefing by weather and intelligence officers, each plane was assigned its position in its squadron, each squadron its position in the group, each group its position in the wing, each wing its position in the division, and each of the three divisions its position to form the Eighth Air Force.

As we prepared for takeoff, most of us followed some superstitious ritual. In my case, as soon as I swung up through the nose compartment's escape hatch into my flying position, I placed my officer's hat over the drift meter until we took off. On one mission when I forgot and left my officer's hat in my locker, our plane was shot up pretty badly. Everyone in the crew knew why—I had deviated from my ritual. I never did that again.

Our three twelve-plane squadrons took off one plane at a time, then circled around the Kings Cliffe radio beacon in East Anglia while gaining altitude and forming our group at ten thousand feet. This early portion of the flight could be quite challenging, beginning with takeoff, because if the target was deep inside Germany, the B-17s were heavily loaded with fuel and bombs and occasionally stalled and crashed at the end of the runway in a fiery explosion. Congestion in the air was even more of a problem as many groups assembled with hundreds of bombers in that relatively small space over East Anglia. This assembly process through the area's typically thick cumulus cloud cover demanded extraordinary alertness and luck. I will always recall the time, during our group's assembly, when our B-17 was caught without warning in prop wash created by B-17s we could not see through the heavy cloud cover. We suddenly dropped several hundred feet and barely missed crashing into numerous other planes that were circling below us. That miracle of survival was aided immeasurably by the superior flying of our two pilots.

On most missions, the Eighth Air Force would fly about one thousand bombers in precision formation, creating a giant assemblage of planes tightly packed together horizontally and vertically. The logistics of fitting all those planes together was daunting because each thirty-six-plane group had to fit into its assigned position in the overall Eighth Air Force formation, with two-minute intervals between each group. Each group had to arrive at its assigned position by the assigned moment to depart Britain and, following the mission route, eventually arrive at the designated point united to begin the bomb run to the target. All of this customary but complex forming and meshing over East Anglia for each thirty-six-bomber group required about one and a half hours.

These massive formations must have been something to behold from the ground. However, as a navigator, I was an extremely busy participant and had no opportunity to enjoy the spectacle when I was embarking on a mission.

Fighter planes joined the bomber armada over the English Channel and escorted us as far as their fuel allowed. We had P-38s and P-40s with limited range for fighter protection on our early missions, but the newer long-range P-47s and P-51s soon vastly bolstered this cover because their extra fuel enabled these "little friends" to accompany the bomber formation all the way to even our most distant targets.

Each B-17 defended itself and the other bombers in its squadron or group solely through concentrating the fire of its thirteen .50 caliber machine guns. The bombardier had twin machine guns in the nose; the navigator fired guns on either side of the nose. The ball turret gunner and the top turret gunner both fired twin guns. The two waist gunners fired single guns from opposite sides of the center of the plane, and the tail gunner lay on his stomach armed with .50 caliber guns protruding from the B-17's tail. The inside of a B-17 was a relatively small space, packed with men and motion. When the crew opened fire on German fighters, the noise was deafening.[3]

When the .50 caliber machine gun firepower of each B-17 was combined with that of others flying in tight formation, our relatively slow bombers had the chance to fend off attacking Nazi fighter planes, primarily Messerschmitt-

A B-17 navigator's working area was rather cramped, especially for a tall, lanky guy on a ten- to twelve-hour mission. (Love family archives)

109s (ME-109s) and Focke-Wulf 190s (FW-190s), despite their blazing speed, maneuverability, and considerable firepower. Our best defense was to fly so close together that our wings almost touched. Tight formations helped prevent German fighter planes from picking off any sloppily flown B-17 and also gave us tight bomb patterns. Each B-17 in a squadron dropped its bombs when the bombardiers saw the lead crew plane's bombs drop, thus producing a tight bomb pattern. The tighter the bomb pattern, the greater the damage inflicted on the target.

If the lead plane was shot down, the deputy lead would take over. If the latter was also shot down, the remaining B-17s in the squadron would attempt to mesh with another squadron in the group and drop their bombs off of its lead plane. Only lead and deputy lead bombers were equipped with the Norden Bombsites, an advanced guidance system that, according to Army fliers, "was accurate enough to guide a bomb from a plane into a pickle barrel."[4]

No B-17 was pressurized. Each flier was supplied with his own oxygen and heat via an oxygen mask, which was strapped on at 10,000 feet, and an electrically heated flying suit and boots. If anything happened to a crew member's heated suits or boots while flying at 25,000–30,000 feet in a −50° Celsius cabin, he faced certain frostbite or freezing with possible to probable amputation of the most severely frozen extremities. I experienced this danger in September 1944 on a mission over Germany. When flak ripped through the nose of our B-17, flying glass damaged the heating element in my uniform and my toes began to freeze. Only fast action by a crew member prevented serious damage to my feet.

En route to our target, we were often attacked by flak fired from the enemy's deadly accurate 88mm antiaircraft guns on the ground and by German fighter planes, predominantly ME-109s and FW-190s. When the Luftwaffe fighters swooped in, the interior of each B-17 burst with noise and action as we frantically fired our machine guns and blasted away at the German fighters that buzzed around and through our formation, their guns blazing away at us. The B-17 was by no means soundproof, and the reverberating racket of our machine guns could be deafening. Spent shell casings flew through the air and stacked up on the floor as we returned fire.

Such battles added to the complexity of my job, because I had to fire two machine guns, one on each side of the B-17's nose, while doing my primary job of calculating our precise location at each moment in order to hit all points on course, on time, and eventually on target. Thick clouds and strong, shifting winds posed additional challenges to my efforts to calculate drift and ground speed.

The Germans had the good sense to concentrate their fire on our lead and deputy lead planes, knowing that the other planes in the squadron and group relied on them to maintain a tight formation and to time the release of their bombs. And, as mentioned above, in each twelve-bomber squadron, only the lead and deputy lead planes were equipped with Norden Bombsites.

As we approached a target, flak became a major concern. The Eighth followed a bombing procedure based on flying a straight and unwavering path from the Initial Point, or IP, which was about fourteen minutes from the target, on through to the target. After a seemingly interminable passage of time on this hellish bomb run and after the bomb bay doors had been opened, the Lead bombardier would release his bombs and shout through the intercom, "Bombs away!" The planes in each squadron dropped their bombs at the moment they saw the Lead plane's bombs drop out of its bomb bay, then headed for home, still in formation and without taking individual evasive action.

The Germans, of course, had studied our tactics and had developed radar to provide their antiaircraft flak batteries with our precise altitude and airspeed. They installed large arsenals of 88mm antiaircraft guns around all of their major facilities and calibrated them to fire into the flight patterns of our bombers. The bomb run to a well-defended target was a time of magnificent violence, with black clouds of exploding 88mm shrapnel all around as we plowed steadily toward the target. One minute a plane manned by ten friends would be flying wing to wing with you; the next minute, it would explode in flames and you would look anxiously, albeit fleetingly, through the smoke and metal and pray to see some parachutes.

Inside, the crew members could only concentrate on their jobs, testing their discipline in remaining calm and focused, despite the chaos all around. Men with a duty to perform learned to control their fear, assuming, as young men will, that *their* plane would not be among those to be shot down. During these missions I felt powers of concentration that I have experienced few other times in my life. I was so determined to do my job as nearly as I could to the imperative, required perfection that there was not time—there simply was not space in my mind—for fear when we were being attacked.

Crews that were shot down and survived faced a harrowing ordeal. Capture meant a prison camp for the duration of the war. If not captured, downed crew members sought the help of the Underground in returning to England or in finding refuge, eventually, in Switzerland, Spain, or Sweden. Those who made it back to Polebrook subtracted one more mission as they disembarked wearily, joyously, from their B-17, often gazing at the gaping holes in the fuselage and marveling that they had made it. The group photographer took pictures of the lead crews upon landing, often as long as twenty hours after we had sped down the runway on takeoff. The group doctor met officers with stout shots of whiskey to calm their nerves, then quickly sent them to debriefing by the group intelligence officers. Finally, after a long-awaited meal at the officers' mess, we went to bed, hoping to avoid recurring, vivid combat nightmares while resting up for the next mission, which might come the next day or the next week.

Nightmares were hard to avoid, given the harsh realities of aerial combat. The flak and the Luftwaffe's ME-109 and FW-190 fighters succeeded in so badly damaging our B-17s that a rugged Flying Fortress typically flew only nine missions before it was retired from combat and scrapped, its parts cannibalized for other bombers. The men inside these bombers knew that they would be hit often and hard. One question mattered above all others: would the plane survive this particular raid and return its crew safely to Polebrook? I suffered at least seven close calls during my twenty-five missions. I also watched others, not as lucky as I, go down with their planes. We had no choice but to accept the randomness of the answer to the fundamental question of who would live and who would die.

Such a general description of life in the air cannot do justice to the personal experiences of each man as he flew each mission. I have never before or since felt the intensity that accompanied aerial combat. I came to accept in the abstract that I was willing to die for my country in a war against Hitler's oppression of innocent people. But even with death all around me, I seldom, if ever, acknowledged the realistic possibility that I might not survive the war.

After returning from each mission, I recorded brief, cryptic notes about it in a small pocket diary. Years later I looked back at those notes and expanded them to include more detail. What follows is meant to supplement the general narrative above with the more personal account of the twenty-five missions flown against Hitler by Benton F. Love.

1. JULY 28, 1944	My B-17 officer crew:
Target: Merseberg, Germany	2nd Lts. Allen Barnhart, Jack Hoskins, and Alex Wodje

Arose at 00:30 for mission briefing and preparation. German ME-109s attacked 351st Bomb Group at target; medium flak. (Ben Smith, author of

Chick's Crew, described Merseberg's synthetic oil plants as the "heaviest defended target in the Third Reich with over a thousand flak guns."[5]) Flak hole appeared just above my head when shell burst near our B-17's nose. About twelve German fighters attacked our formation twice and shot down one of our B-17s.

Experiencing my first attack by German fighters—firing and diving through our "lumbering" 150 mph bombing formation at more than twice our speed—indelibly certified in my mind the necessity to fly tight formations.

Awarded my first combat citation, the European Theater Campaign Ribbon. That night I sought reassurance in the Twenty-third Psalm, beginning a nightly ritual that provided me with spiritual strength and physical courage throughout my combat tour.

The Lord is my shepherd, I shall not want . . .

II. JULY 29, 1944   My B-17 officer crew:
   Target: Merseberg, Germany   2nd Lts. Barnhart, Hoskins, and Wodje

Very heavy flak put ten holes in our B-17. Target smoking from previous day's bombing. Flying off my right wing was a B-17, piloted by my friend Cal Bragdon, a sunbaked twenty-year-old who had grown up on his father's ranch in Arizona. Suddenly, flak blew his Flying Fortress to pieces and they were gone, paying the ultimate price for their country. *Rough!* Our bombardier refused to fly another mission after seeing friends die when their B-17s blew up.

He maketh me to lie down in green pastures . . .

III. AUGUST 1, 1944   My B-17 officer crew:
   Target: Chateaudun Airport, France   2nd Lts. Barnhart and Hoskins

Our bombardier refused to fly so we toggled (released) our bombs when the 510th Squadron's lead bombardier dropped his. Good bomb pattern. Ran into accurate flak at the French coast. Intelligence briefed us that we might be hit by new super-fast German fighters powered by revolutionary jet engines. We saw none—a good thing because our B-17 formation always flew 150 mph.

Fourteen hours without food, but steaks after landing at Polebrook. Awarded my second combat citation, the Normandy Campaign Battle Star.

He leadeth me beside the still waters, He restoreth my soul . . .

| IV. AUGUST 3, 1944 | My B-17 officer crew: |
| Target: Saarbrucken, Germany | 2nd Lts. Barnhart and Hoskins |

Good visibility. Saw Brussels, Rotterdam, lots of Europe. We again toggled our bombs when the 510th Squadron lead bombardier dropped on Saarbrucken's rail marshalling yards. Accurate flak hit us on the coast entering Europe, but only one B-17 from 351st Bomb Group blew up. Damned good mission! Hit target junction of Metz-Trier railroad yards, at 15:20. Fourteen hours between meals.

He leadeth me in the paths of righteousness for His name's sake . . .

| V. AUGUST 4, 1944 | My B-17 officer crew: |
| Target: Anklam, Germany | 2nd Lts. Barnhart and Hoskins |

Awoke at 05:30; flew eight hours over North Sea and Baltic, the latter populated with convoys of Russians fleeing to Anklam, on the northeast coast of Germany. Hit target solidly and left it burning badly. One B-17 from our squadron exploded. Saw Sweden, Norway, and Denmark. *Good mission.*

Yea, though I walk through the valley of the shadow of death . . .

| VI. AUGUST 6, 1944 | My B-17 officer crew: |
| Target: Berlin, Germany | I was reassigned to a lead crew. On this mission I flew 351st Bomb Group lead with Capt. Olsen, Capt. Allen Behrendt, and Col. Robert Burns. |

The sky over Berlin was black with flak and planes blowing up as we flew through a wall of shrapnel and hundreds of German fighters. Three ME-109s concentrated their fire on a B-17 in our squadron being flown by my friend Bill Boyd, a clean-cut, twenty-year-old All-American guy who had volunteered during his sophomore year at Baylor University. Suddenly, Bill's plane exploded, killing all ten crew members. In my 510th lead squadron, seven of our twelve B-17s blew up. I saw close friends killed and a few others parachute from their burning planes. We flew through this death trap. Those of us lucky enough to live hit our targeted aircraft and diesel factories dead center. My roughest mission to date. Fortunate to survive since our plane landed at Polebrook full of holes. At age nineteen, I am maturing! Hitler protected Berlin with flak and fighters unlike anything I could imagine. I was awarded the Air Medal for this mission.

I will fear no evil . . .

VII. AUGUST 11, 1944   My B-17 officer crew:
    Target: Brest, France   Capt. Keller, 510th Squadron commander

Our mission was to wipe out German fortifications blocking the advance of Allied troops toward German-occupied Brest. I flew 510th Squadron Lead with heavy-browed, ramrod-erect Capt. Keller. We hit the target hard with excellent bomb pattern and results. Took off from Polebrook at 13:15 hours; landed at 19:00. A milk run compared to Berlin. Even so, I hope the war is over soon. Flak tore through our tail gunner's parachute, but we did not know flak had also damaged our landing gear until it collapsed when we landed at Polebrook . . . then skidded off the runway. The resultant noise, vibration, and shock revealed how tense we were—even after a so-called "milk run"—because we nearly jumped out of our skins before skidding to a stop on the grass. We were quickly surrounded by wailing sirens from two fire trucks dispatched to help if we caught fire. This mission resulted in my being awarded a Northern France Campaign Battle Star.

for Thou art with me . . .

VIII. AUGUST 14, 1944   My B-17 officer crew:
    Target: Stuttgart Airfield, Germany   Capt. Keller, 510th Squadron
                             commander

Awoke at 03:15 hours, long before sunrise. Briefed as usual by 351st Bomb Group commander Col. Robert Burns, an all-business, seasoned leader I really respect. When the curtains were pulled, the giant map of Europe revealed that our mission was the heavily industrialized region around Stuttgart. Along the black-lined route to the target were the usual large red splotches denoting the flak battery concentrations that we would confront as we executed our flight plan. The flak concentrations did not look bad . . . and it turned out that our intelligence officers were right. It was an easy mission. We hit the target and damaged it severely. No 351st Bomb Group planes lost. We landed at Polebrook at 15:30—twelve hours without food. But we returned

Our ninth mission was to bomb a major bridge at Namur to prevent the German Seventh Army's retreat from Belgium. Although my diary records the results as "fair"—based on what I could see from twenty-nine thousand feet with seven-tenths cloud coverage—this photo, taken at the moment of impact and developed later, reveals that we knocked out the bridge completely. (Love family archives)

unwounded and completed our mission expertly, so being a little hungry and bone-tired is nothing.

Thy rod and Thy staff they comfort me . . .

IX. AUGUST 18, 1944
    Target: Namur, Belgium

My B-17 officer crew:
Maj. Fishburn, Capt. McClusky,
Lts. Gulnac and Craig

Flew wing lead. Our target was a major bridge across which the Seventh German Army was retreating from Belgium into Germany in a desperate attempt to escape from the Falise Gap and, thereby, fight again. Our Eighth Air Force Wing encountered heavy cloud coverage but lighter-than-usual flak. We bombed from twenty-nine thousand feet and obliterated the escape bridge. On the ground, the U.S. infantry is advancing slowly but surely. Allied forces are only twenty-five miles from Paris! Maybe the war will be over soon.

Thou preparest a table before me in the presence of mine enemies . . .

X. SEPTEMBER 4, 1944	My B-17 officer crew:
Target: Ludwigshafen, Germany	Maj. Fishburn, Capt. McClusky,
	Lts. Gulnac and Craig

Flew wing lead. Our target was the I. G. Farben Chemical Works, which produced numerous war materials (including, we learned later, the gas used to exterminate six million Jews in German concentration camps). Over the target, we were prevented from dropping our bombs because we could not see the Farben plant due to cloud cover. Thus, we had to circle 360° and get back into formation at the "tail end" and make another bomb run. By the time we could complete this maneuver, the 351st Bomb Group was twenty minutes behind the rest of the Eighth Air Force instead of the two-minute interval that customarily separated the bomb groups. The sky was orange and black with exploding flak. Other than at Berlin, I had never seen so many enemy fighters.

Our thirty-six-plane group was literally alone as we reentered the exploding sky en route to the Farben plant. Without hesitation at the Initial Point, Lt. Craig opened our bomb bay doors. We flew our bomb run heaving from the constant concussion of exploding flak as the shells burst into our bomb group—or what remained of it. We were being decimated by the minute.

Just as Craig dropped our ten five-hundred-pound bombs, our plane violently lurched as a flak burst hit us. Both right engines and the right wing caught on fire. We immediately began a slow, out-of-control spin, burning as we fell. The vibration of the two runaway propellers threatened to shake the B-17 apart or, worse, send the propellers flying off and crashing through the nose or the cockpit. Each second seemed an eternity as we fell. I had seen too many other B-17s explode as they had been shot out of formation not to know that we were near death.

Unable to feather the two vibrating right engines, and expecting the fire to ignite the wing fuel tank at any second, Maj. Fishburn gave the order to "bail out" as we helplessly spun down. But the spin toward earth was so steep that centrifugal force held us in our seats. None of us could move toward our escape hatches despite superhuman effort. We were certain the plane would explode at any second.

We fell thirteen thousand feet, but the rapid fall miraculously snuffed out the fire. Getting some control and leveling out at that point, we feathered the two right engines, continuing to lose altitude all the while. All of this consumed mere seconds, but it seemed like an eternity since we had been hit.

We radioed "Mayday! Mayday!" for fighter protection because German fighters were notorious for shooting down cripples . . . and our B-17 was a visible cripple, smoking and losing altitude as we struggled to fly back to England on only our two left engines, dropping steadily, all alone. By a miracle, two P-51 Mustangs heard our distress call and location, found us, and flew beside us for about thirty minutes until their fuel ran low, forcing them to return to their base in England. This left us alone again—still over German-occupied territory, still losing altitude despite throwing all our .50 caliber machine guns, ammunition, and everything else detachable out of the plane in order to lighten it.

As time dragged on, our spirits vacillated from despair to slight hope. We initially feared being spotted by German fighters . . . we were now totally defenseless. Then we expected to crash-land in German-occupied territory. Then we hoped to make the English Channel and ditch in the water. Throughout the ordeal, however, that marvelous B-17 Flying Fortress held together and yielded each foot of altitude grudgingly. Our plane seemed as intent on survival as its crew.

As we began crossing the channel, we had dropped to slightly over one thousand feet . . . and seemed unable to maintain even that. It was turning dusk. We feared if we ditched in the channel, we would drown in its cold, choppy currents.

We cheered when, still airborne, we spotted the east coast of England. Minutes later, we spotted a runway and fired our flares to signal our need for fire trucks and ambulances as we tried to land our severely damaged plane.

The number-one engine failed on approach, but that Flying Fortress earned its name and landed, powered by only the left inboard engine.

The customary landing picture taken of the 351st Bomb Group's lead crew reveals the strain in our faces—and the delirious joy! We were alive! We were home! We literally kissed the ground . . . and none of us was embarrassed

Pictures of the lead officer crew were customarily taken upon landing after a mission. This "customary" landing picture from my tenth mission, to bomb the I. G. Farben Chemical Works in Ludwigshafen, Germany, reveals an "uncustomary" strain in our faces—and the delirious joy—of landing after a mission we had scant hope of surviving. After getting shot up over Ludwigshafen and subsequently separated from our bomb group, we limped back alone across the English Channel, losing thirteen thousand feet along the way, with two engines feathered, a smoking, visible target for German ME-109s. We finally landed at Polebrook powered by only the left inboard engine. Standing, left to right are: Maj. Fishburn, wing commander; Lt. Love, navigator; Lt. Craig, bombardier; Capt. McClusky, pilot; and Lt. Gulnac, navigator. (Love family archives)

to do so. Yes, we had survived against all odds. That night I said the Twenty-third Psalm, as was my bedtime custom, but I never repeated those lines with more gratitude.

I awoke late the next morning, dressed, and walked out of the barracks. Never before had I remotely been as conscious of the pure, sweet, fresh air. Never had the grass been so green, the warm sun so inspiring, the trees so beautiful, the morning so invigorating and crisp, the wonders of God's nature so gloriously evident. I shall always remember that high-pitched sensitivity to my surroundings—it continued for weeks. At age nineteen, I was joyous and thankful to be alive.

Thou anointest my head with oil, my cup runneth over . . .

XI. SEPTEMBER 10, 1944   My B-17 officer crew:
    Target: Merseberg, Germany   Capt. Hillebrand, Lt. Alan Reed

My mission assignments are becoming spaced at wider intervals because I am exclusively flying as a member of the lead crew, heading ever-larger formations, progressing from the 510th Squadron (twelve B-17s) to the 351st Bomb Group (thirty-six B-17s) to our Wing (108 B-17s) to the 1st Division (324 B-17s).

Today's target—once again—was the huge synthetic oil plant at Merseberg. We were assigned to fly deputy wing lead . . . or number-two-position lead for 108 B-17s.

The weather was perfect . . . absolutely clear. I saw more of Europe today than on any previous mission. Our bombing altitude was twenty-eight thousand feet, $-44°C$. We flew formation at the customary 150 mph.

Still climbing toward our assigned bombing altitude, our formation crossed the Rhine River. Hitler's industrialized Ruhr region was heavily defended by flak batteries that fired incessantly at our wing as we flew to Merseberg.

About 11:45, we came within range of the flak batteries guarding Merseberg. The sky was orange and black with flak as we commenced our bomb run. Then, for the first time, I realized that I was *really* on edge about the flak— Ludwigshafen (September 4) and Berlin (August 6) had taken a toll on my nerves. But I was able to maintain composure by totally concentrating on doing my job perfectly as we proceeded at 150 mph through the wall of exploding fire and shrapnel that hit our plane and others in the wing.

We dropped our ten bombs at 12:30. I felt lucky to live through that bomb run, as we blasted Merseberg's synthetic oil plant once again (my third mission to Merseberg!). Hitler's tanks, planes, and trucks would be starved for oil from Merseberg until his slave labor units, working twenty-four hours daily, could rebuild it one more time.

When we landed at Polebrook we counted fifteen gaping holes in our plane. After Ludwigshafen, I had been thinking too much about the fact that the average Eighth Air Force combat crew was killed on its fifteenth mission. I had just completed my eleventh mission with fourteen more to fly.

Surely goodness and mercy shall follow me all the days of my life . . .

XII. SEPTEMBER 22, 1944   My B-17 officer crew:
  Target: Kassel, Germany   Capt. Hillebrand, Lt. Reed

Today's daylight briefing was somewhat of a relief. We were bombing Kassel— not Berlin, or Ludwigshafen, or Merseberg!

The intelligence officer advised us that Kassel was defended by seventy-eight flak batteries. Hillebrand, Love, and Reed would fly deputy wing lead again.

The targets, armored vehicle and motor vehicle factories, were covered with several thousand feet of clouds. We bombed by sighting the shape of the target through a new technological wonder called Pathfinder Force, or PFF, which could "see" through the thick clouds with a radar device. What a miracle!!

The flak batteries concentrated on a B-24 Liberator Bomb Group two minutes in front of our 351st Bomb Group of B-17 Flying Fortresses. We lost no planes. I kept fear in check by concentrating totally on perfectly executing every mission, yet I was still shaken (inwardly) from our close call at Ludwigshafen. I am truly thankful to fly a mission without being shot up. For this mission, I was decorated with the Air Medal Oak Leaf Cluster.

and I will dwell in the house of the Lord forever.

XIII. SEPTEMBER 28, 1944   My B-17 officer crew:
  Target: Magdeburg, Germany   Capt. Keller, Lt. Reed

Our target was an oil refining complex at Magdeburg. Flying deputy wing lead once again, we completed our formation assembly and flew over the English Channel, "on time, on course," as we climbed toward our assigned bombing altitude of twenty-nine thousand feet.

Near the target, German ME-109 fighters hit the group behind us, shooting down several B-17s. Despite heavy cloud undercast, we bombed the target satisfactorily. Although we encountered no flak over the Rhine—for a change—we did experience heavy flak at Magdeburg. Yet, our plane returned to Polebrook with only one hole in the fuselage. "Lucky 13" (or mission "12B") was now behind me. We were *plain* lucky!

The Lord is my shepherd, I shall not want . . .

XIV. OCTOBER 2, 1944
   Target: Kassel, Germany

My B-17 officer crew:
1st Lt. Jim Purcell, Capt. Hillebrand, Lt. Reed

When all the officers flying this mission assembled at 0300 hours in the briefing room, we saw that our mission was the huge ordnance plant on the outskirts of Kassel—a tough one!

Our crew was assigned to lead the 351st Bomb Group. The weather officer predicted moderate-to-heavy cloud coverage at Kassel . . . and he was correct. But the flak was heavier than the cloud cover. Over Kassel, the Plexiglas nose of our B-17 was shattered by flak. My face was hit by flying glass, my heating element was shot out, and my toes began to freeze within twenty minutes. Alan Reed tucked my freezing feet into his undamaged heated jacket, saving my toes from possible amputation.

From what I could observe as we flew away from the target, our incendiary bombs (the first incendiaries dropped on my missions thus far) hit target "only fair." Photos taken thirty minutes later proved that my assessment was too pessimistic; the reconnaissance photos showed the Nazi ordnance plant burning fiercely.

We landed safely at 15:00 hours. My good luck continued, however, because my eyes and face had not been damaged. Roughest mission, besides Ludwigshafen, ever.

Six days later, orders arrived from Eighth Air Force headquarters promoting me to 1st lieutenant. I had been flying combat missions for slightly more than two months, six weeks away from my twentieth birthday.

He maketh me to lie down in green pastures . . .

XV. OCTOBER 3, 1944
   Target: Nuremberg, Germany

My B-17 officer crew:
Capt. Hillebrand and Lt. Reed

Our target was the railroad marshalling yards in the center of Nuremberg. Nuremberg was the home of Europe's largest outdoor arena, from which Hitler delivered his famous speech mobilizing the Nazi party in 1938. Col. Burns, our briefing officer, advised that 109 flak batteries protected our target.

We encountered moderate flak over the target, but shrapnel pierced our Plexiglas nose and wing . . . otherwise a milk run. (Evidently, I am becoming accustomed to having our B-17 battered by flak!)

Of the thirty-six B-17s in our 351st Bomb Group, flak damaged nine. Our results were "fair." We encountered cloud coverage throughout the mission, complicated by a ninety-five-knot upper atmosphere gale over Germany.

He leadeth me beside the still waters . . .

XVI. OCTOBER 19, 1944   My B-17 officer crew:
    Target: Cologne, Germany   Maj. James Gorham, Capt. Jim
                                           Gibbons, 1st Lt. Fred Ralph

Col. Burns announced that our target today was the Ford Tank and Armed Vehicle plant on the northern outskirts of Cologne. Cologne was in the Ruhr . . . and Hitler's flak batteries were there in vast numbers to guard Germany's concentrated manufacturing facilities supplying his war machine from the Ruhr.

Our crew was assigned by Col. Burns to lead a "lone wolf" mission; in other words, the 351st Bomb Group would not fly as a part of the usual one-thousand-plane Eighth Air Force formation on this mission.

Due to atrocious weather conditions on the continent, we were forced to deviate repeatedly from our flight plan. We improvised our route to Cologne, but arrived at the target with a precision that caused me to note in my diary that evening, "*Did best job I have ever done . . . all in all, a damned good mission.*"

Henceforth, Jim Gibbons, Fred Ralph, and I became inseparable friends and flew most of our remaining missions together as a "highly regarded lead crew."

He restoreth my soul . . .

XVII. OCTOBER 22, 1944   My B-17 officer crew:
    Target: Hanover, Germany   Col. Robert Burns, Capts. Eickhoff,
                                           Lyttle, and Maltby

This was my second mission flying with the 351st Bomb Group's base commander, Col. Robert Burns. He had long ago completed his tour of combat missions and now flew only when the 351st had an unusually important mission. Today's was such a mission. The 351st was assigned to lead twelve wings, and Colonel Burns selected me to be a member of his lead crew.

Our target was an armament plant located on the edge of Hanover. At the pre-mission briefing, intelligence officers warned us that we would encounter heavy flak and weather officers forecast a thick undercast.

While light flak pecked at us all the way in and out, we experienced a big surprise because the mission turned out to be a milk run! We bombed with the new technological miracle—PFF—that could "see through" the undercast well enough to generally identify the target area. Pattern bombing did the rest.

We are hitting German armament plants now, which are gaining equal target priority with the synthetic oil plants.

He leadeth me in the paths of righteousness for His name's sake . . .

XVIII. OCTOBER 30, 1944	My B-17 officer crew:
Target: Munster, Germany	Maj. Davies, Capt. Gibbons,
	1st Lt. Ralph

Jim Gibbons, Fred Ralph, and I flew Wing Lead on this strike against the railroad marshalling yards of Munster. As we neared Munster, we encountered bad weather at twenty-eight thousand feet, −52° C. Flew to the target through a ten-mile corridor with heavy flak on both sides and used our PFF radar on the bomb run because 100 percent cloud cover obscured the target.

Considering flak and weather, this was one of the best missions I ever flew, in terms of instituting constant flight plan alterations due to the weather while keeping our formation tightly united and eventually hitting the target.

For this eighteenth mission, I was awarded my second Air Medal Oak Leaf Cluster.

Yea, though I walk through the valley of the shadow of death . . .

XIX. NOVEMBER 7, 1944	My B-17 officer crew:
Target: Frankfurt, Germany	Maj. Gorham, Capts. Gibbons and
	Warren Steitz

Today's target, Frankfurt, was our first visual target in a long time. We encountered "not too much flak," although our plane was hit in the nose section.

But what German flak and fighters failed to do was made up for by the horrible weather we met as we flew back toward England. We flew formation at the standard 150 mph, but our ground speed was at a "snail's pace" because we were flying into 100-knot headwinds. This cost us precious fuel. Ultimately, we were diverted to an airbase at Beecles to refuel, then finally landed at Polebrook at 20:30. Having arisen for the mission at 02:30, we should have been tired . . . and we were!

I will fear no evil . . .

XX. NOVEMBER 12, 1944   My B-17 officer crew:
     Target: Metz Fortress, France   Capts. Dennis and Gibbons,
                                           1st Lts. Ralph and Cook

This was the only low-level "tactical" mission I was ever assigned to fly—and this was against the Metz Fortress, a bastion of the Maginot Line that had been occupied by Nazi troops in 1940. (All of my other flights were high-altitude strategic missions against targets that were generally some distance from Allied troop concentrations on the ever-moving front lines.)

The French had constructed the "impregnable" Maginot Line after World War I to protect it from German aggression. Hitler's Panzer tank divisions proved the Maginot Line otherwise in 1940, outflanking and overrunning the fortification in a matter of weeks. Four years later, the Germans turned its impressive bulwarks against Allied troops advancing toward Germany from the west after D-Day (June 6, 1944).

Gen. George Patton yearned to be the first general to lead Allied troops into Germany across the Rhine, but in November 1944, he could not move past the Metz Fortress. He demanded that the Eighth Air Force obliterate the fortress so that his army could resume its headlong drive into Germany.

Jim Gibbons, Fred Ralph, and I led our 94th Wing into France, assigned to bomb Metz at twelve thousand feet, the lowest altitude from which any of us had ever bombed an enemy target. The heavy cloud coverage grew progressively thicker as we flew east.

We remembered the tragedy immediately after D-Day when a wing of the Eighth Air Force was ordered to provide low-level bombing support to Allied infantry, whose advance into France had been stalled by the German army.

With no training or experience in low-level bombing, they missed the Germans and hit the Allies, killing hundreds of U.S. infantrymen, including the U.S. field commander, Lt. Gen. Lesley J. McNair.

Lacking low-level bombing experience and rapidly approaching a target that was socked in by undercast and surrounded by Patton's army, we were confronted with a potentially pulverizing decision with a tight deadline. Patton had demanded that we knock out the Metz Fortress. But we could not *see* the Metz Fortress. To drop our bombs where our dead-reckoning navigation indicated Metz to be located invited a situation where we might pulverize Patton's troops instead of the German-occupied Metz Fortress.

Every mission flight plan had a *secondary* target in case of bad weather. Rarely had we been forced to bomb the secondary target, but after circling our primary target area several times and finding no break in the undercast, Gibbons, Dennis, Ralph, Cook, and I decided we could not drop our bombs blind and risk hitting Patton's advancing troops in the vicinity. So, we flew past Metz to Saarbrucken, Germany, and hit our secondary target.

We landed at Polebrook at 14:00 hours, disappointed that weather had been the ultimate enemy in our attempt to accelerate Patton's advance toward Hitler's Germany.

for Thou art with me. Thy rod and Thy staff they comfort me . . .

XXI. NOVEMBER 26, 1944
    Target: Hanover, Germany

My officer crew:
Maj. Leonard Roper, wing commander; Capt. Gibbons, 1st Lt. Ralph

At today's predawn briefing, Col. Burns announced that the 351st Bomb Group would lead the 94th Wing and that our target was the heavily defended oil refinery at Misberg, outside of Hanover. One week earlier, I had reached my twentieth birthday.

As we flew the fifteen-minute bomb run from the Initial Point to the target, all hell broke loose. The German flak battery commanders not only had their 88mm guns accurately trained on the 351st, but they concentrated on the lead plane in the lead group in our wing. That was us!

Fred never seemed to notice the exploding steel that laced the sky around us. He flew the plane from the IP with his Norden Bombsite, sighting the target through the smoke below and carefully adjusting the crosshairs to get a fix that compensated for our altitude (thirty thousand feet), speed (150 mph), drift (resultant from wind velocity and direction), and other factors in order to decide the precise moment for "bombs away."

Our plane was continuously buffeted by the tremendous concussions from nearby explosions of flak. The violent lurching made it even more difficult for Fred to focus on the target, but he kept his head glued to the Bombsite through our run. After "bombs away," a flak explosion tore four gaping holes through our Plexiglas nose, destroying the Norden Bombsite Fred had been using a split second earlier. That split second was the difference in Fred's head being blown off!

Suddenly, I felt dizzy, then keeled over and passed out. Fred must have responded instantly. He first jerked off my flak jacket looking for a bloody wound, then saw my oxygen tube swinging loose, completely severed by the shrapnel. He grabbed the portable oxygen, strapped it on my face, and I quickly revived.

When we landed at Polebrook, we counted thirty-five big holes in our B-17 . . . our roughest mission yet besides Ludwigshafen.

Thou preparest a table before me in the presence of mine enemies . . .

XXII. JANUARY 6, 1945   My B-17 office crew:
    Target: Bonn, Germany   Capts. Dennis and Gibbons,
                                   1st Lt. Ralph

When Sgt. Robicheaux opened the door at 03:15 hours, Fred and I sprang out of the sack. We were ready to fly!

German Field Marshal Gerd von Rundstedt had launched an all-out tank, artillery, and infantry attack against Allied forces during December, in a final offensive intended to drive Allied ground forces back to the English Channel. In what came to be known as the "Battle of the Bulge," our troops had been reeling backward in subzero weather . . . beaten and freezing.

The 351st crews had been on standby for three weeks hoping to fly low-level tactical bombing missions against von Rundstedt's supply lines and troops, but the atrocious weather kept the entire Eighth Air Force grounded. German meteorologists called the right weather for von Rundstedt—we could not take off. From daily intelligence reports, we wondered if we might lose the war. The Battle of the Bulge was that serious. The Allies were losing it.

So, we were really ready to fly when this mission was assigned to the 351st Bomb Group this cold, cold morning. We were elated when Col. Burns identified the target as being a critical German supply route bridge over the Rhine, together with troop and supply concentrations near the Bonn railroad marshalling yards. These were the resources von Rundstedt depended on.

Jim Gibbons, Fred Ralph, and I were designated to fly another wing lead.

Weather conditions over Europe were still forbidding, a frigid −55°C at bombing altitude of twenty-nine thousand feet, and so socked in that we were forced to bomb PFF due to a solid 10/10 undercast. We encountered a little flak at Koblenz, but not much. I rated our bombing results as fair, but our desire was intense to help our retreating, freezing, besieged ground troops battling under us in the "Bulge." God's weather seemed to be on Germany's side.

Thou annointest my head with oil . . .

XXIII. FEBRUARY 19, 1945
  Target: Munster, Germany

My B-17 office crew:
Col. Stewart, commander;
Capt. Gibbons, 1st Lt. Ralph

Today's target was the large synthetic oil plant and huge railroad marshalling yard located side by side in Munster. As with earlier missions to Merseberg, nothing crippled Hitler's airplane, tank, and troop mobility more than a shortage of oil. For the Germans, no oil, no war. Hitler concentrated his dwindling flak batteries to defend Germany's large synthetic oil plants because we had knocked the core of Air Marshall Hermann Goering's Luftwaffe out of the air.

Jim, Fred, and I again flew 94th Wing Lead. The heavy clouds and overall weather conditions were not conducive to a visible target . . . but we flew our best mission yet and knocked out the oil plant and rail yards with our best bomb pattern in a long time. Really bad flak hit us en route and over the target. I was lucky—again—not to be wounded seriously (or killed) when a piece of the steel shrapnel from a flak burst bounced off my steel helmet over the target. Krupp Steel versus U.S. Steel. U.S. Steel won that battle! The sole casualty was my throbbing head, but a single aspirin handled that when we landed at Polebrook.

My cup runneth over . . .

XXIV. FEBRUARY 28, 1945
    Target: Soest, Germany

My B-17 officer crew:
Col. Clint Ball, commander;
Capt. Gibbons, 1st Lt. Ralph

At the pre-sunrise briefing, Col. Clint Ball (West Point '38) announced that our target was the marshalling yard at Soest and that he had chosen the Gibbons-Ralph-Love team to fly Lead for the First Division—which would itself lead the Eighth Air Force. Col. Ball would be in command.

This was Jim Gibbons's and Fred Ralph's twenty-fifth—and final—mission. Jim was a slender, imperturbable, quiet Californian who had received his pilot's license before World War II started and whose self-effacing modesty balanced his uncommon competence in a B-17. My admiration, appreciation, and affection for this unassuming, unflappable, skilled man were complete. Fred enjoyed life; his jaunty walk and dashing mustache suggested fun. Above all, this man from Barre, Vermont, was unquestionably the ablest, coolest bombardier in the 351st Bomb Group. Both had always shown complete faith in me . . . and I knew that I was flying with the best when I flew with them. Yes, how fitting that they should fly their last missions leading the Eighth Air Force!

Coincidentally, Soest may have been the best job I ever did. I shall always remember crusty Col. Ball telling me on the intercom a couple of times that I had lived up to his expectations. Coming from Clint Ball, that was really something. It's a funny thing . . . occasionally the prospect of getting killed was of secondary importance to receiving a commendation from a seasoned combat veteran like Col. Ball, a senior officer all of us liked and respected.

For this mission, I was awarded the third Oak Leaf Cluster for my Air Medal. When we landed at Polebrook, Col. Ball stated that he thought my performance on this mission was worthy of the Distinguished Flying Cross (DFC) and that he was recommending to the Eighth Air Force headquarters that I be decorated with the DFC for the Soest mission, together with "a couple of other missions" for which my individual performance had received "special commendation."[6]

Col. Burns and Col. Ball were also instrumental in my promotion to captain. The orders for that promotion came from Eighth Air Force headquarters on May 15, 1945, approximately six months after my twentieth birthday.

Surely goodness and mercy shall follow me all the days of my life . . .

XXV. MARCH 17, 1945   My B-17 officer crew:
    Target: Zeiss Optical   Capts. Dennis and Poston and
    Instrument factory near   Lt. Burr
    Moblis, Germany

Two members of our three-man Lead Crew, Jim Gibbons and Fred Ralph, had completed their tour of twenty-five missions and headed home, but only *after* I adamantly refused their persistent offers to fly one more mission in order for me to complete my twenty-fifth with them.

Their offer was a concrete certification of the exceptional bond we felt for one another, but if one of them had been wounded—or killed—by flying this extra mission, and if I survived, I could never have forgiven myself. So, I determined to fly my twenty-fifth mission with other officers, including Capt. Dennis, with whom I had flown before.

Everyone was superstitious about his final mission. I was no different. I had lost too many friends to fly this mission with "carefree abandon."

First Division commander Brig. Gen. Lacey appeared in the briefing room with Col. Burns to define the objective of today's mission: the Zeiss Optical Instrument factory near Moblis, Germany.

Although the Luftwaffe's fighter planes had been largely destroyed or rendered inoperative due to shortages of both fuel and pilots at this juncture of the war, German flak continued to be heavy and deadly. Nor did the day's weather over Europe welcome our one thousand bombers: the target was totally obscured by clouds. However, we sighted the outline of the factory on our miraculous PFF radar and dropped our bombs, hoping the bomb pattern would envelop Hitler's Zeiss Optical Instrument factory.

About three hours later, when we landed at Polebrook, I realized it was over! I had done my duty! I experienced a profound surge of relief and rejoicing when I jumped from my escape hatch to the tarmac.

For me, World War II in Europe had ended, even though Germany did not surrender for seven more weeks. That night, as was my ritual, I went to sleep thankfully reciting the Twenty-third Psalm. With renewed conviction and thanksgiving, I silently repeated, "I will fear no evil. . . ."

. . . and I will dwell in the house of the Lord forever."

★ The Eighth Air Force had instituted a policy of having its top lead crews train beginner lead crews, and I invested much of my time between missions in this endeavor, primarily flying over Great Britain, observing and teaching the newer lead crews. After my twenty-third mission, having almost completed my twenty-five-mission tour, I was held back from finishing my last few missions so that I could train the relatively inexperienced replacement lead crews. This training continued between my twenty-fifth mission and VE Day.

Germany's surrender on May 8, 1945, set off an explosive celebration all over Europe and the United States, and Polebrook was no exception. The night the news came over the radio, the base came alive with lights, music, and a huge victory party! Local citizens—restricted from the base throughout the war—poured in to help the Yanks celebrate. One of the severest tests of my ability to navigate came in the wee hours of May 9 as I walked from the Officers Club to my quarters.

Then on May 10, as though nothing momentous had just occurred, we received orders to fly to Linz, Austria. Each of our thirty-six B-17s was designated to transport twenty-five French prisoners of war back to France. They had been captured by the Germans when the "impregnable" Maginot Line fell in May 1940. We were ordered to repeat this exercise on May 12. Although Patton's tanks had rushed through the city a few days earlier, no Allied medical teams had arrived by the time we landed. We were not certain what we would find in Linz, but nothing could have prepared us for what we encountered there.

The French officers were ecstatic to see us. Their uniforms were worse for wear, but the men were healthy and overjoyed at their good fortune to be returning home. All had been in German POW camps since the Maginot Line

On May 10, 1945, two days after VE Day, my 351st Bomb Group was ordered to fly to Linz, Austria, to transport twenty-five French prisoners of war back to France in each B-17 bomber. In this picture, the three men in the center are French officers, ex-POWs, who had been captured by the Germans when they overwhelmed the French Maginot Line in May 1940. Our pilot is on the left, and I am on the right. (Love family archives)

had been flanked, breached, and captured in May 1940. One French officer pulled me aside and said, "Lieutenant, if you want to be sure you know what this war has been about, walk across the field. There," he confided, "is the Mauthausen concentration camp."

I cannot recall being briefed—throughout my years of service—on Hitler's concentration camps. Several weeks earlier, I had read the news accounts and seen photographs of the large camp at Belsen that British tanks had stumbled across on April 15, but this assuredly did not prepare me for the reality of Mauthausen. That pitiless, merciless confirmation of Hitler's savagely incomprehensible cruelty will forever be stamped in my memory.

Men, women, and children, dressed in ragged, rough, striped burlap uniforms, leaned against the formerly electrified fence or lay helpless on the ground, their bodies wasted away by disease and starvation. They were emaciated beyond what any photograph could portray. Most were too weak to stand and hardly more alive than the two hundred thousand other Jews who, we learned later, had died in the gas chambers of this camp that we slowly walked through.

I had endured the flak, the fighters, the pressure to execute bombing missions precisely as assigned, and the loss of so many friends in the deadly skies over Germany fighting Hitler. But it was not until two days *after* combat ended in Europe that I truly understood why we fought World War II. Mauthausen will always provide me with indelible proof of man's capacity for inhumanity to his fellow humans if mesmerized by a leader like Adolph Hitler.

After I concluded my twenty-fifth combat mission, I was uncertain for a time about signing up for an additional tour of duty in the Pacific. I had done my job, and the thought of permanently returning to the States was very tempting. Since my tenth mission over Ludwigshafen, I had sensed vaguely that I was living on borrowed time. I also experienced a brief period of disillusionment when my promotion to captain seemed to be delayed, either because of my comparative youth or because scarce promotions often went to pilots instead of navigators. Assuredly, the lead responsibilities assigned me were those normally carried by captains or majors, who were a bit older. But my promotion did come through on May 15, 1945. And in a burst of patriotism that exceeded my sense of self-preservation, no doubt encouraged by the end of the war in Europe and my visit to Mauthausen, I volunteered for another combat tour, this one to be waged against Japan in the Pacific.

There was one more chapter to my tour in Europe, a three-day flight from Polebrook back to the United States via Wales, Iceland, and Labrador. We left England on June 8 and began our thirty-five-hundred-mile trip home with a short hop to Wales. Tragically, almost inconceivably, one of our 351st Bomb Group's B-17s crashed into the Wales hills, killing a crew of brave men who had valiantly fought and survived their combat missions.

We did not fly in formation on this "homerun," so our B-17 was alone in facing the navigational challenges posed by this trans-Atlantic trip. (Please recall that Charles Lindbergh's historic nonstop flight had been accomplished in 1927, only eighteen years earlier.) Now we were taking a bomber, loaded with twenty-five 351st Bomb Group personnel—including Col. Caraway, who had selected me to be his navigator—on a trip across the Atlantic that would require three stops for refueling. In addition, we flew so far north that my compass gyrated wildly due to the northern magnetic fields. My principal means of navigating was an unsophisticated drift meter through which I tried to gauge the wind velocity and direction by "reading" the whitecaps and then calculating how much the wind would force us off course. I had never done this type of ocean whitecap navigation, and everyone in the plane knew that if my calculations were incorrect, we might run out of fuel, off course, and be forced to ditch in the cold waters of the North Atlantic. To the immense relief of all on board, including myself, I hit each refueling stop with pinpoint accuracy.

From Wales, we made a six-and-one-half-hour flight to Meeks, Iceland, on June 9, arriving late in the evening, but with the Northern Lights literally turning night into day. The next morning, it was on to Goose Bay, Labrador, to refuel before making the final leg of our trip to Bangor, Maine.

When we landed in Maine, after a very long day in the air on June 10, I went to the PX and ordered a quart of sweet milk, two ice-cold American beers, and a heaping bowl of chocolate ice cream. I had not had any of these delicacies for eleven months, and I consumed them simultaneously and ravenously. It was wonderful to be back in the United States.

After a thirty-day leave with my mother in San Antonio, I was assigned to the 243rd Army Air Force base at Great Bend, Kansas, to train on the B-29 Superfortress in preparation for joining the war against Japan. Throughout the spring and early summer of 1945, U.S. bombers had been hammering away at targets on the Japanese mainland, preparing the way for an invasion. Our experience in "island hopping" in the Pacific had included fierce and bloody combat on virtually every landing, and U.S. planners assumed that the invasion of mainland Japan would be extraordinarily costly in losses of men. Indeed, estimates of one million American casualties were generally accepted as the price we would pay to invade Japan.

However, such considerations came to an abrupt halt when President Harry Truman ordered the newly developed atom bomb dropped first on Hiroshima on August 6, 1945, and then Nagasaki on August 9. Fred J. Olivi, who had first learned to fly with me in the College Training Detachment class in early 1943 at Ada, Oklahoma, copiloted the B-29 that dropped the atom bomb on Nagasaki.

Decades later, critics argued that Truman was wrong to authorize these new weapons, and that Japan could have been convinced to surrender without the terrible destruction of atomic weapons. Along with most of my generation, I strongly support Truman's decision. This country's decision to enter war against Japan came only after Japan's devastating sneak attack on the

U.S. Pacific fleet at Pearl Harbor. Four years of fighting around the globe had killed and wounded far too many Americans to contemplate a horrible and bloody invasion of Japan, if there was any other option.

As I looked back at those who second-guessed Truman, I am reminded of my own optimism recorded in my diary in August 1944: "Maybe war will be over soon." Four months later, the German advance into the Ardennes shoved our forces back on their heels in the Battle of the Bulge, killing tens of thousands soldiers on both sides and raising at least momentary fears that Hitler might gain a stalemate that would greatly prolong the war or enable Germany to negotiate a peace treaty with the Allies. Like most Americans who had sacrificed for the war effort—both on the battlefront and the home front—I had learned the sharp turns that a war could take. No victory is safe until the other side stops fighting. General Eisenhower had demanded "unconditional surrender" by Germany. He was our leader, and he was right.

I was relieved when Japan surrendered in August 1945, without an invasion, after our two atomic bombs struck. I would not be flying missions over Japan in a B-29. Instead, I could go home and resume my real life.

In the fall of 1945, as I waited for my discharge, I enjoyed two weeks of sightseeing in Atlantic City, New York, Philadelphia, and Washington, D.C. I also took a side trip to visit an aunt and uncle in Casper, Wyoming, and fell in love with the open West. My adjustment to civilian status began on these trips, and it moved forward sharply after my discharge on December 10, 1945, at Sioux Falls, South Dakota. My service in World War II had been packed with enough danger and drama to last a lifetime, and I was eager to return to my "real life" and whatever it would bring.

NOTES

1. Eric Hawkinson, *When Did We Quit—8th Air Force,* reprinted in *Congressional Record,* 102nd Cong., 1st sess., 137 (March 21, 1991). Also, Charles N. Stevens, *An Innocent at Polebrook: A Memoir of an 8th Air Force Bombardier* (Bloomington, Ind.: 1stBooks, 2003), and Brian D. O'Neill, *Half a Wing, Three Engines and a Prayer* (New York: McGraw-Hill, 1998).

2. When I married Margaret McKean in Austin on September 20, 1947, our very first wedding gift came from my beloved pilot Jim "Hoot" Gibbons, who had returned to California after the war. Throughout my life, it has been a great pleasure to renew these wartime friendships whenever possible.

3. Years after the war, I had the pleasure of accompanying my grandson Benton on his first tour of the inside of a B-17. His immediate impression was that it was "so tight and cramped."

4. Joseph E. Persico, *Roosevelt's Secret War: FDR and World War II Espionage* (New York: Random House, 2001).

5. Ben Smith Jr. *Chick's Crew: A Tale of the Eighth Air Force World War II* (Tallahassee, Fla.: Rose Printing Company, 1983), 128.

6. I was awarded eleven combat decorations, including the Distinguished Flying Cross.

The three missions cited in the Eighth Air Force General Order #321, issued April 16, 1945, decorating me with the Distinguished Flying Cross were for two missions to Munster, Germany, flown October 30, 1944, and February 19, 1945, and one to Soest, Germany, flown February 28, 1945.

I returned to the University of Texas in January 1946, a twenty-one-year-old Air Force captain-turned-sophomore determined to get a good education and eager to move on with my life. A four-thousand-dollar nest egg from my service pay and poker winnings, a part-time job, and the GI Bill would help make it happen. The Ben Love who returned to Austin was older than his years and more committed than ever to securing the education he needed to succeed in life.

The University of Texas had also changed dramatically by 1946. Although the buildings, and even many of the professors, were the same as they had been in 1942, the tone and the student body were not the same. The educational assistance provided by the GI Bill flooded the university with students who helped transform UT and other state universities in the postwar years. We were not kids fresh off the farm. We were not in awe of our professors. The war had given us maturity and a hard edge. We were anxiously eager to learn and respectfully demanding of those who taught us. The air in Austin in those years buzzed with energy and urgency as we set about making up for lost time in the classroom, in our social lives, and in our personal lives. We were lucky to be alive, and we were crammed with a zest to live and a desire to achieve.

I moved back into the Deke fraternity house, and I returned to work at The Toggery on the Drag for four or five hours a day to conserve my nest egg. Before the war, I earned the prevailing wage of twenty-five cents an hour. After the war, I earned the prevailing wage of sixty-five cents an hour, a nice increase but still a material reduction from a captain's flight pay.

Pre-law had been my major before the war. As a boy, I dreamed of becoming a lawyer and eventually entering politics. Although that dream still had appeal, its glow was dimmed by the prospect of five more years of school. Frankly, I was itching to put my nest egg to work, so I transferred to business. This was a decision I have never regretted, thanks in no small part to the superb training I received at the UT Business School.

Among the many outstanding professors I had, one stands out. William Paxton Boyd taught a course called "Business Letter Writing," which also turned out to be a study in business psychology, precise written communication, and salesmanship. He was the toughest teacher imaginable. I do not know whether he could sing, but I do know that Mr. Boyd preceded Frank Sinatra in demanding "All or Nothing at All." Any miscue in expressing convincingly, concisely, clearly, and completely how good your product *really* was, and you were shot down, his aim as unerring as a Messerschmitt-109's at a B-17. With Mr. Boyd, your letter was either right or wrong, A or F. Like many of his other students, I confess to experiencing a love-hate relationship with him. I hated him at moments, but I loved what I was learning. My "A" in his course is a happy conclusion I still savor.

But student life was not all study. I pitched intramural softball for a Deke team with a roster of returning servicemen that included such athletes as Tom Landry, Ralph Ellsworth, George McCall, and Lewis Holder. All were outstanding UT varsity football players who could also hit a softball and run exceptionally fast. I believe they would join me—were all of them still alive—in acknowledging that at moments in our various contests on the softball diamond, winning that particular game seemed almost as important as winning World War II. In any event, the Dekes did not lose a game, and the University of Texas intramural athletic committee selected me as the UT intramural all-star pitcher. That accomplishment was the peak of my climb up the athletic ladder.

The University of Texas offered me a superior education at a price I could afford, and the Dekes, in electing me president of the fraternity in 1946, gave me another practical lesson in leadership. I enjoyed my years at UT both before and after the war, but I have to admit I was ready to move out into the world when I graduated in June 1947 with a Bachelor of Business Administration.

★ MY MAIN CHANCE

After the war, so many veterans were entering the workforce at the same time that companies did not need to recruit college graduates. Procter & Gamble was the only company that came to interview at the University of Texas in both 1946 and 1947. It is a great company, and I must have passed the interview because the district manager asked me to accompany him and a salesman to see what they did. This included going to small grocery stores and stacking Oxydol, or whatever P&G product needed stacking. Was this the job for me?

Well, maybe I hoped I could do more than sell soap. Maybe I had gained self-confidence by achieving my captaincy in the Air Corps six months after I turned twenty. Maybe my dreams for a future had been overenergized by those visionary Houston businessmen who had driven the Ellington Air Force cadets around town on Saturday afternoons and excited us with their conversations about the future of the Ship Channel, about the Texas Medical Center, about what lay ahead for a city whose industrial production had more than doubled for wartime and promised to keep right on going in peacetime. I had grown up in the Depression on a farm where there was no hope of a way out except by making good grades. Well, I had made good grades, and I had become infatuated with Houston as a heady place of promise where, if you worked, you had some chance for material success. Houston was inclusive. There was energy here. Those businessmen were progressive and positive. They were not jealous of one another. "We *can* do this," they would say. "We *can* do that." This was an ambitious city clearly on the move. I believed them, and I wanted to participate. I was coming to Houston in search of my main chance.

★ POSTWAR HOUSTON

World War II had pushed a city that was built on cotton and shipping, and oil after Spindletop in 1901, to a new stage of development. The wartime boom had been fed by the expansion of oil, petrochemicals, oil tools, natural gas, and steel vital to the Allied victory. The reconversion to peacetime, though not always smooth, moved quickly in the wake of the all-out war effort that had wrought fundamental changes in the city's industrial organization. The Houston I encountered in 1947 was obviously poised for a postwar boom, and I hoped to find a way to ride this explosion in pursuit of my own ambitions.

Houston was by no means a finished metropolis. That was part of its appeal. Walking streets filled with newcomers who had been drawn by the hope of better opportunities, I could feel the possibilities. I could sense that this was not a place where an ambitious young man would be forced to wait in line for decades before being accepted as a mover. I learned later about Houston's historical openness to outsiders. Those who migrated to the city and brought with them ideas and a willingness to work had always been quickly accepted as "Houstonians" because not too many residents were actually born here. This was particularly true during the amazing era of sustained expansion that was to transform Houston from a good-sized city of 384,500 in 1940 into a major metropolitan area of more than 1.2 million in the twenty-five years after World War II,[1] and I was lucky to arrive just as it entered this boom.

★ MAGNOLIA PAPER COMPANY

Of course, to participate in this boom, I had to find work. In 1947, this proved tricky because the economy still suffered from shortages and dislocations as the conversion to peacetime production moved forward. My job search led me to the Houstonians I knew best. I had been in navigator training with Ralph Schnitzer Jr. His grandfather, Max Schnitzer, had founded Magnolia Paper Company, a wholesale paper and packaging distributor, in Houston, and Ralph urged me to talk to his father about a job. After deciding to build a more college-educated sales force, Mr. Schnitzer not only hired me, but also hired two of my fraternity brothers at the same time.

In June 1947, I started work at Magnolia Paper Company for two hundred dollars a month as a commissioned salesman. My territory was one the established salesmen did not want. I drew the mom-and-pop stores in less prosperous, out-of-the-way areas. Transportation was my first hurdle. I had to have a car. My college roommate, Webb Carnes, was one of the other new Magnolia Paper salesmen. His father, who owned an automobile agency in San Antonio, found a used 1938 Chevrolet sedan in good condition and sold it to me for about two hundred dollars. I was fortunate to find an automobile at all because none had been built during the war. Even getting a secondhand car took some pull.

My next hurdle was driving that car in Houston traffic. Even though I had conquered fear in combat situations with a 32 percent casualty rate, Houston traffic absolutely scared the bejesus out of me. All of those damned cars seemed to honk at me at the same time I was wondering if my own vehicle was about to break down!

However, I leapt those hurdles and began making sales, and my compensation steadily increased to about $600–$650 a month. The Chinese-, African-, and Italian-American storekeepers I called on seemed to like this young guy who was just starting out and working hard, just as they were.

★ MARGARET MCKEAN

Two or three weeks after I returned to the UT campus from the war, I met Margaret McKean in the receiving line at a Kappa Alpha Theta open house held for the Dekes. One of my fraternity brothers, Dick LaRue, had, for some reason, mentioned me to her, and I remembered her picture from a copy of the *Daily Texan,* the campus newspaper, that a cousin had sent me while I was in the UK. She had been one of five finalists for "Sweetheart of the University of Texas," and I had immediately thought, "Well, *that* is a pretty girl." When I finally met her, I found that the photograph told only half the truth—and she made good grades, too!

But getting beyond "pleased to meet you" was not easy. As I said, she was in the receiving line, and she *stayed* in that receiving line for a long time after seating me on the sofa next to the homeliest girl I think I have ever seen. Finally, Margaret completed her duties and sat down beside me.

Then I called her for a date every day for a month. She was always busy. On my "final" effort, her Theta little sister, Margie Thalaneus, cut in on our conversation and said, "Try next Thursday." Then I asked Margaret, "Well, all right, how about next Thursday?" That worked.

It was sometimes difficult for me to revert to a "white-oxford-cloth, buttoned-down-collar schoolboy," having carried the responsibility of flying combat missions with the Eighth Air Force as lead navigator. I occasionally became restless and yearned for the romanticized solitude of Wyoming, deciding I could escape from being a schoolboy and eke out a living there as a cowboy. Margaret materially assisted in reorienting me to the real world by encouraging me to complete my courses at the University of Texas. Anyway, I doubt that I would I been much of a cowboy.

Even after I had found my mate for life, we were engaged for more than a year because my yearning for economic self-sufficiency was a deterrent to marrying any sooner. Margaret's family had been financially well-off, and I could not be proud of myself if I could not provide for us. Margaret was from an old Austin family. Her father had a wholesale dry goods distributorship

Margaret McKean and I were married on September 20, 1947, beginning a strong partnership that has lasted to this day. (Love family archives)

that sold directly to retail stores all over Texas. He died before we met, but her mother, a beautiful and intelligent lady, viewed me with a "correct coolness." I do not blame her a bit, because my prospects at that moment must not have seemed conspicuously promising.

Margaret and I never discussed finances, but on the eve of our wedding on September 20, 1947, she did inquire, "Do you mind if I ask how much you make?" I said, "Why, of course not. Two hundred dollars." After a long silence, she asked, "How often?"

Housing in Houston was scarce due to the World War II restriction on residential construction. In the four months I worked in Houston before our marriage, I had lived downtown at the YMCA on 1600 Louisiana. I finally found a house on Ruth Street that would be available in September. The landlady said she would hold it for us *if* I paid her a four-hundred-dollar cash bonus, up front, in June. Well, that took a bite out of my four-thousand-dollar nest egg, but at least we had a place to live. However, in September, when we came to occupy the home, she declared that no such agreement or cash transaction had occurred. We finally found an upstairs apartment on Brandt Street.

★ GIFT-RAPS, INC.

After about two years with Magnolia Paper Company, I failed to find the kind of profit potential in the wholesale paper business that would have inspired me to continue that pursuit for the rest of my life. I became restless. I wanted to build something of my own, to manufacture something, and I knew that I had the passion and ambition to succeed if only I could find the right opportunity and product. I had no connections and very little capital, but I did detect something Magnolia was not doing and was not interested in doing. I decided that I might build a successful new business if I could find an opportunity that would:

Yield healthy profit margins
Attract other underemployed ex-servicemen as salesmen
Develop a national demand through retail stores
Be sufficiently superior to competitive products to attract chain stores
    and large department stores
Feature a distinctive brand name, product value, and price that
    customers would recognize and seek
Be a project that I could finance.

Bill Crutcher, Magnolia Paper Company's sales manager, with twenty-five years of experience in the paper industry, and Margaret's stepfather, Harold Lawrence, an attorney, were enthusiastic about going into business with me. In 1949, we pooled our resources, which totaled twenty-five thousand dollars, and incorporated in Texas as GIFT-RAPS, Inc.

Little did I know at the time that I was entering a sixteen-year period in which I would pour myself into the task of building a successful company and then merging it into a larger enterprise. I lived through the classic cycle of a small business start-up. My company was nurtured by sweat equity, the team spirit of a small group of dedicated employees, a clear sense of strategy, and a willingness to think creatively about all phases of the business. As it grew, I had to find ways to retain the momentum of its early years while learning the specifics of manufacturing, marketing, finance, and motivation that would push the company forward. Then I had to decide what to do as its success drew the attention of older, larger competitors.

Finally, I chose to sell the company. I then negotiated a merger with a larger, New York Stock Exchange–listed company where I learned a higher level of the art of business systems and management. During the entire cycle, I worked with a passion to build a company I could be proud of; in the process, I became an experienced entrepreneur and businessman.

Of course, my initial goal was much simpler. I wanted to survive and, in time, to prosper. The key to success was a basic hunch that I had identified a unique product in a market with potential for growth. At the time, all gift-wrapping paper was sold in 26″ × 20″ sheets, three sheets to a package, usually folded, but occasionally rolled on a tube. My idea was simple: I would *not* cut the paper into the standard 26″ × 20″ sheets. Rather, I would wrap one continuous sheet on a roll and add a label proclaiming, "Just cut off the size your package requires!" This product offered several advantages:

- There would be no splicing for large packages. Our paper products were 26″ × 60″ in one continuous roll versus Hallmark's three 26″ × 20″ sheets.
- There would be scant wasted paper or leftover end pieces because our product was one long sheet.
- There would be no wrinkles. Our paper was rolled, not folded.

We decided to print a retail price of twenty-five cents on each label versus the competition's three-sheet packages that retailed for twenty-nine cents.

Before GIFT-RAPS opened for business, I discussed my idea with an officer of one of the large downtown banks. The gentleman who counseled me said, "You know, you seem like a nice young man, and you've saved some money. You should invest it wisely." Then he added, "This gift-wrap business— goodness, nobody's going to pay any real money to buy something they just tear off a package and throw away."[2] This was the first of several "discouraging words" I was to receive from conservative bankers.

I went counter to his advice. With our twenty-five thousand dollars in capital, GIFT-RAPS, Inc. leased an eight-hundred-square-foot masonry building in a multi-use, commercial-residential area on Fairview Street. Then we established contacts with suppliers, bought a modest amount of equipment, called on prospective customers, hired employees, manufactured our continuous-sheet rolls of paper, and went to work filling orders.

Our major suppliers were Queen City Paper Company in Cincinnati, Ohio, which wholesaled Champion Paper Company's coated papers in master rolls, and H. D. Catty Corporation, a Connecticut-based intermediary firm that laminated aluminum to paper, then printed the foil. At first, GIFT-RAPS bought raw material through these middlemen, but as our volume grew and we established a payment record, we petitioned Champion and Revere Copper & Brass Company to sell to us directly. After much discussion, they agreed, and that saved us about 20 percent on our raw material.

Ours was a "by-hand" operation. We rigged up long tables, each equipped with a sliding cutting razor on a rod and a sturdy holder for the 26-inch-wide, 150-pound master rolls of paper. Our employees cut and rolled the paper, labeled, and wrapped the rolls in acetate, all by hand, and packed fifty rolls in corrugated boxes for shipping to our retail customers.

Bill, Harold, and I were the salesmen. Harold Lawrence, whose health was never good, concentrated on Texas sales from his home in Austin. In addition to buying all the raw materials, hiring employees, and planning production schedules, I was also the chief financial officer. If production became a problem, I cut and rolled paper. If shipping became a problem, I expedited shipping. I think this style of management could be called leadership by example in its simplest form.

We could afford to pay only minimum wage, but we hired steadfast, honest, hardworking people, we worked alongside them, and we included them in our frequent conversations about sales and quality workmanship. We were a team. We had only three employees at first, one warehouseman–truck driver and two office-production workers, but we built up to about one hundred and fifty workers during the fall seasonal upsurges.

Before long, I was working such long hours that Margaret and I rarely saw each other. One day she said, "Why don't I come over and see what I can do?" She saw the need for a telephone receptionist and bookkeeper and went to work as our fourth employee. She had earned her degree in nutrition (UT '47, with honors) and had never taken a course in accounting, but she mastered the assignment expertly and continued working for about three years. Nor were her contributions entirely of the "white collar" variety. A hurricane roared into Houston in 1949, and Margaret joined the rest of the staff as we boarded up the plant for the storm. Fortunately, the next day dawned bright and sunny, because I had to rush her to the hospital. Our first child, Jeffrey Benton Love, was born on October 4, 1949.

Mother helped out, too. She had been teaching near Austin when Margaret and I married, but she moved to Houston after she retired in 1949 and pitched in at GIFT-RAPS to audit our increasingly voluminous motor freight shipments and freight bills.

Before the end of our first year in business, Bill Crutcher asked to be bought out. Concerns about the company's survival, the stress, the long hours, and related hardships caused him to conclude that he needed a job with more certainty. His request imposed on us an unexpected need for funds, a modest amount, but everything financial was in relationship to our ability to provide funds. Indeed, during that first year, GIFT-RAPS became a real mom-and-pop-and-son-and-mother-and-father-in-law operation! At the end of 1949, after a few months in business, we tallied up thirty-two thousand dollars in sales.

Our first customers were the Sears and Foley's department stores in Houston. Their response was enthusiastic. Our product was new, and their customers liked it and bought it. We had no competition, and we were off to a fine start. Soon the manager of the downtown Houston Woolworth's store, Herbert Hocher, began noticing people walking through his store with rolls of GIFT-RAPS paper sticking out of their Foley's shopping bags. So he went to Foley's, bought a roll, read the label, called us, and placed an order. Mr. Hocher's sales of our individual 26″ × 60″ rolls soon caught the attention of the district buyer, Ray Wooden, and he placed orders for thirty-eight Woolworth stores in this region.

That new business was wonderful, but it overwhelmed our capacity to produce. In 1950, we leased a fifteen-hundred-square-foot plant nearby on Hyde Park Street, an unheated, un-air-conditioned structure with dirt floors throughout. Every cent we could find, including modest loans from River Oaks Bank (secured by some U.S. government bonds Margaret's father left her when he died in 1938), was invested in inventory.

By 1952, we had ten employees and had outgrown the Hyde Park facility. Harold and I decided to construct our own plant, get it financed, and start building equity. We formed a separate partnership and erected a handsome one-and-one-half-story redwood facility at 2445 Bartlett Street that seemed to offer plenty of room to grow. Within a year, however, we needed more space. The lot next door was available, and we bought it and constructed a comparable building that put fifteen thousand square feet of double-decked space under our combined roofs.

By 1955, with one hundred and fifty exceptionally loyal, able, unbelievably hardworking people on the payroll—including a superb design artist—we had built a two-story masonry plant within one hundred yards of our two redwood facilities on Bartlett. We even managed to purchase additional equipment during this period, including a complicated, automated rolling machine that never did prove as efficient as our "by-hand" operation for the sixty-inch retail rolls.

And in 1962, at the time of our merger with NYSE-listed Gibson Greeting Cards, we began to negotiate with Gibson to construct a spacious new plant on Seamist Street, in a beautiful industrial section in northwest Houston. During the first years, we operated within our personal resources and with what credit we could get from our suppliers. We were able to secure some ninety-day invoice payment dating on materials, which was very important. This left it up to us to manufacture that material into final products, sell, bill, collect, and pay our suppliers within the ninety days or the agreed payment period, which at times was even longer. Instead of ordering enough for three or four months, we might order almost on a weekly—certainly no more than a monthly—basis. Our capital would suffice only if we kept turning that inventory, and turning it and turning it. Fast!³

When I needed advice about inventory financing, I did not approach the downtown banker, who had seemed to discourage a young guy trying to get started. Instead, I turned to a banker at the suburban River Oaks Bank. However, the equally skeptical officer there offered this advice: "Well, you shouldn't try to get credit from suppliers. You want to pay cash for all your raw materials upon delivery or in advance."⁴

Once again, a traditional, conservative banker and I differed on a matter of business. Here I was, a twenty-something guy, writing letters to establish relationships with big suppliers. To ask them to deliver my orders on a cash-on-delivery basis would make my operation seem so amateurish and so lacking in concept that I did not think they would have answered me. Thus, I ignored that banker's advice and demanded credit from my largest raw material suppliers.

At first, I got no response. But I kept up a steady barrage of letters and phone calls, and finally, one paper supplier's district sales manager showed up at our business and asked, "How much do you think you can sell?" I stated, "125 reams." This was a very modest amount, and he sold me the material on open account.

We gradually built up the confidence of our suppliers because we always paid our bills exactly as agreed, never one day late. Although we discounted every invoice, we would negotiate very diligently, extremely hard, for invoice dating. And once we reached an agreement, we always kept it precisely. As Mother would say, "We made our word as good as a government bond." We never lost a single discount.[5] In the process, we convinced our much larger suppliers that we were hardworking, honest professionals who should be taken seriously.

Our small size at times caused problems. We gave our customers a 2 percent discount on invoices paid within ten days, and we required them to pay us by then. Most of our chain store customers realized that we were a small firm with a unique product and accommodated us. But when our larger competitors, such as Dow Chemical's Benmont Papers, began shipping Christmas goods in September but not asking for payment until after Christmas, our customers began petitioning us for the same terms. Large retail organizations, such as Sears, wanted to receive invoice dating from their suppliers just as we did from our suppliers, but there was no way our capital could stretch to accommodate them.

One time, a very large company's purchasing department accepted our terms, but the treasurer's department wrote that they were going to take dating. We had to risk losing that important relationship and tell them again that we could not extend dating. They did not believe us, did not pay us, and we charged them interest on the invoices that were not paid on time. This finally convinced them that we meant business. Fortunately, we did not lose that business.

In about 1951, searching for additional efficiencies, I began talking to our raw material suppliers' mill foremen about coordinating our orders with their most efficient production routines. For example, at Champion headquarters in Hamilton, Ohio, the head foreman told me that the coated paper we were buying in 150-pound rolls could be produced by the mill considerably more cheaply in 500-pound rolls. Although the larger rolls meant we would need to buy a Clark lift truck to handle them, our 20 percent savings on this critical raw material made the cost of the forklift more than feasible.

At Revere Copper & Brass Company in Brooklyn, New York, I learned that, rather than basing their prices on their own most efficient production methods, the company's sales department drew up their price lists and included prepaid motor freight to the customer's destination in their quotations. At that time, motor freight ran $4.58 per one hundred pounds, whereas shipping by water from Brooklyn into the Port of Houston cost ninety cents per one hundred pounds—and took just thirty days longer en transit. Well, that was a no-brainer. We asked the company to rebate the freight charges to us. We would ship by water and pay our own transit costs. Revere's lawyers finally agreed that departing from their published price list in our case would not violate existing federal law, and we thus reduced our raw material cost from Revere by a very meaningful $3.68 per one hundred pounds.

Then the plant foreman told me that Revere could cut its production costs considerably if we ordered quantities geared to what the Revere plant could produce on one machine in one eight-hour shift with no interruptions. I negotiated with Revere to split the savings with us on such orders. I emphasized that this would produce a "win-win" result. Again, the lawyers had to make sure that passing these savings along to us would not violate federal law. Eventually they agreed, and we gained another raw material cost advantage over our national competitors.

Finally, I learned that Revere had slack seasons during early and midsummer when its plant did not operate at capacity. I negotiated to place our orders during their slow times if Revere would date our invoices as of December 31. This made financial sense to the company, and it gave us time to collect from our own customers before our Revere bills were due.

We subsequently negotiated these same ordering and shipping arrangements with our other suppliers. As a side benefit, this put raw material into our plant all year long and helped us level out our own production schedules.

Throughout this fast-growing period, my thoughts were preoccupied with the efficient use of our capital. I think we earned concessions that few comparable firms received, from suppliers on one end and customers on the other. Stated briefly, our financial plan was predicated on negotiating delayed invoice payment terms with our suppliers and insisting on our own short terms in promptly collecting our own customers' accounts receivable. These agreements were not easy to negotiate. I had to think like a big corporation in buying and selling, but I had to reduce raw material costs and control expenses in the most frugal manner imaginable.[6]

I concentrated our purchasing with the suppliers that offered us the best products and accommodations, and we were very loyal. But we were tough customers because we negotiated skillfully, firmly, knowledgeably, and intelligently on price, terms, and quality. I discovered that these negotiations were akin to combat.

★ SELLING WITHOUT A SALES FORCE

At the beginning of each year, I calculated painstakingly the dollar volume and units of each product I thought we could sell, and every component of our costs and profit margins. From this, I developed a series of production schedules. By multiplying sales on top of the solid foundation of product cost control and by maintaining our profit margins without expanding our overhead disproportionately, we increased profits year by year.

We initially thought that stores in the large cities in Texas would generate the volume to support our operation, but soon it became obvious that we needed a broader market. We decided that the first thing we would *not* do was spend money to build a national sales organization. The best way I know to create immediate overhead and delayed returns is to invest in a large sales force, especially with capital already strained. Harold and I decided that the two of us would do all the selling.

Because two people could not possibly call on thousands of individual stores, we decided to call on buyers who purchased for, say, twenty stores. One sale equaled twenty sales. We started in Houston, then identified chain operations throughout Texas, then ventured into Oklahoma and eventually into St. Louis. We called on these large retail chain operations and tried for all the business we could get, limiting a single customer to 10 percent of our annually expanding volume.

Finally, we tackled New York and the national chain stores like S. H. Kress, Newbury, and W. T. Grant. At first, these tough buyers were dubious about the ability of this upstart Texas company to compete with their large, long-established suppliers. In fact, Kress even sent their buyer, M. L. Roberts, a really likeable man, to Houston to see if we had the capacity to handle their account. Fortunately, he decided we could and placed orders for the entire chain. With this contract, we added a second shift and began working ten to eleven hours per shift.

★ YOUNG PRESIDENTS' ORGANIZATION

While GIFT-RAPS was growing rapidly, there was little time for civic or community work. I joined the ex-students association of the University of Texas Business School soon after I moved to Houston; I made time to throw baseballs to my son Jeff from the time he was old enough to hold a bat; and I attended his Boy Scout meetings. But that was about it. I spent fifteen hours a day at the plant, focusing all my efforts on building a successful business. However, I did belong to one group that had a significant impact on me then and continues to do so today—the Young Presidents' Organization (YPO).

YPO was founded in 1950 by a young man who was thrust into the president's chair of his father's large manufacturing company after only one year with the company. He was twenty-eight at the time, and he knew he needed help. Finding few mentors from a board of directors that was of his dad's generation, he looked around for other young men who had been forced to take on large responsibilities. And thus YPO was born as a teaching and learning organization for its members, one that sometimes functioned as an informal board of directors.[7]

The Houston arm of the Texas YPO was organized by a friend of mine, Bud Adams, who was then the Phillips Petroleum franchisee for the Houston area. A YPO member had to be under thirty-five years of age and president of a company that generated one million dollars in annual sales. Bud's wife, Nancy, and Margaret were close friends and sorority sisters. Bud had been after me to join, and when GIFT-RAPS's sales finally reached one million dollars in 1957, I joined. I was thirty-three.

At that time, there were only twelve YPO members in Houston, but our group quadrupled by the next year. The energy and enthusiasm of the group foretold the success of its members and of the city. We were fortunate to come into contact with each other at formative times in our careers. Lloyd Bentsen was president of Lincoln Liberty Life Insurance Company. Both Duncan brothers belonged. Charles was running the family business, Duncan Coffee Company; John was cofounder of Gulf & Western. George Mitchell, as president of Christie, Mitchell & Mitchell, was a geologist just starting to build his oil and real estate empire. Bill Lane was president of River Brand Rice Mills, with offices in the American General building. Robert Herring was president of Valley Gas Transmission, Inc.

Our meetings were open and stimulating because we all faced related challenges, whether it was marketing, or production, or attracting the right people, or operating on limited capital. We all worked hard, and it was not always "behind-the-desk" kind of work, either. Bud's father, who was chairman and CEO of Phillips Petroleum headquartered in Bartlesville, Oklahoma, had assigned his energetic son to develop the Houston franchise. On days when a new Phillips station opened, Bud would be out pumping gasoline with the rest of his crew.

One day, John Duncan suggested that we tour each other's plants to look around and make suggestions. The group's reaction to their visit to GIFT-RAPS is one I will never forget. My fellow YPO members actually thought we wrapped gifts for stores like Foley's and Neiman Marcus and employed hundreds of women to cut ribbons and tie beautiful bows. Imagine their astonishment when they walked into an assembly-line operation and dodged forklift trucks hauling 500-pound rolls of paper! John and the other YPOers exclaimed, "I didn't realize GIFT-RAPS was *that* kind of operation!"

At regular meetings, we might discuss problems or hear a motivational speaker, such as Ben Woodson, president of American General, who had joined founder Gus Wortham in building an extremely large international insurance company. The regional YPO organization sponsored annual conferences with terrific guests like the dean of the business school at the University of Southern California and the nation's most successful corporate CEOs.

My fellow YPO members steadily became better established. Lloyd Bentsen was elected to the U.S. Senate. Bud Adams founded the American Football League Houston Oilers professional team, which is now the Tennessee Titans of the National Football League. George Mitchell built a business empire around Mitchell Energy and The Woodlands. When Duncan Coffee was sold to Coca-Cola, Charles Duncan became president and director of Coca-Cola, then later served as U.S. Secretary of Energy under President Jimmy Carter. John Duncan moved forward when Gulf & Western merged with Paramount (later Viacom). Bill Lane's company evolved into

Riviana Foods, with international scope. Robert Herring became chairman of Houston Natural Gas Company after his company was acquired by this major utility.

As we succeeded in business and politics, our shared experiences in helping one another build successful business enterprises forged bonds that held us together for a lifetime. At a critical time in our lives, we traded ideas and encouragement that helped us create thriving businesses. The web of friendships woven among these "young presidents" continues strong today as we work together to do things for the city. Indeed, many of my fellow young presidents remain my oldest friends.

★ GIFT-RAPS AND CHAMPION

A moment of consternation occurred in the mid-1950s when one of our suppliers, Champion Paper Company, announced to me that they were going into competition with GIFT-RAPS. The officers of this huge company then backed off and said they would consider buying GIFT-RAPS instead. Champion proposed to close our relatively small operation and incorporate our customers and knowledge into their headquarters at the mill in Hamilton, Ohio. It meant nothing to them that GIFT-RAPS had created a significant new use for their Krome Kote and Colorcast papers. Kent cigarette packages were wrapped in Krome Kote, yet we bought more Krome Kote tonnage than did Kent.

Neither Harold nor I was interested in selling the business—and Margaret was not interested in moving to Hamilton, Ohio. But I failed to dissuade them. Marshalling its vast financial resources, its nationwide distribution system, and its state-of-the-art printing equipment, Champion set up a division in direct competition with GIFT-RAPS.

That did not bode well for us. In fact, I thought it was so unfair that I wrote Senator Ralph Yarborough[8] and sent a copy to the CEO of Champion, Ruben Robertson, and the sales manager, Sterling Browning. This may have given them pause because, bless his liberal Democratic heart, Senator Yarborough was very sensitive to small business. He wondered if our situation might be of interest to the Justice Department, and if new legislation should be introduced. We were probably on shaky ground, but Senator Yarborough did take great interest in us, and his interest did seem to moderate the ardor of Champion's ambitious competition.

Jeffrey Benton Love was born on October 4, 1949. Today he is managing partner of the Locke Liddell & Sapp law firm's Houston office of 175 lawyers. Jeff graduated from Vanderbilt (where he still holds the school's all-time batting record) and the University of Texas Law School. He was elected president of the UT Law School Association, the youngest person ever elected to that position. (Love family archives)

 GIFT-RAPS AND GIBSON

Champion's action was fair warning for us to decide whether to grow GIFT-RAPS and compete nationally or to start looking at merger partners. We had no competition in our particular facet of this industry when we started, but by 1960, more than twenty identifiable companies—plus our own suppliers—crowded the field.[9] I had invested every penny I owned and could borrow in the business. The years were passing. Margaret, who valiantly worked by my side when we first started, had given birth to three children.[10]

I worked at GIFT-RAPS seven days a week during the August-through-December busy season and six days a week during the "slow" season. Profitable and growing, the business rang up three million dollars in sales in 1962. But we knew that competition would come eventually from other primary producers if we became a really large operation.

We had preliminary discussions with many prospects, including investment bankers and such firms as Sun Chemical Company, Dow Chemical

Jan, our older daughter and a Phi Beta Kappa, married Tom Simmons, managing director of Spencer Stuart in Houston. She serves actively on the development board of the Casa de Esperanza de los Niños, a group that provides a home-like setting for abused and neglected children until they can be placed in a real home. (Love family archives)

Company, and American Greeting Card Company. My friend from the University of Texas and the Eighth Air Force, Jim Bayliss, manager of the local Rauscher Pierce office, finally located a perfect partner for GIFT-RAPS in Gibson Greeting Cards in Cincinnati. Gibson was second in volume to Hallmark. Its stock was listed on the New York Stock Exchange. It had a magnificent printing operation and a sales organization that spanned the United States; we had neither. Its president, Max Weaver, was one of the finest businessmen I have ever known. He was extraordinarily kind to me.

In December 1962, after several months of discussions, we agreed to exchange all of our stock for 16,472 shares of Gibson.[11] Our personal real estate partnership would retain ownership of our plants and properties, and Gibson would build GIFT-RAPS a new plant on Seamist Street. I had already talked to my friend Gerald Hines about constructing such a plant and recommended Gerry to Gibson.

Upon the completion of our merger, Harold Lawrence retired and I executed a three-year employment contract with the company. Excluding real

This picture of Julie, our younger daughter, was taken at her debut. Julie was a real estate banker, the youngest female senior vice president at Republic National Bank. (Love family archives)

estate, Harold and I received about eight hundred thousand dollars in Gibson stock for GIFT-RAPS.

After the merger, I distributed GIFT-RAPS catalogs to the company's three hundred sales reps, and a veritable tidal wave of new orders soon forced our factory to work three shifts, seven days a week. Our local business with Sears became nationwide. We began manufacturing all of Montgomery Ward's gift wrapping paper under its "Tower" label.

Gibson discovered that we were buying our raw material, which was comparable to theirs, at lower prices, despite their much larger purchases. Perhaps because of this, Gibson figured that our group could accommodate a three-hundred-man sales force versus our erstwhile two-man effort and somehow assimilate that explosion in orders. Not so! We were literally exhausted.

Max counseled me not to work so hard. Then the Gibson salespeople called, demanding to know where their customers' orders were. My natural response, after investing more than a decade of my life in the business, was to produce more, work harder. Finally Max, in his wonderful way, suggested that I really did need to bring in a professional financial officer. When I told him we could not afford one, he said, "Well, you let me worry about that. We haven't made a short-term investment here. We want this division to grow." And so I finally hired a chief financial officer. That was a huge help!

★ GIBSON AND CIT FINANCIAL CORPORATION

In 1963, the CIT Financial Corporation made a cash tender offer to Gibson of $45.00 per share, substantially above the $37.37 price of Gibson's stock.[12] Gibson accepted the offer. It benefited all of the Gibson stockholders, including us.

The CIT transaction brought another hero into my life, Walter Holmes, chairman and CEO of CIT. Within two or three months after the completion of the acquisition of Gibson by CIT, our need for the larger plant became critical. The plans for the Seamist facility we had submitted to Gibson were in the works for the future, but we were drowning in business *now*. Max told me, "I know you want that new plant. Walter Holmes will be in Cincinnati next week. I want you to come here and tell him what you need."

Walter was a very warm, friendly man. I told him it would take a plant three times the size of ours just to fill the orders for the fall. He asked if I had

This "MBA" was my farewell gift from Walter Holmes, chairman and CEO of CIT, the ultimate acquirer of GIFT-RAPS. (Love family archives)

taken bids, reminding me that CIT never built without bids. I told him no, but I had talked to a builder I trusted (Gerry Hines) and that if I fooled around and got bids we would not be able to fill the orders. Then I launched into a chauvinistic lecture on Texas honor and integrity—even threw in the Battle of San Jacinto and the heroism of Texans winning their freedom from Mexico against heavy odds!

Finally, this New York executive could take no more. He laughed heartily and asked, "How much will it cost?"

"Four hundred thousand dollars," I responded.

"What if there are overruns?"

"That's where we put our faith in Hines. There won't be overruns."

Finally he laughed again, slapped Max on the back, and said, "Let's give the young man what he wants." Then he shook his finger at me and said, "But you'd better not run over four hundred thousand dollars!"

We didn't.

If I had been in Walter's shoes, I would have fired me on the spot. I was a hardheaded, entrepreneurial Texan, tough to manage, but because of their commitment to us, I broke my back in every way to live up to their expectations. Walter and I became great friends, but at the end of my three-year contract, I felt I was being taken increasingly away from Houston. I wanted to do more in Houston. Walter invited me to New York for a farewell visit and gave me a plaque that read: "I got my MBA at CIT."

And that plaque was absolutely right. My three years with Gibson and CIT were tremendous learning years. The superb financial planning, budgeting, and controls at Gibson and CIT were systematic and professional. I was especially impressed with top management and the systems employed to organize and finance these large, geographically diverse firms. The lessons learned with them supplemented and reinforced the lessons I had taken from my experience within the exceptionally efficient Eighth Army Air Force. But the most useful of all for me was the time invested in building my own company, GIFT-RAPS, Inc. There I learned how to survive and prosper in a competitive industry. From marketing to manufacturing, from hiring new employees to motivating them, from competing with larger companies to negotiating with them, my years as an entrepreneur in Houston after World War II prepared me to meet the challenges ahead of me.

NOTES

1. Walter L. Buenger and Joseph A. Pratt, *But Also Good Business: Texas Commerce Banks and the Financing of Houston and Texas, 1886–1986* (College Station: Texas A&M University Press, 1986), 4.

2. *Innovator in Industry and Banking,* transcribed interviews with Mr. Ben F. Love, interview by William Howard Beasley III, Oral Business History Project, Graduate School of Business, the University of Texas at Austin, sponsored by Moody Foundation Grant #70-30, 1971, 21.

3. Ibid., 23.

4. Ibid., 21.

5. Ibid., 23.

6. Ibid., 24.

7. In 2002, YPO had more than eighty-five hundred members in one hundred and seventy chapters in seventy-five nations. Members must apply before age forty-five (formerly, thirty-five) and be the chief executive of a company of a certain size. The fact that YPO members must "graduate" at age fifty has spawned a robust World Presidents' Organization. See www.ypo.org.

8. Ralph Yarborough, as an Austin attorney, had represented Margaret in a trust case while we were still students at the University of Texas. He served as U.S. senator from Texas between 1957 and 1971.

9. *Innovator in Industry and Banking,* 34.

10. Jeff was born in 1949; Jan, in 1953; and Julie, in 1955. Jeff graduated with honors from Vanderbilt and has a law degree from the University of Texas. He is managing partner of the Houston office of Locke Liddell & Sapp LLP, a four-hundred-lawyer firm headquartered in Texas. Julie, an MBA with honors from UT Graduate Business School, joined Republic Bank and became its youngest senior vice president. Jan, a member of Phi Beta Kappa, has an undergraduate degree from the University of Texas.

11. "Gibson Greeting Cards Discussing 2 Acquisitions," *Wall Street Journal,* December 5, 1962.

12. "CIT Plans to Buy Gibson Greeting for $36.4 Million," *Wall Street Journal,* January 10, 1964.

After my three-year contract with Gibson-CIT expired in 1965, I took the "MBA" I had earned during my sixteen years in business and sought to apply it to the challenge of banking. Armed with my observations as an outside director on the River Oaks Bank & Trust Company[1] board since 1956, the opportunities in banking increasingly captured my imagination. Although I hoped I might become qualified one day to head a large downtown bank, I concluded that I should start at a smaller institution because my banking experience (other than serving on the board of River Oaks for nine years) was as a depositor and business borrower.

In 1965, River Oaks was a $22 million institution owned by Jimmy Lyon, a friend who had joined YPO when he bought the bank in 1961. A very successful real estate developer, Jimmy left his bank in the hands of an executive vice president. Although he was both president and chairman, he showed up only for board meetings—and then usually came late. There were no pretenders for the job of chief executive officer.

I remember quite well that day in November 1965 when I decided to approach Jimmy. I asked to be president of River Oaks Bank & Trust, with the understanding that I be given a free hand to run the bank for three years using the financial planning, management, and marketing principles I had learned in my own business and Gibson-CIT. Savoring the chance to make money if my ideas worked, I also proposed buying 10 percent of the bank's stock from Jimmy with the agreement that I would sell it back to him at a discount to the then-market price if I left before three years.

Jimmy was no banker, but he was a shrewd, able businessman. My proposals were not offensive to him, yet he did gulp once or twice before saying, "Fine." That decision took an act of faith on his part, because running a bank like a business ran counter to the way banks were typically operated in those days, and Jimmy had invested a sizeable amount of his net worth in River Oaks Bank. Here he was, taking on somebody with no bank management experience and granting him total authority to implement entirely new ideas.

My three-year Gibson-CIT contract was up thirty days later. I had given my friends Max Weaver and Walter Holmes (CEOs of Gibson and CIT, respectively) proper notice, worked hard until my last day, led my Texas-based operation to record growth, and oriented my successor. And in December 1965, I joined River Oaks Bank & Trust Co., at 2119 Westheimer in Houston, as president and CEO with, I believe, the goodwill of my former employees, employer, suppliers, and customers.

★ PAST EXPERIENCE WITH RIVER OAKS BANK & TRUST COMPANY

At the time I joined the bank's board of directors, I was working long hours trying to launch GIFT-RAPS's products into the national market. I spent my days struggling with budgets, negotiating with suppliers, calculating product and labor costs to the penny, seeking new customers, and expanding production facilities. But when I stepped into the bank's board meetings, time stopped. The hustle-and-bustle world of competitive business gave way to the slow-paced world of banking, which had become a tightly regulated environment during the Great Depression, when the watchword of banking was "safety." There were no annual budgets, no apparent goals, no orientation toward profitability, no marketing or business development programs. Instead, meandering conversations went on and on about automobile loans or whether this borrower or that would repay his loan. I became increasingly curious about whether banking had a mystique that no mortal manufacturing businessman could understand or whether it could yield itself to the same principles that other businesses followed.

As I learned more about banking, I came to understand that the industry continued to be shaped by the attitudes and reforms of the Great Depression. The devastation that had visited my own family with the failure of our local bank in Vernon had scarred Americans throughout the nation. Widespread bank failures had generated panic, and legislators reacted with a sweeping wave of reforms that heavily regulated commercial banking and also separated commercial banks, investment banks, and savings-and-loan institutions into three distinct industries. The result was the "sedation and segmentation" of financial services, as regulators rebuilt a devastated banking system around the central concept of deposit security. This was a natural response to the economic dislocations of the Great Depression, but the impact of laws passed in the panic of the 1930s continued long after depression was replaced by postwar boom.

In effect, commercial banks operated as if they were public utilities. Regulators "sedated" competition by setting the interest rates banks could pay on savings deposits. Federal law "segmented" competition by blocking commercial banks from investment banking. Worse yet, the strictly enforced unit banking law in Texas held banks to a single location, limiting their capacity to grow and compete aggressively for business outside of their immediate location. Indeed, the lesson held over from the 1930s was that competition in banking could cause more harm than good.

Such an industry was not likely to attract risk-takers. Security-conscious individuals found refuge from the competitive marketplace in the quiet lobbies of banks. In the postwar era of regulated stability, most bank officers showed little concern for their shareholders. The most successful commercial banks in Texas cultivated long-term relationships with a limited number of major industrial customers and individual depositors. The primary work of the loan committee was to serve the needs of each bank's "blue-chip" customers and to protect the bank's depositors by making only the safest of loans. Few banks in Texas had active calling programs. Beyond the construction of stately, secure buildings, "marketing" was limited. Indeed, most bankers seemed to find it distasteful.

The downtown Houston banks worked under severe constraints to their growth. The money center banks, located primarily in New York City and Chicago, dominated major financing in the region. With a long head start due to history and geography, these institutions were much larger than even the biggest Texas banks and could make much larger loans. For example, in the two decades after World War II, First National City Bank in New York, a leading money center bank and a predecessor of Citibank, was fifteen to twenty times larger than the National Bank of Commerce, one of Houston's leading banks. When the largest Houston companies needed substantial loans, they turned to the money center banks. At times, Houston banks would participate by supplying a small portion of these loans, but they did not have the resources to take them on without help from the money centers.

River Oaks Bank & Trust, like other suburban banks in Houston at that time, had much the same relationship to the downtown Houston banks that those banks had to their counterparts in the money centers. In 1960, for example, deposits held at River Oaks were less than 5 percent of the total then held at Houston's National Bank of Commerce. In 1965, when I entered the world of banking as head at River Oaks Bank & Trust, I stepped onto a relatively low rung of the ladder in an industry where regulation and tradition made it most difficult to climb quickly through rapid growth.

That being said, it was clear that the postwar boom of the Houston region presented excellent prospects for banks of all sizes. Oil, gas, petrochemicals, industrial construction, residential construction, and manufacturing all expanded rapidly, and local banks participated in this growth to the extent that they could, given their limited deposits and legal loan limits and the geographic restrictions of unit banking.

During this era, the most aggressive of the downtown banks sought size through mergers. By the 1950s, six major banks dominated Houston banking. By the early 1960s, mergers had reduced this number to four. In the same years, the rapid population growth in outlying areas of Houston opened competitive space for banks located outside of downtown. Clearly, there were banking opportunities in booming Houston, but few of the existing banks seemed willing to shake clear of the safe, traditional Depression-era approach to banking and exploit these opportunities.

My challenge, as I saw it when I walked through the door at River Oaks Bank & Trust, was simple: to find ways within existing laws and traditions for the bank to grow. It was past time for banking to be run more like a business. I knew that banking was a highly regulated, conservative business; I had experienced firsthand the conservatism of two traditional bankers in the formative years of GIFT-RAPS. But, to repeat, I still believed that banking was a business. As a businessman, I felt that I could run a bank more profitably and achieve greater growth than that being generated by the traditional approach taken by the bankers at River Oaks who sat at their desks all day, gazing across the lobby and stifling yawns.

 ## THE SIXTEEN MONTHS AT RIVER OAKS

The job at River Oaks proved to be paradoxically easy and hard. It was easy because my business experience had taught me there were actions that would generate productive results immediately: a budget, an organization chart, quantified goals, a marketing plan, and a customer calling program that required our bankers to rise from their desks and visit customers and prospects at *their* places of business. In contrast, banking was hard because it presented a new vernacular, a new idiom, and a new environment to absorb.

Judging credit—analyzing balance sheets and income statements—was not entirely foreign to me, because GIFT-RAPS had granted credit to huge AAA-rated operations, such as Sears, Montgomery Ward, and the Federated Stores, as well as to many more marginal businesses. However, the technicalities of real estate construction financing, for example, did occasionally make me feel like I was in a foreign country. During those times, I did not attempt to speak the language. I just listened. I have since learned that there were not as many mysteries as I had earlier supposed, but I do know that listening played a large part in my learning process.

River Oaks Bank had needed a new home for some time, and Jimmy owned a prime piece of real estate on the corner of Kirby Drive and San Felipe since 1959. He wanted to build a first-class office tower as a home for the bank with lease space for tenants. Although the building had been a topic of conversation (and the project of several architects) for six years, nothing had been accomplished in the way of construction. In my first week at the bank, I hired a new architect, but the project languished because there were more pressing challenges.

River Oaks needed new ideas and new business practices more than it needed a new building. It was easy to create job descriptions because River Oaks had none; organization charts, none; budgets, none; profit goals, none; a customer calling program, none. To prosper, the bank needed fundamental changes in its traditional operations. From the start, I understood that the bank's officers and directors would be skeptical of change. To succeed, I would have to present them with a coherent plan for growth, persuade them to give it a try, and then show them real, numerical results.

I found that River Oaks guarded information jealously and shared it grudgingly. That was *not* the atmosphere for achieving long-term, statistically oriented performance goals. So we changed the atmosphere. Central to greater growth would be the collection of data that would affect results, the analysis of these data to identify opportunities for improvement, and the aggressive use of statistical measures to define and reach financial goals. This meant testing the management and the marketing lessons I had learned at the Eighth Air Force, GIFT-RAPS, and Gibson-CIT in the laboratory provided by River Oaks Bank & Trust. I was eager for the challenge.

My primary goals were the same as those that had always guided bank managers: asset quality, asset growth, and, finally, asset profitability. However, we reordered the priority of these goals. Profitability moved from the bottom of the old list to parity with asset quality and asset growth. This new decentralized, market-oriented, businesslike approach to banking proved as suited to the mid-1960s as the old, highly personal and centralized approach had matched the needs of an earlier, less competitive era.

River Oaks had always tried to achieve good profits, but it was impossible to measure whether results were better or worse than the goals because there were no goals. We defined clear, simple objectives for asset profitability, asset growth, and asset quality, and we made this information available to directors, employees, and customers alike.

The bank's deposits had been stalled at a $19 million to $22 million plateau for three years. What was the bank's deposit potential? In terms of profits and loan quality, where was it going and in what period of time, statistically defined? It seemed like fundamental management practice to define these goals and set them forth for everyone in the bank to see. We projected that River Oaks's deposits could easily reach $25 million by the end of 1966 and $50 million within three to five years. This could not happen, however, if the bank's officers sat at their mahogany desks and waited for customers to walk through the doors.

So a call program was born. Each officer was assigned to make fifteen outside calls per month on customers and prospects and write reports on each call. Soon, those erstwhile office-bound "order takers" found it was not so bad to stop relying on the "drop-in trade" and get out and visit customers in their places of business. Our clients concluded that their bankers knew more about their banking needs after touring their premises. They also came to feel that the bank cared enough about their business to reach out to them and learn their needs.

I drew up a budget and proposed it to the River Oaks board. One of our directors, Henry Beissner, a successful investment banker, questioned this change. He said, "Ben, you can't do a budget for a bank. You have no control over too many variables such as interest rates and loan demand. It won't work, and you'll make yourself look bad."

I persisted, "We may not be able to control interest rates, but we can control expenses and margins. The budget will help us do that."

When I persevered, Henry was good enough to say, "Well, try it, Ben, but I've given you my best advice."

During another budget presentation to the board of directors, Bill Davis, who was head of Montgomery Ward in the Houston area, enthusiastically volunteered: "I'll tell you what I'll do. The director in this boardroom who comes closest to predicting the actual year-end deposits and earnings will win the biggest color TV Montgomery Ward makes!" Well, that color TV did the trick! If a budget can be designed so that it is not a yoke around the ox's neck, it can be fun, and it can focus attention on specific, quantified goals at the same time.

Next, we hired an advertising agency to establish an image for River Oaks Bank. We adopted an oak tree standing by a river as our advertising logo and drew up a marketing plan to replace the almost nonexistent one then in use. We did not have a large marketing budget, but it did not require a vault of money to buy several junior-sized billboards in our market.

Our people's capabilities far exceeded the beauty of our building or the size of our deposits, so our message was about our people. We did not post a picture of our building on our billboards, as most banks did at the time (our advertising account executive advised: "We are not trying to sell the building!"), and we did not post our relatively modest resources. Instead we posted pictures of our directors, along with a tagline inviting viewers to ask them about the bank.

This novel approach to bank advertising borrowed from a lesson I had learned during my Army Air Corps days. When I had plotted the 351st Bomb Group's navigators' log entries on that huge map of Europe during the debriefing sessions held immediately after each mission, the pressure from their own crews forced the navigators to compile more complete logs and save lives. The same basic principle applied to posting pictures of the River Oaks directors on billboards. At River Oaks, as in the Army Air Corps, our focus on individuals fostered responsibility in those individuals. My purpose was to get our directors deeply involved in the bank—and we did. When their friends saw those billboards and began asking questions, my directors had to come up with the answers or call me for the answers to those potentially business-building inquiries about the bank and its products.

I'll never forget the day that Jack Harris, treasurer of Great Southern Life Insurance Company, came to the board meeting with a list of questions in his pocket. He said, "People see my picture on those billboards. They start asking me about the bank, and I don't know the answers." Well, we remedied that situation in a hurry! This happened repeatedly, but as directors became comfortable talking about the bank, they became more involved and grew genuinely enthusiastic about helping us build it. And our deposits, loans, and profits just took off.

Later, that same kind of peer pressure would apply to the statewide Texas Commerce organization in the form of quarterly "Blue Book" reports. These ranked and published the performance-to-goal numbers of each member bank for all to see.

Another vigorous flow of new business came from the six highly respected, aggressive go-getters in my general age bracket, late thirties and early forties, who doubled the size of the River Oaks board during this period. These included Bill Lane, president and CEO of Riviana Foods; Gene Murphree, owner of Gene Murphree Corporation, a general contracting firm; Mike Tomforde, owner of A. M. Tomforde & Co., an insurance firm; Bill Davis, head of Montgomery Ward in Houston; Dr. Tom Anderson, a leading pediatrician; and Harvey Houck, an independent real estate investor. These men brought energy and ambition, as well as experience in competitive industries, to the board. They joined me at the bank to help it move forward. Combined with our advertising and our calling program, these young, aggressive directors gave us a new image as an organization on the move.

We involved customers, too. I wrote a mass-mailed, individually addressed letter, sharing with each customer our goal to reach $25 million by the end of 1966. Then we followed up with another letter forthrightly detailing our results-to-goal numbers for the quarter. These short, one-page compositions also included information about the economy or new products.

One letter discussed certificates of deposit (CDs), a relatively new product for the banking industry at the time.[2] CDs offered higher rates on large deposits held for specific terms, and they were guaranteed up to the limit allowed by the Federal Deposit Insurance Corporation. Previously, banks had few deposit options for individuals beyond checking and savings accounts, and all banks were required to pay the same interest rates. We decided CDs would be a big hit with our security-minded, affluent customers, and we touted "the highest interest the law allows."

My letters to our ever-expanding base of customers appealed for their help in a novel effort to recruit them for the team, to get them pulling for us to reach our stated deposit objectives for the upcoming quarter. We knew that the successful people who lived in our market did most of their banking downtown, but we wanted River Oaks Bank & Trust to be their neighborhood bank. We knew it would take all of us—directors, employees, and customers—working together to make it happen. We all had to leave behind the passive stance of a traditional bank and, instead, aggressively seek growth.

Our first budget was fairly ambitious, but we performed considerably better than planned. By the end of 1966, we reached $29 million in deposits, exceeding our original goal of $25 million. We were just fourteen hundred dollars short of $30 million in April 1967, on the day I left. Better yet, our profits were up a whopping 270 percent, and our loan quality remained top-drawer.

TABLE 5.1: *Year-end Deposits of River Oaks Bank & Trust Company*

1960 $17,140,181	1964 $22,666,883	1968 $31,457,982
1961 $17,278,594	1965 $22,349,395	1969 $31,194,056
1962 $19,102,504	1966 $29,567,994	1970 $37,770,424
1963 $20,098,153	1967 $30,193,974	

"Bank Call Reports," Houston Chronicle, *January 6, 1961; January 5, 1962; January 6, 1963; January 5, 1964; January 6, 1965; January 5, 1966; January 6, 1967; January 5, 1968; January 6, 1969; January 6, 1970; January 5, 1971.*

★ JOINING THE TEXAS NATIONAL BANK OF COMMERCE

When I joined River Oaks Bank & Trust as president, I told Jimmy Lyon, the bank's controlling stockholder, that I wanted to stay for three years maximum and then go to a large downtown bank. I suggested we might do that in one of two ways: he and I would buy a bank, probably not one of the large banks, or I would simply join a downtown bank. We often talked about purchasing a bank, but the idea was never seriously considered because we had so many other things going at River Oaks in terms of our own building projects and programs we were initiating, implementing, and achieving. More and more, I thought about joining a large downtown bank.

Before leaving Gibson-CIT, I had thoroughly studied the banking industry in Houston. First City National, the city's largest bank, was a fine organization, but Texas National Bank of Commerce came to my mind consistently as a quality institution. I think most people have an affinity for certain environments, and I liked the atmosphere in that bank. The Gulf Building, its home, had a prominent presence near the center of the city. I felt that the bank was cast in the image of the man whose portrait hung on the wall of its magnificent lobby, the great Houstonian Jesse Jones, who had been its

Jesse Jones's Gulf Building was the "paramount office structure of the South." It opened in October 1929 as the home of Gulf Oil Company and Jones's bank, the National Bank of Commerce. (Photograph courtesy Houston Endowment Inc.)

The banking lobby is an "immense space, 70 feet by 112 feet, the walls of which rise sheer and unobstructed to a ceiling 43 feet from the floor . . . the walls are of French limestone, embellished with fluted pilasters . . . panels of especially fabricated glass and metal ribs . . . supply the entire room with a flood of mellow daylight." ("A Book Describing the Gulf Building," a leasing brochure published by the Jesse H. Jones Interests, courtesy Houston Endowment Inc. Photograph © Aker/Zvonkovic Photography, Houston.)

primary stockholder from 1919 until his death in 1956. I respected the bank and was convinced that I would enjoy being associated with it.

While I was still at River Oaks, my YPO friend John Duncan, who was liquidating his holdings in Gulf & Western, offered a proposition: he would invest those funds to buy a major position in First City National Bank if I would to run the bank. John Duncan and Charles Bluhdorn cofounded Gulf & Western, a very successful, NYSE-listed, diverse conglomerate, so John would be equipped with sufficient funds to proceed with such an offer.

Well, I was dumbfounded. I will never forget the offer, because this was no "cocktail comment." John was perfectly serious. He had already consulted with his lawyer at Vinson Elkins, David Searls, who, as managing partner of the law firm that represented First City, was the best possible source to determine whether this action was feasible. After giving the proposition serious thought, I asked John not to pursue it. His offer nonetheless was an incredible vote of confidence. In the many years since, I have often told him that he was the only director, friend, stranger, or anyone else who ever offered to buy a bank for me to run!

Whether I would have been happy at First City, I do not know. Looking back at the question today, I think that moving to a new position is somewhat like a marriage. You have to ponder whether there is only one woman in the world for you. Your answer, having married, is that there *is* only one woman for you. So having "married" Texas Commerce, I will say that this was the only bank for me. I knew that I was marrying into a "blue blood" family: "Jesse Jones's bank" had a well-earned reputation as the leading corporate bank in Houston.

At about this same time, sixteen months after joining River Oaks, one of my ablest directors, Bill Lane, gave me the exciting news that John Whitmore, president and CEO of Texas National Bank of Commerce, had noted River Oaks's performance and would like for me to visit with him.

Texas National Bank of Commerce had been created by a merger in 1964 between the National Bank of Commerce and Texas National Bank. The merger produced an $800 million contender for the top spot among Houston banks. However, two years later, with deposits down to $754 million at year-end 1966, TNBC was still feeling the aftereffects of a difficult merger that had created serious tensions among the officers, directors, shareholders, and customers of the two banks.

John Whitmore was looking for a commercial banking manager who could effectively help set the bank on a growth track, someone not closely identified with either predecessor bank. However, a move to TNCB would be professionally challenging for me: the bank had a strongly embedded conservatism in its approach to banking. Moving would also be personally costly. At TNBC, my salary would be the same as my salary at River Oaks—thirty thousand dollars. However, the move would entail a two-hundred-thousand-dollar financial sacrifice on my part, in that I would have to sell my River Oaks stock back to Jimmy Lyon at a discount because I would not be fulfilling my three-year agreement.

I emphasized to Mr. Whitmore as he was recruiting me: "I will come downtown if I have a chance for the top job when you retire—provided I perform ably, of course." He assured me that this would be the case. He also pointed out that I would be coming as a member of neither the Texas National nor the National Bank of Commerce camps. Nor would I arrive as an interloper: the other senior officers, for various reasons, did not want the top job. If I could perform, I would be considered for it.

On April 22, 1967, I joined Texas National Bank of Commerce as senior vice president in charge of the Houston Metropolitan Division. I arrived at the age of forty-two, brimming with enthusiasm to address the myriad opportunities presented by my new position. I felt change was in the air for the world of banking, and I was eager to help build a new environment of more aggressive, competitive bank management. My experience at River Oaks had convinced me that I could make a difference. I believed that my past had prepared me well for my new job, and I knew that if preparation, ambition, and hard work were the keys to success, I could contribute materially.

NOTES

1. River Oaks Bank & Trust Company was chartered as Hampton Oaks State Bank in 1947. It changed its name to River Oaks State Bank in 1951, then to River Oaks Bank & Trust in 1962. This institution, located in a thirteen-story building at Kirby Drive and San Felipe since 1970, had reached nearly $500 million when Compass Bank bought it from Jimmy Lyon in 1991.

2. Certificates of deposit were introduced by First National City Bank of New York in 1960.

At Texas National Bank of Commerce I joined a major downtown Houston bank with a strong past but an uncertain future. The bank had been created by a merger of two of the city's traditional banking leaders, Jesse Jones's National Bank of Commerce (NBC) and Texas National Bank (TNB), one of the oldest and most aggressive banks in Houston, to form Texas Commerce Bank (TCB).[1] Their union in 1964 had produced the city's second-largest bank, with vast promise for growth. But despite its initial potential, the merger had not lived up to its promise. As a new officer who hoped to someday run this bank, I faced several clear challenges. First, I had to establish a sound position for myself within an institution still trying to come to grips with a largely unsuccessful merger. Second, I had to convince a traditional, conservative bank to allow me to try to introduce more competitive practices into its operations. Finally, I had to prove that my more aggressive approach to banking could produce results.

★ THE TROUBLED MERGER OF THE NATIONAL BANK
OF COMMERCE AND TEXAS NATIONAL BANK

The merger united two banks with historic pedigrees. The larger bank was the National Bank of Commerce, which Jesse Jones had helped build into one of Houston's dominant corporate banks. After moving to the city in 1898, Jones had quickly established himself as an important force in economic and civic affairs. His business career diversified from lumber into construction, banking, and publishing. He was a director and stockholder of several predecessors of Texas Commerce, but his longest association was with NBC. He began as a founding director in 1912; by 1919, he was its largest stockholder; in 1922, he became its president; and in 1930, he took the chairman's title and held it until his death in 1956.[2] To house his bank and the Gulf Oil Company, Jones constructed the most majestic of his downtown Houston office buildings in 1929. The thirty-four-story art deco structure re-

The announcement of the merger of National Bank of Commerce and Texas National Bank was front page news in the Houston Chronicle on July 16, 1963. The merger was completed at the close of business, January 17, 1964. (Houston Chronicle Publishing Company, © 1963, reprinted with permission, all rights reserved)

mained the tallest building in the city until Exxon's forty-six-story skyscraper went up in 1962.

Government service and politics occupied Jones's middle years. He served as finance chairman of the Democratic Party in 1924 and persuaded the party to hold its 1928 national convention in Houston. In 1932, President Herbert Hoover appointed Jesse Jones to the board of the Reconstruction Finance Corporation (RFC); Franklin Delano Roosevelt named him head of the RFC in 1933, a position he held until he left Washington in 1945. During World War II, he was also secretary of commerce. While he lived in Washington, however, Houston and his bank were never far from his thoughts.

Jones left his bank in the hands of the able management team of A. D. Simpson, "Mr. Outside"; Robert P. Doherty, "Mr. Inside"; and Sam Taub, chairman of the loan committee. He telephoned his lieutenants almost daily about one matter or another. As one of the most visible representatives of business in the country, Jones came into daily contact with executives throughout the nation. He regularly introduced his friend A. D. "Dee" Simpson to the nation's corporate leaders, and Simpson followed up on these leads and brought business into NBC. Jones was particularly adept at identifying able young Houston businessmen such as Gus Wortham, founder of

This 1958 photograph of an aged A. D. Simpson and Robert P. Doherty standing in front of a portrait of the recently deceased Jesse Jones aptly summarizes the management succession problems common to many Houston banks in the 1940s and 1950s. The top managers were growing old, yet they remained in the shadows of the giants of the previous era. (Walter L. Buenger and Joseph A. Pratt, But Also Good Business: Texas Commerce Banks and the Financing of Houston and Texas, 1836–1986, *Texas A & M University Press, 1986. Photograph courtesy Houston Endowment Inc.)*

1886–1986

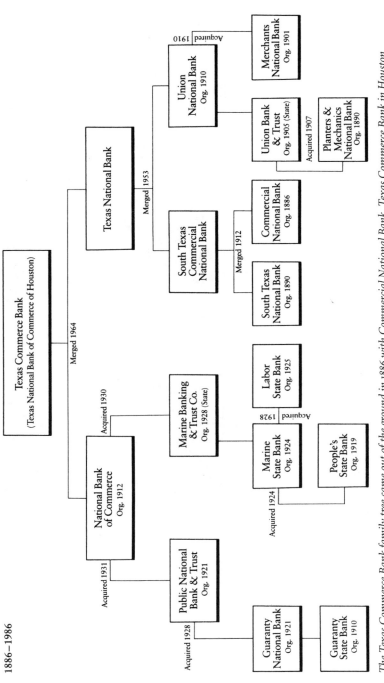

The Texas Commerce Bank family tree came out of the ground in 1886 with Commercial National Bank. Texas Commerce Bank in Houston matured through merger in 1964, then founded Texas Commerce Bancshares, Inc. in 1971, the statewide, multi-bank holding company. (Ben F. Love, "People and Profits: A Bank Case Study," master's thesis, Southwest Graduate School of Banking, Southern Methodist University, 1967.)

American General Insurance, and convincing them to conduct their banking business at NBC.

Throughout his years in Houston banking, Jones figured that what was good for Houston was good for his bank. By helping make Houston a better city, he encouraged its dynamic economy, which attracted thousands of people and hundreds of businesses. He was confident that NBC would get its share of the action.[3] After Jones and his wife returned to Houston following the war, they expanded their philanthropic activities, bequeathing their sizeable fortune to Houston Endowment to continue doing good works for the city they loved. When he died in 1956, Jones was widely known as "Mr. Houston." His bank basked in his reputation as Houston's leading citizen; NBC's list of blue-chip businesses and individuals and its reputation as a premier corporate bank reflected Jones's standing in the city's business community.

The pedigree of NBC's merger partner in 1964, Texas National Bank (TNB), reached even further back into Houston's history. TNB had been formed in 1953 by the combination of two longtime friendly competitors, South Texas National Bank and Union National Bank. These two traditional Houston institutions shared conservative management philosophies and ties to an area economy that was based on cotton and railroads and stretched beyond the turn of the century. Prominent, old-line families named Rice, Baker, and Carter held large blocks of stock in South Texas and Union, and members of these families had served as officers and directors at both banks over the years. The presidents, S. M. McAshan and R. M. Farrar, were even neighbors who took walks together in the evening.

The glory days for both banks came before the mid-1930s, and the deaths of their longtime leaders in the early 1940s further slowed the expansions of both. In 1953, South Texas sought to grow through a merger with its neighbor across the street. The new Texas National Bank soon moved into a tall, modern building at 1200 Main Street with Continental Oil Company.

The South Texas president, Harris McAshan, held the same job at Texas National. A fourth-generation banker, he had witnessed firsthand the problems of management succession caused by the early death of his father, S. M. McAshan, and promptly instituted a program to recruit and train young managers. When he was forced to retire prematurely in 1959, at age fifty-three, one of these young managers, the thirty-seven-year-old J. W. (Bill) McLean, stepped up to run the bank. He quickly won the support of a strong chairman, Dillon Anderson, a partner in the major law firm of Baker, Botts,

Shepherd & Coates, who had served as national security adviser to President Dwight Eisenhower. Anderson's national reputation combined with McLean's dynamism gave the bank a presence in the regional and national financial community that contributed to its image as a vigorous, enlightened organization on the move.

Texas National sought business from the small and midsized companies that often felt lost among the bigger accounts attracted by the larger banks. TNB also offered the first bank credit card program in the city. It launched an innovative public relations campaign to reinforce its public image as an organization on the move. Despite all this, however, Texas National remained a distant fourth among Houston banks in the race for deposits. When the National Bank of Commerce proposed merger in 1964, Bill McLean commented to his executive committee on the difficulties of gaining market share and making percentage gains against the larger banks. He said, "After running as fast as we can these past few years, we have not even stood still, but rather have slowly slipped further behind." He considered deposit growth as a primary objective for accepting the proposal and made a strong case in favor of the merger.

The idea of merging these two banks was greeted favorably by regulatory officials. U.S. Controller of the Currency James J. Saxon cited the exuberant growth and diversification of Houston's economic base since World War II as strong reasons for its approval. He noted that this region, boasting the world's largest concentration of oil, gas, and petrochemical refining, processing, and manufacturing plants, was one of the fastest-growing industrial areas in the nation. "However," he added, "while metropolitan Houston's banks are growing rapidly in number, perhaps they are not growing fast enough in size." He charged that the state's anti-branch banking laws hindered the growth of Texas banks and prevented them from amassing the capital needed to finance the growth of the region.[4]

The unit-banking laws then in effect in Texas required merged banks to occupy a single building, so Texas National Bank moved in with the National Bank of Commerce. At 9:00 A.M., Monday, January 17, 1964, Texas National Bank of Commerce of Houston opened for business at 712 Main Street. Texas National's forty-one-year-old president, Bill McLean, was named president of the new institution, with the expectation that he would be elected chief executive when the seventy-two-year-old chairman Bob Doherty retired.

But this succession plan was not implemented. Tensions between the two banks quickly undermined any hope for a smooth transition to a unified new bank. McLean was gone within a year, along with many of the TNB directors, most of the young Texas National managers, and several substantial customer relationships. By the end of 1965, deposits had declined by 8 percent during a year when most major Houston banks recorded large increases.

Despite the impressive heritages of both banks, this was not so much a merger of banks as it was a merger of banking eras. The Jones management ran a superb bank for the 1950s. But banks were run differently in the 1960s, and NBC management, being extremely loyal to Jesse Jones even after his death in 1956, clung to the traditions and attitudes that had succeeded in earlier times. Those who did not follow this path were deemed unfit for leadership. On the other hand, Texas National's young management ran a bank for the 1960s, one of the most forward-thinking, marketing-oriented institutions in Houston.

And so, when the dust cleared from a merger that NBC had initiated for new managers, it was perhaps ironic to see a senior officer of the old National Bank of Commerce, John Whitmore, emerge as president. The fifty-seven-year-old Whitmore had been with NBC for eighteen years. A real estate specialist, he had attracted a large following of mortgage companies to the

TABLE 6.1: *Year-end Deposits of Large Houston Banks*

YEAR	NBC	TNB	BSW	1ST CITY
1962	$495,051,283	$278,371,486	$479,436,378	$816,979,834
1963	472,513,408	272,867,361	468,712,838	785,755,036
1964	778,722,638		535,384,405	900,319,456
1965	713,041,791		587,400,656	911,702,256
1966	753,634,759		593,336,436	922,481,296
1967	838,435,986		626,108,584	973,549,668
1968	925,397,598		687,743,270	1,018,648,054
1969	939,349,565		648,866,690	1,041,471,627
1970	1,138,661,301		688,696,587	1,151,392,874
1971	1,252,031,477		781,146,629	1,364,504,325

"*Bank Call Reports,*" Houston Chronicle, *January, 6, 1963; January 5, 1964; January 6, 1965; January 5, 1966; January 6, 1967; January 5, 1968; January 6, 1969; January 6, 1970; January 5, 1971; January 5, 1972.*

bank. Now he faced the job of guiding the merged banks through a difficult, emotionally charged transition by salvaging as much benefit as possible from the merger and bringing a new generation of management into the bank. A builder, not a firebrand, he did a superb job of putting the bank back on the path to growth and profits. Under his leadership, deposits turned around in 1966 and began a steady climb.

★   MEETING THE CHALLENGES AT TEXAS COMMERCE

This was the situation on April 22, 1967, when I walked into the Travis Street door of Texas Commerce Bank (TCB) as senior vice president of the Houston Metropolitan Division and crossed that magnificent lobby to my office, one that had once belonged to the man referred to as Jesse Jones's "Mr. Outside," A. D. Simpson. At first, I had a lot of visits from older customers who came by just to be in the environment that man had created— and Mr. Simpson had passed away seven years earlier! He must have been a most engaging person.

Although much of the work of healing the breach from the merger had already been done, it quickly became apparent that intense feelings still existed. The bank officers remained split into two discernible camps, with the Texas National forces subordinate to those of the National Bank of Commerce. Clearly, effort was needed to rekindle the enthusiasm and loyalty of the Texas National officers and customers. I was from neither group, and it appeared that I could be a bridge between the two and help bring some up-and-coming businessmen into the bank simultaneously.

One of my first challenges was to solve the mystery of how a big bank operates. TCB's loan portfolio boasted an impressive array of blue-ribbon customers that included very wealthy individuals and select large companies. It also contained smaller businesses that reached into every corner of the region's economy, from retailers to scrap-metal producers to stockbrokers. Real estate and oil lending records were kept separately, as were national accounts, correspondent bank accounts, and our small international portfolio, but most everything else was lumped together under the label "metropolitan" lending. The Houston Metropolitan Division also included customers headquartered throughout the Southwest.

I learned that Texas Commerce Bank's credit policy functioned very well.

During the 1930s and 1940s, as the bank grew too large to rely on the memory of a few officers and directors, it had set up credit files on every Houston company and businessman the bank might be asked about. I also learned that the bank was very picky about accepting new customers. They could come to the bank, but the bank would not go to them. I found an aloofness that bordered on arrogance in the bank's view that officers calling on prospects in the marketplace for the purpose of producing business—of selling—was akin to prostituting the institution. Certainly TCB never actively solicited other banks' customers. What was ours was ours; what was theirs was theirs.

In short, Texas Commerce operated as a larger, statelier version of River Oaks Bank, with no budget, no organization chart, no quantified asset or profit goals, and no marketing plan. The bank presented a huge opportunity to organize human resources in pursuit of statistical objectives, and I had no hesitancy about redirecting people and procedures. From the 1930s through the 1950s, in times that valued safety above all else and measured performance more by deposit size than any other single factor, NBC had operated splendidly. In fact, from 1950 through 1955, until City National and First National merged to form First City National Bank in 1956, NBC was the largest bank in Houston. In the next few years, however, it struggled to retain its competitive position, even slipping to third place among Houston banks, behind Bank of the Southwest (BSW).

In response to changing times, I developed organization charts, defined statistically quantifiable goals for officer calls, established budgets and reporting channels of communication, and monitored and posted results for all to see. My aim mirrored that of Jesse Jones: to build the premier bank in Houston. He was ever-present in my mind. I never walked into that lobby of the Gulf Building in the morning without figuratively tipping my hat to the heroic portrait on the wall of the majestic figure of Jesse Jones. I believe that he would have smiled approvingly at my efforts.

★ BUILDING A MORE COMPETITIVE BANK

When I had been at Texas Commerce for about a week, I asked Terry Shirley, an assistant cashier, if the bank had an organization chart. We had vice presidents, assistant vice presidents, and assistant cashiers, but nobody seemed to report to anyone else. Terry said no, and in great frustration commented that the bank was not organized the way he had studied at Louisiana State University while earning his MBA.

I said, "Well, what about Bill Pugh? He's a senior vice president. Who does he manage? Surely a senior vice president has vice presidents reporting to him."

Terry said, "No. There is no reporting structure. When we have an important matter that needs a decision, we go to Mr. Whitmore."

That system might have worked well for a small institution, but for organizing to grow our market share, for defining those segments where we could become proficient, and for assigning people to certain segments, we needed a formal organization chart and written job descriptions. Vice presidents had to be accountable for quantified, budgeted goals; they needed people reporting to them who could assume parts of that result-oriented responsibility.

My frustration was probably a carryover from the Eighth Air Force, where everything was organized: squadrons consisted of twelve planes; three squadrons made a group; three groups made a wing; three wings made a division; three divisions made the Eighth Air Force. Certainly, organization charts had been useful tools at Gibson and CIT, too. Taking heart from these three worthy models, I organized the Houston Metropolitan Division: units reported to groups, groups to sections, sections to divisions, and divisions to departments.

This hierarchy equipped the "vice president" and the "senior vice president" titles with authoritative meaning and organizational importance. It let us decentralize authority among officers who had statistical accountability and cut the umbilical cord attached solely to the man who sat in the chairman's office.

★ ESTABLISHING A CALL PROGRAM

Even in the best-run businesses, a good organization chart cannot take the place of a well-directed, well-executed marketing strategy. Traditional banks had become too comfortable to pursue business; they emphasized security of deposits over marketing strategy. When I entered TCB in 1967, Bank of the Southwest was the one downtown bank that made calls on prospects and customers. They sent out business development officers who brought in leads and turned them over to lenders. Although Dee Simpson had been powerfully productive at NBC in following up on Jesse Jones's leads among huge, blue-ribbon corporations, that system of business development was less geographically widespread, less industry focused, and less encompassing of both junior and senior officers than the one we organized beginning in 1967.

At Texas Commerce, I found no system for surveying the market and identifying firms that might be potential customers. Nor did we have a system for analyzing whether we *should* be doing business with any of those firms. So the call program we instituted might be likened to taking census, with one important difference: this census was a way to build a prospect list *and* determine which prospects were creditworthy.

A call program had worked at River Oaks, and I wanted Texas Commerce bankers out making calls. Let me emphasize this: I wanted the people who made the loan decisions, lenders, to make the calls on customers and prospects—*not* business development officers. This was an important change. I suppose this idea came from my years of sitting on the other side of the desk and suffering glad-handers who came by as "bank business development officers," wasting my time and not being able to do anything for me.

If the idea of Texas Commerce Bank making calls was not radical enough, the idea of actual lenders getting out and making calls nearly stirred up a revolt. "What if I'm out on a call when a big customer comes in?" more than one officer asked. That was a valid protest from officers who were accustomed to sitting at their desks waiting for "drop-in trade." So we assigned back-up officers to each account and required back-up officers to be in the bank when primary officers were out making calls. In addition to his other duties, a back-up officer's job was to become familiar with his primary officer's accounts. For example, if Wyatt Boiler Works's CFO came in while Bill Mann, a senior vice president, was out on a call, the back-up officer could help the customer effectively and report to Bill, in writing, what he had done.

Then we broached the subject of numbers. How many calls should we make? Another uproar! I calmed the fears of lending officers, though, when I told them that I had no specific number in mind, that they would participate fully in establishing the number of calls each man should complete every month. After some discussion, we arrived at one hundred and fifty calls per officer per year—just three calls a week. (Our call quota later moved up to four per week.)

I remember that my first call at TCB was with Bill Mann on the aforementioned Wyatt Boiler Works. The company was located eight miles west of downtown off the Hempstead Highway. As we drove past business after business, I asked, "Bill, who has this account? Who has that account?" He did not know, so I started writing down the names of those companies.

Then I said, "Bill, we're early. Let's stop at this U-Tote-Em store and use the outside pay phone. I want to call the bank and find out who is assigned to all of these companies we just drove past. Who do I talk to?" I was still the "new boy on the block" and knew relatively few bank people at the staff level.

Bill laughed and said, "Nobody. No one person knows who is assigned to each account."

I responded, "Surely there's someone I can call."

He replied, "There is nobody to call."

Well, that opened a door of opportunity! We added officer assignments to the customer-prospect files in the Credit Division. Next, we tried organizing the call program using Procter & Gamble's geographical method: "Maximize the number of calls by minimizing the drive time." Officers turned in the names and addresses of their accounts, and then my assistant, Margrette Anawaty, plotted colored pins, by officer, for all of those accounts on a large map of Houston.

When I unveiled this map, all of the lenders in the room could readily see that their accounts were strewn from Katy to LaPorte. Our officers discussed the map, but concluded, wisely, that while assigning accounts on a geographical basis might improve efficiency, the principle, strictly applied, would not work for a bank because good banking is about people. It would uproot too many account relationships. Strike one!

Then we looked at broad industrial groupings—retailing, wholesaling, and manufacturing—thinking that if a group of officers were assigned to manufacturing, for example, they might become really proficient at financing manufacturing companies. But this was a flawed concept because the categories were too broad. For example, a plant that makes sheet metal is a vastly different animal from a bookbinder, but both are manufacturing companies. Strike two!

Then Carl Galloway, a senior vice president, hit a home run. He said, "Ben, what about trying Dun & Bradstreet's Standard Industrial Classification?" SIC codes break the major industrial groups down into manageable segments. That seemed just right, and our bank officers accepted it.

We assigned certain SIC codes to specific division managers who were responsible for developing relationships within these codes. For example, the transportation codes included rail, airlines, trucks, and other forms of transport. The Transportation Division manager would divide these codes, in manageable portions, among the section, group and unit managers reporting to him. Our lenders, indeed, began to develop expertise in certain areas. I recall that one prospect who owned five boats told me he was dissatisfied with his bank because they did not understand the transportation business. I was able to point to a TCB officer and say, "Why, we have a transportation expert over here. Transportation has been his industry assignment for the past two years."

We began by organizing our customers by SIC codes and by geographical location, supported by a central file of account assignments for each officer. The segmentation by account size came later. Our system did result in some account reassignments, but we worked to minimize this uprooting. We certainly did *not* reassign productive, long-term relationships from an established officer to another officer who happened to be assigned that SIC. For example, if Bill Pugh was entrenched with Brown & Root, we would not move that relationship to another officer even though Brown & Root might be in the latter's SIC responsibility.

What constituted a call? Our lenders were expected to make an appointment, go out to the customer's place of business, and discuss solid, well-thought-out ideas for ways TCB could benefit his company. That was a call. Each call required a substantive, written call report, not just a superficial, "Saw Joe and everything is okay."

I did not expect the most senior officers like Pete Rehrauer, a vice chairman, to come into the program, but senior vice presidents like Bill Pugh and Bill Mann did join this organized, monitored push, along with the other officers in the Metropolitan Division.

All of this took a lot of selling inside the bank. "Sell not tell" was a philosophy I had had to learn as a young businessman with a tendency to dictate rather than persuade. Selling takes more patience and effort, but selling your ideas, rather than making demands that lack consensus or support or may not be understood fully, means your organization will function infinitely more productively. John Whitmore put the same philosophy in different words: "You achieve results through happy people rather than unhappy people."

As we achieved good results, our people bought into the new approach.

Officers turned in their call reports promptly, and I read as many as possible on weekends. Margrette Anawaty tracked the number of calls each officer made against their cumulative loan and deposit balances and disseminated monthly written reports on results generated per officer versus his previous month's totals. And sure enough, the volumes of deposits and loans began to grow in proportion to the number of calls made.

These monthly reports evolved in sophistication and scope over the years, becoming the monthly and quarterly "Blue Books," so called because of the color of their covers. Publicizing performance and profit information had not been done at Texas Commerce before. I believe that sharing results with the people who are charged with producing results creates more unity in moving toward an objective.

As I said, all of this took a lot of selling inside the bank. But just as in plotting the 351st Bomb Group navigators' log entries on that huge map of Europe promptly after each mission for all to see, these monthly reports sold the "doubting Thomases." Officers could read the reports and see for themselves the correlation between the number of calls they made and the growth in deposits and loans. They began to enjoy making calls. I did not have to sell them anymore.

Our target prospects were people in their forties who ran their own companies. We wanted to do business with them and forthrightly said so. Doing business this way takes an attitude and a certain amount of courage. You cannot be afraid that you will be trapped if you tell somebody you want to do business, because you must say the occasional "No." But first, you need a sufficient number of choices to have somebody to say "No" to. You ask people to let you look at their business to determine whether you can bank it better than their existing bank. You say, "I want to do business. Let's see if we can be your banker."

An associate and I once called on the president of a large chain retail grocery operation. After we talked for a while, he said, "Oh, you don't want to do business with us. You turned us down several years ago." This is another way a call can bear fruit: it gives you a chance to correct old, wrong impressions. We said, "Yes, we do!" and sat there and debated for thirty minutes about whether we did or did not want to do business. Finally, I said, "Okay, test us." They did and found that we *did* want their business. Ultimately, they transferred a substantial amount of their relationship to us because we backed up our invitation with the competence of this bank. Better yet, the president began recommending his suppliers to us because he felt we were the most progressive bank in Houston. That was a complete turnaround.

An encompassing call program, a clear desire, and the ability to perform are the three basic ingredients of business-building success. Billboard, radio, and television advertising all provide invaluable support, but a successful business does not lean on advertising. Rather, it depends on personal contact. If a well-informed banker desires to do business and makes enough calls, he will begin attracting more than his quota of customers. And when the customers come, I'll wager that this kind of banker can counsel those customers and make them profitable accounts. As I said, one purpose of the call program was to stir up enough prospects in the marketplace so that we did not have to grab at every opportunity we uncovered. If we saw a potential problem, we let some other bank make that loan. I firmly believe this was an important reason for Texas Commerce's solid success in the years to come.

We started the call program in 1967 and, although many improvements have been made since, we had the foundation laid by the beginning of 1969. We gradually established the fact that our bank would compete for business by going out and talking to potential customers about their needs. As had been the case at River Oaks, our systematic approach to calling on customers laid the solid base for future growth.

★   BUDGETING

Texas Commerce had neither budgets nor the staff to construct budgets that could clearly identify what we should be achieving in terms of return on equity, return on assets or earnings per share, or any of the other statistics that are a normal part of the vocabulary of managers today. Nor did many other regional banks prepare detailed budgets. When I first came to TCB, I recall asking the president of a rather large Houston bank how they prepared budgets. He laughed and said, "Budget! All I do is tell the board at the beginning of each year that we'll make 10 percent more than we made last year. I don't fool with tying up my time in budgets. Banking isn't that kind of operation."

Despite the fact that I had budgeted expenses, revenues, and profits to the penny at GIFT-RAPS and later absorbed the more professional budgeting methods employed by Gibson and CIT, my personal abilities required professional help. TCB auditor Charles Smith understood what I wanted to do. Charles had joined TCB from a large public accounting firm about the time

I came aboard, and he helped me establish comprehensible goals for the Houston Metropolitan Division. This may have been the bank's first budget, a simple quantified document that addressed only expenses and revenues. Later, Charles McMahen, another TCB import from a large public accounting firm and Texas Commerce's future chief financial officer, greatly perfected and sharpened our objectives. Within about three years, we had completed enough study on the performance of other banks our size to identify reasonable goals for return on assets, return on equity, and increase in earnings. Our next step was to hitch our goals to our call program. How many calls does it take to generate a loan? How many dollars in loans to generate one cent on the bottom line?

★ REACTION TO CHANGE

Initially, these changes generated major protests. Having spent seventeen years in business for myself and with Gibson in Cincinnati and CIT Financial in New York (both NYSE-listed firms), my marketing, budgeting, and organizational procedures did not seem revolutionary to me, but they alarmed the "old school" bank executives.

When John Whitmore heard about the call program I had painstakingly developed and instituted in the Metropolitan Division, he called me to his office. It never occurred to me to run the idea past him first. I certainly had not intended to bypass authority; I had learned *that* lesson in the Air Force! I had been hired to build deposits and loans to reverse TCB's erosion in size vis-à-vis our two major competitors, and that was what we were doing.

With obvious conviction, Mr. Whitmore asked, "What do you mean starting a call program? Any customer worth having already knows about TCB. Any customer worth having will come to us. By going out and asking for business, all you'll do is bring in trashy loans. You are simply elevating our risk."

Fortunately, I had brought along several months of records showing how our calls had already brought in some first-class business. I admitted that, although the older officers had objected to making calls at first, they were now sold on the idea and seemed to enjoy it. Our customers certainly did! In fact, many had told us it was the first time a banker had ever been out to see their business.

He said, "Well, you can try it for a while, but if I feel our reputation is being damaged, you'll have to stop."

I said, "Yes sir; fair enough; we will proceed."

Later, when we quantified our profit goals and got the budget installed, I was called in again. "Why are you talking to your officers about profits?" he asked. "This bank doesn't talk about profits. We talk about our deposit size and we talk about service!"

Again, I had brought along my charts showing how our calls were generating deposits, loans, and, yes, profits, and he finally said, "Well, all right. Keep it up for a while."

It is a remarkable tribute to John Whitmore that he let me stay in his organization, because my vision of what a bank ought to be doing differed totally from the one that he had inherited. I may have grown up in the Great Depression, but he had lived through its ravages as an adult. He knew where banking's cocoon of safety had come from—and why. Conversely, I had run a successful business and knew that a bank could be run more like a business.

We had surprising support from the seasoned bankers on the loan committee, like vice chairmen Pete Rehrauer, often called the "Dean of Houston Banking," and E. O. Buck, the petroleum engineer who had established the bank's Oil Department after World War II. Mr. Buck, a wise old Aggie, could be direct in voicing his opinions. He often said, "Banking is a business that's in the business of analyzing other businesses."

At board meetings, my most vocal supporters were the businessmen such as Riviana Foods CEO Bill Lane (my YPO friend I had recruited for the River Oaks Bank board), who had joined the TCB board in January 1968, nine months after I came to the bank. Big Three Industries CEO Harry K. Smith also backed me, as did oilman John Blaffer, who owned a lot of TCB stock and was interested in getting the price up so he could make more money. Independent oilman Bob Mosbacher was another booster. I remember Bob came into my office one day and said that he had been on the board nearly ten years and had never been asked to do anything. "Now, you're working me to death!" He loved the action.

★ GUS WORTHAM'S SUPPORT AS A MENTOR

I was also to earn the support of one of Houston's leading citizens, Gus Wortham, founder and chairman of American General Insurance Company and a major stockholder. I had met Mr. Wortham, who was to become my valued mentor and friend, after I came to Houston. My wife's family, the

I have always been a proponent of strong boards, and in 1971, Texas Commerce had its first "Billion Dollar Board." Members included Bill Lane, president and CEO of Riviana Foods, Inc., and Bob Herring, chairman of Houston Natural Gas Corporation, both close friends from my Young Presidents' Organization days. (Texas Commerce files)

McKeans, had known the Worthams for many years in Austin; in fact her uncle, Lonnie McKean, had introduced Mr. and Mrs. Wortham to each other.

But my own relationship with Gus Wortham began one evening in 1968 when, as president of Houston's University of Texas alumni association, I served as master of ceremonies at the annual dinner, held in the packed Emerald Room at Glenn McCarthy's Shamrock Hotel. I told a story that brought the house down. (Every now and then, you do hit a home run, and that evening I hit a home run.) Gus Wortham happened to be in the audience. He was a great civic leader, and he believed that chief executives ought to be seen out in the community. The next morning, John Whitmore told me that he had had a call from Gus Wortham. "You know, I didn't go to that function last night. There are just so many. I guess I should have," he said. "But he asked if I knew what a good speaker you were; he said you related a story that was as well told as any he had ever heard."

As silly as it sounds, I believe that my funny story was the first time I caught Gus Wortham's attention. He always looked out for young people. One of his protégés was Bill Lane, my friend from YPO whose company,

"To my friend Ben Love, the most effective younger bank president that I have ever known. Gus S. Wortham 1974." Thus was inscribed a portrait of the best friend a young man like me could ever have. (Love family archives)

Riviana Foods, had offices in the American General Building. Bob Herring was another. Bob was chairman of Houston Natural Gas when I talked to him about becoming a TCB director. I will never forget the joy in Wortham's voice when I told him that Bob was resigning from another bank board and joining Texas Commerce. He asked, "Would it be appropriate for me to call Bob and tell him how wonderful this is?" Of course, getting a phone call like that from Gus Wortham would be a tremendous compliment to anyone.

Gus Wortham enjoyed the marketing side of business. He loved to produce profitable business, and that is what I enjoyed, too, so we understood each other on that front as well. When he became aware of the business that was coming our way, he began inviting Margaret and me to small dinners at his home and introducing us to important members of the Houston community. The Worthams did extraordinary things for us.

Gus Wortham's relationship with the bank was long and close. According to a story he relayed to me in 1969, this relationship began in about 1925 when he decided to start American General and went to see his father's rather awe-inspiring friend, Jesse Jones, about investing start-up capital. He was a young man with a head full of plans and a briefcase full of projections. When he walked in, Jesse Jones was working at a desk piled high with papers. He never looked up but said: "Sit down, Gus."

Gus sat down.

"What do you want, Gus?"

He said, "Mr. Jones, I want to start an insurance company."

"How much, Gus?"

"Well, Mr. Jones, I want to capitalize it for $300,000, and I hoped you'd buy 25 percent, or $75,000."

"Okay."

Gus was so taken aback by this abrupt response that he stammered, "Well, Mr. Jones could I just clear a little place here on your desk and show you my pro formas?"

Jesse Jones looked up for the first time and he said: "Gus, I've given this matter all the time I'm going to."

And that was the first direct business relationship Gus Wortham had with Jesse Jones. Mr. Wortham joined the board of Mr. Jones's bank a year later, beginning a long association during which he progressed from its youngest to its oldest member. Likewise, TCB's relationship with American General was to grow into one of the bank's largest and closest.

Then in 1968, Gus Wortham repaid Jesse Jones's favor. Jones's great fortune, including his majority ownership in the National Bank of Commerce, had passed to his nonprofit, charitable foundation, Houston Endowment, at his death in 1956, and even after NBC's merger with TNB in 1964, the endowment remained the bank's largest single stockholder, with a 35 percent stake. By 1966, the endowment began facing a variety of governmental pressures to exit the banking business, and its officers began looking around for buyers for its bank stock and other commercial properties as well. The first possibility was John Mecom, who had parlayed his fortune as an independent oilman into diversified business holdings. The $85 million deal he struck with Houston Endowment included nearly eight hundred thousand shares of bank stock plus the *Houston Chronicle,* the Rice Hotel, and several other properties.

On December 6, 1965, Mecom gave Howard Creekmore, the head of Houston Endowment, a $1 million earnest-money check and promised to make complete payment in six months. On January 20, 1966, John Mecom was named chairman and chief executive officer of the bank, replacing Bob Doherty, who moved up to honorary chairman. On June 6, 1966, the purchase option expired and the deal fell through.[5] At the June board meeting two weeks later, President John Whitmore was named the bank's chief executive officer, and Ben Taub, a beloved Houston business leader and philanthropist and a director of the bank since 1956, was named chairman of the board.

After the collapse of the deal with Mecom in early 1968, Gus Wortham and American General Insurance Company stepped up and purchased the Texas Commerce Bank stock from Houston Endowment. In a typically succinct speech to TCB's employees after the purchase, Wortham summed up the historical ties between these organizations: "I'm an early depositor and the oldest borrower this bank has. Had it not been for Jesse Jones, there would be no American General."

Wortham did not plan to involve himself in running the bank. In fact, he went to great lengths to assert his complete confidence in the bank's current management: "I've known John Whitmore since he's been with the bank," he said. "It's been interesting to watch this man grow. I've found that when people of ability are elevated to positions of great responsibility, you can see them grow."

Then, just when the question of control of the bank's largest block of stock seemed resolved, the law governing bank holding companies was changed and the matter was reopened. On December 31, 1970, the Bank Holding Company Act of 1956 was amended so that any company that owned 25 percent or more of the voting stock of a bank was subject to the same regulation as a bank.

Of course, John Whitmore and TCB's lawyer, Charlie Sapp, had been planning for this change for some time because of its impact on American General. When the act passed, it was clear that American General would have to sell its TCB stock. But if the stock went to one individual, we might set up another "Mecom" situation, and we did not want that. We favored the amendment because it offered a way for the bank to grow and control its own destiny. However, the amendment posed a serious dilemma to American General and to the bank: How could they dispose of one-third of the bank's stock without destroying the price of that stock in the market?

And so, with the Federal Reserve's approval in 1972, American General converted its stock into Class B Non-Voting Common Stock and agreed to divest these holdings by 1980. The Fed also decreed that no American General officer could serve on the board of TCB, which meant we lost the daily counsel and advice of two of our most valuable directors, Gus Wortham and Ben Woodson, president of American General.[6]

American General fulfilled the terms of this agreement by divesting the Class B shares as stock dividends to its own shareholders and by selling debentures that could be exchanged for Texas Commerce stock after ten years. (The Class B stock reverted to regular voting common stock at divestiture.) The dissemination of this large block of stock into the hands of numerous smaller investors also marked a significant step in the transition of the bank from the control of owner-managers to hired, professional managers. This transition was completed in 1974 when Texas Commerce was listed on the New York Stock Exchange.

Gus Wortham did one other good turn for Jesse Jones's bank before he left the board. He established a retirement policy for the directors and officers. One day soon after I was elected president, he met with John Whitmore and me and emotionally recounted how much being a director of the bank had meant to him. During the next board meeting, Mr. Wortham opened the proceedings by declaring: "I look around this boardroom. A lot of us are getting old, and the bank has no retirement policy. I'm concerned about that. I realize that I have served on this board longer than anyone else has, and while I may not be the oldest, I am certainly in that category. Therefore, because of my length of service, because I am affected, and because American General owns 35 percent of the bank, I am the only one who can make this motion." With that, he proposed a retirement policy that called for officers to retire at sixty-five and board members at seventy-two. "Think about it," he said. "But do not delay. Let's proceed." And the board did.

★ MY PROMOTION TO PRESIDENT

I joined the bank in 1967 with the understanding that, if I did my job properly, I would have a shot at the top job when Mr. Whitmore retired. He assured me that no one else at the bank wanted the spot. I was aware that Bob Gerrard, senior vice president and senior loan officer in 1967, was a candidate for this position, but Bob had driven to my home one Sunday afternoon while I was interviewing with TCB and told me that he had no ambition to be CEO. He said he liked credit, was good at it, and did not enjoy the social and business activities required of the CEO. Soon after I arrived, however, Bob changed his mind. He had worked at the National Bank of Commerce since he graduated from college in 1952, so he would have been a comfortable choice for the board and management.

One afternoon about a week before the January 1968 board meeting, Mr. Whitmore came to my office and advised me that the board would promote Bob to executive vice president at the next meeting, and I would remain a senior vice president. Well, that was a shock. The "new" Houston Metropolitan Division had brought in a tremendous volume of A+ business. My system was working, and morale was excellent. Yet, I was being passed over for a key promotion.

About this time, my friend Dan Arnold, an attorney with Vinson Elkins, contacted me. He had read *People and Profits: A Bank Case Study,* my thesis on the history of TCB, written for the Southwest Graduate School of Banking at Southern Methodist University, and he wanted me to talk to David Searls, who was the attorney for my friend John Duncan, the cofounder of Gulf & Western. As managing partner of First City National Bank's law firm, Vinson Elkins, David was on that bank's board and headed its senior officer recruiting committee. First City was looking for a president. We visited several times and got along very well. David said he would recommend me to First City chairman Jim Elkins.

As it turns out, David was also Gus Wortham's personal attorney and naturally mentioned our conversation to one of his most important clients. Much later, Ben Woodson, the president of American General, told me that Mr. Wortham had then called Whitmore and emphatically identified me as "our next president." He said it was the only time Gus Wortham ever told the bank what to do. I owe a great debt of gratitude to Gus Wortham and Ben Woodson, and I cherish their memories and the opportunities they gave me. Everybody needs a mentor. They both were that to me.

In January 1968, Bob Gerrard was named executive vice president and manager of the Administration Department. And in April 1968, I was promoted to executive vice president and manager of the Commercial Banking Department. This added the National Division, the Petroleum Division, the Chemical Division, the Correspondent Banking Division, and the Family Banking Division to my Houston Metropolitan "home base," which was renamed the Houston Southwest Division. In January 1969, Bob and I both were elected to the board of directors.

On December 17, 1969, John Whitmore moved up to chairman and chief executive officer, and I was elected president of the bank. Two and one-half

TCB's new chairman and CEO, John E. Whitmore, and its new president Ben Love strode down Travis Street on the day of our promotions, December 17, 1969. (Bankers' Hours, 27: 6 (1989), Barbara Eaves's archives)

years after joining TCB, I had earned the opportunity to run the bank. To succeed, I would need to continue the initiative to make the bank more competitive in the marketplace and more highly organized internally. That called for completing the transition from performance measured by growth in deposits to performance measured by growth in earnings per share. In essence, I had to complete the transformation of a traditional, regulated bank into a more competitive business organization willing and able to more aggressively enter the marketplace for banking services.

NOTES

1. Texas National Bank of Commerce of Houston was the legal name of the bank formed by the merger of Texas National Bank and the National Bank of Commerce on January 17, 1964. The name "Texas Commerce Bank" was soon adopted for marketing purposes and became the legal name of the bank in 1970. In this book, "Texas Commerce Bank" indicates the bank after the 1964 merger.

2. Ben F. Love, "People and Profits: A Bank Case Study" (master's thesis, Southwest Graduate School of Banking, Southern Methodist University, 1967), 43–44.

3. Walter L. Buenger and Joseph A. Pratt, *But Also Good Business: Texas Commerce Banks and the Financing of Houston and Texas, 1886–1986* (College Station: Texas A&M University Press 1986), 3.

4. "Deposits Have Tripled Since War," *Houston Chronicle,* February 16, 1964.

5. "Mecom Lets Sale Option Run Out; Stock Dip Cited," *American Banker,* June 9, 1966.

6. Federal Reserve chairman Arthur Burns and American General chairman Gus Wortham, together, had worked out the agreement whereby American General would relinquish control of Texas Commerce. Specifically, its terms called for the company to sell its TCB stock and resign from the board. Ten years after the terms of this agreement had been met, I wanted to reinstate formal board ties between the two "old friends," and, after gaining agreement from Harold Hook, Ben Woodson's successor as chief executive of American General, I submitted the request to the Federal Reserve. The Fed's general counsel turned us down.

Because I had never seen a copy of the original agreement, I wrote to Arthur Burns (who was ambassador to Germany at this time) about it. Ambassador Burns replied that the agreement was a verbal one between him and Gus Wortham; no one else was in the room, so no one else would know what it contained. He stated that the terms of the agreement had been satisfied and saw no reason to deny our request. But nothing happened.

A year or so later, I ran into Ambassador Burns after a meeting and he asked, "Did you ever get that matter with American General straightened out?" I replied that the Fed's general counsel still would not budge. Now, this was a minute detail for someone of Arthur Burns's standing to bother with, but he said, "Ben, you let me handle this." Sure enough, the matter was soon fixed, and Harold Hook was elected to the Texas Commerce board in 1982.

This episode with Arthur Burns reaffirmed a lesson my mother had taught so well: "Let your word be as good as a government bond." In other words, never—no matter how big you become—disregard an agreement you have made.

My broader responsibilities as president gave me the opportunity to extend throughout the bank the organizational structure, the officer calling program, the quantified goals, and the budgets that had worked so productively in the Houston Metropolitan Division. I worked with Chairman John Whitmore and a good group of officers to broaden the bank's marketing program, open new lines of customer communication, and further consolidate and coordinate the still-feuding internal NBC and TNB camps. We also recruited and trained extraordinarily smart young managers who had excelled academically prior to joining TCB. In this way, we increased our ability to compete with the giant money center banks.

A healthy economy is the single most critical factor in the success of any bank. Between 1968 and 1972, Texas Commerce was operating in the healthiest economy in the nation. Real estate construction was probably the most visible growth industry of this period; it was hard to overlook the complete generation of downtown skyscrapers it produced. Houston's new big city skyline fit its rank as the nation's sixth-largest city in 1970, one with an increasingly diverse economy that could no longer be easily categorized as cotton- or oil-based.

Oil had been the glamour industry of the southwestern states immediately after World War II, but a sustained decline in exploration and production began in the early 1970s as petroleum deposits in the Middle East proved larger, easier to find, and less expensive to bring out of the ground. Although local oil production was not the business it had been, the expertise and infrastructure for this by-now international industry was increasingly headquartered in Houston. A boom in the cross-country shipment of natural gas came after the war, and the largest natural gas transmission companies were based in Houston. The war effort also incubated a vast petrochemical complex in Houston, one that accelerated its growth after the war and made the city the geographic center of one of the nation's fastest expanding industries.

The bank was well positioned to take advantage of the resulting opportunities. An excellent group of bank officers led the way. The urbane Lew Brown moved from National to head Houston Southwest, while Charlie Beall, an Ole Miss gentleman and scholar, was promoted to manage the National Division. Correspondent Banking was led by Grant Byus, who had run small banks and understood them well. John Townley, a shrewd, hardheaded Aggie petroleum engineer, followed E. O. Buck as head of the Energy Division. W. N. (Bill) Davis put his impressive industry experience to work managing the new Chemical Division. Family Banking was run by Warner Rogers, an exceptionally innovative retail banker with finance company managerial seasoning. The courtly George Ebanks, one of the first Texas bankers to travel to Japan after World War II, was in charge of International and reported to Bob Gerrard. George ran a one-man show and did a notable job, considering his limited resources in manpower, comparative competitive size, and locations. Real Estate was managed by Lloyd Bolton, a man of uncommon common sense, who reported to John Whitmore.

★ BUILDING ON TRADITIONAL STRENGTHS
IN ENERGY AND REAL ESTATE

Oil lending at TCB did not dip as dramatically as the drilling rig count in the 1970s because the bank generally made loans secured by proved producing reserves, rather than more speculative loans related to drilling for oil. John Townley's division also lent to such energy service giants as Hughes Tool Company and Schlumberger. Pipeline and transportation companies constituted another important component of his division's portfolio. We made very few loans secured by drilling rigs. As a matter of fact, if a young officer brought a rig loan application to vice chairman E. O. Buck, he referred that officer to the junkyard to get the price of scrap iron, because Buck, a veteran of the oil patch before he became a veteran oil banker, declared that a rig would be worth only its weight in scrap iron during the inevitable cyclical drilling bust.

With local oil production on the wane, TCB looked within the industry for other opportunities and found that the Texas Gulf Coast plants were producing 40 percent of the nation's petrochemical supplies. John Whitmore tapped Bill Davis, an experienced chemical engineer, to build a new Chemical Division around several accounts previously served by the Energy and National divisions. Bill joined the bank in 1967, about the same time I did.

As oil-led development fueled Houston's expansion, two postwar building booms brought nearly 10 million square feet of office space on stream. This construction virtually doubled the city's architecturally acclaimed central business district, vastly expanded a Texas Medical Center that was well on its way to housing more doctors per square foot than any other seven-hundred-acre plot on the planet, then created from scratch the retail blockbuster Galleria and many other commercial and retail developments.

Several factors made TCB particularly well suited to participate in this growth. First, John Whitmore had established a large, profitable business in mortgage warehousing at the National Bank of Commerce. Next, Texas National Bank, under T. O. Taylor and Lawrence Lee, had taken the lead in real estate construction lending in Houston. The merger brought these strong capabilities together under T. O. Taylor in perhaps the only instance where a Texas National banker managed a division in the merged bank. But the most important factor was that Jesse Jones, a world-class, exemplary developer, controlled the National Bank of Commerce from 1919 until his death in 1956. It was from him that TCB inherited its appetite for real estate lending.

One of Texas National's early customers was my friend Gerald Hines, who came to Houston in 1948, after World War II, with a degree in mechanical engineering from Purdue University, and began constructing small buildings and warehouses as investments. One of his early projects was to design and construct the manufacturing plant for GIFT-RAPS. Interim construction financing from local banks, coupled with long-term takeout loans from insurance companies, was sufficient for his early projects. At that time, Houston banks extended funds based on a builder's personal worth rather than on the value of the project itself. As Gerry's projects outgrew his personal worth, he found it increasingly difficult to arrange financing, although he did do some business at Texas National with T. O. Taylor and Lawrence Lee, who offered construction loans secured by mortgages and deeds of trust.

By the late-1960s, with the fifty-story One Shell Plaza on the drawing board, Gerry stepped into a clearly different league. He sought financing at money center banks and again was confronted with demands from these banks to encumber the personal worth of all of his partners in this project. This was unacceptable. So he decided to put together a consortium of all the major banks in Houston to handle this $30 million deal. First City took the lead and Texas Commerce was a significant participant in a loan that was, at the time, the largest construction loan totally funded by Houston banks. Earlier, most of Houston's large downtown buildings had been constructed by oil companies, with financing supplied by their East Coast banks. First National Bank of Boston was a leader in construction lending. It offered resources, experience, and contacts with long-term lenders that the Houston banks could not yet match.

When Gerry developed his visionary plans for the Galleria, we joined as a visible participant in a loan package headed by First Boston. The Galleria included a major hotel, three levels of shopping (featuring retail stores including Neiman Marcus) overlooking an Olympian ice-skating arena, and a high-rise office tower. Assembling the various parcels of land and the airspace to the satisfaction of the many tenants proved anything but easy. In fact, Gerry later acknowledged that the Galleria required one of the most complex construction loans ever made up to that time. First Boston's King Upton, a dean of construction lending, orchestrated this process. Lloyd Bolton headed much of this loan structuring for Texas Commerce. Knowledgeable, able, sound Lloyd had trained to manage the Real Estate Division under John Whitmore, Pete Rehrauer, T. O. Taylor, and Lawrence Lee.

So Texas Commerce came of age in real estate lending by financing projects "from gas stations to Gallerias" for people of exceptional vision, ability, and character, like Gerry. Other clients included Kenneth Schnitzer, who built the 127-acre Greenway Plaza office and entertainment complex, and our two large mortgage-warehousing customers, John Dunn, CEO of Mortgage & Trust, and Jake Kamin, CEO of American Mortgage, who also resoundingly proved his skill in development. These were just four of scores of customers who constituted the bank's absolutely first-class borrowing base. Texas Commerce had the highest-quality real estate customers in Houston, and that was extremely important in this type of lending, where credits are typically large and risks are correspondingly high.

Meanwhile, bank real estate officers continually called on customers and brought in interesting projects. Lloyd Bolton always looked at the character of the borrower first. If he concluded that the people involved were not top-notch, no matter how good the project seemed, he would say, "These people are not Grade A." That's all it took. We let another bank make that loan. Lloyd was a terrific judge of character. He contended, "Banking is like flying in an airplane. The only time it's exciting is when everything is going to hell. You want it to be dull." Recalling the excitement of my tenth mission flying over Ludwigshafen, Germany, in September 1944, when our B-17 Flying

Fortress bomber was so damaged by flak that we barely made it back to England, I could identify with that.

Gerry, Kenneth, John, and Jake (and many, many others) provided the lessons for our real estate lenders; First Boston supplied the tutors; and Texas Commerce was the active student participant—initially. Several years later, Texas Commerce was lead bank on phase two of the Galleria and First Boston was a participant. Importantly for us, the roles had been reversed.

★ THE QUEST FOR SIZE: FAMILY BANKING CENTER

In the mid-1960s, John Whitmore and senior management looked at the competition from suburban banks and at the rise in the disposable dollars in the pockets of families that were being formed by World War II babies. They and Warner Rogers, who had come to the bank in 1966 as head of our new installment loan department, concluded that Texas Commerce had financing to offer suburban families even though we were a downtown bank. Thus, with full-page ads running in the *Houston Chronicle* and the *Houston Post* on Sunday, July 23, 1967, Texas Commerce opened the Family Banking Center, a new marketing concept calculated to give young families a reason to come downtown to bank.[1]

We located the first Family Banking Center in a small alcove off the main lobby. The furnishings were homey and informal because we projected that some people might feel uncomfortable in the strictly business surroundings that characterized the bank's awesome lobby and forty-four-foot-high leaded-glass ceiling. This cozy "little bank inside the big bank" offered fifty-three specific banking services and was staffed with "personal bankers" who were ready, able, and willing to compete aggressively with the cozy suburban retail banks for personal and family business. We knew that most customers might not use more than two or three services at the outset, but we also projected that many customers would prosper and require astute direction involving trust and investment advice in the future.

Two new facilities quickly followed. In January 1969, a full-service mini-bank opened for extended hours—from 7:30 A.M. to 5:30 P.M.—on the corner of Rusk and Milam as a convenience for people who worked downtown. In April 1970, the thirty-thousand-square-foot, full-service, permanent home for the Family Banking Division opened two blocks away. This was as far

TEXAS *National Bank of* **COMMERCE**

changed to

TEXAS _{BANK OF} NATIONAL COMMERCE

then was modified to

TEXAS/COMMERCE

TEXAS NATIONAL BANK OF COMMERCE

and from there to *

TEXAS COMMERCE BANK

TEXAS NATIONAL BANK OF COMMERCE

and finally to

TEXAS NATIONAL BANK OF COMMERCE

The Texas Commerce logo began with the cumbersome Texas National Bank of Commerce signature that came out of the Texas National–National Bank of Commerce merger in 1964. In 1966, TCB adopted the very recognizable Texas Commerce flag. (Bankers' Hours, 8:3 (July 1968), Barbara Eaves's archives)

from the minibank as a separate facility could be and still comply with existing Texas anti-branch banking laws.

The Family Banking Center was a material source of deposits. Within three years, it grew to $154 million, larger than all but the top four Houston banks. Had we been so inclined, we could have spun off Family Banking and formed the fifth-largest bank in Houston.

Between 1968 and 1972, Texas Commerce Bank thrived amidst the booming regional economy, propelled by vigorous calls by bank officers offering innovative, first-class service to active and prospective customers from Bellaire to Bahrain and generating ever-increasing and measurable profits for the bank. Even the bank's image was new. To supplement TCB's newly invigorated marketing program, John Whitmore retained Ketchum, MacLeod & Grove advertising agency and its masterful account executive Bill Allison. Soon the bank had a new name (Texas National Bank of Commerce of Houston became Texas Commerce Bank), a new logo (the TCB flag), and a warmer persona. And its advertising won the Houston Advertising Club's Grand Prix awards three years in a row, an unprecedented feat.

In this environment, I anticipated that Texas Commerce Bank, relying on its young, well-trained, energetic staff, should prosper more than most large banks in unit-banking states. Of the bank's 160 officers, about 40 percent were under thirty-five years of age. This officer contingent would be available to TCB in the 1970s and 1980s, during the most productive years of their lives and during the era of the bank's greatest expansion of assets, profits, and facilities.

<h2>★ THE CHALLENGE OF SIZE</h2>

As the decade of the 1970s dawned, our major challenge was mustering the deposits to fund big loans. Texas bank deposits might have been doubling every ten years, but these deposits were fragmented in a profusion of different banks, and each bank was a separate institution with its own board and its own individual lending capacity. At this time, twelve hundred banks were domiciled in Texas, more by far than any other state, and new banks were springing up every day in the booming suburbs. But growth in numbers was not accompanied by growth in the size of the state's large banks vis-à-vis money center banks. Indeed, not one Texas bank ranked among the twenty-five largest in the country in size or in profits. In fact, just 21 percent of the state's deposits were concentrated in its five largest banks. This translated into $6 billion in deposits in all five banks combined, giving each bank an average loan limit[2] of $10 million per customer—a totally inadequate financial capacity for a bank trying to persuade Shell Oil to move its headquarters to Houston from New York City, where the huge money center banks were located. Only Iowa, Kansas, and West Virginia had lower levels of deposit concentration, and their financing needs hardly compared to those in Texas.

This situation focused our full attention on one sobering fact: operating under the state's unit banking law, Texas banks could not muster the capital to finance the increasingly large Texas corporations that created the jobs responsible for the state's growth. It was that simple. As a result, Texas companies were forced to turn to money center banks and take their place in line for loans behind those banks' local customers. How much more beneficial it would have been for the Texas economy if, instead of fragmenting our financial resources among the ninety-odd banks in Harris County alone, we could have consolidated these bank deposits and financed Texas's growth.

The Federal Reserve Bank of Dallas agreed. In the early 1970s, the Fed interviewed forty-two of the one hundred largest businesses in Texas and confirmed that strong working ties existed between most of these Texas-based companies and large, out-of-state, money center banks. The survey concluded: "The main reason for this outflow of business from Texas is clearly the size of Texas banks. Banks in the state are simply too small to compete effectively with large out-of-state banks."[3] But if Texas banks were to grow larger, the Texas Constitution would have to be changed, because the primary engines of bank growth—branch banking and interstate banking—were banned in the state constitution of 1876. In 1970, the only option for growth was to merge two unit banks and move them together under one roof, in one location.

Texas banks occasionally finessed this "one roof" problem. For example, South Texas and Union National banks sat across Main Street from each other. When they agreed to merge and form Texas National Bank, South Texas already had a new home under construction. Regulators approved the merger quickly, contingent, of course, on the two banks moving into a single location. Well, the new building was not finished in time, but rather than make two moves, the bankers noted a 1950 decision by the Texas attorney general that allowed a bank to open a drive-in across the street if the two buildings were connected by a permanent tunnel. At an expense estimated around $50,000 and a slight inconvenience to traffic on Main Street, a small, permanent tunnel was dug between the two banks. Once a single message traveled through the tunnel, the two buildings were officially proclaimed to be a single site for regulatory purposes. The merger was completed and the tunnel was never used again. Texas National carried on business as usual, in both buildings, until the new facility opened. And society was again "protected" from the dangers of branch banking. In the late 1960s, however, a merger (with or without a permanent tunnel) was a moot point because there remained no logical downtown partner big enough to make much difference.

★ INTERNATIONAL BANKING:
TEXAS TALK AROUND THE GLOBE

Lending to oil-related businesses also contributed significantly to the bank's international efforts. For decades, Texas Commerce officers had followed major customers into Europe, Latin America, and the Far and Middle East, traveling extensively to extend international banking services that usually required the participation of a large New York bank. By the late 1960s, we made a decision that committed TCB to a more aggressive international posture. In August 1968, Texas Commerce purchased 35 percent of an established merchant bank in London. This was the first of several steps that created a footprint from which to grow internationally by establishing geographically diverse offices, by building an increasingly experienced international staff, and by creating an image as an emerging competitor with the expertise to bank our Texas-based customers wherever in the world their business took them.

The problems we faced at the outset of our move into international banking may be illustrated by the "Big Three Industries Story." That company's chairman and active Texas Commerce director, Harry K. Smith, had taken the welding equipment supply and industrial gas company he inherited at age thirty-eight and built it into one of the largest oxygen and nitrogen supply companies in the world. Eventually, he needed financing beyond TCB's meager loan limit, so I called Harold Young, an officer at Chase Manhattan in New York City, seeking the "participation" of that large money center bank in the credit. A participation worked in this manner: we brought in the business; Chase and TCB structured the loan; we kept a "participation" in the loan, never to exceed our legal loan limit; and Chase booked the rest. This was quite a deal for Harold and his New York bank.

A few months later, Big Three needed another loan, this time in Eurodollars,[4] to finance a transaction in Europe. I called Harold about a Eurodollar technicality, and he responded, "Look, Ben, don't go out there and call on Big Three anymore; you'll just mess things up. I'll be down in a couple of months, and I'll let you participate in whatever Chase works out."

He would *let us* participate? Remember, I had initiated that call! Big Three was *our* loyal customer! Worse yet, Harold called back in a few days and said it would be best if Chase took over as Big Three's primary bank because the company was expanding far beyond our loan limit and overall capabilities. Well, that was like being punched in the nose by an ostensible ally. However, it clearly exemplified the problem of our lacking the lending capacity and international expertise our Texas-based customers needed—plus the inevitable risk of losing those customers to the money center banks. We could do little about it unless Texas banking laws were modified. I felt no sense of inferiority in terms of the caliber of our people vis-à-vis the out-of-state, money center bankers, but I did feel inferior about the puny-sized loans we could legally offer our Texas-based, high-growth business customers and

TABLE 7.1: *Texas Commerce International Offices*

1968 — Burston & Texas Commerce Bank, Ltd., merchant bank

1969 — Nassau, branch

1969 — New York Edge Act office

1971 — Mexico City, office

1972 — Tokyo, office

1973 — London, branch

1974 — TCB acquires Burston's 65 percent interest in the merchant bank
and renames it Texas Commerce International Bank, Ltd.

1976 — Bahrain, office

1977 — Hong Kong, office

1977 — Caracas, office

1978 — São Paolo, office

In the decade between 1968 and 1978, Texas Commerce established nine international facilities: one merchant bank, full branches in Nassau and London, an Edge-Act office in New York, and six loan production offices.

those large out-of-state companies that were considering moving their major headquarters to Texas. And "Eurodollars"? Why, that word was almost excluded from the Texas banking vocabulary!

To change this situation, TCB pursued an opportunity to buy into a merchant bank in the heart of London's financial district. London was the financial capital of the world, the headquarters for trading in gold and Eurodollars, and the clearing point for financial transactions all over Europe, the Middle East, and the rest of the world. London was the compelling choice for TCB's first operation outside the United States, and this bank, Burston, Howard De-Walden & Co., Ltd., was located at 41 Moorgate in "The City," just two blocks away from the Bank of England. Although the bank was small, it was just right for our appetite. With the Big Three/Chase situation chafing in my recent memory, I pushed hard for TCB to make this investment, and in August 1968, we concluded an agreement to acquire 35 percent of what became Burston & Texas Commerce Bank, Ltd. We paid just over one million dollars for our stake, a small price for a big concept. Texas Commerce was the first bank in the Southwest with a facility in London.

Neville Burston, the bank's founder and chief executive, was the son of an innovative London businessman who owned a group of successful retail stores. A Cambridge-educated lawyer, Burston was third in line to become lord mayor of London. He opened his merchant bank in 1955 and, in only eight years, earned the enviable "authorized status" from the Bank of England, which permitted his bank to conduct foreign exchange and other forms of business not authorized for "new" banks. He sought a U.S. partner to give his bank a conduit to new customers and to bolster its capital.

John Whitmore, Bob Gerrard (senior loan officer), Tom McDade (head of the Investment Department and manager of TCB's securities portfolio, a graduate of Baylor and Harvard), George Ebanks, and I all were enthusiastic about the move. We believed we had made an investment in learning to "walk the walk and talk the talk"—and we might even make some money. With Texas-based customers like Big Three, Cameron Iron Works, El Paso Natural Gas, Hughes Tool, and others marketing their products internationally, I felt strongly that we would be left by the side of the road if we did not develop our international banking capabilities. George dispatched his second in command, Mike Gaetz, a seasoned professional, to London as a managing director of Burston & Texas Commerce Bank for two years. Robert Hunter, a University of Texas honors graduate whom I had hired in 1969 from Citibank's office in Seoul, Korea, replaced him when Mike rotated back to Houston to impart the knowledge he had acquired in London to our people here.

Hunter was only twenty-eight years old when I assigned him to London in charge of Europe, but this mature, disciplined Texan from Abilene had international experience with Citibank. My confidence in the capabilities of young men of Robert's age resulted from my experience flying combat missions with the Eighth Air Force over Germany in World War II. Few of those men, who carried out life-and-death assignments under intense pressure, were more than twenty-two years old. I was barely twenty when I completed my twenty-five-mission tour with the rank of captain. In my eyes, a twenty-eight-year-old could be a responsible banker, provided he was mature, equipped with sound judgment, and backed by a strong institution like TCB. Robert proved that he had every trait required.

Robert's reaction to this appointment did surprise me, though. In thanking me for my support, he said: 'You know, Mr. Love, since you are putting all this confidence in me, we need to be on a first-name basis." I recall that I immediately said, "Why yes, of course, Robert." He, however, recalls that I made him sweat for at least a decade before I broke into a grin.

Meanwhile, we intensified our international banking quest from the Texas side. We boned up on international tonnage and traffic traveling through the Port of Houston; we identified Houston firms that were active in international markets and learned what services they needed; and we assigned Jack Moriniere, a smart young TCB officer, to Washington for a year to study the Export-Import Bank's new government-backed trade finance services.

We also learned exactly what a merchant bank could and could not do. This peculiar beast is a combination of an investment bank and a commercial bank. By law, American dollars could not be exported for loans to American companies operating overseas, but Burston & Texas Commerce Bank could muster dollars that were already outside the country—Eurodollars— and lend them, unrestricted by the size of Texas Commerce's loan limit. Our London bank could also raise capital in virtually any foreign currency, and it could underwrite public stock offerings.

The Burston partnership was just the first step. Next came Nassau. In 1969, we opened a branch there to gain direct access into the unregulated Euro-dollar market. Although little more than a post office box managed by a trust company, this branch enabled Texas Commerce to carry out various important international transactions that were constrained by U.S. law. At first, we sent Jim Follis, a retired TCB officer, to Nassau to handle the "arduous" chore of checking the mail each day (applicants lined up out the door for this "tough duty" post). Later, Jim returned home and TCB managed the branch from Houston.

Mexico City was the site of our first loan production office. It opened in 1971, the only U.S. application (out of eight) approved by the government of President Luis Echeverria that year. This reflected the fact that three of us from TCB had campaigned for this office with every regulator in Mexico City and with the assistance of every influential Mexican friend or customer who could help us win approval.

Next we opened an office in Tokyo in 1972, because Japan shipped more tonnage through the Port of Houston than any other country.

We established a full-service commercial branch in London in 1973 to add balance sheet strength and to supplement the investment and wholesale banking activities of the Burston bank. Norman Nolen, another academically outstanding officer in his twenties, replaced Robert Hunter at the Burston bank when Robert opened the new branch. I recall that Herbert Allen, a Texas Commerce director and chairman of Cameron Iron Works, happened to be in the UK at the time visiting his plants in Scotland, and Robert put him to work cutting the ribbon.

The oil business took us to Bahrain in 1976 (where our office opened in the worst sandstorm this East Texas boy had ever seen) in pursuit of the petrodollars needed to fund large loans to customers such as Aramco and companies doing business with Aramco.

Then, in 1977, came Hong Kong, where the chief executive of Esso Eastern, Howard Duncan, introduced me to Hong Kong's foremost investor and Esso's China Light Co. partner, Sir Lawrence Kadourie. Sir Lawrence, among his diverse interests, had developed a technique for breeding huge hogs because he could foresee a shortfall of protein for the population of mainland China. He insisted to me that TCB could set up an office in Hong Kong for $60,000 a year and learn more about international business there than anywhere else in the world, except London. He was right about the hogs, and he was right about the banking office location in Hong Kong strategically.

From there, we went to Caracas in 1977 and São Paulo in 1978. The national oil companies in Venezuela and Brazil eventually established permanent purchasing offices in Houston near the tool and services companies that supplied worldwide markets (again, our customers).

George H. W. Bush's son, Jeb, a youthful, brilliant Phi Beta Kappa Texas Commerce officer who had been extraordinarily effective as my top administrative assistant for two years in Houston, launched our office in Caracas with an opening reception that attracted a whopping eight hundred business leaders as opposed to the fifty or sixty who typically attended any foreign bank opening. The reason was simple. Lady Bird Johnson, a Texas Commerce director, helped host the affair in Caracas. When word leaked out that she was coming, people "asked to be asked." A "secondary market" literally developed for those invitations.

We arrived for the reception a day early to give Mrs. Johnson and another TCB director, Ambassador Edward Clarke, time to rest. But as we checked into the hotel, Mrs. Johnson asked what I planned to do during their "day of rest."

"Make calls," I said.

"What time is your first call?" she asked.

"Eight o'clock in the morning," I responded.

"Would you mind if I went with you?" she asked. I was thrilled but dumbfounded that she wanted to go and our customers were stunned. What a

trouper! She accompanied us on every call that day and then served as a relaxed, charming hostess at the reception that evening.

As the widow of a U.S. president, Mrs. Johnson has full-time Secret Service
protection. I was not surprised to learn that these agents are armed. At first, the
Venezuelan officials said, "No, no, the Secret Service officers cannot be armed
at your reception." Well, Mrs. Johnson could not travel without the Secret
Service, the Secret Service would not go without their arms, and the business
and political leadership of Caracas was already "up in arms" to meet her. The
situation evolved into the "Standoff at the Caracas Corral" until someone
came up with a peaceful compromise. The solution? Both sides "packed iron."

During the reception, the top Chrysler executive in Latin America spoke
to me about the long, memorable visit he had enjoyed with Mrs. Johnson. His
wife said, "Why Henry, we may have talked to her for thirty seconds in the
receiving line." He said, "Really? But the way she fixed her total attention on
me for those thirty seconds made it an unforgettable experience." It was not
the length of their visit but the force of her full attention that made his visit
with Mrs. Johnson unforgettable. She totally epitomizes to me a majestic individual, mentally tough, hardworking, and never, ever, anything other than
gracious. She is a truly lovely lady.

Initially, we invested in the Burston bank as a learning experience, but part
of what we learned was totally unexpected. By 1971, we realized that some of
the areas in which Neville was taking Burston & Texas Commerce posed risks
with which we were not comfortable. I asked my colleague Jack Horner to accompany me to London. Jack had been president of several Shell Oil subsidiaries and had completed his career with Shell as chief financial officer in
New York before joining Texas Commerce as head of Commercial Banking.
Jack was a few years older than I, and his extensive international experience
with Shell included tenure in London. His judgment was superb, and we
were totally comfortable in discussing thorny business matters.

During these negotiations, it became evident that we would have to elim-
inate the risky ventures that troubled us. My friend Neville was unwilling to
make those divestitures, largely influenced by two of his senior officers whom
we would not have hired to be Texas Commerce bankers. Our very vigorous
discussions lasted more than a week and often ran late into the night. Finally,
I hit upon the idea of constructing an agreement involving "puts and calls."
After Neville digested the fairness of this proposal, he agreed on two things:

a price at which we could "put" our 35 percent interest in the bank to him and a price at which we could "call" his 65 percent interest in the bank.

When I relayed that proposal to John Whitmore, he became extremely concerned and brought in Vice Chairman Tom McDade, TCB's chief investment officer, to help him evaluate my proposal. Lengthy conversations passed between John's office in Houston and my hotel room in London, where I had privacy. Tom was very helpful in persuading John that my concept had merit and was a sound method whereby we could either exit the partnership or buy all of Burston & Texas Commerce.

In the troubled times that eventually converged on the Burston bank, along with most other British merchant banks, this legally binding agreement of "puts and calls" became invaluable. In 1974, as the Bank of England was conducting "lifeboat exercises" for the UK's collapsing merchant banking system, the head of that bank's foreign desk, Jim Keough, called and declared that Texas Commerce had a responsibility to take over $70 million in debt that Neville's publicly owned companies could not repay. Well, that was a shock. Fortunately, earlier that year, TCB had "called" Neville's 65 percent interest in the bank. We legally and completely severed those ties prior to any problem Burston subsequently experienced. Otherwise, Keough's contention would have meant a $70 million loss for TCB. Texas Commerce also would have been removed from the London market and effectively denied reentry, if not in perpetuity, for a long period of time. That was not the kind of "learning" we sought when we bought a 35 percent minority position in Burston.

If I look back on anything of major financial import that I might have contributed to our international effort, it would be eliminating from Burston & Texas Commerce Bank those entities Neville subsequently took public. Fortuitously, I had employed Freshfields, a legal firm that also represented the Bank of England, to construct the total divesture of these subsidiaries in language that would satisfy the British judicial system. Freshfields' legal work was decisive—worth about $70 million to TCB, to be precise.

In addition to the merchant bank, we ultimately established full branches in Nassau and London, an Edge Act office in New York, and six loan production offices, which, considering the size of this planet, is not very many, but they were strategically located in those areas of the world that conducted business with Texas and had current or potential ties to Texas Commerce customers.

★ TEXAS COMMERCE SHAREHOLDERS COMPANY:
   SEEKING SIZE IN THE SUBURBS

As we moved around the world in search of expansion opportunities, our quest also took us into the Houston suburbs. Here we built on the earlier efforts of Jesse Jones, who had realized in the 1950s that most of the growth in Houston was coming from the suburbs. Jones led the move to tap Houston's suburban bank deposits. In 1950, he organized Reagan State Bank in the Houston Heights neighborhood and purchased more than 50 percent of its stock through the Commerce Company, his wholly owned operating entity that also held more than 50 percent of the capital stock of the downtown National Bank of Commerce. Ultimately, his Commerce Company held controlling interests in half a dozen so-called "chain banks" in Houston's suburbs, along with the Rice Hotel, the *Houston Chronicle,* and other interests. When Jesse Jones died, childless, in 1956, these holdings passed along to Houston Endowment, together with the rest of his assets, to be managed by his selfless associate Howard Creekmore, a man of great integrity and judgment.

Business associates and personal friends of Jesse Jones served on the chain banks' boards of directors and chaired their loan committees. These suburban Houston banks developed very close, mutually beneficial correspondent relationships with the National Bank of Commerce—referring business, participating in one another's loans, and operating in constructive, profitable harmony. But the structure was not perfect. For example, each bank in a chain remained a separate organization in calculating its legal lending limit. This meant that one link in the chain could not make a loan based on the capacity of the entire chain. That was a serious drawback from the perspective of a downtown bank that was seeking to grow rapidly and compete with larger, out-of-state, money center banks. Thus, the search for legal circumventions of, or alterations to, the state's unit banking laws was pursued energetically.

The Bank Holding Company Act of 1956 gave tacit approval to certain chain banking relationships by requiring any entity that owned 25 percent or more of the outstanding stock of more than one bank to register with the Federal Reserve as a bank holding company. By remaining silent on cases that involved less than 25 percent, this law encouraged the spread of the so-called "24.9 percent banks."

Now, this act hit Houston Endowment squarely in its asset base. Its ownership in each of Jesse Jones's half-dozen banks, including the downtown

Texas Commerce Bank, was considerably more than 24.9 percent. This not-for-profit, charitable foundation had no interest in being regulated by the Fed and thus began selling all of its holdings in for-profit businesses. Much of the chain bank stock went to the chain bank managers and directors.[5]

During the mid-1960s, John Whitmore, with astute legal guidance from Charlie Sapp, managing partner of the bank's primary law firm since the days of Jesse Jones (Liddell, Sapp, Zivley & Brown), created Texas Commerce Shareholders Company (TCSC) to invest directly in suburban banks. This initiative was well underway when I joined the bank, and after I became president, Whitmore involved me deeply in every facet of the move into the suburbs, even as I was taking out initiatives into international banking.

In 1968, the shareholders of Texas Commerce voted to organize Texas Commerce Shareholders Company, a company owned by a trustee for the benefit of the shareholders of Texas Commerce Bank. TCSC was *not* a bank and *could* invest in suburban banks or just about anything else it chose. Logically, the company's first purchases were Houston Endowment's remaining interests in Jesse Jones's chain banks, all located in Harris County. In addition to Reagan State Bank, these included Airline National Bank, Chemical Bank & Trust, First National Bank of Stafford, and Lockwood National Bank. The solid deposit growth of these five banks between 1967 and 1968 versus the growth achieved by the nine major downtown banks also illustrates the strategic value of these investments.

As if deposit fragmentation were not headache enough, a nationwide money crunch began in 1968 and continued well into 1970. As a brake on

TABLE 7.2: *Texas Commerce Shareholders Company*

	% OWNERSHIP	YEAR-END DEPOSITS (MILLIONS)		
		1968	1967	
Airline National Bank	24.9%	$19,429	$16,580	
Chemical Bank & Trust	24.9	14,765	10,008	
First National/Stafford	24.0	7,923	4,169	
Lockwood National	17.9	26,198	22,911	
Reagan State Bank	24.9	46,174	39,120	
		$114,489	$ 92,788	23.4%
Nine downtown banks		$3,383,910	$3,097,231	9.3%

"*Bank Call Reports*," Houston Chronicle, January 6, 1969.

inflation, the Fed curtailed the supply of money, resulting in the prime lending rate being raised five times, from 6.5 percent to 8.5 percent, between December 1968 and June 1969.[6] The Fed then froze the money supply for nine months but did *not* raise the rates banks could pay for deposits. This Fed policy put banks in the untenable position of having to charge high interest for loans while paying low interest for deposits. Meanwhile, to make the equation more perplexing for bankers, customers did not have to leave their money in the bank. Bank deposits dwindled, especially the large, $100,000-plus investments in jumbo certificates of deposit (CDs) that were a critical source of funding for loans.

As a result, TCB entered 1970 with CD funds at a two-year low of $69 million, but with no reduction in our commercial loan commitments. Like large banks everywhere, we were strapped for cash. At Texas Commerce, we innovated to the utmost to meet our customers' borrowing requirements. We directed all of our deposit growth into loans, we reduced investment portfolio reserves, we bought the excess funds of smaller banks and sold them participations in our loans, and we found new domestic and foreign sources for funds.

On the wholesale front, we pulled in Eurodollars first, drawing, on average, some $75 million per day from TCB's Nassau branch, supplemented materially by Burston & Texas Commerce and the open market. But the Federal Reserve soon dampened our enthusiasm for these funds by imposing reserve requirements on Eurodollar deposits that were used domestically, thus increasing the cost of these funds to a marginally profitable level. Next, we turned to Texas Commerce Shareholders Company and issued some $100 million of commercial paper on a daily basis. We bought loans from Texas Commerce Bank with that money. Then the Fed stepped in and set reserve requirements on this type of borrowing by affiliates, too. While the reserve requirements did not stop us from using either source of funds, they did make us groan more when we did so.

On the retail side, TCB's Family Banking Center began offering the most diversified investment program of any bank in Houston, adding Ready-Money Savings, Tax-Deferred Savings, Premium-Rate Savings, and Cash-Reserve Checking to our already-popular Investor Certificates and "Double Your Money" Growth Bonds. We boldly became the first bank in Houston to offer "premiums" for savings deposits in the form of gifts. In keeping with the dignity of the bank, our premiums were sensible *Merriam-Webster's* dictionaries rather than the ubiquitous toasters. These tomes proved to be such a hit that we came back with another heavyweight gift—*McCall's Cook Books*—just in time for Thanksgiving.

Our cost of borrowed funds frequently exceeded our lending rates. Often, and for large amounts, we paid in excess of 12 percent for funds we made available to customers at the 8.5 percent prime rate or slightly above. Our only rationale for "buying high and selling low" was that the expensive funds were part of a broader mix. If loan rates were linked to one particular funding source, an incomprehensible lending rate structure would emerge. Perhaps we rationalized, but we considered Eurodollars as part of the mix, commercial paper as part of the mix, along with the relatively inexpensive demand and time deposits from our own customers. In other words, we funded loans using a weighted average cost of funds.

Our Nassau branch and Texas Commerce Shareholders Company had been formed largely to address the borrowing needs of our customers, but both entities performed magnificently through the funding crisis, abetted by our own officers' concerted calling efforts to attract less expensive deposits from customers and correspondent banks. Remarkably, as the table below shows, we managed to turn in strong earnings through these demanding years. We also passed a significant milestone. On December 15, 1970, for the first time, Texas Commerce's total deposit figure surpassed $1 billion. Two weeks later, at year-end, we had reached $1.14 billion, up 21 percent from year-end 1969.

Finally, on June 24, 1970, the Fed removed the ceiling on the rates that banks could pay for large CDs, and our balances doubled by the end of the year. Tight money had made the quest for size doubly difficult, and we looked forward to the increased competition permitted by the Fed's new policy.

TABLE 7.3: *Earnings per Share*

YEAR	EPS	% INCREASE
1968	$2.76	
1969	$3.17	15%
1970	$3.92	23%
1971	$4.45	14%

Texas Commerce Bank, annual reports.

★ THE BIRTH OF THE MULTI-BANK
HOLDING COMPANY IN TEXAS

Another regulatory change introduced a new era in Texas banking while opening important new avenues for growth for TCB. On December 31, 1970, Texas banks were given a mechanism for intrastate expansion when President Richard Nixon signed an amendment to the Bank Holding Company Act of 1956 that launched the multi-bank holding company movement. As Texas Commerce's 1971 annual report correctly predicted: "The formation of the bank holding company is the most important event in the recent history of Texas Commerce Bank."

The major banks headquartered in Houston, Dallas, and Fort Worth had been lobbying for regulatory change for years. John Whitmore and TCB's lead attorney, Charlie Sapp, led the TCB charge. We were ready to move the minute President Nixon laid down his pen. Texas Commerce Bancshares, Inc., a multi-bank holding company, had been incorporated in Delaware a month earlier, and TCB-Houston was slated to be its first member bank. On February 16, 1971, shareholders approved this action plus the dissolution of the Texas Commerce Shareholders trust and the sale of its stock to Texas Commerce Bancshares, Inc. On July 7, 1971, with the Federal Reserve's blessing, Texas Commerce Bancshares, Inc. became the owner of TCB-Houston and the assets of the Texas Commerce Shareholders Company trust.

Previously, TCB officers could expend repeated efforts and be lucky to bring in a $250,000 account. Now, the newly created Texas Commerce Bancshares had the opportunity to merge with a $50 million bank, a $100 million bank, a $200 million bank. Of course, those "lucky" $250,000 accounts remained a top business development priority of TCB's banking officers systematically calling on customers and prospects, but in terms of achieving size rapidly, clearly, senior management was focused on potential bank mergers. Our incentive was to catch up with First City and the two largest Dallas banks in size, and the entire state, with its twelve hundred banks, was a healthy market for mergers.

John Whitmore and Charlie Sapp made up the initial moving force in conceptualizing the holding company, but as president, I was totally involved even while my primary duties continued. TCB's chief investment officer, Vice Chairman Tom McDade, ably calculated prices that reflected the value of these banks without diluting TCB's earnings. I contacted prospective candidate bank CEOs, negotiated the terms, and worked to persuade the management and directors of prospective merger candidates about the advantages of merging with TCB, with superb support from Tom McDade, CFO Charles McMahen, and chief economist Dr. Jody Grant.

Strengthening ties with our chain banks was an obvious early move, and we quickly acquired the outstanding stock in Airline, Reagan State, North Freeway State (a newly chartered bank), and MacGregor Park National, which had strong ties to Airline. Our first merger announcement, however, was with American National Bank in Beaumont, the second-largest bank in this city of 250,000 people, drawn there primarily by employment opportunities in three of the largest petroleum refineries in the nation. The bank had been founded in 1901, the year that the discovery of oil nearby at Spindletop introduced a new era of oil production into the state and nation. American National had grown and prospered with the region. But now it faced the choice of forming its own holding company, of joining a holding company of banks in midsized cities, or of seeking the best available merger with a major bank holding company.

The bank's CEO, Bill Phillips, a former Arkansas legislator and a progressive banker, was convinced that an emerging holding company headquartered in Houston or Dallas could provide resources, stock liquidity, and management depth beyond his own bank's means—and thus improve its long-term profitability and services to Beaumont customers. He assured me that he was convinced an early merger would boost his bank in its increasingly competitive market. Further, Bill believed that the geography, history, and economy of Beaumont dictated a fit with Houston, not Dallas. Texas Commerce was his logical choice. A farsighted man, Bill Phillips had tentatively approached us about the possibility of a merger even before President Nixon's action legally enabled the formal creation of Texas Commerce Bancshares.

The American National–TCB transaction generated abundant interest among other banks and regulators because it was the first time a major Texas bank holding company proposed to enter a market outside its home city. It was also a learning experience for me, because some of American National's directors were adamantly opposed to the merger. During one heated discussion in Beaumont (the site of all these negotiations), I inadvertently employed the verb "acquisition." Immediately, one opposing Beaumont director pounced on the word. He declared, "Houston just wants to *acquire*

Beaumont!" That taught me an unforgettable lesson in semantics: never say "acquire"; always say "merge." The word "acquire" connotes a master-slave relationship, whereas "merger," a much softer word, implies a mutual partnership, a working relationship. Indeed, we sought mergers.

Price was invariably the key, and the agreement on price was won only after lengthy, sometimes trying, negotiations. But Bill's compelling arguments, supported by the vocal efforts of Tom McDade and me, finally convinced the directors that the long-term payoff of owning marketable stock in a growing, Houston-based multi-bank holding company would be greater than owning stock in a privately owned, independent Beaumont bank whose stock had limited liquidity.

Gaining stockholder approval was tough, but that was not even half the battle. On April 12, 1971, the Federal Reserve, eager to set guidelines quickly for mergers by big city banks with banks in smaller Texas markets, denied the American National–Texas Commerce merger on the grounds that it would be anticompetitive. That same day, it also denied our request to merge with MacGregor Park National Bank in Houston. Oddly, though, it approved a TCB merger with Beaumont State Bank. Now, that was a surprise. American National held a minority ownership in Beaumont State, but neither Texas Commerce nor Beaumont State had even thought about merging with each other. As Tom McDade commented, "It was sort of like asking a farmer for the hand of his daughter and being given her cousin's."

When the dust settled, the MacGregor Park bank merger denial was reaffirmed, but the American National denial was reversed by the Federal Reserve because three other Texas holding companies had reached agreements to acquire Beaumont's third-, fourth-, and fifth-largest banks, thus nullifying the Fed's concern about competition. However, the Fed did make its approval contingent upon our divesting our interest in Beaumont State. It did not take a lot of thought on either side to agree to that. TCB's merger with American National Bank was finally completed in October 1972 after a sixteen-month wait for the regulators' approval. And thus TCB was successfully introduced to a process that was not to become less complex in the future.

Sometimes, unexpected opportunities presented themselves. At a Gulf Oil reception at the Petroleum Club in Houston one evening, my good friend Bill Noel (with whom I served as an El Paso Natural Gas Company director for many years) and I talked about his banks in West Texas. Bill and his partner, E. G. (Rod) Rodman, were in the oil and gas business, but they also owned the controlling stock of banks in San Angelo, Odessa, and Lubbock. They were interested in merging their banks into a much larger one with actively traded stock in order to build some liquidity into their estates. "Banking is not our number-one avocation," Bill told me. "As West Texas continues to develop, it will demand larger and more professionally run banks to finance its increasing capital needs. The bank holding company seems to be an effective way to accumulate capital without breaking the state's constitutional prohibition of branch banking."

Although those markets were not on the top-priority list that Jody Grant had studiously structured, we decided that a presence in West Texas might be useful. Bill liked the concept, and he and Rod both liked Houston's energy leadership. I negotiated merger terms with Bill and Rod in their Odessa offices. We announced the mergers in January 1972 and completed them a year later, soon after I succeeded John Whitmore as chairman and CEO of TCB-Houston and Texas Commerce Bancshares. These West Texas banks were solid from a financial standpoint, but most notably they launched TCB's expansion across the state. Later, San Angelo became a major remote disbursement center of great value to our large corporate customers like J. C. Penney.

We had lined up eight mergers in six months, ready for a fast start. Twelve months later, however, we were still at the starting gate, champing at the bit and waiting for decisions from the Federal Reserve.

The amended Bank Holding Company Act stated that any bank holding company (one-bank or multi-bank) that owned more than 25 percent of even one bank was subject to regulation as a bank. As identified earlier, American General Insurance Company owned 35 percent of Texas Commerce Bank's stock, largely as a consequence of buying Jesse Jones's bank stock from Houston Endowment in 1968. Not wishing to be regulated by the Federal Reserve, it began looking for a buyer as soon as the holding company amendment was signed. Just six weeks after American General announced its ingenious plan to convert its TCB common stock into Class B non-voting common stock and to divest this stock, the logjam at the Fed finally began breaking up. The Federal Reserve first denied our applications to merge with American National and MacGregor Park, but by the end of January 1973, the American National decision had been reversed and we had completed mergers with our three former chain banks in Houston and the three Noel-Rodman banks in West Texas. We had solidly launched Texas Commerce Bancshares.

American General's move also broke up the large block of stock that Jesse Jones had passed along to Houston Endowment, tripling our shareholder base within one year, further increasing the marketability of our stock, and smoothing the way for listing Texas Commerce on the New York Stock Exchange. On September 19, 1974, TCB traded its first shares on the NYSE.

★ THE MOVE UP TO CEO

John Whitmore turned sixty-five in November 1972 and announced his retirement. At the board meeting on December 18, 1972, he moved up to senior chairman and I was promoted from president to chairman and chief executive officer of Texas Commerce Bancshares. John Whitmore was a major influence in my life. He was a complete gentleman, a man respected by his associates. His perception and judgment bordered on shrewdness, in the lofty meaning of that word, and he combined with them a blend of talents that included advertising creativity and the character to make difficult judgments about people and business. It was my privilege to watch John grow for five years. For three of these years, while I served as TCB's president, we worked together on every matter. Our experiences—John's as a lawyer-banker and mine as a businessman-banker—supplemented each other's. My intense, quantified push for TCB's growth and profits occasionally disturbed John because he believed such efforts were beneath the genteel dignity of TCB, but together, with tremendously productive support from our colleagues, we made the partnership work.

And what a busy and productive five years they were. In our quest for size, the bank stepped into the international markets with Burston & Texas Commerce Bank, Ltd., then into the suburbs with Texas Commerce Shareholders Company. Finally, with Family Banking, we had some success in luring suburban customers back downtown. Although these were actions taken on the offensive to build size, they also proved to be useful defensive weapons during the period of tight money. But useful as they were, structurally they were not the ultimate solution.

Finally, the amendment of the Bank Holding Company Act at the end of 1970 gave Texas banks a better tool to serve the Texas economy—the multi-bank holding company. It also forced the broad distribution of the final large block of Texas Commerce stock—the Jesse Jones stock that American General had bought in 1968—greatly expanding and diversifying our stockholder base and symbolizing the transition from "owner management" to "professional management."

NOTES

1. Family Banking Center advertising won the Houston Advertising Club's Grand Prix trophy in 1967 for the best advertising produced in the Southwest. This was TCB's unprecedented third consecutive year to win this prize. In 1965, we won for generally improving the look of the bank's advertising after the 1964 merger; in 1966, for introducing the flag logo and developing its use. *Bankers' Hours* 7, no. 5 (July 1968): 24.

2. The largest loan regulators allow a bank to make to a single customer is called its "loan limit." For national banks, as a general rule, this is 10 percent of its capital.

3. John Stodden, "Their Small Size Costs Banks Business of Large Companies," *Business Review, Federal Reserve Bank of Dallas,* October 1973, 6–7.

4. Eurodollars—U.S. dollars on deposit outside the United States. Included are the deposits and investments of U.S. companies doing business overseas and government payments to other countries, as well as cash spent by American vacationers.

5. Houston Endowment began looking for buyers for its stock in the National Bank of Commerce as well as for its chain banks at the same time. As related in chapter 6, this quest led first to John Mecom, then ultimately to Gus Wortham and American General.

6. The banking system entered 1969 with a prime rate of 6.75 percent then increased to 8.5 percent by midyear. Interest rates remained at this point until March 1970, then started to drop, returning to 6.75 percent at year-end. *Texas Commerce Bank, 1970 Annual Report*, 4.

I was fortunate to be CEO of a major Texas bank during a time of great opportunity, and I assumed my new responsibility with great passion for building TCB into one of the nation's premier banks. Texas Commerce Bancshares took its initial steps toward creating a statewide bank holding company while I was president. Once the regulatory barriers were cleared, a surge of mergers throughout the state propelled the bank into twelve "glory years" of expansion. The pace of change was breathtaking; the results were spectacular. On December 31, 1972, Texas Commerce Bancshares had more than $2 billion in assets in four banks in Houston and one in Beaumont. On December 31, 1984, Texas Commerce Bancshares had $21 billion in assets in sixty-nine member banks throughout the state plus seven foreign banking offices.

This growth did not occur at the expense of earnings. Although Texas Commerce ranked twenty-first in size among U.S. banks in 1984, it ranked tenth nationally in earnings. As stated in that year's annual report: "In every year for the past 19 years and in every quarter for the past 65 quarters, Texas Commerce has increased its earnings per share from the prior year's comparable quarter. This record was unmatched by any other large U.S. banking organization and exceeded by only five of the 1,510 companies listed on the New York Stock Exchange."

As a consequence of this consistent, solid financial performance, Texas Commerce's profitability record ranked number one among the nation's twenty-five largest banking organizations over the 1975–84 decade in the following categories:

Compound annual growth in earnings per share (15 percent)
Average return on assets (1.0 percent)
Average return on equity (18 percent)

During this period, the total market capitalization of TCB's stock occasionally exceeded that of Manufacturers Hanover Trust Company in New York, which, at the time, was one of the nation's premier money center banks.

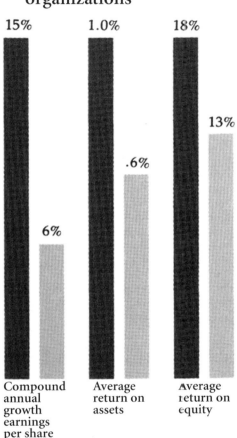

■ Texas Commerce

▨ Average of twenty-five largest U.S. banking organizations

FIGURE 8.1: *TCB's Performance Versus Top 25, 1975–84 (Texas Commerce Bank, 1984 annual report, 2.)*

In 1983, TCB was accorded Standard & Poor's coveted AAA status, one of only two U.S. banks to carry S&P's top rating.

Indeed, the bank's growth and profits improved the price and liquidity of its stock, two powerful factors that enhanced our ability to attract strong, well-positioned banks in growth markets and merge them into TCB. Texas

Commerce had no intention of expanding at costs that would dilute earnings or of entering markets with marginal prospects for growth. Growth in size was important only as it related to growth in earnings.

★ THE PLAN FOR BUILDING TEXAS COMMERCE BANCSHARES

Jody Grant was a guiding force in structuring Texas Commerce's quantified, strategic merger plan. He joined the bank in 1970, recommended by my friend Dr. George Kozmetsky, dean of the School of Business at the University of Texas at Austin. George phoned me about Jody, identifying him as one of his brightest scholars. George advised me that Jody was completing the final academic courses preparatory to receiving his doctorate in economics. He thought I would like to visit with him, and I promptly did so. Luckily for TCB, Jody accepted my proposal to become the bank's economist.

Jody examined every Standard Metropolitan Statistical Area (SMSA) in Texas and defined those components of growth in each market that would be important in building a really healthy bank—population growth, value added by manufacturing, bank deposits, and related economic data. He singled out the metropolitan areas that represented 75 percent of the state's deposit growth between 1960 and 1970 and promised to lead the state in the coming decade. He defined ten of these areas as top-tier markets; the rest were second-tier.

Then we set priorities on the top two or three available banks within each SMSA based on how they might fit TCB's growth and profit strategies and on the probability that the candidate might be interested in merging with TCB. For example, we might not opt for the largest bank in a smaller SMSA, because we would not want an excessive amount of our stock invested in a market that our projections indicated might not have much potential for growth and profitability beyond three or four years out.

Our resultant strategic SMSA plan equipped us with a carefully analyzed, useful map to follow in initiating contacts and responding to opportunities, but it was not an edict that we slavishly followed. We were not flying a bombing formation from which deviation could be lethal!

Finally, the bank's Investment Department manager, Vice Chairman Tom McDade, calculated the likely cost of each candidate. On none did we accept earnings dilution simply to generate asset size.

In those cities where Texas Commerce had a market share in excess of

Dr. Jody Grant was a guiding force in structuring Texas Commerce's broad merger strategy, analyzing each Texas SMSA's economy and the banks within those SMSAs. (Photograph courtesy Jody Grant)

20 percent, or where there was no existing bank in the right location, we chartered a new bank, a so-called *de novo* bank. A de novo bank would dilute earnings slightly at the outset, but if we chose our markets well and installed energetic, talented, productive management, these new banks would quickly grow and contribute to earnings. We projected that every de novo bank should break even in its twelfth month of operation, but sometimes they surprised us. TCB–Katy Freeway in Houston, for example, opened in April 1979 and was in the black within four months. It ended the year with $10 million in deposits.

Jody, Tom, and I poured ourselves into the merger effort. We followed this blueprint while traveling to meet with the management and boards of our top prospect banks, discussing the advantages that a partnership with Texas Commerce would bring to their customers and stockholders. Then we reviewed our analysis with our Long-Term Strategy & Merger Committee, a group made up of TCB's most senior managers and outside directors. I would

In 1984, senior managers included Tom McDade, who was responsible for asset and liability management and who had productively participated in the merger expansion program since the inception of the holding company; Charlie Beall, who, as senior loan officer, was responsible for business production and overall credit quality of Texas Commerce's loan portfolio; and Jim Goodson, who was the senior Texas Commerce representative in the Dallas–Fort Worth Metroplex. Texas Commerce Bancshares 1984 annual report. Photograph © Aker/Zvonkovic Photography, Houston.

not make a merger decision before this committee reviewed and analyzed the pros and cons of the deal, the prospect bank's record, and how we could specifically help it increase returns and become a solid, contributing member of the TCB family of banks. This procedure also educated the committee members, managers, and directors about our merger analyses and strategy.

That was our system, and it worked. If we had it to do again, I do not know how we would do it differently. We acquired forty-two banks during the forty-four quarters between 1972 and 1985, almost one bank per quarter, and chartered twenty-eight de novo banks. Such rapid growth tested our control systems and our management depth.

Banks joined Texas Commerce for several reasons—management, stockholder liquidity, and anticipation of a consistently escalating TCB share price.

TABLE 8.1: *Member Banks of Texas Commerce Bancshares, with Assets and Dates of Acquisition*

DATE	NAME AT MERGER	PRESENT NAME	ASSETS (12/31/85)
1971	Texas Commerce Bank, N.A.	TCB–Houston	$11,969,956
1972	North Freeway State Bank	TCB– North Freeway	69,828
1972	American National Bank of Beaumont	TCB–Beaumont	305,808
1972	Reagan State Bank	TCB–Reagan	314,374
1972	Airline Bank	TCB–Airline	125,792
1973	Citizens National Bank	TCB–Lubbock	156,585
1973	American Bank of Commerce of Odessa	TCB–Odessa	163,509
1973	San Angelo National Bank	TCB–San Angelo	250,318
1973	Lakeside Commerce Bank*	TCB–Lakeside	104,241
1973	Plaza del Oro Commerce Bank*	TCB–Del Oro	70,936
1973	Inwood Commerce Bank*	TCB–Inwood	46,457
1973	Irving Bank & Trust	TCB–Las Colinas	227,296
1974	Kingwood Commerce Bank*	TCB–Kingwood	74,063
1974	Westwood Commerce Bank*	TCB–Westwood	57,047
1974	Texas Commerce Medical Bank*	Texas Commerce Medical Bank	187,537
1974	Plaza Commerce Bank*	TCB– Greenway Plaza	110,269
1974	Guaranty National Bank & Trust of Corpus Christi	TCB– Corpus Christi	182,787
1974	Southeast Bank	TCB–Southeast	81,775
1974	Union Bank of Fort Worth	TCB–Fort Worth	162,059
1974	First National Bank of Hurst	TCB–Hurst	164,002
1974	Arlington Bank & Trust	TCB–Arlington	369,973
1974	Highland Park State Bank	TCB–San Antonio	212,691
1975	Pan American Bank of Brownsville	TCB–Brownsville	412,992
1975	Northwest Bank of Dallas	TCB–Northwest	60,263

(*continued*)

TABLE 8.1 *(continued)*

DATE	NAME AT MERGER	PRESENT NAME	ASSETS (12/31/85)
1975	Casa Linda National Bank of Dallas	TCB–Casa Linda	86,357
1975	Royal National Bank of Dallas	TCB–Preston Royal	55,350
1975	Fidelity National Bank of Dallas	TCB–Park Central	79,002
1975	Village National Bank Association of Dallas	TCB– Campbell Centre	98,524
1975	Commerce National Bank of Conroe*	TCB–Conroe	52,961
1976	First National Bank of New Braunfels	TCB– New Braunfels	105,133
1976	Longview National Bank	TCB–Longview	213,255
1977	Southern Bank & Trust	TCB–Garland	138,553
1977	BanCapital Financial Corp. (Capital National Bank)	TCB–Austin	1,402,067
1977	Tanglewood Commerce Bank*	TCB–Tanglewood	128,631
1977	Main Street National Bank	TCB–Dallas	478,795
1978	First National Bank of McAllen	TCB–McAllen	442,909
1979	Richmond Commerce Bank*	TCB–Richmond/ Sage	45,722
1979	TCB–Katy Freeway*	TCB–Katy Freeway	41,807
1979	TCB–Southbelt*	TCB–South Belt	39,940
1980	TCB–CyFair*	TCB–CyFair	23,256
1981	Banc-Southwest Corporation, Amarillo	TCB–Amarillo	116,732
1981	Gulfway National Bank of Corpus Christi	TCB–Gulfway	58,980
1981	Friendswood Bank	TCB–Friendswood	57,028
1981	TCB–Quorum*	TCB–Quorum	37,221
1981	First National Bank of Stafford	TCB–Stafford	148,667
1981	Hillcrest State Bank, University Park	TCB–Hillcrest	103,184
1982	TCB–Barton Creek*	TCB–Barton Creek	28,013

TABLE 8.1 (continued)

DATE	NAME AT MERGER	PRESENT NAME	ASSETS (12/31/85)
1982	Stone Fort National Bank, Nacogdoches	Stone Fort National Bank	113,916
1982	TCB–Clear Lake*	TCB–Clear Lake	32,412
1982	TCB–Cypress Station*	TCB–Cypress Station	45,937
1982	El Paso National Corporation		
	Border City Bank	TCB–Border City	27,769
	East El Paso National Bank	TCB–East	41,664
	El Paso National Bank	TCB–El Paso	804,408
	El Paso National Bank–Chamizal	TCB–Chamizal	23,747
	First State Bank	TCB–First State	73,287
	Northgate National Bank	TCB–Northgate	50,497
	West El Paso National Bank	TCB–West	28,135
1982	Chemical Bank & Trust, Houston	TCB–Chemical	115,186
1983	TCB–Westlake Park*	TCB–Westlake Park	49,694
1983	TCB–Champions Park*	TCB–Champions Park	22,708
1983	TCB–Greens Crossing*	TCB–Greens Crossing	27,931
1983	TCB–West Oaks*	TCB–West Oaks	15,374
1983	Bank of Pasadena	TCB–Pasadena	25,890
1983	TCB–Sugar Land*	TCB–Sugar Land	22,348
1984	TCB–Northcross*	TCB–Northcross	30,921
1984	TCB–Midland*	TCB–Midland	57,275
1984	TCB–Irving Boulevard*	TCB–Irving Boulevard	68,036
1985	TCB–San Antonio Northwest*	TCB–San Antonio Northwest	15,387
1985	TCB–River Oaks*	TCB–River Oaks	28,375
1985	TCB–Brookhollow	TCB–Brookhollow	3,998

*de novo charters

Financial Accounting Files, Texas Commerce Bank archives.

In terms of management, a controlling stockholder might want to retire or he might decide that his own bank's management needed bolstering. We were the mother lode in terms of able bankers, although the youth of some of our managers did concern numerous prospective merger partners. But there were few experienced, seasoned bankers in inventory at that time because few aggressive, able people had gone into the sedentary banking business between 1930 and 1945. So we sought mature, smart young people. We recruited top college graduates whose academic records could give them a head start, who had demonstrated an ability to work until they solved problems, and, hopefully, who were mature beyond their years and could thus effectively assume bank responsibilities while they were well under thirty years of age. I assigned many young people to senior positions. Scott McLean was president of our bank in Houston's Greenway Plaza at age twenty-six and in downtown Dallas at age twenty-nine. Sometimes TCB directors would shudder at such youth, but the philosophy worked.

In a presentation to the Financial Institutions Subcommittee of the Texas House of Representatives, Bobby Duffey, the dynamic president of Pan American Bank of Brownsville, addressed his bank's need for management as a reason for merging with Texas Commerce. "We have hired an executive vice president, a senior lending officer, and a senior trust officer from Texas Commerce," he said. "These three men are well educated and career motivated. It is my opinion that they would not have joined us in Brownsville had our affiliation with TCB not offered them a broad opportunity for upward mobility."

In terms of liquidity, a significant amount of a large stockholder's wealth was usually tied up in the bank he had spent his lifetime building, but there was rarely a ready market for that closely held block of stock. I recall that Chairman John Whitmore would occasionally call and ask if I knew anyone who wanted to buy a few hundred shares of stock in our bank. The two of us would huddle together, identify prospective buyers, call them, and literally make the market in the bank's stock. If liquidity and marketability were problems for Texas Commerce in downtown Houston, it was a gravely bigger problem for banks in smaller Texas towns. For example, my own employment-investor agreement with Jimmy Lyon had stipulated that I should sell my 10 percent share of River Oaks Bank stock back to him if I left the bank before three years. Although Jimmy owned virtually all of the rest of that bank's stock, he had pledged it as collateral for his real estate projects. He was concerned that if I

Texas Commerce Bancshares common stock was listed on the New York Stock Exchange on September 19, 1974. I bought the first one hundred shares at twenty-seven dollars per share. Here, John Cater, Texas Commerce president, and I are discussing the trade with Merle Wick, right, vice president of the NYSE, and Andrew Corcoran, specialist in TCB's stock. (Texas Commerce archives)

forced my stock into the market at a discount, it would collapse the value of his pledged collateral. And so, to prevent that possibility, when I accepted TCB's offer, he winced, then amicably and promptly bought my River Oaks Bank stock at the over-the-counter price quoted that week in the Houston papers.

This question of the marketability and broad liquidity of Texas Commerce stock was solved constructively on September 19, 1974, when the common stock of Texas Commerce Bancshares, Inc. was listed on the New York Stock Exchange, the first Texas bank traded on the "Big Board," a goal I pushed to achieve. I bought the initial 100 shares traded at twenty-seven dollars per share, a symbolic gesture of my faith in and commitment to the bank as its CEO.

Three years after merging their West Texas banks into Texas Commerce, Bill Noel and E. G. Rodman faced a liquidity situation quite different from Jimmy Lyon's concern about his collateral. Rod died suddenly in 1976, and his estate needed a substantial amount of cash to pay inheritance taxes. Their oil and gas holdings were large but not immediately liquid. Listing our stock on the New York Stock Exchange two years earlier had vastly increased its marketability, and Bill, who was Rod's executor, asked what would happen to TCB's price if he tried to sell Rod's sizeable block of TCB stock at one time. A block of this size had not previously traded on the exchange, and I suspected it might take two or three points off the currently quoted price. But I was wrong. Bill called after the sale, elated, and said, "The market went *up* one-eighth of a point when Rod's TCB stock sold!" The bank's liquidity stood the test.

Because stock was the "currency" of most bank mergers, and because a stock's price reflects the underlying performance of an institution, it behooved Texas Commerce to perform well. And we did. As the *New York Times* said of TCB's growth in the decade of the 70s: "[I]ts earnings per share over the past decade have grown . . . faster than the 50 largest banking organizations in the country." Most of our asset growth was in loans. Here, again, the *New York Times* reported: "[S]ince 1973, [Texas Commerce's] domestic loans have grown . . . slightly less than twice the national average." [1]

The best news was not published in the newspapers, however. Our per-customer loan limit, a primary reason for forming the holding company in the first place, grew from $10 million in 1970 to $189 million in 1984. This same *New York Times* article cited Ched McConnell, a senior vice president with Keefe Bruyette & Woods, as saying that the lending capacity of Texas banks was beginning to keep Texas banking business in Texas.

We felt that all of this added up to a persuasive argument of the potential benefits to prospective member banks in joining Texas Commerce Bancshares. Although we were careful to avoid overpayment for the stock of these banks, we could offer a fair deal to their shareholders. We could also offer a measure of continued self-governance in a decentralized management structure in which each member bank by law retained its own board. In our negotiations, we stressed that our desire to merge with a member bank was predicated on its capacity to grow within its own market. This could be done only if local management remained responsive to local conditions. We stressed that membership in a statewide holding company could bring tangible benefits to local banks as they met the needs of their communities, and that membership could come with representation on the board of the holding company and input into its operations.

However convincing such arguments seemed to us, matters did not, of course, always proceed exactly as we wished. We were breaking new ground and found numerous political and regulatory constraints and substantial opposition from Texas community banks along the way. In these exciting and, paradoxically, trying times, the large Texas bank holding companies had a two-sided challenge: We were fighting legislative threats and political opposition on the one hand and vigorously trying to sell other Texas banks on the idea of merging with us on the other hand. We would appeal to a prospective merger partner, "Let's get together. Let's work together. We can help you increase capacity, as well as human, technical, and financial resources and offer a liquid national market for your stock." Then they would read in the paper about these damnable giant Texas bank holding companies, which were allied with the devil, martyring the Christians.

Almost from the start, the Texas legislature bombarded the large Texas bank holding companies with charges of evil intentions and sinister motives. Urged on by the Independent Bankers Association and the Texas Bankers Association, both organizations historically dominated by small banks, legislators fed the perception that the big-city Texas bank holding companies sought to grow at the expense of the small Texas community banks.

In January 1974, the Texas legislature convened a constitutional convention and called all 181 members of the House and Senate together as delegates to rewrite the state's huge, century-old, unwieldy state constitution. They set a deadline of July 31 to present a document to the voters. Banking law quickly became one focus of intense debate.

Representative Bob Gammage of Houston chaired the convention's General Provisions Committee. On a seventeen-to-one vote, this committee proposed an amendment that would thwart the Texas banks' best efforts to grow and finance the Texas economy by limiting both the number of banks and the percentage of the state's deposits any one bank holding company might accumulate. As initially structured, these legislative curbs were so strict that the larger holding companies would have been forced to divest banks. Thus, we armed for battle.

Our primary, most articulate opponent was John Wilson, a representative from LaGrange. I say this with no disrespect, because I think he savored his role. He rose rapidly to prominence because his "big is bad" issue stirred up considerable visibility and provided him with a platform in the media spotlight. At times, I felt that he was not only *un*informed but also that he did not *want* information. Nonetheless, he proved to be a formidable political opponent.

During one legislative hearing conducted in Austin by this representative, I was characterized one too many times as the epitome of a heartless big-city banker from Houston who neither understood nor cared about the financial needs of average small-town Texans. I decided it was time to set the record straight. Looking the representative from LaGrange in the eye, I advised his committee that I had grown up during the Great Depression; that my father lost everything in the cotton business; that we had moved from a comfortable middle-class life in Vernon to my Confederate grandfather's old worn-out, abandoned farm near Paris; that every summer, beginning at age ten, I had helped my father plow the fields using a single tree plow pulled by one of our mules; that I had ridden my horse Billy twelve miles each day to attend sixth and seventh grades in Paris; that I had worked my way through college totally; and that it astounded me to hear myself depicted as heartless and unknowing insofar as the financial needs of those who had not been born with a golden spoon in their mouth! My lecture moderated the attacks on me, personally, and possibly those on the CEOs of other larger Houston and Dallas bank holding companies, albeit very slightly.

In another speech given to the Texas Bankers Association in San Antonio in March 1974, I tried to summarize the "big is good" argument of the bank holding companies. I include much of the speech here because it seemed to me then, as it still seems so many years later, to get to the heart of the debate.

I see five challenges for Texas bankers for today and through the 1970s.
The first challenge: to finance our economy
The second challenge: to meet increasing competition
The third challenge: to benefit all communities and banks in financing our economic growth
The fourth challenge: to check our alternatives before charting our course
The last challenge: to get involved in the solution

The First Challenge: To Finance Our Economy
Texas is blessed with an abundance of natural resources.

Agriculture. Texas farmers and ranchers outproduce those of forty-seven other states, contributing more than $10 billion per year to the Texas economy. Texas has 185,000 farms in operation, which cultivate 145 million acres. We rank first in production of commodities from cattle to castor beans, from wool to watermelons, from cotton to cabbage. Even if some of our eastern friends might believe that *Texans* aren't the most cultivated, there can be no question that *Texas* is. More than any other country, America should be able to produce agricultural products in excess of internal demands. As we learn to price our food exports the way others have learned to price our energy imports, Texas agricultural production will strengthen the state's economy and the nation's balance of payments—*if financed.*

Energy. In energy production, where federally regulated prices have long suppressed needed exploration, Texas ranks first. Not only do we produce more than 33 percent of the nation's energy, we also have 27 percent of the nation's total refining capacity (the next-highest-ranking state has less than half of our capacity). More importantly, 35 percent of the nation's reserves of crude oil and natural gas lie under Texas soil. This energy will flow out of the ground—*if financed.*

Manufacturing. The largest single contributor to state income is manufacturing. In 1970, the $13 billion in value added by Texas manufacturing ranked ahead of all fifteen southern and southwestern states and behind only the heavily industrialized states of the Northeast. Since the end of World War II, the growth of Texas's "value added" has been the fastest in the nation. In terms of new capital invested in manufacturing, Texas averaged first over the past three years. This dedication of capital to plants is supported by other outlays for raw materials, manpower, finished goods: ingredients that can help the Texas economy—*if financed.*

Construction. In terms of construction contracts, Texas ranks behind only California and New York, our two most populous states. Texas and Texans can continue building—*if financed.*

The question lurking behind each of these opportunities was pointed out by Senator Lloyd Bentsen this month in Austin when he warned:

It has always been relatively easy, in our country, for someone with an idea to get the money to put that idea to work. But it isn't easy anymore. It grows more and more difficult. And, when the day comes that capital dries up, when financing is not available, plants will shut down, businesses will close their doors, workers will be out of jobs, and the prosperity that Americans have enjoyed and shared—and taken for granted—will be at an end.

Our challenge is clear. Are we, as Texas bankers, going to respond to the promise of our economy?

We can do it. The growth in our bank deposits is exceptional, increasing at twice the national average: reaching $35 billion in 1973; ranking fifth in the nation. This is promising. Yet are the hamstrings of our banking system about to be tightened, making Texas jobs even more dependent on the generosity of out-of-state banks? Texas banks appear to be the target of some testifying now before the General Provisions Committee of our constitutional convention.

The Second Challenge: To Meet Increasing Competition
The strength of the Texas economy is just as attractive for non-Texas bankers as it is for Texas bankers. Every day we're seeing increased activity from out-of-state banks and non-banking corporations. The market share of financial services held by commercial banks in the United States as a whole decreased from 56 percent in 1947 to 38 percent in 1972.

Where is this competition coming from? We all know about savings and loan institutions. But what about our friends in the retail and manufacturing fields? They are growing! In 1972, the financial service operations of one of the nation's largest retailers netted profits of over $200 million—greater than the net income of any banking organization. The earnings of this retailer's credit operations alone were $39 million, equal to the total earnings of Wells Fargo, our nation's seventh-largest bank. Does this suggest we are doing our job well? Other corporations are increasingly involved in venture capital, mortgage lending, factoring, leasing, and consumer financing.

No size limits are placed on out-of-state banks and corporations. And the size of our out-of-state banking friends is impressive: Bank of America ($42 billion), First National City Bank ($35 billion), and Chase ($30 billion). Despite all of our growth, Texas banks, collectively and comparatively, are *puny* compared to these behemoths. For example, the deposits of Bank of America are larger than the total bank deposits in Texas . . . $6 billion larger than all thirteen hundred of us put together.

These big, strong banking organizations are coming to Texas. We have twenty out-of-state organizations in Houston right now; twenty-four more will open by the end of the year. Texas jobs depend on these out-of-state banks. Our own Federal Reserve in Dallas recently conducted a survey of forty-two of the largest corporations headquartered in Texas, companies that employ four hundred thousand Texans. Their findings are sobering:

- Most of these companies use Texas banks—but they use twice as many out-of-state banks. And five use no Texas banks at all.
- More than half report that their company's principal banks are not Texas banks.
- These firms maintain more than $600 million in loan and deposit balances with banks in other states.
- Four-fifths of their current loan and credit balances originate outside of Texas.
- Their deposits are three times greater with out-of-state banks than with Texas banks.

"Texas banks are simply too small to compete," these firms told the Fed.

Although the top five Texas banking organizations employ 32 percent of the state's deposits today, these five had 31 percent of Texas deposits twelve years ago. But now, unlike in 1962, the five largest include banks rooted in every section of Texas. Thus, consolidation is happening. That is good. But there is much more to do. We must consider that only Iowa, Kansas, and West Virginia have lower levels of deposit consolidation than Texas—and their states' financing needs hardly compare to ours.

This is no protest against out-of-state competition. Rather, it is a plea to give Texas banks the unfettered ability to compete if they choose. Right now, Texas banking is facing the threat of having its hands tied behind its back—by its own people—and being thrust into the boxing ring with Muhammad Ali and George Foreman. Our constitutional delegates need to evaluate carefully our economy's thirst for financing and let Texas banks maintain the ability to fight.

The Third Challenge: To Benefit All Communities and Banks in Financing Our Economic Growth

We talk about needing sufficient financial resources to compete with large money center banks, but how does a strong holding company movement benefit the individual consumer, his community, and unaffiliated banks?

Some have proposed to let Texas banks serve only consumers and let the out-of-state banks finance our commercial needs. Yet, to consume, a man must have a paycheck. To have a paycheck, he must have a job. To have a job, he must work for some segment of our economy. And that economy must be financed. Should Texas jobs depend solely on out-of-state money—especially in periods of tight money?

Banks attract industry. A bank holding company is vitally interested in developing the communities of its member banks. That is a benefit. Consider, certain parts of Texas need more industry, more jobs. Between 1960 and 1970, 147 Texas counties (57.8 percent) lost population. We cannot be complacent. You and I know that new industry means new jobs.

An active holding company movement increases the alternatives of the shareholders of unaffiliated banks. It is a traditional right of American property owners to determine the disposition of their property. Should bank shareholders be denied the right to join a holding company—or to decide which one to join—by constitutional edict? Should they be denied the right to improve the marketability of their stock? Should they be forced, by constitutional restriction, to be limited in selling their stock to the too-typical non-banking promoter? The poor management of these promoter types has been a principal contributor to bank failures in Texas.

Not only will bidding by strong bank holding companies enhance the price of a bank's stock, but the identical price would be paid to all shareholders, including minority shareholders.

Do bank holding companies benefit only Houston or Dallas? No. Since the formation of Texas Commerce Bancshares in 1971, we have seen the opposite. Our ownership has expanded across the state as banks have joined the holding company. In fact, if our pending mergers are approved, some two-thirds of our stockholders will be non-Houstonians. Control will be in the hands of Texans who do not live in Houston. Our board membership has broadened as well. Seven Texas Commerce directors from Odessa, Corpus Christi, Austin, Beaumont, and Kingsville have joined our board in the last two years. More Texas cities will be represented later this year. Thus, today, we are finding ourselves with a board, shareholders, and management with statewide interests. This is decentralization, not centralization—and the entire state benefits.

The Fourth Challenge: To Check Our Alternatives before Charting
Our Course

Let's not confuse branch banking and bank holding companies. Branch banking allows any bank to enter your community without knowing your community or paying a price to enter. This is not so with bank holding companies. They pay the hometown stockholders a considerable price to enter. No stockholder sells out; rather, he broadens his ownership from one Texas bank to several Texas banks.

Fact #1: Membership. A bank holding company means membership in an organization—and I stress the word *membership.* Both the board of directors and all shareholders must vote to join a holding company. Then when a positive vote is taken, the hometown bank board remains unchanged, management continues to be elected by that board, and loan decisions continue to be made by that hometown bank. Autonomy is enjoyed by the member bank in both the legal and operational sense. The local management's knowledge of his community and customers— as well as the fact that autonomy is an effective management principle— dictates that autonomy makes good sense.

Fact #2: Regulation. Why does banking need constitutional control when banking is already one of the most regulated industries? Today, banks operate under the:

1. State Banking Department
2. State Attorney General's Department
3. U.S. Justice Department
4. Comptroller of the Currency
5. Securities & Exchange Commission
6. Federal Deposit Insurance Corporation
7. Federal Reserve Board.

The competitive aspects of all proposed mergers are closely examined by these regulatory bodies to assure that they are in the best interests of the community. Texas Bankers Association president Truett Smith, speaking to a TBA meeting in Houston, noted that one segment of the banking industry was being singled out for "somewhat punitive action" without much debate or study. He called a meeting of the TBA's Legislative Committee last Monday that voted unanimously against the proposed constitutional restriction on Texas bank holding companies and voted unanimously to retain the branch banking ban.

No matter what you or I decide to be the appropriate course of action, our alternatives must not be restricted by the state constitution. In today's times of change, we must maintain flexibility, with control being exercised through the legislative process.

The Fifth Challenge: To Get Involved in the Solution
And what involvement lies ahead! Our Texas economy will provide for its citizens—if we finance it. Out-of-state banks are occupying facilities on our once protected courthouse squares—can we compete? Our communities and our stockholders look to us for leadership—will we discharge their trust? Our alternatives are being proposed by those who seek to regulate us further and regulate us beyond any other industry. Shall we silently abdicate our rights and responsibilities?

Unfortunately, such arguments did not sway many of our opponents. Regardless of how the state ranked nationally, as measured by the size and multifaceted dimensions of its economy, and regardless of the thirst of Texas business for Texas bank financing, these legislators decided that "big was bad." The fear that the major bank holding companies would "gobble up" any and all small-town banks bordered on paranoia. The two sides battled through a succession of proposed bills at the constitutional convention. After six months of considerable effort by delegates and lobbyists alike, the convention expired on July 31, 1974, just three votes short of the two-thirds majority it would have taken to present the revision to voters. In succeeding legislative sessions, the debate continued, but finally, the "born again" TBA's legislative committee reversed its "anti-big-bank" position, the amendment was recalled, and we won that battle. But it was a tough fight.

★ REGULATORY CHALLENGES

Regulatory politics was another challenge. To read accurately the mood of regulators at the Federal Reserve and the Office of the Comptroller of the Currency in Washington required vigorous effort. Tom McDade built a solid relationship with the Federal Reserve staff in Dallas; I lobbied the regulatory agencies in Washington, trying to keep tabs on the Fed's ever-changing bank merger policy. Bank holding companies were new. Both sides were finding their way.

Importantly, I was named to represent all banks in this Federal Reserve District as one of twelve members nationally serving on the Federal Reserve Advisory Council. The Advisory Council met with the Federal Reserve Governors for a day each quarter in Washington, D.C. Dr. Arthur Burns was chairman of the Fed during my three terms. Dr. Burns was a truly great man, intelligent, fair, wise, informed, and we became solid friends.

In the early 1970s, Texas Commerce had negotiated a constructive entry into Austin via Austin National Bank, the largest bank in the state capital. Many of TCB's directors had long and close ties with their counterparts at Austin National. Former Texas governor Allan Shivers, chairman and a major stockholder of that bank, had also served on Texas Commerce boards from 1957 to 1976. Negotiations between the two banks proceeded smoothly, and in August 1973, a preliminary agreement to merge was announced. Both bank boards ratified the merger agreement in May 1974. And thus ended the easy part.

Our experience with American National Bank of Beaumont taught us that merging with the largest bank in Austin would be intently scrutinized by the Fed. Therefore, we prepared the formal merger application with painstaking care, we mustered an impressive array of informal contacts between influential friends of the banks and government officials, and we presented our case in strict compliance with existing regulations and with compelling logic. Our timing was unfortunate. In January 1975, the Fed denied permission to complete the merger.

Between our announcement in 1973 and the Federal Reserve Board's decision in 1975, the rush of mergers had been slowed considerably by something that came to be known as the "Tyler Doctrine." In December 1973, after two years of rapid expansion by Texas bank holding companies, the Federal Reserve Board denied the application of Dallas-based InterFirst Corporation, the largest Texas bank holding company, to acquire Citizens First National Bank of Tyler, the largest bank in that East Texas city. The Fed argued that the merger would adversely affect competition in the Tyler market, that competition would be enhanced if InterFirst entered Tyler "underneath" the city's dominant bank. Interpreting this new Fed policy, one could only conclude that the largest, or second-largest, bank in a market could not merge with one of the major Texas bank holding companies.

However, with frequent policy exceptions and periodic policy shifts, the Fed undermined the enforcement of its own policy. For example, in 1976, the

Fed approved Texas Commerce's merger with Capital National Bank, the second-largest bank in Austin. Six years later, the Fed allowed Austin Banc-shares to merge with InterFirst, which united the largest bank in Austin with the largest bank holding company in the state. So much for the theory of potential competition in practice.

In 1976, the Fed rejected TCB's merger with Bexar County National Bank in downtown San Antonio, defying regulatory precedent and delivering the most illogical and unfair decision imaginable. I could visualize that decision being authored by a young Yale Law School graduate who had never traveled south of the Mason-Dixon Line. The author opined that Texas Commerce had a trust department in New Braunfels, and, from that vantage point, thirty miles north of the San Antonio city limits, TCB was poised to conduct trust business in San Antonio. He suggested further that our Highland Park State Bank, which was located in a moderate-income suburb in southeastern San Antonio, cut off from the central business district by a major freeway, gave us full and ready access to San Antonio's downtown business community. So the regulators in Washington, D.C., turned down TCB's proposed merger with Bexar County National Bank, a merger that could have given us a significant point of entry into downtown San Antonio. Compounding this injustice, the Fed approved Bexar County National Bank's merger with the large Republic Bancshares in Dallas a year later.

That Fed policy inconsistency was really a blow to TCB in San Antonio because there were not many alternatives in that city. As Mayor Henry Cisneros told me, TCB was the first holding company to enter San Antonio; we had been unusually sensitive to the needs of San Antonio's small businesses and progressive in lending to them; and we had been alert in bringing energized banking services to an underbanked area of San Antonio. Instead of being rewarded for pioneering an array of big-city banking services far out on the southeast side of San Antonio, we were punished!

However, I do not fault the Fed totally. On the whole, the Federal Reserve was constructive. They had a tough job. Considering the monumental responsibilities of its board for carefully constructing the nation's monetary policy, it was ludicrous for its seven governors to be investing their time poring over the banking environment in Port Neches, Texas, for example, and determining whether Texas Commerce should have a bank there. (By the way, the Fed turned down TCB's proposed merger with First National Bank of Port Neches because TCB had a bank in Beaumont, about fifteen miles down the road.)

The Fed's policy began to change in the early 1980s when Mercantile Texas Corporation, a Dallas-based holding company, decided to fight "city hall," taking the Fed to court over a decision about merging with a bank in El Paso. Mercantile won their case. From that point forward, the Federal Reserve decided to let the marketplace work out some of these matters instead of having its own board of seven governors in Washington, D.C., formulate every merger decision in Texas.

Changes were becoming apparent elsewhere as well. In April 1982, when I was elected president of the Association of Reserve City Bankers—composed of the 170 largest banks in the nation—U.S. Attorney General William French Smith made a speech declaring that the new competitors in the financial services arena were *not* banks and had no regulated or restricted geographical boundaries, as banks did. Pointing specifically toward Sears, American Express, and Prudential Bache, he said, "As a consequence of this new competition, as a consequence of the competition from foreign banks in this country, the point about adequacy of competition in a marketplace is moot. There is more competition in the marketplace today than ever before. Therefore, it no longer makes sense to shackle banks with geographic limitations." In short, the marketplace had rendered the McFadden Act and the Douglas Amendment restrictions on interstate banking obsolete. That was strong language, especially considering the source.

At that same meeting, a day earlier, Comptroller of the Currency Todd Conover, in commenting on the explosion in the number of banks, projected there would be twenty-five hundred banking institutions in the United States by the year 2000. So the heads of two major regulatory agencies in one meeting projected that there should—and would—be widespread consolidation of banks throughout the nation.

In the fall of 1983, events began moving rapidly. The Federal Reserve approved a merger between Mercantile, the third-largest banking organization in Dallas, and Southwest Bancshares, the third-largest in Houston. This suggested that the Fed would no longer block mergers of any size as long as potential anticompetitive impacts could be resolved by divesting certain banks in specific markets. Whereupon, the two largest Houston banks and the two largest Dallas banks began eyeing each other warily.

In 1985, we had discussions with Republic that began with a conversation between our director, Harry K. Smith, and Republic's largest stockholder, Bum Bright, and continued with numerous phone conversations between

Republic Bancorporation's CEO, Jim Berry, and me. As talks progressed, Harry, Charles Duncan (the head of TCB's Long-Term Strategy and Mergers Committee), and I, along with Marc Shapiro (TCB's CFO) and Charlie Beall (TCB's chief lending officer), flew to Dallas on a Sunday afternoon to meet with Bum and Jim. I got along well with Bum, but it was evident that Jim Berry did not want to merge. I had drawn up prospective organization charts and job descriptions that showed Jim and me as co-CEOs of the merged company—Jim would head trust, marketing, and one other major department; I would manage banking, finance, and another department. Each of us would name three vice chairmen. This would create a bank run by two co-chairmen and six vice chairmen.

Jim took unexpected offense at this proposal. However, he had done no preparation on the organization, which suggests that he was not too sincere about merging in the first place, even though Bum was very sincere and constructively positive on the prospective merger. In order to break the deadlock, I said, "Look, Jim, there is only one way to resolve this. Assign me the three jobs I proposed for you and you accept the three duties I thought you would prefer for me to handle." I recall that Bum commented, "Well, Ben, that's bending over backward to make this thing work."

After three hours of negotiating, we took a break, and wise old Harry K. Smith said, "Ben, Jim is going to do everything he can during this recess to wreck the deal." Sure enough, Jim Berry came back and said that he had talked to his three executives—Charlie Pistor (chairman-CEO of Republic Bank of Dallas), Joe Musolino (vice chairman of Republic Bancorporation with company-wide responsibility for general banking), and Jerry Fronterhouse (president and chief operating officer of Republic Bancorporation)—who had not participated in the discussions but were in an adjoining room. He said his three top men were not interested in our organization or our merger proposal. With that, Jim turned down a proposal that had been initiated by his largest shareholder without presenting it to the Republic board of directors.

About this time, we also held discussions, and did some due diligence, at InterFirst with CEO Bobby Stewart. Bobby was very interested in merging. He was a classy guy. He and Dewey Presley were the best banking team I ever ran up against: Dewey was "Mr. Inside" and Bobby was "Mr. Outside." Bobby really wanted to merge with TCB, but our due diligence exposed problems there that would have posed an insurmountable burden to the TCB organization, so I regretfully advised Bobby that we were unable to merge with InterFirst.

If either merger had gone through, we probably would have had to sell some banks and consolidate others because of over-concentration in certain markets, but with the regulatory climate at that time, if we could prove that such a move would strengthen Texas banking, I think we might have made the case that this was a sane, constructive action.

TCB and Republic would have made a particularly interesting match. Indeed, it would have created the dominant bank in Texas and the twelfth-largest in the nation. The agreement on the exact exchange value presented complex, yet surmountable, questions, but the management structure raised a more serious quandary. TCB had outperformed Republic in every measurable category; yet, influenced by the ancient and emotional Dallas-versus-Houston competitive atmosphere, management issues could not be resolved in the minds of our Dallas managerial counterparts.

★ BUILDING A PRESENCE IN THE
DALLAS–FORT WORTH METROPLEX

Some markets were harder to enter than others. The Dallas–Fort Worth Metroplex turned out to be one of our most difficult challenges. Dallas banks could readily gain a foothold in Houston, which was home to several medium-to-large banks. But the choices in the Metroplex were meager. Dallas had three giant banks and virtually no medium-to-large banks. Moreover, rather than being potential partners, Republic, First National, and Mercantile were our strong competitors in acquiring banks. We talked with many of the smaller Dallas banks, but none provided what TCB needed in terms of size or location at a price that would not materially dilute the earnings of our entire group. This left only banks so small that the Dallas business community would scarcely notice if TCB merged with one.

Adding further complexity to our challenge, the Metroplex was not only huge, it was also fragmented. It had two major financial centers (in the rival cities of Dallas and Fort Worth) and several smaller, active Mid-Cities enclaves. A significant presence for TCB in either Dallas or Fort Worth required, at a minimum, a $100 million bank. There were none available.

We had avoided unfriendly mergers by design. Banking is a peculiar business, because you compete vigorously with other banks and yet, at the same time, you work together and share loan risk through participations. It is often a love-hate relationship, which is especially obvious if you are the first in a market with a new idea.

We focused first on Dallas. When that did not work, we hit on the new concept of entering the Metroplex through one of the major Fort Worth banks. This approach proved tremendously shocking—and therefore offensive—to First United Bancorporation, a strong, well-run organization with which we initiated merger discussions first in 1980, then again in 1982. After its chairman, Paul Mason, thought over our offer for about a year, he began to see some advantages in merging, but we were at a disadvantage because we had been first in line with a "revolutionary" concept. The fact that we were from the Metroplex's traditional rival, Houston, did not help much, either. So First United put the black hat on TCB of Houston and, in 1983, accepted a merger proposal from InterFirst of Dallas.

We journeyed through a similar process later in 1983 with the $5 billion Texas American Bank (TAB), Fort Worth's other large bank, which ranked seventh in Texas. Its chairman, Lewis Bond, owned twelve thousand of the bank's nine million shares outstanding. He took exception to my proposal that TAB and TCB join forces, a proposal I personally presented to him in his Fort Worth office. Such a merger would have given our $19 billion Texas Commerce banking organization—at that time composed of sixty-five banks—a meaningful position in Fort Worth; it would have also given Texas American a meaningful position in Houston, in Austin, in El Paso, and elsewhere in Texas; it would have made us both infinitely stronger in Dallas. That added up to a network of banks in five of the six major Texas markets, leaving only San Antonio. We would have been much stronger together than apart.

Lew Bond and I had been banking friends for several years. I respected his tough-minded demeanor and was sympathetic with his desire to remain independent. This product of West Texas did not want someone from Houston telling him how to run his bank. Lew was a skilled manager, and I had no intention of "moving in" and telling him what to do. In fact, TCB's foreign and domestic bank expansion absorbed so much of my days that it would have been virtually impossible for me to intercede meaningfully into Texas American operations, even if I had been inclined to do so. In an attempt to ease Lew's apprehension, I proposed that he become vice chairman of the entire Texas Commerce organization with responsibility for all TCB banks in the northern part of Texas, "anchored by your flagship bank in Fort Worth." He would be positioned to succeed me as CEO should I be "hit by a truck." Perhaps the prospect of greatly increased travel or of managing a geographically far-flung foreign and domestic banking organization did not appeal to Lew. Or, perhaps he had already determined that he did not want to consider any merger.

Thus, when Lew declined to let me make any merger proposal to his board of directors, I was left with two alternatives. First, I could forget the merger. Second, I could send Lew Bond and the TAB board an offer in writing. I chose the second option. I called my friends Perry Bass and William Fuller, who served as Texas American directors and were among its largest shareholders. In addition, Texas Commerce director Lady Bird Johnson contacted her friend Perry Bass on our behalf. Finally, we wrote the most tactful proposal we could compose. Still, Lew considered the offer unfriendly. He was adamant and again refused to give me an opportunity to talk to his board. Based solely on his strong operating record (certainly not on his strategic vision for banking or on his recognition of the fact that the consolidation of the industry would let no Texas bank remain "status quo"), Lew's board supported his recommendation to reject our offer decisively.

Lew Bond notified me by letter, hand-delivered by TAB's vice chairman to me in my Houston office, that the Texas American board rejected TCB's "*un*solicited, *un*welcome and *un*wanted offer." Simultaneously, he issued a press release from Fort Worth announcing his bank's rejection of Texas Commerce's offer and reaffirming Texas American's intentions to remain an independent bank. This was duly reported in the *Wall Street Journal* and *New York Times,* as well as in most Texas newspapers.

And there you have a textbook situation where one CEO, with twelve thousand shares of stock, was not ready for a strategic concept involving structural change and rejected an opportunity for the owners of the other nine million shares outstanding. These same stockholders subsequently regretted that their bank had not merged with TCB when Texas American failed in 1989.[2] If the nation had adopted interstate banking at that critical time, if Chemical Bank of New York had proposed to Texas Commerce (as TCB had proposed to Texas American) and offered a 40 percent premium for TCB's stock, and if Chemical had a long performance record that logically certified that the 40 percent premium TCB offered TAB would not be likely to disappear due to inept management, then I, as TCB's CEO, would have presented that offer without hesitation to my stockholders for their decision.

It would have been my duty as a "hired hand" to represent the best interests of all the owners rather than presume that the decision was mine to make unilaterally.

A few years later, TAB director William Fuller confided to me that the worst business decision of his long and successful career was in not taking the initiative during that Texas American board meeting to effect my proposed TCB-TAB merger.

Interestingly, Tom Frost, a major stockholder and CEO of the Cullen Frost banking organization headquartered in San Antonio, told me later that he had initially reacted as Lew had to a similar offer. But as he backed off and disengaged from his emotions, he concluded that his bank could not go it alone in the rapidly developing interstate banking market, that it had to merge, and that he preferred to merge with a large Texas bank now rather than with an out-of-state bank later. Thereupon, Cullen Frost agreed to merge with First City. However, the transaction failed to meet the Fed's capital requirements and was subsequently turned down in Washington.

And so Texas Commerce evolved a new strategy for DFW. If it is not feasible to merge with a big bank in the Metroplex, then build one. In 1972, I met with a successful, entrepreneurial, extremely likeable, progressive businessman and banker named Gene Engleman, the major stockholder of the $29 million Union Bank of Fort Worth and the $31 million First National Bank of Hurst, an affluent Metroplex Mid-Cities community. Gene wanted to build Union into a major downtown Fort Worth bank, and he believed Texas Commerce would help do it. Gene and I shared the goal of building stockholder values.

The right opportunity came in 1977 when Charles Tandy, a pioneering businessman who ran a billion-dollar company based on electronic gadgets and hobby wares, cast his dream of revitalizing downtown Fort Worth in $80 million worth of concrete and glass called Tandy Center. Union Bank leased the first floor of one of the Center's two nineteen-story towers. Then it ran "The Last Ad You'll Ever See from Union Bank," changed its name to TCB–Fort Worth, added specialized energy lending expertise, activated its trust powers, and began marketing the $7 billion strength of the Texas Commerce organization. These moves, plus an aggressive marketing effort that activated directors and officers to call on old customers and new prospects, nearly doubled the bank's deposits within a year.

Earlier, we had completed mergers with major banks in other Metroplex communities, the $62 million Irving Bank & Trust (1973), the Wilemon family's $92 million Arlington Bank & Trust (1974), and the $22 million Southern Bank & Trust in Garland (1977). Texas Commerce CFO Charles McMahen shouldered the initiative in Irving, and the usual three (McDade, McMahen, and I) carefully established TCB's negotiation guidelines and assumed primary responsibilities in making our presentations to the individual boards of all three banks. All of these banks adopted the TCB flag as their own when they joined the Texas Commerce organization.

At last, in October 1975, TCB entered Dallas through businessman and banker Cam Dowell's five suburban banks. We completed five mergers on one day at five concurrent board meetings to add the perception of heft to their aggregate $51 million in combined assets. Cam was a strong, crusty bank investor and CEO about the same age as Tom McDade and me. The three of us "talked the same language" in building the market value of TCB through Cam's five Dallas banks.

Two years later, we added one more bank to our Dallas roster, the $28 million Main Street National Bank, located on the outskirts of downtown Dallas. This bank was controlled by Ron Steinhart and Richard Strauss, able investors. Building a presence in the Metroplex was slow going, but throughout these strenuous, sometimes lengthy negotiations, we held to our "no earnings dilution" principle, without deviation.

Soon after we announced our merger with Main Street, a four-building complex, the Plaza of the Americas in downtown Dallas came to our attention. With twin twenty-five-story towers flanking a luxury hotel, the glamorous facility stood out on the downtown Dallas skyline. It was convenient to major freeway access; the developer agreed to name the south tower Texas Commerce Bank; and the city's commitment to that area of Dallas, through construction of a new symphony hall and art museum, indicated a prosperous future. In mid-July 1978, we struck a deal.

Through all of this, calling officers from TCB-Houston's National Division had been emphasizing the strength of the $7 billion Texas Commerce Bancshares organization in the Dallas market while funding Dallas loans out of Houston. In 1978, Tommy Cox and Lee Straus, two customer-oriented, effective commercial bankers from TCB-Houston, moved to Dallas and opened a Texas Commerce commercial loan production office directly across the street from the Plaza of the Americas.

Finally, by 1979, most of the pieces were in place: five suburban banks, one downtown bank, and a commercial lending facility in Dallas, plus downtown banks in Fort Worth, Irving, Arlington, Hurst, and Garland—a total of eleven banks throughout the Metroplex, more than any other banking organization. By then, TCB-Dallas had grown to $40 million in assets, but it looked, and acted, like a much larger bank. Our cannon was loaded. Now it was time to fire. It was time for visibility.

Visibility meant television, and television meant money—a lot of it. Texas Commerce Bancshares footed the bill for production, and the Metroplex member banks contributed to a pool to pay for time for TV commercials that depicted the high-quality management of our Metroplex banks and stressed our many locations there. To follow up, TCB-Dallas devoted an unusually large portion of its 1980 marketing budget to television advertising. With new quarters, new people, new capital, and new television commercials, TCB-Dallas was ready to make its premiere. And what a premiere it was! Working with Paramount Pictures, through the affiliation of my very close friend and TCB director John Duncan (a cofounder of Gulf + Western Industries, which owned Paramount), TCB Marketing's Barbara Eaves originated and Pat Callaway executed the "world premiere" concept. TCB-Dallas invited the celebrities (the "stars" of the Dallas business community), rented the strobe lights, rolled out the red carpet, and premiered two new thirty-second minimovies that talked about Texas Commerce, its by-now $9 billion in financial strength and its cast of thousands of banking specialists. Two thousand Dallas business and community leaders attended.

By 1981, nobody in the Metroplex asked how big Texas Commerce was. The new downtown quarters and television advertising gave us a "big bank" image in Dallas and in Fort Worth, too. People in both cities watch the same television stations, so the TCB-Dallas commercials gave a real boost to the Texas Commerce flag regardless of which building it flew over in the Metroplex.

Directors were of critical importance in building our Dallas presence, but recruiting the directors we needed, CEOs of prominent Dallas-headquartered companies, was not easy. We began our search for five directors from a list of the CEOs of the twenty-five largest Dallas companies for the Texas Commerce Bancshares board, but most of these CEOs were tied in with the three large Dallas banks. Every director prospect we invited— except Forrest Hoglund, who was CEO of Texas Crude Oil & Gas Corp.— turned us down. Forrest broke the ice. He was attracted by TCB's strong quarterly performance. TCB and Texas Crude, in their respective industries, were unrivaled performers. And thus, with Forrest, we had an outstanding Dallas CEO as a director.

We then tried the younger generation from prominent Dallas families, and there we hit home runs. Berry Cox, Harlan Crow, and Robert Murchison, who became three of Texas Commerce Bancshares' hardest-working directors, came from this effort.

Between 1980 and 1984, more than twenty Dallas business leaders joined Texas Commerce boards. Of these, Dallas insurance executive Jim Goodson certainly became the most involved—in fact, he joined TCB as a vice chairman. Jim became a key factor in turning Texas Commerce into a "Dallas bank."

As a senior manager with the Southland Financial Corporation and CEO of its founding life insurance subsidiary, Jim led that firm in developing what began as the Hackberry Ranch (four hundred acres of "low hills and wildflower prairies veined with meandering creeks") into twelve thousand acres and a new city, Las Colinas, located inside the city limits of Irving, Texas. Jim joined the board of TCB-Dallas in December 1980 and Texas Commerce Bancshares in July 1981. Three years later, on one September day in 1984, he retired from Southland Financial and Southland Life in the morning and came aboard Texas Commerce Bancshares in the afternoon as vice chairman responsible for nurturing the growth of our seventeen banks in the Dallas–Fort Worth Metroplex, as well as TCB's bank in Longview, his hometown. Long an integral figure in the Dallas establishment, Jim was a highly respected civic leader, an able executive, a truly likeable man, and a World War II hero.

One of Jim's early actions was to move the charter and deposits of our by-then $182 million downtown Irving bank into booming Las Colinas ("where," TCB-Irving president Rusty Workman told me, "all of our new business is coming from") and to install a new bank charter downtown to continue serving Irving's downtown customers.

When Jim joined Texas Commerce, I delegated to him, carte blanche, the responsibility of selecting staff for the Dallas banks. One day in 1985, he asked about Scott McLean. He wanted Scott to move to TCB-Dallas as president, to work with vice chairman Terry Wilson, an established Dallas banker. Although Scott was doing a superb job as chairman of TCB–Greenway Plaza, the difference in the size and complexity of the two bank markets was con-

Texas Commerce bankers joined Trammell Crow dignitaries to announce the new, fifty-five-story Texas Commerce Tower in downtown Dallas. From left to right, Texas Commerce–Dallas chairman Terry Wilson; Trammell Crow partner Harlan Crow; Greg Young, leasing and marketing partner of Crow's Dallas office division; Texas Commerce Bank president Scott McLean; and Texas Commerce Bancshares vice chairman Jim Goodson. (Bankers' Hours, 24: 1(1986), Barbara Eaves's archives)

siderable—and Scott was only twenty-nine years old. I suppose, initially, I reacted to Jim's proposal much as John Whitmore had responded to me twenty years earlier, when I had proposed sending the twenty-eight-year-old Robert Hunter to London, because I recall asking, "Jim, do you know how old Scott is? Are we asking too much of someone that young to assume the escalating responsibilities assigned to the president of TCB-Dallas?"

But Scott performed superbly. Jim then quickly selected a relative "old-timer," the thirty-one-year-old Martin Cox, to transfer to Dallas from our New York office. Scott, Martin, and Jim identified the largest companies in Dallas and devised a two-phase calling strategy that assigned contacts at both treasurer and executive levels. Jim, our "Good Housekeeping Seal of Approval" in Dallas, made the introductions; Scott and Martin made the calls and quickly fit into that city's rather closed business community.

Jim also made TCB more visible in the Dallas skyline. Soon after he joined the bank, he said, "Ben, when I tell people I've joined Texas Commerce, they ask me, 'Where is that?' Republic, First National, and Mercantile, our competitors, all operate out of multistory towers with their names on them. TCB has lease space on the second floor of the Plaza of the Americas." He noted that Trammell Crow had a new skyscraper coming out of the ground, an architecturally recognizable, fifty-five-story centerpiece for the Dallas skyline. In size and prestige, the building would provide far greater visibility than the Plaza of the Americas. Trammell was looking for tenants, and we wanted to do more business with him. Jim approached him about moving the bank there if we could put our name on the building. Trammell agreed, and I thought it was a terrific idea. We were able to terminate our lease with the Plaza of the Americas in a deal that was doable within our then-level of profitability, so the move offered tremendous potential to add to our bottom line in the long term without seriously affecting our immediate return.

In 1986, TCB-Dallas had become what could be called a "top tier" bank in Dallas, ranking as the seventh largest of 196 banks in the city. But top tier was not good enough. We wanted to be number one. We had been presenting TCB-Dallas as a bank that could offer all the resources of a banking organization headquartered in Houston. But that just was not selling. Dallas wanted a Dallas bank. Thus, we made the commitment to invest in people and facilities to make Dallas a major decision-point for Texas Commerce.

In 1987, as Jim Goodson began "phasing out" toward retirement, Texas Commerce Bancshares vice chairman John Adams, the hard-driving, productive, inspirational president of TCB-Houston, accepted responsibility in Dallas as chairman and CEO of TCB-Dallas, and the bank moved into Trammell Crow's stunning new Texas Commerce Tower. Later that year, when Texas Commerce and Chemical Bank of New York completed the then-largest interstate banking merger in U.S. history, Chemical's Southwest regional office, led by third-generation Dallasite Bob Thornton,[3] merged its eight officers and its customers into TCB-Dallas. And, as John Adams observed at the time, "TCB in the Metroplex became a regional bank with money center bank capabilities."

Other big events followed quickly. In 1988, First Republic (so named upon the 1986 merger of Republic and InterFirst, the two largest Dallas banks) and MCorp failed, wiping out much of the city's financial and community leadership, while TCB stood firm. Dallas businesses that wanted to bank with a Dallas bank realized that Texas Commerce was the sole major Texas bank to survive the state's devastating economic downturn, and our energetic prospect calls, our visibility in downtown Dallas, and our community activities for the preceding twelve years began to pay off. Business poured in, and the entire TCB-Chemical organization benefited. Dallas ended the year $1.6 million in the black rather than $1.5 million in the red, as originally budgeted. Sixty-five of the top corporations in Dallas banked with TCB-Dallas at year-end, up from thirty-three in just over a year. More than 375 smaller companies also moved to TCB-Dallas during 1988. Demand deposits (inexpensive checking accounts) took off and reached nearly $1 billion by year-end. Even loans were up. TCB-Dallas was one of only five Texas Commerce banks to report increased loans in 1988.

I cannot say enough about the contributions Jim Goodson, John Adams, Scott McLean, and Martin Cox made in leading TCB to the banking forefront of the Dallas market. Of course, they were aided by the times, but they had made calls on Dallas businesses and had, simultaneously, become deeply involved in the Dallas community. When the opportunity came, TCB was ready. I will never forget the day when A. H. Belo's CEO, Robert Decherd, called me from Dallas and asked if he could approach John Adams about taking on even more time-consuming civic responsibilities. What a thrill it was to take that call, because it certified that, at last, the Dallas business community had accepted TCB as a major Dallas bank. Over the next few years, John was elected chairman of the Greater Dallas Chamber of Commerce and the Dallas Methodist Hospital; Scott became the youngest leader ever to head the Dallas United Way campaign in 1991, a successful $40 million drive in a tough year. Later, as president of the SMU Alumni Association, Scott served on the school's prestigious board of trustees. John, Scott, and Martin worked well together; they worked well with Jim Goodson. The chemistry was right, the times were right, and they executed their mission with unforgettable distinction.

★ BEYOND TEXAS INTO THE MID-AMERICA ENERGY BELT

In a world that might include aggressive interstate banking, I envisioned Texas among the three states destined to become one of the nation's "Big Three" financial centers. The other states were obvious: New York and California, maybe Illinois. Indeed, in the half-dozen years leading up to 1984, Texas Commerce initiated concrete steps to create a banking region among states with kindred interests and economies, a Mid-America Energy Belt, as an essential bridge to nationwide interstate banking.

Energy was our logical common denominator, and the oil-producing states contiguous to Texas made up our natural region. We did journey north up to Wyoming, however, because Texas firms were investing there, buying leases, and drilling. This eight-state Energy Belt produced 60 percent of the oil and 90 percent of the natural gas in the nation. It accounted for almost three-fourths of rotary drilling rigs in operation in the country at the time.

The case for regional bank holding companies within the Energy Belt was further supported by Texas Commerce's ability to serve this market. With a lending capability sufficient to meet the needs of any corporate customer, with the ability to provide technical financial expertise, and with Houston's position as an energy and international center, Texas Commerce's natural business transcended state lines and was irrevocably linked with the economies of states throughout the Energy Belt.

In 1983, by state law, we could buy up to 4.9 percent of an out-of-state bank. We quickly determined that, if TCB's return on equity was 20 percent, investing in out-of-state banks would dilute our earnings, because our return would consist of the dividends yielding no more than 6 percent on the stock we owned. We also recognized that a 4.9 percent investment in these banks was a long way from control, but we worked diligently to develop relationships with each bank's management so that, when interstate banking did come, we would at least have our foot in the door. On a worst-case basis, if Citicorp appeared a more desirable merger partner to United Banks of Colorado, for example, then Citicorp would presumably find our 4.9 percent stake important for them to own and would pay a reasonable price for it.

We could not be certain that we would be welcome, but if we were welcome, maybe we could produce some additional business and improve the return on our equity. We went to Wyoming first, and we were welcome there. David Johnson, chairman of Wyoming Bancorporation, the largest banking organization in that state, was quoted in the *New York Times* as saying that our investment was the greatest thing that ever happened to them. Not only did we invest capital, he said, but we also expanded their lending capacity so that they could make the loans that had been leaving Wyoming, and TCB provided the energy lending expertise that Wyoming Bancorporation lacked.

In this campaign, I visited the CEOs of our choice of the best banks in Oklahoma, Louisiana, Arkansas, New Mexico, and Colorado. At the conclusion of each discussion, we were invited to buy the maximum 4.9 percent of stock then allowed by Texas banking law. Then TCB jumped from the Energy Belt states to Sun Banks in Florida, because I began to believe that we might, down the road, also merge with that fine bank if the restrictive interstate banking laws were to change, as I felt would eventually occur. Through these investments and the cultivation of these managements, I believed our interstate strategy had taken its first step.

I will always believe that, when the Texas economy collapsed in the mid-1980s, we would have fared better with a diversified geographical reach than by being confined to the area between the Red River and the Rio Grande. It has always been a mystery to me why TCB could have offices in Tokyo and Caracas and Bahrain but not in Tulsa and Albuquerque and New Orleans.

As a matter of fact, Treasury Secretary Nicholas Brady[4] later cited Chemical's successful merger with Texas Commerce as illustrative of the benefits of geographic diversification. "If a bank had money spread all over the country, it wouldn't be so hard-pressed when one region's economy got into trouble," he said. He then specifically cited Chemical, noting that, although there was economic weakness in the Northeast, the improving health of the Texas economy "has made Chemical, as a whole, stronger." He was speaking in favor of the Treasury's proposed modernization of the banking system, which provided for, among other things, interstate banking.

★ LOOKING TO THE FUTURE IN 1983

In 1983, thinking ahead ten years, I listed my top priorities as follows: (1) for Texas Commerce to be in the six major markets in Texas in a meaningful way; (2) to accomplish this while maintaining the bank's quantified, top return on assets, return on equity, asset quality, and asset growth; and (3) to consolidate TCB's resources with those of the banks we had chosen for investments in the Mid-America Energy Belt and Florida, if the Texas legislature ever approved interstate banking. These investments, and the strategy they represented, concretely established both our geographical foothold and our plans for future expansion. I preached these priorities to TCB bankers, from tellers to CEOs, as I traveled regularly to visit TCB banks all over the state.

Of course, I knew that my three priorities might need to be revised if the financial world continued to deregulate and change. Insurance companies, American Express, and retailers such as Sears, with all of their financial strength, facilities, and lack of regulatory restraint, challenged the ability of any bank—with its onerous regulatory burden—to compete. In such a situation, I would not hesitate to recommend to TCB's board that this bank join forces with, say, Chemical Bank. If such a merger proved necessary, I wanted to deal from a position of strength.

I lectured myself each day that I would betray TCB's proud heritage if I accepted the "easy way out" proposition that TCB was destined to be a small, albeit statistically impressive, operation confined to Texas. But I also was not interested in being the biggest just for the bragging rights. If becoming the biggest entailed *not* producing superior operating results that would enhance TCB stock, I would consider myself a total failure as a CEO. Even though I would prefer for TCB to be the largest, I was irrevocably unwilling for the bank to sacrifice asset profitability or asset quality simply to attain asset size. Those three factors had to be kept in balance. TCB would not launch a growth binge by risking inferior loans. Paradoxically, I would not set quality standards so high that we sacrificed all growth. And I would not want either of these to overwhelm our profitability.

In 1983, Elvis Mason, at that time the CEO of InterFirst Corporation, paid a price for the rather sizeable Peoples Bank in Tyler and Fannin Bank in Houston that would have required a 1.9 percent return on assets (ROA) in order not to dilute InterFirst's earnings. Bear in mind that Texas Commerce's ROA was 1.2 percent, and we led the nation's top twenty-five banks in this area. In other words, the historically high price InterFirst paid for these two middle-tier banks set a new benchmark price that every prospective bank merger candidate in Texas henceforth demanded. Again, we were confronted with the perpetual question: Should we sacrifice asset profitability to gain asset size? We could not hope to increase our 1.2 percent ROA to 1.9 percent except by making risky, high-yield loans. This represented a policy dilemma, and I promptly sought a policy decision from our diverse, universally seasoned directors.

"We have come to a fork in the road, and we need your guidance," I said. "TCB has been a product of growth, but we have maintained our asset profitability and asset quality objectives among the nation's twenty-five largest banks even while rapidly growing. Among the nation's twenty-five largest banks, we ranked number one in asset growth, asset profitability, and growth in earnings per share and number two in loan quality, as determined by loan charge-offs as a percentage of total loans (behind only J. P. Morgan). We analyze those elements during our due diligence, before we establish our offering price for any prospective bank merger candidate.

"Now, the marketplace has been totally changed by the 1.9 percent ROA that InterFirst paid for these two medium-sized banks in Tyler and Houston," I continued. "I do not know how to maintain Texas Commerce's decade-long financial growth and stability if we pay on a formula of 1.9 percent ROA for banks. Yet InterFirst has set this new pricing formula for banks in the Texas market. If we pay this much for banks, we will dilute TCB's earnings. If we could recoup dilution within a year, we might do it, but I don't see that vastly escalated asset profitability potential in today's environment. Thus our quandary: We can pay the new prevailing market price for more banks and dilute earnings, or we can maintain earnings at the expense of growth through additional mergers."

I spoke soberly. This was one of the most important policy questions I ever put to the TCB board. Their vote? "Stay the course." It was unanimous, except for the nationally respected and beloved Barbara Jordan, who had recently retired from Congress. She declared in her forthright manner, "I'm for growth. We must keep our bank merger program in high gear."

After 1983, the excessive prices for banks combined with the faltering economy had virtually halted our merger program. All of our subsequent external growth—except for the merger with the $21 million Bank of Pasadena in Houston—was by *de novo* banks. The TCB board had reaffirmed our non-dilution earnings merger policy. Management accepted an additional duty to generate future expansion through internal growth, relying entirely on the banks already in the TCB family. Our call program, advertising, and overall marketing became increasingly critical in propelling TCB's growth.

We had reached the end of a dozen glory years of change during which we had experienced a heady mix of quantifiable success in operations and solid consolidations. All of this had been propelled by the expansion of Texas Commerce Bancshares, a multi-bank holding company, operating in an economy deemed to be among the strongest in the nation in virtually every way an economy can be measured.

During these years, Texas Commerce increased its assets tenfold, expanded to sixty-nine locations in every major market in the state, established seven foreign TCB offices, and turned in a performance that ranked number one among the largest banks in the nation as measured by return on assets, return on equity, and growth in earnings per share. Everybody won. Texas Commerce stockholders enjoyed exceptional growth in earnings and dividends; more than one million individual and corporate TCB customers enjoyed access to more capital and better services; and TCB's employees enjoyed above-market wages and benefits.

But in 1984, after a decade of compound annual growth in earnings per share of 15 percent, the price of oil plummeted, problem loans were appearing, margins became exceedingly tight, inexpensive demand deposits dwindled, volume became the name of the game, and every blessed penny we earned was precious. We were able to achieve our sixty-fifth quarter of uninterrupted, year-over-year earnings increases, but only by the skin of our teeth. Yet ours was a record matched by only 5 of the 1,510 companies listed on the New York Stock Exchange—and by no other bank. Merriman Morton, then president of Texas Commerce's banks in El Paso, said at the first quarterly Executive Council meeting in 1985, "Folks, we get two minutes to enjoy last year. . . . Okay, that's it. Now let's work on next year." The next few years proved extremely challenging indeed.

NOTES

1. James R. Pierobon, "The Southwest," *New York Times,* January 8, 1980.

2. Joseph M. Grant, *The Great Texas Banking Crash: An Insider's Account* (Austin: University of Texas Press, 1996), 207, 208. TAB operated independently until "5 P.M., July 20, 1989, [when] representatives from the OCC and FDIC arrived in the office of Joseph M. Grant, chairman and CEO of TAB, and he surrendered Bank Charter #3131 issued to the Fort Worth National Bank on March 4, 1884, signed by Comptroller of the Currency John Jay Knox."

3. Bob Thornton's grandfather, R. L. Thornton, founded what became the third-largest bank in Dallas, the Mercantile National Bank, by lending money on mules and automobiles. Later, as a mayor with the motto "Keep the dirt flying," Thornton played a large part in expanding the airport, enlarging city hall, increasing the city's water supply, and more. The R. L. Thornton Freeway was named for him. *The Handbook of Texas,* vol. 3, edited by Eldon Stephen Branda (Austin: Texas State Historical Association, 1976).

4. Interview with Treasury Secretary Nicholas Brady, *Good Morning America,* February 6, 1991.

Chapter 9 A NEW HOME FOR TEXAS COMMERCE

When I arrived at Texas Commerce Bank in April 1967, one of the first things I was told was that we needed a new building. Lloyd Bolton, who later became head of the Real Estate Group, was then in charge of TCB's properties. He agreed. "Jesse Jones moved the bank into his new Gulf Building in 1929," he said. "Today, the pipes are rusty and breaking." So, the idea was planted. I agreed with Lloyd because Texas Commerce was not the same bank it had been in 1929, and we needed space badly because we were growing and adding people. By 1977, ten years after I had arrived, TCB had become a $6.6 billion statewide organization with thirty-five banks in thirteen markets and more to come. Meanwhile, in the Gulf Building, more than the pipes were failing. We were faced with a decision: Renovate or raze?

The case for renovation was strong. First, the Gulf Building was the bank's traditional home. An elegant, historic building, it served as the centerpiece of Jesse Jones's empire. At thirty-four stories, the Gulf Building was Houston's tallest building for more than thirty years until the forty-six-story Exxon Building finally surpassed it. More practically, space in a renovated Gulf Building would be cheaper than space in a new, Class A structure. Space in a Class A structure, however, would be easier to lease.

Renovating around our major tenant, Gulf Oil Company, posed a daunting problem. But Gulf, which occupied twenty floors, solved that problem by deciding to move into a new building in Houston Center, leaving TCB with a much more vacant structure in which to work. In addition, the significant investment tax credit that TCB could earn for restoring a landmark building was financial icing on the cake.

And so, we decided to renovate the Gulf Building and list it on the National Register of Historic Places. I proposed that we build two new buildings, the Texas Commerce Tower and the Texas Commerce Center. These moves would preserve a landmark, keep most of the Banking Department in its traditional home with its glorious lobby, provide Trust and Operations with the space they needed to grow, save money on rent, equip the bank with a modern, efficient garage, and provide a striking headquarters for the multibillion-dollar statewide organization TCB had become. The decision, although tough to make at the time, seems obvious in retrospect.

Work began on the $50 million restoration of the Gulf Building in 1981. It was completed in 1986, in the bank's centennial year. At the same time, planning for the new Texas Commerce Tower proceeded apace. The growth of downtown Houston was marching to the south and west of Main Street, led by skyscrapers for Shell Oil, Humble Oil, Tenneco, Bank of the Southwest, and Houston Natural Gas, to name just five. This exodus left the north end of Main Street looking dowdier and dowdier. I thought we might materially anchor the traditional core of downtown Houston by turning toward the city's historic northern border. By that time, Jones Hall had allayed the stampede away from the heart of the old city and laid the foundation for what is now the Performing Arts District. Gerald Hines had crossed the street from Jones Hall and built Pennzoil Place, designed by the internationally acclaimed architect Philip Johnson.

★ ASSEMBLING THE LAND

Ironically, Jesse Jones, a man who had died twenty-five years before work began, delayed the construction of the Texas Commerce Tower. Initially, our preferred site for the new building was Block 68, the block on Main Street between Jones's prized Gulf Building and Rice Hotel. Fearing that this attractive property could fall into the hands of a competing bank that might construct a building to rival his two prized possessions, Jones had bought part of the block and engineered the subdivision of the rest among his friends. This left us with fourteen separate landlords to deal with, some as far away as Mexico City. "Nobody," Jones had said, "will ever be able to put that block together again!"[1] He was nearly right.

It took almost ten years and the hard work of two superb commercial real estate professionals to purchase 95 percent of that block. All that remained was one twenty-one-foot tract on Main Street owned by the Levit brothers.

Land assemblage began in 1967, when Howard Horne, a commercial broker, learned that the Montgomery Ward property on Capitol and Travis, across the street from the bank, was up for sale. Following the old real estate adage "Talk to the owner of adjoining land first," he called John Whitmore.

John did not dismiss the idea out of hand. The price of forty-seven dollars per square foot was attractive, and this site represented about one-fourth of the block, but John had detected the shift of major buildings away from Main Street. However, when Howard offered to put the entire block back together, John agreed to the Montgomery Ward transaction and to buy any other lots on Block 68, provided no one knew the bank was the buyer and that the property was assembled in order, working clockwise from the Montgomery Ward plot. We did not want to be saddled with odd lots surrounded by property that we could not buy.

The Montgomery Ward step was easy. Next came the Milby Hotel, which was *not* easy. It was not for sale. Howard told me it took him five minutes to learn that fact and three years to gain the confidence of Charles Milby, whose family had run this institution across from the Rice Hotel for fifty years. Finally, in early 1970, perhaps because the hotel business on the north end of Main Street was not getting any better, we bought that property for sixty dollars per square foot. And thus TCB controlled more than half of Block 68.

The next transaction took two years. This ten thousand-square-foot tract included Kelley's Oyster Bar, Houston's first New Orleans–style, stand-up eatery, a venerable institution that Cleve Brown, its owner, dearly loved. This transaction, for seven hundred thousand dollars, brought us around to Main Street.

Just before the Brown transaction was complete, Howard turned over his Block 68 file to R. E. "Buddy" Clemens. Buddy, a native Houstonian, was well acquainted with the old-line, wealthy families that owned most of the remaining properties, consisting of ten tracts with Main Street store frontages ranging from fifty to ten feet wide. Although the financial return on most of this land was declining, all of the properties held increasing sentimental value to the owners. To complicate matters further, word leaked that Texas Commerce was buying Block 68. Of course, prices went up. Everyone knew the bank was a bottomless pit of money!

It seemed it would take forever to put this block together. Meanwhile, the TCB directors had promoted me from president to chairman and CEO in December 1972, the bank and the holding company were growing rapidly, TCB was running out of space, and we needed an image-building headquarters that could take us into the next century.

About this time, a longtime TCB customer and the CEO of Allright Auto Parks of Houston, A. J. (Jay) Layden and I launched discussions about TCB buying Allright's Block 67. Jay Layden's company owned the entire block and used it as a parking lot, which meant we could start construction almost immediately on unencumbered land. Block 67 also had prestigious neighbors—Jones Hall, the *Houston Chronicle,* Pennzoil Place, and Block 68. Indeed, Block 67 offered a number of benefits, and TCB took an option on the property at ninety dollars per square foot, somewhat above market at the time. However, the idea of building away from Main Street still had questionable appeal. After all, Texas Commerce had helped build Main Street. So I let that option lapse.

Buddy continued working on Block 68, appealing to the owners' civic pride as well as to their pocketbooks. Finally, in 1977 (after we overcame the death of one owner, who left his property in the hands of First City National Bank's trust department), TCB had acquired all of Block 68, except that twenty-one-foot frontage occupied by Levit's Jewelers.

But we could wait no longer. Fortunately, Allright was still interested in selling Block 67. By then, the price had risen to one hundred dollars per square foot, but that seemed reasonable and a sound business decision compared to the headaches and costs of completing the acquisition of Block 68. And so, as had often happened in the past between sellers and Jesse Jones, a trade was struck among friends. We transferred several nearby pieces of property to Allright in exchange for Block 67, the future site of the Texas Commerce Tower. Jay Layden and Durell Carothers, the founder of Allright, handled this transaction for Allright, and I concluded the deal for TCB.

Meanwhile, we still needed space for TCB's Operations Center, and the Main Street Block 68 was perfect for that purpose. However, Maurice Levit sensed that the center could not be built unless he capitulated, and he drove a hard bargain with us. By this time, Buddy and Howard had exhausted their superhuman efforts and turned the problem back over to the bank. I must have negotiated with Maurice Levit thirty times. Finally, he came to terms we could live with—and still make the project financially plausible. We built an operations center and a parking garage on Block 68, as well as a new home for Levit Jewelry Store, in concert with the design and construction of the seventy-five-story Texas Commerce Tower on the block across Travis Street.

Texas Commerce needed more space, but in considering a major new facility, the lurking question was whether we could fill the new building with enough tenants to make it economically feasible. I talked to developer Gerry

Hines about joining TCB as a partner. He agreed, and before moving ahead, we signed up El Paso Natural Gas (EPNG) for the top floors of the building. I served on that company's board of directors at the time.

Howard Boyd, CEO of EPNG, a TCB director, and a major tenant, insisted that the building be named the El Paso Natural Gas Building. If giving up naming rights was a requirement for the economics to be sound, I would agree, but I tried to persuade Howard that naming that building The El Paso Tower would not be of discernable benefit to EPNG because his company did not sell to the general public in Houston or in Texas. Conversely, I argued that Texas Commerce *would* benefit, every day, within the corporate community and among individual bank customers, because such a landmark building would denote the stability and security of TCB to our Houston and Texas clients. My impassioned plea fell on deaf ears. But a costly liquefied natural gas experience in Algeria gave Howard a financial reason to rethink his earlier commitment.

Hugh Roff, CEO of United Energy Resources, then stepped up and leased all of the EPNG space and allocated the naming rights to TCB. The name chosen was the Texas Commerce Tower in United Energy Plaza. That pleased all of us at TCB immensely. Since 1929 the bank had been housed in the Gulf Building. Now, at last, we would have facilities bearing the bank's name.

★ DESIGNING THE BUILDING

Next came the selection of the architect. Gerry and I came up with an innovative procedure for doing this. We narrowed the list to eight; three were from Houston, others were internationally famous. We proposed to pay each of them fifteen thousand dollars to submit a concept. If, after three months, they had no concept, they would still get the fifteen thousand dollars. At first, most were insulted by our meager monetary offer, but when Cesar Pelli agreed to the toe-to-toe competitive procedures, the other seven quickly entered the fray. In order to arrive at an even-handed decision, we invited all of the architects to present their proposals on the same day and allotted one hour and fifteen minutes for each presentation. Gerry and I would then evaluate the proposals and make a prompt decision.

From these, we chose I. M. Pei. His enthusiasm for our project, his self-taught knowledge of our history, and his international reputation for design impressed both Gerry and me. The Houston firm of 3D/International was se-

Texas Commerce Bank/Bancshares 1978 Annual Report

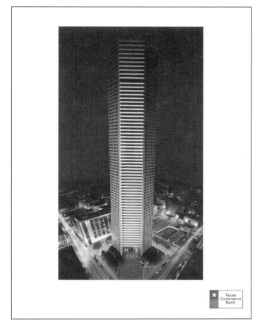

Photographer Joe Aker superimposed a photograph of the Texas Commerce Tower model onto the Houston streetscape in 1978, the year in which construction began. At the time, the seventy-five-story tower was the tallest building under construction in the world. It symbolized Texas Commerce's commitment to Houston and Texas. (Texas Commerce Bancshares 1978 annual report. Photograph © Aker/Zvonkovic Photography, Houston.)

lected to complement Pei's New York architectural firm, and Colaco Engineers, Inc., also of Houston, was selected as the structural engineering firm.

My original concept was for a forty-story building that would cover the entire block, but I. M. played the critical role in modifying that idea. Gently, persuasively, he asked me one day: "What do you think are the greatest cities in the world?" I responded, "London, Paris, Rome . . ." I. M. interrupted. "Stop right there. Have you ever thought that the reason you consider them great is not because of their solids, but because of their voids? Why don't we leave a void—an open space—in this site? Downtown Houston architecture is impressive, but it has one weakness. Most buildings are built sidewalk-to-sidewalk." Then he proposed, "Let's allocate three-quarters of the block for a beautiful plaza enhanced by a major sculpture, Bartlett pear trees, fountains, and benches for people." And so we did.

When that decision was made by I. M., Gerry, and me, it became necessary to build a tower soaring seventy-five or eighty stories to provide the space we needed and believed we could lease. I am not going to pretend that, subconsciously, the aspiration to build the tallest building in Texas did not exist, but the original concept was born more of commercial, rather than creative, considerations. Early and continuing goals I assuredly shared with Gerry were to recruit enough tenants to guarantee that the project would be financially successful and to provide adequate space for TCB's growing needs. However, after construction, when Texas Commerce Tower *was* the tallest building in Texas, the tallest building in the United States outside of New York and Chicago, and the tallest *bank* building in the world, we were visibly and vocally enthusiastic, as were TCB's employees, member banks, and the Texas Commerce Board of Directors.

A sixtieth-floor sky lobby, unique in Houston at the time, not only offered a splendid public platform for viewing the city (as the Empire State Building provides for viewing the scope and majesty of Manhattan), it also freed up a considerable amount of lease space because people traveling to the upper floors had to change elevators at the sixtieth floor. This space-saving concept let one shaft service two sets of elevators.

The decision about whether to construct a seventy-five- or eighty-story building was made easy by the Federal Aviation Authority. It decreed that the building's height should be limited to seventy-five stories because going higher might interfere with landing patterns at both of Houston's major airports. I quickly agreed because I had firsthand knowledge that airplanes can fly into tall buildings. After World War II, while awaiting separation from the Air Force in Sioux Falls, South Dakota, two of my buddies from the 351st Bomb Group took off in a B-25 to deliver a lieutenant colonel to New Jersey. The pilot, Lt. Col. William F. Smith, evidently got lost in heavy weather on his return and catastrophically flew into the Empire State Building.

I had always envisioned that the tower and the operations center, both designed by I. M., would be clad in gleaming white travertine marble, but I. M. counseled that marble was a comparatively porous, soft building material—an expensive maintenance nightmare. Instead, he recommended dignified, hard, gray granite and showed me two samples. I made my selection, then inquired casually where the stone was from. When he said, "Rock of Ages in Barre, Vermont," I nearly fainted. That company was run by Fred Ralph, the bombardier on most of my combat missions bombing Hitler's Germany! During the war, Fred and I had been such close friends that I had given him my cigarette ration, a valuable commodity for a serviceman. I did not smoke, and Fred did love his cigars. That granite coincidence subsequently led to the first reunion between Fred and me since World War II. He and his wife

Joan Miró's Personage and Birds *was originally cast in bronze, but Texas Commerce Tower architect I. M. Pei felt it should be colored to add whimsy to Houston's dark and serious streetscape—and Miró agreed. I. M., developer Gerald Hines, United Energy chairman Hugh Roff, and I traveled to Miró's studio in Spain for the unveiling of the colored Personage* maquette. *In this picture, I. M. discusses color with Miró while Hugh and Eileen Pei look on. We later donated the maquette to the Museum of Fine Arts in Houston and displayed the five-foot bronze casting in the Tower's sixtieth-floor sky lobby along with another Miró sculpture we had considered. (From the Hugh Roff archives. Reprinted with permission.)*

planned to attend the Tower dedication, but he died the week before, sadly, from the effects of a lifetime of smoking cigars.

★ MIRÓ'S *PERSONAGE AND BIRDS*

When I. M. completed the design of the Tower, the search began for a monumental sculpture. We finally selected Joan Miró's *Personage and Birds*. Our objective was to enliven street life in downtown Houston and focus

BANKERS' HOURS

Volume 20, Number 2, 1982

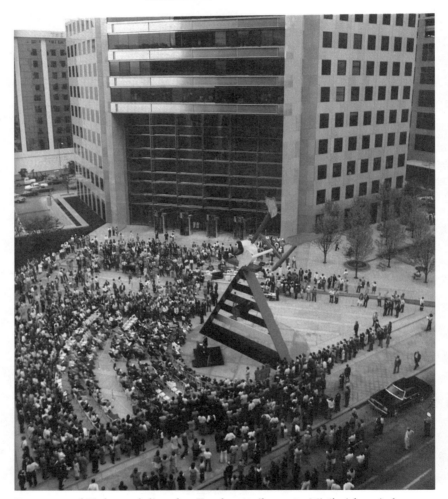

Personage and Birds *was dedicated on Tuesday, April 20, 1982, Miró's eighty-ninth birthday. He had planned to attend the dedication but was too ill to do so. I. M. Pei's decision to increase the five-foot sculpture to nearly eleven times its original size was determined by the plaza site. The squared arches of Jones Hall (across Milam Street from the Tower) are sixty-five feet high and so is the glassed-in lobby of the Tower. At fifty-two and one-half feet,* Personage and Birds *optically fits under the arcade and the lobby. (Photograph © Aker/Zvonkovic Photography, Houston)*

At the dedication, I. M. Pei spoke of making the Texas Commerce plaza a space for people. The building sits on a mere one-third of the block, freeing the remaining area for sculpture, trees, fountains, and open space. Here, former first lady Lady Bird Johnson and former president Gerald Ford, both directors of Texas Commerce Bancshares, sit in the front row at the dedication of Personage and Birds. *(Copyright 1982,* Houston Chronicle Publishing Company. *Reprinted with permission. All rights reserved.)*

national attention on Houston's cultural achievements. Gerry, Hugh Roff, and I became serious students of contemporary sculpture, with Ann Holmes (arts editor of the *Houston Chronicle*), and I. M. Pei as our tutors. We learned that, although other prominent sculptors were well represented in the United States, Miró, one of the world's foremost living artists, had just one major outdoor work in our country, and that was in Chicago.

"We were not searching just for form," I. M. said. "It was Miró's mischievous spirit that appealed to me." We considered another work by Miró for a while, but it was not appropriate for the space. Finally, I. M. saw a five-foot, unpainted cast bronze of *Personage and Birds* in the artist's New York gallery and projected the work upward nearly eleven times in scale in his mind to a soaring height of fifty-two feet. "Color became the right thing to do," he said. Then the three "students," Gerry, Hugh, and I, traveled with I. M. to Spain to meet Miró and see the model he had colored. Miró accepted our invitation to attend the dedication, but he became too frail to travel. He died, at ninety, on Christmas Day 1983.

At the dedication, on April 20, 1982, I called that sixty-one-ton sculpture a "whimsical piece." Gerry declared, "It adds a sense of humanism to the city since it sits there in front of a serious banker's gray granite building. Frankly, it tickles my funny bone." And Hugh said, "That's one sculpture that will be noticed. It should liven up the place, all right. I'd be disappointed if some didn't say, 'What's that?' I have not been disappointed."

★ CONSTRUCTING THE TEXAS COMMERCE TOWER

The engineering of this building attracted as much attention as its aesthetics. We broke ground in October 1978 and, in 1981, the Texas Commerce Tower won the highest award given by the American Consulting Engineers Council for "the integration of architecture and structural and foundation engineering." Its Grand Conceptor Award for Engineering Excellence went to McClelland Engineers, Inc., geotechnical consultants, and CBM Engineers, structural consultants.

It won for three reasons.

First, although at 1,049 feet, the Texas Commerce Tower was the tallest bank building in the world, unlike other soaring structures, it was not built on bedrock because Houston has no shallow bedrock. Rather, it was built on a thick deposit of compressible soil. We had to build our own bedrock, so to speak, in a sixty-three-foot excavation nearly twice as deep as that required for the Empire State Building and with enough concrete to cover eleven and one-half miles of highway.

Second, its "fifth side," I. M.'s "lopped-off" corner that opened up the park space, was designed to be free of columns, giving offices on that side of the building uninterrupted, eighty-five-foot vistas completely unimpaired by support columns.

Finally, acknowledging that the Texas Commerce Tower is located near one of the city's most important cultural centers, its main lobby is sixty-five feet high, the same height as the squared arches in the adjacent Jones Hall for the Performing Arts.

Our contractors also set a record for pumping concrete. Turner Construction Co. and Hercules Concrete Pumping Service, Inc., both with Houston offices, improved on a powerful pumping method created by a German manufacturer, Schwing, and pumped concrete one thousand feet straight up, exceeding the previous record by almost 40 percent.

Remembering that the windows had popped out of the John Hancock Building I. M. designed in Boston, I told him that the one thing I wanted was 20 percent more steel than that called for by his engineers. I had read that this serious window-popping problem in the Boston building was related to the building's structure. With the Texas Commerce Tower soaring so high into the Gulf Coast sky, I did not want our building "popping windows" when a hurricane hit Houston. TCB would have been forever in the courthouse if that happened. And sure enough, in 1983, a year after the building was dedicated, Hurricane Alicia gave it a severe test. Glass cascaded onto the sidewalks and streets from Tenneco's acclaimed building and other downtown Houston skyscrapers, but Texas Commerce Tower withstood that violent storm, undamaged and undaunted.

The Texas Commerce Tower was, for Houston, the "last train out of the station" before the economic downturn. The building was 99 percent leased and occupied, a financial success from day one.

NOTES

1. John Bloom, "Three Gentlemen, One Ghost and a Skyscraper," *Texas Monthly,* May 1980, 117.

Chapter 10 THE ECONOMIC DOWNTURN AND
MERGING WITH CHEMICAL BANK, 1983–89

I spent my first fifteen years at Texas Commerce building a nationally prominent bank amid an oil boom, a vigorous regional and state economy, and an expansive bank holding company movement. I spent much of my last six years there working to defend the gains we had made in the 1970s and early 1980s. From 1983 through my retirement in 1989, I led a team of bankers determined to pull TCB through a time of turmoil caused by a severe downturn in the oil industry and heightened by far-reaching regulatory changes. Looking back on these events with more than twenty-five years of perspective, it is clear that we were in a race with history to create a new "money center" banking system in Texas. Unfortunately, we came up short. But I remain proud of the efforts that led TCB to a merger with New York–based Chemical Bank, making it the only one of the five largest Texas banks to avoid bankruptcy or a forced marriage to a larger bank.

The 1980s brought two giant waves of change to our business. The first big change was in the New Deal banking legislation of the 1930s, which abolished most rate restrictions and minimums on deposit accounts plus phased out the differences in products offered by banks, savings and loans, brokers, and other financial institutions. Modified forms of interstate banking also emerged in the 1980s. Equally important for a bank based in Houston was the second big change, the fall in the price of oil. After a quarter of a century of relative stability, oil prices zigged as high as forty dollars per barrel in the 1970s and zagged as low as ten dollars in the 1980s. The resulting economic devastation to Houston and to Texas rivaled that of the Great Depression. With its broad exposure to all segments of the oil-based economy, banking was particularly hard-hit by the unexpected and unprecedented oil bust.

In 1983, the impact of such changes on banking became clear. InterFirst lost money, Republic and First City reported drops in earnings, and Texas Commerce's earnings per share managed to grow just 3 percent, as opposed to the 17 percent compound annual growth in earnings per share we had generated over the past decade.[1] Earnings increases remained tough to produce in 1984. TCB eked out a growth in earnings of 3 percent, thereby extending our record of consecutive year-over-year quarters of expansion in earnings per share to sixty-five, but we labored mightily for every precious penny. Finally, in the first quarter of 1985, our record was broken. We did not lose money; in fact, we earned $29 million, but we earned less than the $45 million it would have required to beat TCB's first quarter of 1984. Our people's heroic struggle to generate earnings continued on into 1986 until, in the fourth quarter, Texas Commerce experienced a loss. It was to be the first of seven consecutive quarters in the red before TCB made it back into the black in the third quarter of 1988. Throughout, the organization remained united, steadfast, and determined to return to the good old years of top performance.

With the collapse in the price of oil and the closely associated collapse of real estate—indeed, of all business all over the state—it slowly dawned on me that there was an element of déjà vu to this situation. My father had been a cotton broker during the era of King Cotton. As I was growing up, he bought cotton from farmers in West Texas and Oklahoma and exported it through the Port of Houston. In the eighteen-month period between early 1932 and mid-1933, the price of cotton dropped from twenty-nine cents a pound to six cents a pound, exports through the Port plunged, and business of all types throughout Texas collapsed or teetered on the brink of failure. As an impressionable youngster, I had seen King Cotton decline to "peasant" status. It had a profound effect on me because my father was absolutely wiped out. The culprit then was a commodity—cotton. Now, another basic commodity—oil—was in trouble. Could Texas Commerce be similarly devastated fifty years later as the price of oil collapsed from thirty-five dollars to ten dollars a barrel? In the 1930s, I remember that my father and mother looked worried all the time. In the 1980s, I would lie awake at night worrying if history might repeat itself.

My paramount concern for the safety of TCB's stockholders, customers, and employees was the factor that guided me to consider merging Texas Commerce with a larger money center bank. But that was coupled with my long-held belief that Texas banks should not be, could not be, confined between the Red River and the Rio Grande because Texas business was no longer concentrated exclusively between the Red River and the Rio Grande.

★ THE LOAN SITUATION

Texas Commerce entered the downturn with no seasoned problem-loan banking staff and no specialized systems for handling voluminous problem loans because, simply stated, we previously had so few problem loans. In 1971, for example, loan charge-offs were practically zero—0.07 percent of total average loans. Every year in the twelve years between 1970 and 1982, TCB's charge-offs were less than two-thirds of the average for the nation's largest banks.

In 1982, energy prices took a big hit and then gradually improved. But in 1985, the rig count dropped 28 percent and the overbuilt real estate market was slugged hard by a crash in property values. Retail sales simultaneously plunged. Disaster struck first in Houston, later in Dallas, later still in San Antonio and elsewhere, but never in El Paso. Austin lagged two years behind all the other markets because state government and the University of Texas stabilized the economy there. When real estate hit bottom in Houston, Austin was still building homes and office buildings.

At the end of 1982, 26 percent of our overall loan portfolio directly related to energy in some way—primarily in loans collateralized by proven, producing reserves and loans to the major international energy firms. We generally steered clear of lending to oil tool suppliers and contract drillers. Thanks to our chief energy lender, that wise, stubborn old Aggie John Townley, TCB's experience in the industry was materially better than any other large bank in Texas. We eventually charged off $125 million in energy loans, 7 percent of our peak energy portfolio (as of December 31, 1982). Because that was spread over seven years, the average charge-offs of one percent per year were manageable. The other large Texas banks charged off 40 percent or more of their energy portfolios because they had lent more to the riskier segments of the industry, contract drillers and oil-service and supply companies.

TCB's big problem was real estate. Long a leader in commercial real estate lending, we held more than 30 percent of our overall portfolio in construction and mortgage loans. Although this was a large concentration of loans in one sector, we did *not* concentrate loans to a few borrowers within the industry as some other banks had. Where First Republic had thirty real estate relationships of more than $100 million, we had three or four with the premier Texas-based developers, Gerald Hines, Ken Schnitzer, and Trammell Crow. Our chief real estate lenders, the sensible Lloyd Bolton and his succes-

John Adams ran the Banking Department at TCB-Houston and was responsible for business development in all member banks; John Townley oversaw Texas Commerce's energy lending; and Lloyd Bolton supervised the loan administration and real estate lending functions of the company. (Texas Commerce Bancshares 1984 annual report. Photograph © Aker/Zvonkovic Photography, Houston.)

sors, Jim Savage and Steve Field, placed great emphasis on developing lasting relationships with the strongest builders in each Texas market. We further protected ourselves by lending on a project-only basis. We also conducted our own thorough cost analysis before approving a loan and then periodically inspected construction sites and the progress of projects vis-à-vis the builders' draws against their loans.

The one element that no one fully perceived at the time, however, was just how much everything in the Texas economy was tied together. One much-publicized study released in early 1986, for example, suggested that the decline in oil prices cost the Texas economy approximately one hundred and thirteen thousand jobs in manufacturing and mining-related businesses from 1981 to 1985 and concluded that each additional decline of one dollar per barrel in the price of Texas oil would cost the state twenty-five thousand additional jobs and $100 million in state and local tax revenue.[2] The energy industry lost two hundred thousand jobs in eighteen months in Houston alone, a telling decline. Energy problems incubated many of the real estate problems, because many oil companies had decided to build during the boom. Of course, an office tower generates no cash flow from rents while it is under construction, and as most of our customers had deep pockets, it took even longer for TCB to start feeling the effects of real estate problems. Hotels were also tied to energy, and TCB had financed several big hotels. Oil-related business travel plunged into depression along with the oil industry, and when a hotel's cash flow dries up, appraised values do not mean a thing.

But land loans represented TCB's most formidable challenge. Half of our real estate charge-offs were in undeveloped land. Real estate lending had become so competitive in the late 1970s that, in order to make a construction loan, a bank had to get aboard a project early and make the land loan. Then, when the music stopped, that land had nothing built on it. Some of these properties were worth no more than twenty-five cents on the dollar by the time the stressful downturn slowed. The similarities of the "Oil Depression" of the 1980s to the "Great Depression" of the 1930s were inescapable.

Altogether, TCB's real estate losses between 1985 and 1993 amounted to more than $1 billion—29 percent of our total real estate portfolio in December 31, 1985. Although these numbers imply severe problems for TCB, we fared considerably better than many of our Texas peer banks. First City, for example, evidently did not apply the strict real estate underwriting standards of the "Jesse Jones bank," nor did it vigorously reappraise (and write down) the value of the properties they held as collateral when the market was collapsing. This may be one reason why our major Houston competitor did not recognize the gravity of the looming problem as early as TCB did.

One reason TCB avoided some of the most serious problems of the mid-1980s was its response to earlier examinations by the Office of the Comptroller of the Currency (OCC). Even though TCB, among the twenty-five largest U.S. banks, had ranked second only to J. P. Morgan in loan quality for the previous ten years (as measured by loan charge-offs as a percentage of total outstanding loans), the OCC concentrated on TCB—first in a series of "qualitative" examinations of Texas banks its regulators launched in late 1984 and then in a follow-up with real estate audits a year later. We did not agree with the catastrophic projections insistently advanced by these young examiners. In fact, TCB's real estate lending officers reasoned with and subsequently argued vehemently with the OCC examiners in daylong meetings, resulting occasionally in the OCC reversing its dour positions on the credits of several long-term and able customers who were experiencing temporary disruptions in cash flow attributable to the economic conditions. As circumstances turned out later, some could have repaid TCB in full if the examiners had extended a modicum of patience and forbearance. But some could not, as the economic downturn grew worse and lasted longer than banker or borrower could have imagined.

Although these two exams taxed us mentally and physically, they did serve as a wake-up call. We realized that the OCC examiners did not believe that TCB's bankers knew how to lend money, and this goaded us into defensive maneuvers two years earlier than our competition. We further beefed up our loan management systems in 1984 and, in the fourth quarter of 1985, we strengthened the bank's capacity to withstand potential problems by quadrupling TCB's loan loss reserve.

★　PLAYING DEFENSE

From the beginning, truly capable bankers handled problem loans for TCB, but we had only three such specialists—John Bemrose, Bruce Shilcutt, and Tony Torres—working *only* on problem loans. As the Texas economy spiraled down, we enhanced our accounting control systems and monitoring procedures, and we formed a "defense team" of bankers to work with problem assets. These moves freed our "offense team" to continue building business selectively, despite the harsh times.

We tapped Robert Hunter, manager of the National Group at the time, as the "defense" captain of TCB's overall loan portfolio. From a standing start of the aforementioned three specialists, he assembled 164 lending professionals and equipped them with the systems and procedures to manage, foreclose, and otherwise work out a problem loan portfolio that peaked at $1.4 billion in mid-1988.

He began with TCB's network of seventy separate member banks and a review system that relied on strong credit quality systems and controls at the front end—that is, when loans were put on the books. Traditionally, each

Robert Hunter played a superb game of "offense" in International and National Banking before transitioning to the defense during the Texas economy's downturn as TCB's very able head of Loan Administration. (Photograph © Aker/Zvonkovic Photography, Houston)

TCB member bank had used its own loan committee and its own CEO to interpret Texas Commerce's written credit policy up to that member bank's legal loan capacity. Each lender was responsible for monitoring his or her own loans, audited periodically by TCB. This system had worked efficiently and effectively during good times, but when the Texas economy started coming unglued, we revised the credit policy manual to fit the not-so-good times and placed new emphasis on the ongoing assessment of the entire loan portfolio. TCB management required greater consistency in underwriting and tougher loan grading standards in member banks; we decisively strengthened the loan review function to identify problem credits early; we continuously centralized control over problem loans in real estate and energy in order to manage the collection or sale of foreclosed assets; we made even more certain that each TCB bank's accounting treatment—in terms of performing status, reserves, and projections—was appropriate and consistent.

Harriet Wasserstrum added her considerable organizational skills and computer literacy to Robert Hunter's defense team and created an invaluable tool, a computerized system to monitor TCB's loan portfolio and identify potential problems early, at a point when many could be remedied before becoming losses. This often proved to be as constructive for the customer as it was for TCB.

I assigned many seasoned TCB lenders to these tough defense jobs. Among these was Larry Shryock, the veteran head of Houston middle market lending who ran TCB-Houston's Loan Administration effort for a couple of years before returning to manage the Commercial Banking Department. TCB's insightful International Banking manager, Keith Oldfield, followed Larry in Loan Administration. Tommy Cox, an experienced National Division lender, set up TCB-Houston's first loan workout team. He was joined later by Bob Bishop, a no-nonsense energy lender, whose team also assumed responsibility for energy loans.

When Austin's economy began imploding in 1986, Tommy Cox went there to set up TCB-Austin's first workout unit. In 1987, newcomer Hall Webb brought strong experience in commercial workouts from Chemical Bank. He was soon joined by TCB's own Jim Hibbert, an unflappable mainstay of the Real Estate Group. In 1989, Bob Bishop moved to TCB-Austin as president and, together with Tommy Cox, prepared for the worst real estate downturn in the state. Todd Maclin and John Doyal took over the real estate problem loans, and Joe Holt and Steve Lea handled commercial loans and recoveries. Terry Gunter was in charge of loan review in Austin, the Dallas–Fort Worth Metroplex, and the remainder of Central and West Texas. Carole Creeden headed loan review for the rest of the state.

These are but a few of the 164 TCB bankers who played "defense" at the depths of the Texas economic downturn, and they played a magnificent game. Most later returned to the "offense," better for their "Great Depression II" experience. One conclusion is unassailable: they knew their customers and they knew their credits! Todd Maclin, for example, returned to real estate financing in a new investment banking function in Houston. He then moved to Dallas, where, after serving as president and chairman in that market, he was named CEO of the Chase South Region in 2002. In 2003, Todd moved up to head middle market lending for the nationwide Chase organization. Jim Hibbert, for another example, became Chase's middle market real estate credit executive for all of North America.

In the fall of 1986, at the time I began negotiating our possible merger with Chemical Bank, TCB's nonperforming loans had reached the abnormally high level of $840 million, or about 6.5 percent of total loans, as the Texas economy continued to deteriorate. They were to grow another $600 million by mid-1988.[3]

Just as important as mounting a strong defense was separating the "good bank" from the "bad bank." This decision allowed most of the organization to concentrate on building business without getting bogged down in problems, a strategy that enabled TCB to increase market share as troubles escalated at our competitor Texas banks. In 1984, for example, Texas Commerce's "offense team" made more than 115,000 calls on prospective and current customers, identifying ample quality lending opportunities that enabled TCB selectively to make only the best loans. TCB had a lot to sell because we were still the healthiest bank in Texas, as measured by capital and other critical financial criteria. When the other large Texas banks failed, TCB's offense team had already contacted their customers and was there to capture and effectively service the creditworthy business.

Indeed, at year-end 1988, when we finally eked out a $2 million profit after seven miserable quarters in the red, TCB counted more than seventeen hundred large and small Texas companies as *new* customers—along with their loans, their deposits, and their fees from trust, cash management, and investment banking services. As financial reporter Greg Seay wrote in a *Houston Post* story in 1990, Texas Commerce was the only major Texas bank to emerge from the downturn "without a dime of federal deposit insurance or taxpayer money . . . to assist [it] over the . . . hump."[4]

★ STATE LAW BECOMES MORE PERMISSIVE

I had been driving to Austin since 1974 to meet with the Texas legislature's Banking Committee, trying to persuade its members to bring a bill to the floor that would permit interstate banking in Texas. I started first by proposing a regional confederation of ten (later reduced to a more "politically digestible" seven) energy-producing states rather than aiming for coast-to-coast interstate banking. The other Texas bank holding companies wanted to push hard for branch banking, too, but I pleaded with them not to introduce that emotional subject into the volatile environment of the time, one marked by the fear small independent banks professed of the five large Texas bank holding companies.

But both points were moot. Neither the bill for a confederation of ten producing states nor the bill for branch banking ever moved out of the Banking Committee because, to repeat for emphasis, the independent banks, the small banks, were concerned that the large banks would acquire power that would work to the disadvantage of smaller institutions. That was not what we wanted at all. We didn't want to "gobble up" the First National Bank in Chillicothe. We wanted to compete with Citicorp in New York City. But every time either bill came up in the Legislative Banking Committee, the independent bankers would descend on Austin in hordes and literally pack that Banking Committee room, emotionally vocalizing their fears and swaying committee deliberations.

In those days, correspondent banking relationships were important and profitable to the large Texas banks. As my holding company compadres grew more and more fearful of losing those relationships, they became less and less enthusiastic about interstate banking, thereby leaving Texas Commerce, which was less reliant on correspondent business from other banks, to become known as the strong proponent in Texas of interstate banking freedom. Although the other holding companies favored interstate banking to varying degrees, many times not one senior officer from those other five major banks would appear with me in Austin at the Legislative Banking Committee meetings.

Walter Mischer was an exception. Walter, who headed the state's sixth-largest bank holding company, the $10 billion Allied Bancshares, was a particularly important CEO, not only because of the size of Allied, but also because he was very active and influential politically. Between 1974 and 1984, Walter and I went to Austin together four or five times to reason with key Texas legislators, seeking fewer restrictions on Texas banks, but we were always outnumbered by the CEOs of small independent banks who controlled important voting blocs in their regions of Texas. We never got a bill out of the Banking Committee. It was defeat after defeat after defeat. Meanwhile, legislatures in North Carolina and other states unshackled their banks, and those banks quickly diversified their markets and increased their size through interstate banking mergers.

By 1986, the Texas economy was under severe pressure. There was a widespread sense that Texas was confronted with an inescapable banking crisis and that we needed more flexibility to merge, diversify our market geographically, and import capital. Texas Commerce had a strong capital base and was still a strong institution, but clearly the industry as a whole was under stress. Surmising that branch banking might relieve some of this stress, Texas independent bankers approached me with the proposition that they would now support interstate banking if I would support branch banking. I felt like the rabbit thrown into the proverbial briar patch. It sure did not take any heavy thinking to say yes to that. Finally, working together, we got both bills passed. The smaller banks got branch banking, which they wanted, as did we. We also got legislation authorizing complete nationwide, coast-to-coast, interstate banking.

The Liddell, Sapp, Zivley & LaBoon law firm (now Locke Liddell & Sapp) had worked with Texas Commerce on political matters for many years, and one of its ablest senior partners, Bruce LaBoon, joined Texas Commerce Bancshares on March 1, 1986, as vice chairman responsible for Loan Administration, headed by Robert Hunter. Bruce also served as corporate general counsel, as senior officer of the Trust Department, and as head of Security.

Shortly after Bruce arrived, we went to work with Governor Mark White, Lieutenant Governor Bill Hobby, various members of the Texas legislature, and the Texas Bankers Association to craft a bill that would permit full interstate banking and change the state's 150-year-old constitutional ban on branch banking. The governor called a special session of the legislature for that summer and agreed to put these two issues on the agenda.

Bruce and the Liddell Sapp attorneys drafted this legislation, working closely with the legislative council of the Texas Bankers Association— Charles McMahen from MCorp, Charlie Hrdlicka from Victoria Bank, and Lowell A. "Stretch" Smith from Rio Vista, president of the TBA. Even the Independent Bankers Association eventually joined this coalition to make sure that whatever passed was reasonable from their perspective.

Because the bill had been agreed to by every interested entity by the time it reached the floor of the legislature, it sailed through during the last few days of the special session. Walter Mischer's attuned political influence was particularly helpful in setting the stage for this quick action. The journey to Austin for Governor White's bill signing ceremony was one of the shortest 162-mile trips Walter, Bruce, and I ever made.

On November 3, 1986, 73 percent of Texans voted overwhelmingly for the convenience of countywide branch banking,[5] and on November 21, just eighteen days later, Texas Commerce was among the first major Texas banking organizations to apply to branch, first in El Paso, then in San Antonio, Austin, Corpus Christi, Dallas, Houston, and San Antonio—in nearly every county that then had more than one Texas Commerce bank.

Actually, TCB got into the branching business even earlier than we expected. On Monday, January 26, 1987, about three weeks after we announced our merger with Chemical Bank of New York, the FDIC invited TCB to bid for Montgomery County Bank, a failed $48 million bank just north of Houston. We were the only Texas bank invited to bid, probably because of our comparatively solid balance sheet and the additional strength implied by our by-then pending merger with Chemical. We turned in our bid on Wednesday; we learned we'd won by noon on Thursday; three hours later the regulators closed the bank and Benny Pitzer, president of TCB-Conroe, assumed responsibility for TCB's new branch. On Friday morning, Montgomery County Bank—renamed TCB–The Woodlands—opened just fifteen minutes late (we had trouble with the new locks), dispensing all of the strength and services of the $19 billion Texas Commerce organization to a new, affluent market. Deposits grew by more than one million dollars on the first day.

★ PUTTING THE NEW INTERSTATE BANKING LAW TO USE

Under previous law, TCB had already purchased 4.9 percent interests in major banks in Colorado, Oklahoma, Wyoming, New Mexico, Arizona, Louisiana, and Florida. We now faced a strategic choice: How would we use the long-sought freedom of full interstate banking now permitted by the Texas legislature?

Work began quickly. After discussions with senior managers and the Long-Term Strategy & Merger Committee[6] composed of Texas Commerce Bancshares directors, we concurred that it would be in the bank's best interest to begin the process of searching for a merger partner that offered financial strength, new products, and geographic diversity. As discussed in chapter 8, we began by thoroughly exploring the possibility of mergers with the two largest Dallas-based banks, InterFirst and Republic. Neither of those partnerships would offer TCB broader geographic diversity, new products, or new resources. Afterward, in August, we drew up a list of prospective part-

Charles Duncan was U.S. secretary of energy and deputy secretary of defense in the Carter administration. Earlier, he held various executive positions with the Coca-Cola Company before becoming its president in 1971. Charles chaired Texas Commerce Bancshares's Long-Term Strategy & Merger Committee through a busy, challenging time. My friendship with Charles—and his brother, John—dates back to our Young Presidents' Organization days. (Photograph © Aker/Zvonkovic Photography, Houston)

ners that included the ten largest U.S. banks and two or three large British banks and met with our investment banker, John Gutfreund, CEO of Salomon Brothers in New York.

We carefully analyzed banks that would be logical and complementary fits; banks that were solid organizations not heavily dependent on oil and gas; banks that were big enough to provide capital to help TCB better withstand the energy-induced storm on the horizon. TCB wanted to be a significant part of the prospective merger partner, but not so large that our temporary problems would become serious problems for that bank. As it turned out, when the fuller impact of Texas's real estate crisis became obvious in 1988, those problems were larger than we envisioned, but none of us perceived the full extent of the real estate debacle in Texas in 1986.

Our first serious discussion was with Dick Flamson, chairman and CEO of Security Pacific on the West Coast. He was originally from Texas and flew to Houston to meet with us following my visit with him in Los Angeles. But Dick became increasingly apprehensive about the impact of falling oil prices on the Texas economy, and he decided Security Pacific wanted no Texas exposure, even with TCB, the strongest large bank in the state.

Another key member of the Long-Term Strategy & Merger Committee was Harold Hook, chairman and CEO of American General Corporation, the fourth-largest stockholder-owned insurance firm in the nation. Harold became CEO in 1978, and, by 1983, American General's revenues had more than doubled. (Photograph © Aker/Zvonkovic Photography, Houston)

Concurrently, TCB director Charles Duncan, who had previously been president of Coca-Cola in Atlanta and served on the board of Coca-Cola at the time, traveled to Atlanta with me to visit Bob Strickland, chairman and CEO of the Trust Company of Georgia, to discuss a possible merger. But the risk Bob saw in the Texas economy was greater than his appetite to expand by merging with a Texas bank. So that breakfast was a one-shot deal. With genteel language, Bob sent us back to Texas.

I initiated discussions with two other major banks on the West Coast, another in Chicago, and then we turned to New York, where our receptions by the money center banks ranged the gamut. Citibank chairman John Reed turned two senior TCB officers and me over to one of his executive vice presidents, who dismissed us on the spot. Morgan treated us wonderfully well. Morgan's chairman and CEO, Lew Preston, assembled his top officers and explored a Morgan-TCB merger thoroughly, although Morgan had made a policy decision earlier, which subsequently became clear. At one time, Morgan had considered expanding into two states—Florida and Texas—but then decided to veer from commercial banking and emphasize investment banking. Lew stated unequivocally that, had Morgan decided to embark on an interstate banking expansion, TCB would have been at the top of his list.

We did not meet with Manufacturers Hanover. My old friend John McGillicuddy, chairman and CEO, was beginning to encounter lending problems there, and I simply did not want to embarrass him by talking about a merger that might extend his resources further. At Bankers Trust, Al Brittain, chairman and CEO, could not have extended a warmer welcome, but he advised us that Bankers Trust also had problems to solve before it could consider venturing into Texas waters. Then we visited Chase to confer with my close friend Bill Butcher, chairman and CEO, and began a serious, constructive dialogue that continued from August through October with many discussions and visits.

Finally, at Chemical Bank, chairman-CEO Walter Shipley welcomed us enthusiastically. Walter had gained a thorough understanding of Texas and Texans during his eleven years of traveling in the state, and we had become exceptionally close banking and personal friends over his twenty years with Chemical. I have always been tremendously impressed with Walter. In fact, I tried to hire him twice for a top position at TCB when he was a junior officer at Chemical.[7]

★ A WARNING FROM THE FED

During this time, I flew from New York to Washington to see Bill Taylor, chief of staff at the Federal Reserve, to discuss the idea of such a merger. Many people found Bill brusque, but I really liked him, and I needed a straight answer. In 1986, the Office of the Comptroller of the Currency regulators were transparently biased against Texas. In fact, the OCC examiners repeatedly demonstrated an anti-Texas bias, emphasizing that the Texas economy was faring worse than the major Texas banks believed. They seemed to be doing everything in their power to "educate" us with their version of a "reality check."

A thirty-six-year-old rather junior banker from Oregon named Todd Conover, whom Ronald Reagan appointed Comptroller of the Currency, made embarrassing judgmental mistakes about Penn Square Bank in Oklahoma City. Penn Square was a minor, ineptly managed suburban bank where a banker named Bill Patterson reportedly frequently entertained customers by drinking beer out of his boot. He had plunged Penn Square into serious difficulty with ill-conceived energy loans and somehow managed to lure Continental Illinois and First National–Seattle into his storm. Penn Square's loan limit was $10 million. If it originated a $100 million loan, Continental Illinois might periodically fund the $90 million overline. Continental Illinois was a large, conservative bank, but Patterson managed to gain access to a few officers in Continental's energy department and, when the price of oil dropped, both banks plunged into a whirlpool of defective energy loans. These problems brought Conover before the House Banking Committee, where he was roundly berated by the committee chairman, Representative Fernand St. Germain of Rhode Island. Two or three examiners later told me that Conover sent tapes of that brutal interrogation to all of his twelve OCC regions with word that this was never to happen to him again. Each region's examiners were to lean hard on energy lending banks, and the Texas economy, being hinged to the collapse of oil in Oklahoma, was the next up.

Now Penn Square's operation differed completely from that of Texas Commerce, as witnessed by TCB's outstanding record in energy lending in good times and bad. Nevertheless, the OCC examiners descended on us with a seeming intent to destroy, in order, ostensibly, to preserve and protect Conover's position in Washington, D.C.

About this time, the OCC was conducting a routine examination of TCB-Houston. I remember that Sam Golden, a man imbued with the threat from above, was in charge. In making his report to a room filled with our senior officers, he demanded that we charge off the loans of long-term and historically able customers, many of whom were experiencing temporary disruptions in cash flow attributable to the economic conditions. He also charged TCB with extending "preferential loans" to two of our outside directors, and he delivered a stern, self-enhancing lecture on morality to that group of TCB's senior officers. After proclaiming that those allegedly preferential loans were made by TCB's "ethically flawed" bankers, he suggested that our senior officers should have been raised by his daddy . . . and on and on. I never forgot that, and I never will. It was an insult to the parents of every officer assembled in that room. But we did not say anything. Every TCB banker in that room was as upright as the day is long, but Sam held the power of the OCC regulators. To defend our parents or our obvious ethical standards would have been fruitless and probably would have boomeranged, resulting in the OCC examiners taking even more capricious actions against TCB.

This happened in early 1985, just as we were preparing to mail TCB's 1984 annual reports. I said to Sam Golden, "Sam, I do not feel comfortable sending out our annual reports until you have finished your OCC exam. I want TCB's information to be absolutely 100 percent correct from *your* perspective. I don't want to mail those annual reports and then afterward have you tell me about a matter that you unilaterally decide would constitute the need for additional loan reserves, something that would require TCB to restate 1984 earnings, reprint the 1984 annual report, and reschedule the 1984 annual stockholders' meeting. If I have to postpone TCB's annual stockholder meeting because your examination is not complete, I will postpone that meeting immediately, without protest."

I will never forget his answer: "Oh, Mr. Love, we have almost completed our examinations. We don't want to come in here and delay your annual stockholders' meeting."

Well, by that time, I was leery, and I responded, "Sam, it bothers me not in the least if we have to postpone our stockholders' meeting. I can have those 1984 annual reports reprinted. I am telling you now, in front of my staff, I am happy to do it." He said, "No," and I made him repeat it three times. Only then did we mail TCB's 1984 annual reports and proxy material to stockholders.

In less than two weeks, word came down from the OCC regulators in Washington that TCB had inadequate loan loss reserves and ordered the bank to restate earnings for 1984! Specifically, the OCC directed TCB-Houston to increase its reserve for loan losses at December 31, 1984, by $27.7 million and the year-end reserves of three member banks by an aggregate $500,000. But TCB-Houston, which constituted 60 percent of the assets of the parent company, was so material to Texas Commerce Bancshares that the SEC filed against us to restate the holding company financials as well. The OCC singled out four or five large loans that, in their opinion, should have had larger reserves. Of course, the examiners had the benefit of hindsight. The loans we made in 1984 were examined in 1985, by which time the economic situation had changed along with the condition of these loans. We argued vehemently. We started with Sam Golden and appealed all the way to the top of the OCC, with no success. Our outside auditors had certified TCB's 1984 results. The head of our outside, independent, large national audit firm even wrote a strong letter of protest to the Comptroller in Washington, but to no avail.

So there was, I would say, hell to pay, because it appeared that TCB had misrepresented its December 31, 1984, earnings statement and balance sheet and that its outside auditors had erred in certifying both. Two years later, on

August 17, 1987, the SEC issued a consent decree stating that the charge that TCB extended "preferential loans" to two of its directors was dismissed with no fine and no finding of fault. But as one outside director, an attorney, commented in a TCB-Austin board meeting, "It doesn't matter now that the OCC has dismissed its allegation. It has been widely reported in the media for about two years. That charge has damaged this bank."

Later, when the large East Coast banks were having their own real estate problems, I remember receiving a call from Bill Brown, who was chairman and CEO of First National Bank of Boston. Bill said, "You know, Ben, I've heard you talk about how unfair the regulators were to Texas banks. I'm going to tell you, we're good friends, but I tended to dismiss what you were saying, thinking, 'Well, Ben's a Texan, and that's the way Texans are.' Now these regulators are here in Boston. Did they ever take loans that were performing like clockwork and make you set up special reserves—and classify all or part of them as nonperforming?"

I answered, "Yes, Bill."

"Did you ever have an OCC examiner named Sam Golden?"

I answered, "Yes, Bill."

That was the regulatory atmosphere at the time. Personal. Destructive. Inequitable. That was how I felt about it then, and that is how I feel about it today. But looking back on things, I realize that Sam Golden probably did us a favor, albeit inadvertently, because he so exercised his authority that we turned TCB's ship around on a dime and steamed full speed ahead on defense as well as offense. Yet the 110 percent constructive, energetic contribution of virtually every banker on TCB's staff was the major factor that preserved the bank.

Our loan management systems grew so strong that the OCC, in carrying out examinations in the northeastern United States in the late 1980s, is rumored to have told bankers there to call TCB for advice. Now *that* was a real compliment, albeit one from a source that had lost my respect. Such was the regulatory backdrop for our exploration of a possible merger with a money center bank.

In 1986, when I stopped over in Washington to visit with the Fed chief of staff, Bill Taylor, our prospects for merger with both Chemical and Chase seemed realistic at the time. I recall like yesterday that Bill said: "Ben, if you can merge with Chemical or Chase, you fly back to New York within the hour and get that done!"

I replied, "Bill, we may or may not want to do that. I wouldn't have started all of this, and I wouldn't be here seeing you, if I didn't feel that it might be our best course of action. The banking industry is consolidating, and I've been preaching my 'consolidation sermon' to the Texas legislature for years, trying to convince that body to allow Texas banks some form of interstate banking. But I'd always envisioned we'd be a buyer, and Texas would be one of the nation's three financial centers consistent with the state's gross domestic product and population. Now, our currency [our stock] is not at a price where we could buy anything, so we'll have to be a seller."

Bill said, "Ben, you Texans always think what you have in Texas is worth one hell of a lot more than any of the rest of us do."

I said, "What do you mean? The New York banks—any of them—are far more exposed to LDC loans [loans to less developed countries] than TCB. Are you telling me that you think a loan we have in Houston on Republic Bank's new building, which is 98 percent occupied, is not as good as a loan to some banana plantation in Latin America?"

He said, "Ben, I've told you all I'm going to. Don't worry about those Latin American loans. The ten largest banks in this nation are not going to fail. As an element of federal government policy, the Federal Reserve will not let them fail. That's the way it is. But I will tell you one other thing: If we think it is proper, we *will* let any Texas bank fail because not one Texas bank is among the ten largest banks in the nation."

Well, that was definitively and unequivocally strong, coming from one of TCB's major and most respected regulators. Hence, after that discussion, I was certain about Federal Reserve policy. The Fed examiners were topflight. I respected their objectivity. But I continued to worry about TCB's 8,300 employees, 18,400 stockholders, and hundreds of thousands of loyal customers. All were potential preys of the OCC examiners' decisions. At night, I experienced acute insomnia when I pondered my choices and courses of action over and over again.

★ COURAGEOUS CHEMICAL

By mid-November 1986, Chase had decided not to bid on Texas Commerce. Chemical did bid. Bill Butcher delivered the Chase news in a princely manner—face-to-face. Bill, who had been wounded by some decisions that went wrong during his administration, flew from New York and came to my office in Houston. We talked for an hour, then he flew directly back to New York. He would not even stay for lunch. His message was this: "I've decided the risk in Texas now is too great for Chase."

At that point, for TCB, Chemical Bank of New York was the remaining active merger prospect. We could have turned to a foreign bank, I suppose, but with Chemical we had the right combination. As one of the nation's top ten banks, Chemical would survive any downturn. Further, Chemical was extremely interested in Texas Commerce, had the capacity to do the right thing, and had Walter Shipley.

About a week before Thanksgiving, Bruce LaBoon, TCB's chief legal counsel, Marc Shapiro, TCB's chief financial officer, and I flew to New York and met with Walter and Ken Lavine, his chief financial officer, and essentially negotiated the price. On Tuesday, we arrived at a handshake deal for what would create the country's fourth-largest bank. At the time, it would be the largest bank merger in the history of the United States.

Mulling over those eventful days on the flight back home, I knew I had made the right decision. This was no shotgun wedding. Our capital was strong. At the time, we believed that TCB could survive despite the temporarily beleaguered Texas economy and the OCC examiners, but the fact that we did do something was consistent with the way we'd stretched geographic boundaries in the past. Despite the prospect of criticism, I believed strongly that our depositors should not have concerns about the safety of TCB amidst the Texas economy's storm and that TCB should continue to position itself so that our customers, stockholders, and employees had full confidence in the bank. Merging with one of the top ten money center banks would be constructive for our customers, our stockholders, and our employees. It would clearly result in TCB being impregnable.

Indeed, the Texas recession continued longer than most, including me, anticipated, and it took longer than we had expected to get our earnings increases accelerating again. That could be read two ways: (1) TCB acted prudently in merging with Chemical when we did, or (2) if Walter Shipley had waited, Chemical might have acquired TCB at a lower price. Even though Chemical had a due diligence team analyzing TCB's loans for six weeks, *American Banker* ridiculed Walter for paying "so much" for Texas Commerce. That publication and many others, the *Wall Street Journal* included, implied that Chemical could have bought all four of the other largest—but failed—Texas banks for half of what it paid for Texas Commerce. I immediately advised Walter that I was totally committed, as was the terrific, proven TCB team, to the proposition that merging with TCB would be one of the best business decisions he and Chemical would ever make.

We negotiated hard on the terms. Walter Shipley was fair and firm throughout our negotiations, a man I continuously respected. Thus we agreed, eventually (and amicably), that Chemical would pay TCB stockholders a package of preferred stock, equity, and cash valued in the range of $34.00 to $36.00 per share. I believed our directors and stockholders would approve because TCB stock had sold as low as $16.50 during 1986 when Wall Street relegated all large Texas banks to the scrap yard.

This was a productive match, dollar-wise. It was structured to enable shareholders on both sides to realize the gains from a hoped-for recovering Texas economy over the next five years while minimizing the downside risk to Chemical stockholders. In fact, various conversion triggers in the package of securities called for the two institutions to operate at arm's length until 1992.

This was a first-of-its-kind transaction in many ways. On merger day, one share of Texas Commerce common stock bought five items. Three were simple to evaluate. Two were not, but our investment advisors estimated the valuation of the "not simple" two pieces at between $11.00 and $13.00. These five items were:

- Cash, worth about $7.00
- 0.09 shares of Chemical common stock (worth about $4.00, based on the closing price of Chemical stock on March 20, 1987)
- One share of Chemical Series C preferred stock with a stated value of $12.00
- One share of Chemical Class B common stock
- One share of National Loan Bank stock

The Series C adjustable rate preferred stock gave TCB shareholders a security with a measurable market value without diluting Chemical's common stock. It paid a quarterly dividend structured to keep the stock trading near its stated value of $12.00. After five years, Chemical had the right to repurchase this stock.

The Class B stock was a kind of new idea designed around a "good bank–bad bank" concept. It provided TCB stockholders the ability to do better in case TCB did better, and it gave Chemical stockholders some protection in case TCB fared worse. And so, from the merger date, May 1, 1987, through 1991, Texas Commerce was to be accounted for as a separate entity. Anytime after March 1, 1992, Chemical could convert the Class B stock into regular Chemical common stock at a rate based on TCB's earnings during that period.

Our nonperforming loans proved to be a serious sticking point, but the merger team developed an ingenious solution. In fact, the concept has been used several times since then. The problem was this: Chemical believed TCB was still carrying $300 million in uncollectible loans on our books and wanted us to reserve for them. We believed strongly in the accuracy of our balance sheet and were convinced we could ultimately collect most of these loans. The solution was for Chemical to identify the loans that troubled them and divest those loans to TCB shareholders in some fashion. That seemed fair, so I countered by proposing, "If Chemical doesn't place any value on those loans, give them to TCB shareholders. They won't cost you anything. We'll keep them."

Next, we needed to conceptualize and then develop a vehicle to hold those loans because, of course, Texas Commerce was going to be merged into Chemical and there would be no residual charter. Coincidentally, we had begun branching, so we kept one of our member bank charters—TCB–River Oaks was selected arbitrarily—and used it to form the National Loan Bank (NLB). NLB's sole purpose was to collect those $300 million in "bad" loans, distribute the proceeds to TCB's former stockholders, and liquidate the NLB. On the day before the completion of the Chemical-TCB merger, those $300 million of bad loans were transferred to NLB and distributed to TCB stockholders, one share of NLB stock for each share of TCB stock.

NLB was the final piece of the financing puzzle. Harry K. Smith, the chairman-CEO of Big Three Industries and a retired Texas Commerce director, agreed to serve as president and chairman of NLB. He and TCB bankers David Ivy and Bob Giles did a magnificent job of fighting the battles and doing the work of collecting $300 million in bad loans that turned out to be not as bad as originally thought. We wrote down these loans to a "fair value" of $113 million—in other words, we expected to be able to collect $113 million from this $300 million portfolio. In fact, we collected $176 million, more than 50 percent more than the fair value.

The Chemical-TCB match was based on more than money, however. The officers of the two institutions had known one another for a long time and

Richard Hickson was responsible for business with large corporations throughout the eastern and western United States; Joe McKinney headed corporate business in the southwestern and southeastern United States; Gary Wright succeeded John Townley as manager of energy lending activities; Steve Field followed Lloyd Bolton as manager of Texas Commerce's real estate lending; and Larry Shryock headed commercial banking in Houston. (Texas Commerce Bancshares 1984 annual report. Photograph © Aker/Zvonkovic Photography, Houston.)

shared comparable policies and philosophies. When we looked beyond our borders and began considering New York banks, I recalled hearing comments from the TCB officers who had traveled in the national markets, bankers like Gary Wright, John Townley's thoughtful successor in Energy Banking; John Adams, the former National Group manager who did such a terrific job as TCB's CEO in Dallas; and Joe McKinney, who made our Southwest Division rank A-one, then applied that same energy to the demanding job of developing the San Antonio market for TCB as CEO of our banks there. They chorused: "If we're going to expand, we hope you'll look at Chemical." Both banks had strong desires to be the best; both had deep corporate and institutional customer relationships; both had robust regional banking franchises; both believed in relationship banking; and people from both banks genuinely liked one another.

After TCB structured the transaction with Chemical, and before we called the stockholders' meeting to seek approval for the prospective merger, I visited two of our oldest and largest stockholders. I anticipated that they might object to Texas Commerce merging with any larger bank, especially one headquartered in New York.

One was TCB director Bill Japhet. To my surprise, this man who, as a boy, had received his first ten shares of stock in the National Bank of Commerce from the hand of Jesse Jones himself, listened and asked whether I believed TCB could make it without merging. I told him that our capital and our loan portfolio were in better shape than the other four or five large Texas banks, but I felt an overriding responsibility to be 100 percent sure, due to the trust that our stockholders, employees, and customers had placed in us. Over the years, I had met all of the board members of all forty-two banks that had joined Texas Commerce, and I could certify that they voted to merge with TCB because they trusted us. Many of these member bank directors had invested nearly every penny they could spare from their own businesses in Texas Commerce stock.

I thought back to that 1930–34 period when I was a youngster, and the impact the cotton market crash made on me. If the same sort of economic collapse toppled TCB fifty years later and financially damaged the Sam Silvermans and other TCB-Brownsville directors or all of TCB's member bank directors in San Angelo who had finally voted to join Texas Commerce, to cite just two member bank cities—if they wound up losing everything they had invested in TCB stock—I could not have lived with myself. At one time, I wondered if we should really try to ride out the oil price collapse from a risk measurement standpoint, but the overall Texas economy continued to decline. Our loans were concentrated in Texas. I knew TCB was now in a high-risk position because no one could guarantee if or when the price of oil would recover, and the bank was being battered by the ripple effect of oil in real estate and other lending sectors.

I also visited with Houston Endowment's veteran CEO, Howard Creekmore, thinking it would be a major hurdle for him to contemplate Jesse Jones's bank combined with a large New York bank. Howard listened, just as Bill Japhet had listened, thoughtfully, without interrupting, to what I was describing—the pros and the cons—and he gave his blessing: "If that's your judgment, Ben, you'll have my support."

★ APPROVAL BY THE BOARD

On December 5, 1986, TCB outside director Charles Duncan, in his role as committee chairman, convened a meeting of the Long-Term Strategy & Merger Committee to consider the Chemical merger transaction. Receiving that committee's approval, I then called a TCB board meeting for Sunday, December 14, 1986, to consider the proposed TCB–Chemical Bank merger, one that would create an $80 billion bank holding company, the fourth largest in the United States. Attendance was remarkable. Although we could place no telephone calls before the market closed on Friday, thirty-seven of the forty-three Texas Commerce Bancshares directors arrived by 2 P.M. on Sunday with less than two days' notice. Director Rudney Atalla flew all the way from Brazil.

A substantive, unemotional discussion ensued, one that ran three hours and fifty minutes. Management and outside directors talked about the fact that Texas Commerce had thrived on change for one hundred years. TCB had responded to change and expanded, through internal growth and, yes, through fifty-seven mergers, to be ranked as one of the nation's twenty-five largest banks. We discussed the fact that, since 1970, Texas Commerce had effected mergers with forty-one banks in Lubbock, San Angelo, McAllen, Longview, El Paso, and elsewhere as those smaller banks opted for the strength and resources brought by consolidating with Houston-based TCB. And so our proposed plan, entailing the merger of TCB with Chemical, was consistent with action we had taken for the past one hundred years.

No voices were raised in heated opposition. Directors asked, instead, intelligent questions. What would be best for Texas Commerce shareholders? What would be best for customers? What would be best for employees? Directors approved a motion for the TCB board to meet then with Chemical Bank CEO Walter Shipley.

At that meeting, Don Jordan, chief executive of Houston Industries, asked

Walter Shipley, Chemical Bank CEO, and I were taking one last look at the TCB-Chemical merger document when this picture was taken. (Photograph © Aker/Zvonkovic Photography, Houston)

Once again, a Texas Commerce merger was front-page news for the Houston Chronicle—
*and for many other newspapers as well. At the time, the TCB-Chemical transaction was
the largest interstate merger in the history of U.S. banking. (Copyright 1986,* Houston
Chronicle *Publishing Company. Reprinted with permission. All rights reserved.)*

what kind of relationship we would have with Chemical. Walter Shipley responded, "Texas Commerce is the best-managed banking organization in the
South. We are merging so we won't have to send our people here to run it."
Barbara Jordan, a lawyer, the LBJ Centennial Chair in National Policy at the
LBJ School of Public Affairs at the University of Texas, and a former U.S. congresswoman and Texas senator, asked: "After you announce this, Mr. Shipley,
do you think your stock will go up or down?" Barbara posed the question in
a way that might lead the witness to say, "Up, because I think so much of you
and Texas." But Walter said: "I think ours will go down a point or two. . . ."
Before he could say another word, she responded: "Good! That means Ben
Love has done a good job for our stockholders in negotiating with you."

　　Our directors considered the alternatives and decided that the merger
with Chemical was the forward-thinking, prudent action to approve. TCB
directors Harold Hook moved and Jon Newton seconded the motion to
merge TCB into Chemical, and the motion passed unanimously.

Texas Commerce and Chemical Bank flags flew at Chemical's headquarters on Park Avenue in New York on Monday, December 15, 1986, to celebrate the merger. (Texas Commerce archives)

On Monday, December 15, 1986, at 7 A.M., the press release was issued. Walter and I addressed our member bank CEOs and the press, then flew to New York City (where the Texas Commerce flag flew alongside Chemical's at the bank's headquarters at 270 Park Avenue) to meet with financial analysts. Then we returned to Texas. Walter and I immediately embarked on three extremely busy days of meetings all over the state with every TCB member bank board of directors, with employees, stockholders, and customers. Walter's warm sincerity and visible forthrightness won the hearts and minds of everyone on that energized tour.

★ DUE DILIGENCE

For six weeks beginning on January 5, 1987, more than fifty Chemical lenders with sound credit skills and thorough banking knowledge—truly first-class people—examined the loan policies, procedures, and loan portfolios at sixteen of the largest Texas Commerce banks. Other Chemical officers came from Internal Auditing, Trust, Legal, and Finance to meet with their TCB counterparts. Bruce LaBoon and Robert Hunter coordinated the due diligence from TCB's point of view; Chemical's chief credit officer, David Eyles, was in charge of the New York team. In examining TCB's $9 billion in loans, one of Chemical's jobs was to select $300 million in TCB loans to cede to the National Loan Bank.

Chemical and TCB had similar approaches to credit grading and lending philosophy, which I believe helped David feel comfortable with TCB's portfolio. It was not that there were no troubled loans, because there were, but he was comfortable with TCB's assessment of the risk. Chemical was not aggressively engaged in land loans, but we convinced them that real estate lending and construction loans were essential parts of doing business in comparatively underdeveloped, fast-growing Texas. I recall that Robert Hunter quipped: "They have no land loans in New York because they have no land. They'd have to tear down a building to find any!"

Both banks were overly optimistic about when the Texas economy would turn around and how long it would take to improve some troubled TCB loans, particularly real estate loans. TCB encountered, but was relatively unscathed by, energy loan problems; however, we were increasingly confronted with real estate problems. Chemical had evaluated all of TCB's loans and reached the same conclusions we did. It would be another year, at least, before it became clear that real estate loan problems were of much greater magnitude than either partner had surmised earlier.

By the end of March 1987, the Federal Reserve and the Securities and Exchange Commission had approved the TCB–Chemical Bank merger and the proxy material. This good news caught up with Walter and me in Austin, in

After Texas Commerce Bancshares's sixteenth—and last—annual meeting, on April 24, 1987, Bruce LaBoon and I talked to stockholders. I recall that one man said, "This is a historic moment in our one-hundred-year history—for those who have held stock in this organization for several generations and for those of us who have joined more recently." (Bankers Hours, 25: 3 (1987), Barbara Eaves's archives)

the midst of another statewide whistle-stop tour to visit TCB bankers, directors, and customers. Probably the most intriguing of the many questions asked on this trip came from TCB-San Antonio director Jack Willome, president of Ray Ellison Homes. He asked Walter: "A year from now, how will we be the most surprised?" Well, Walter was stumped, but he is as quick-witted as any Texan, so he handed off the question to me! Before I could say a word, however, Jack answered his own question: "I was a customer of Highland Park Bank when it merged with Texas Commerce in 1974. After a year, I found that nothing had changed, except the bank had much greater resources. What had been a little bank on the south side of town had, after merging with TCB, become a major competitor in the city." To that, Walter quickly responded, "That's the right answer."

In Dallas, an employee, Bill Bogart, asked: "Given Chemical's success in retail and investment banking, how soon will Chemical's products be offered to Texas Commerce customers? I'm already being asked by customers."

Walter replied, "Seems your people want to pick up the consolidation pace a bit, Ben! Bill, if your customer needs one of our products before it's installed at Texas Commerce, call us. We'll do what needs to be done." (And they did.)

On April 24, 1987, Texas Commerce shareholders approved the merger. On April 28, 1987, Chemical stockholders did likewise. And on May 1, 1987, the merger was completed. This union, at that time the largest merger in U.S. banking history, created the country's fourth-largest banking institution with $80 billion in assets and twenty-eight thousand banking professionals around the globe.

This was a win-win combination of the unique strengths of two strong, geographically diverse institutions. It created an entry for Chemical into the rich Texas marketplace and provided the New York bank with a superb Texas marketing force and an extensive customer network throughout the Southwest. It strengthened Texas Commerce through a partnership with one of the country's most diversified banks. Chemical's solid financial resources gave TCB a leg up when legislative and economic changes opened new opportunities that could reward aggressiveness, innovation, and wherewithal. The partnership also equipped TCB with expertise in strategically important areas of technology, the consumer market, and commercial, international, and investment banking. The merger-day button every Texas Commerce Banker wore captured this message in three words: "Even Stronger Together."

Customers did not wait for the merger to begin moving to TCB. The announcement alone paid off immediately in market share. This was triggered by the concern Texas companies were experiencing about long-term relationships at other large Texas banks, *plus* TCB's strong credit rating, *plus* the convenience of branch banking. We were the first major Texas bank to branch fully by several months. Within months after Texas voters opted for the convenience of branch banking, Texas Commerce had branched as much as possible in Austin, Corpus Christi, Dallas, El Paso, Houston, and San Antonio. Large national accounts had historically divided their business between TCB and other big Texas banks. We began attracting the "other half." Smaller businesses that had been loyal elsewhere for years saw TCB in a new light. This was a window of opportunity that comes once in a lifetime.

There is no secret about the way we took advantage of this opportunity. TCB banking officers called on prospects and customers at their places of business—twenty per officer per month. Then, in June 1987, we launched a statewide television campaign to support all of that shoe leather. The rallying cry? "Texans are moving to Texas Commerce."

In December 1987, we followed up with another TV campaign aimed at the individual customer. It also emphasized TCB's strength, convenience, and desire for their business. In April 1988, we rolled out OnePlus, the Texas version of Chemical Bank's wildly successful ChemPlus, a retail banking product that bundled all of a customer's accounts into one relationship, then paid higher rates and levied lower fees based on the total relationship. As one of TCB's marketing people noted, "OnePlus is the way people used to bank." Obviously, people wanted to bank that way again, because ten days after its launch, OnePlus blew through targets set for the first full month.

The results of the TCB–Chemical Bank partnership were profound, and they were fast in coming. We took count at the end of 1989. TCB's share of commercial middle market businesses had shot up from 16 percent to 25 percent; on the retail side, OnePlus had attracted $3 billion in deposits since its introduction, more than one hundred and ten thousand relationships.

Perhaps the most cherished payoff came in the third quarter of 1988. After two years of unacceptable, unaccustomed quarterly loss after quarterly loss after quarterly loss, TCB bankers returned to black ink with a $6.8 million profit. By the end of the year, counting all four quarters, we were still writing in black ink—a $2 million profit. Our tradition and our pride were slowly recovering.

But despite all of this good news, the drag of nonperforming assets, particularly real estate, hamstrung profits on into 1989. Finally, in the third quarter of that year, TCB's partnership with Chemical really paid off when the decision was made to add $350 million to our reserve for possible loan losses. This enabled TCB to step beyond our problems and, in 1990, to produce our first $100-million-profit year in six years.

★ CLOSING REFLECTIONS ON THE MERGER

Our merger with Chemical worked well in terms of people compatibility and shared philosophies. Walter Shipley proved absolutely true to his word that TCB would retain autonomy. His faith was rewarded when TCB's earnings increases finally resumed before I retired, at age sixty-five, on December 1, 1989.

Texas Commerce might have made it on its own, I will never know. But we made the soundest decisions we were capable of making with the facts and economic conditions confronting us at the time. I do know that we were right about the basics. The industry was, and still is, consolidating, and, as I have emphasized, Chemical treated our people sensitively and with respect. I will be forever grateful to Walter Shipley and to Chemical for having confidence in us and stepping in when our ox was heading toward the ditch then occupied by all of the other large Texas banks.

Life is full of possibilities, some of which we never have the opportunity to explore. I had committed twenty-two years of my life to building Texas Commerce into a national power. My ultimate vision was for TCB to lead the way in establishing Texas as a national center of finance. What if I had been able to convince the Texas independent bankers and politicians in the 1970s to support our efforts to equip our state with three or four financial institutions that could and should compete with Citicorp and the other major money center banks that were invading the Texas market?[8] What if the timing of the oil bust had been different, or its impact had been less severe? What if federal regulators had treated our bank in a more evenhanded way? What if several of the major Texas banks could have found their way to a merger that would have created a strong Texas bank? Such questions are interesting to think about, but as the person responsible for the fate of Texas Commerce and its shareholders, I had the responsibility to act in the 1980s. As in my days playing poker at Polebrook, I had to play the cards dealt me. TCB's merger with Chemical was the best bet I could find in the perilous days after the energy bust. All these years later, I look back with pride at the outcome. I also feel, though, a certain sense of frustration and even sadness that I did not have the chance to finish the job of building an internationally competitive bank based in Houston.

NOTES

1. Texas Commerce Bancshares *1983 Annual Report,* 2.

2. "Study Warns Oil Slump Could Cost 25,000 Jobs," *Houston Chronicle,* February 9, 1986.

3. "In 1972, loan chargeoffs were practically zero—0.05% of total loans. For the decade following, chargeoffs averaged a mere 0.18%. Today, they're 1.86%." Barbara Eaves, "What Went Up Is Finally Coming Down," *Bankers' Hours* (November 1990), 1.

4. Greg Seay, "TCB Has Critics Changing Their Tune," *Houston Post,* October 22, 1990.

5. Federal courts decreed the Texas countywide branch banking statute unconstitutional in June 1988, and branching became statewide.

6. In July 19, 1983, Texas Commerce Bancshares formed a new Long-Term Strategy & Merger Committee under the leadership of two extremely able directors, the Coca-Cola Company's Charles Duncan and American General's Harold Hook. This committee was to consider new products, new structure, and new geographic regions that could positively affect TCB's performance in short, intermediate, and long terms. Charles, who served as secretary of energy and deputy secretary of defense in the Carter administration, had been chairman and a major stockholder in the investment banking firm of Rotan Mosle after he retired as president of Coca-Cola. He was also on the board of American Express and several other NYSE corporations. Harold was the chairman of American General Insurance Company and also a director of several NYSE firms. During his five years at the helm, American General grew fivefold in assets and sixfold in profits as he acquired insurance companies, a savings and loan association, and a consumer finance company.

7. Interestingly, over the next thirteen years, Chemical Bank merged with three of the banks we visited at this time: Manufacturers Hanover Corp. in 1991, Chase Manhattan Corp. in 1996 (Chemical adopted the better-known Chase name at that time), and J. P. Morgan in 2000.

8. Jim Barlow, "Texas No Contender Among Banking Heavyweights," *Houston Chronicle,* April 21, 2002.

When I joined Texas Commerce in 1967, I had the unshakable belief that the bank owned all of my time except Sundays. Because
the bank owned my time, I reasoned, it seemed imperative to work
on matters that would, much like Jesse Jones expressed, create a
healthier, larger business climate for the city. His theory was that if we in the
bank were intelligent enough, alert enough, energetic enough, and productive enough, the bank would get its share of the business. As usual, his theory
was correct. No company can consider itself a success unless it strikes a balance and invests in the welfare of its region *and* its industry *and* its profits
(long range *and* short range). And no company will be in business for long
unless it keeps close tabs on its political and regulatory environment.

★   INTEREST IN POLITICS

When, as a ten-year-old farm boy, I paid that bedazzling visit to my uncle O. K. Allen in the Louisiana governor's mansion, politics instantly became
my primary goal in life. I was absolutely smitten. In high school, I debated
and stumped for local candidates, and in college, before I turned eighteen
and enlisted in the Army Air Corps, I devoured pre-law courses.

But World War II had a maturing effect on many veterans (including this
one) that spurred us to accelerate any remaining college education and get on
with life. Returning to the University of Texas, I noted that a business degree
offered me a three-year road to "life" (versus law's five-year road), and that
was the end of young Ben Love's "bedazzling" career in politics. I switched
majors.

Politics had little impact on my life for many years after the war, but that
changed when I joined Texas Commerce in 1967. It changed quickly, and it
changed personally, because Lloyd Bentsen ran against Ralph Yarborough for
the Senate in 1970. Lloyd and I had become very close friends in the Young
Presidents' Organization when he was chairman of Lincoln Liberty Insurance

Ben — As always in the middle of the action, Lloyd

After the dust of the merger settled, Walter Shipley and I had lunch in the Senate Dining Room with my longtime friend, U.S. Senator Lloyd Bentsen. (Love family archives)

Company in Houston. Senator Yarborough had represented my future wife successfully in a trust case while we were at the University of Texas, and I had gotten to know him well after Margaret and I were engaged. I also wrote letters to him protesting when GIFT-RAPS's major raw material supplier, Champion Paper Company, threatened to compete directly with our small company. Senator Yarborough empathized with my "small-versus-large" competitive dilemma (and so communicated to Champion). Reciprocally, I made modest contributions to his political campaigns for years.

Lloyd faced an uphill battle. With maybe 3 percent name recognition across the state, he was running against a well-known senator who had been in office since 1957. Lloyd was a conservative Democrat; Senator Yarborough was a liberal Democrat. By 1970, I was deeply involved in the daily process of trying to earn a high return for the bank's stockholders, trying to create more jobs, and I believed that Lloyd's conservative philosophy was in the better interests of the Texas economy and TCB.

Barbara Jordan was among the powerful civic leaders on the Texas Commerce board, which she joined after she retired from Congress. A lawyer and recipient of twenty-five honorary doctorate degrees, she served six years as the U.S. representative from the Eighteenth Congressional District of Texas and six years as a member of the Texas Senate. (Photograph © Aker/ Zvonkovic Photography, Houston)

Lloyd's victory over Yarborough in the 1970 primary, and over Republican George H. W. Bush in the general election, launched a distinguished career in the U.S. Senate that lasted until 1993, when he resigned to serve as secretary of the treasury. Lloyd was identified several times as a presidential candidate; in 1988, he was nominated for vice president on the Democratic slate against the Republican ticket of George H. W. Bush (again) and Dan Quayle. Lloyd's sterling character, astute business acumen, proven patriotism, unquestioned intelligence, genteel manner, and warm personality contributed to his becoming a leader in the national Democratic Party.

Banking issues abounded in politics at both state and national levels. Admittedly, Texas Commerce was small potatoes compared to the distant money center banks, but from time to time we needed politicians on the national scene to be sensitive to certain components of our business so that TCB would not be disadvantaged by its money center competitors. Closer to home, we were continually aware of attempts (primarily by our own Texas legislature) to limit the growth of the larger Texas banks.

In any political relationship, the key word is "access." Former congresswoman Barbara Jordan, in perhaps the shortest, most straightforward political speech I've ever heard, perfectly described the importance of that key word, access. She had been asked by Bob Fluor, CEO of Fluor Corporation,

Bob Fluor, an effective contributing board member, was chairman, president, and CEO of Fluor Corporation, an international energy-related engineering, construction, and natural resources company. (Photograph © Aker/ Zvonkovic Photography, Houston)

headquartered in Los Angeles, and a Texas Commerce Bancshares director, to address the topic of congressional access by business at one of TCB's quarterly board luncheons. Fluor competes for huge engineering projects with companies all over the world. Many of these foreign business counterparts receive government subsidies, a situation that even today places American companies like Fluor's at a competitive disadvantage. Bob sought insight into what a businessman could do to get his point of view over to Congress so that an American company like his might compete on level ground with, say, a German company for a project in the Middle East.

Barbara was blessed with an incisive mind and a solid understanding of business. I had called on her when she was in the Texas legislature and had made modest personal contributions to her campaigns for years. I will never forget her response to Bob Fluor's question. All of her words had pop. They had zip. They were laced with common sense and penetrating intellect. She said:

I have been asked to talk about how those of you in business can better get your views known to members of Congress. If you think I am going to give you some high-blown, theoretical response, you are wrong. I am going to tell you how to do it. When Ben Love called me on a matter, I always returned his call. When he wrote me on a banking matter, I read those letters personally and I responded personally. Why would I do that when I couldn't answer all of the letters or telephone calls that came into my office? It is very simple. Early on, I got financial support from Ben Love. You may not like that answer. I was not for sale, but I owed it to somebody who had supported and helped me to listen to his or her concerns. That is the way democracy works. And that is the end of this speech.

With that, she opened the floor for questions. There were none.

That was the most forthright, most direct, most practical response I have ever heard to the question of how John Q. Businessman can get the ear of any elected official, whether at the local, state, or national level.

Along with access, you need to factor into the political equation the "sifting process." In other words, do your homework. You need to meet candidates, study their backgrounds, and, if you detect someone with an ethical wiggle, let them fall through the strainer. Sometimes it takes inordinate effort and good luck to find a Lloyd Bentsen or a Barbara Jordan — political figures you trust with your life's work and with the goals of those who work with you, politicians in whom you really believe. Yet, if we ever lose faith that there are truly fine people who want to be in public service, then we have become disillusioned with our entire democratic process. And the alternative? As Winston Churchill said: "Democracy is the worst form of government except for all those other forms that have been tried from time to time." The United States will be saddled with the occasional scoundrel, but this country has been and will continue to be served, overall, by excellent, judgmentally sound, honest citizens in government, who deeply care about our nation and its people.

As legislative issues arise, you win some battles and you lose some battles. My inability to convince the Texas independent bankers and the Texas legislature of the economic benefit to Texas of interstate banking, long before the state's economic downturn, was a battle I lost. Nevertheless, it is crucial for any business to be involved in the political arena and to understand the nuances of proposed legislative actions in local, state, and national governments, especially any business that is, or may be, affected by government regulation.

★ PARTY POLITICS

I grew up a Democrat. The majority of those who were battered through the Great Depression, as I was, especially anyone from the South, were Democrats. My parents believed that Herbert Hoover, a Republican, was a "do-nothing" president; that, despite the misery across the land caused by a 20 percent unemployment rate, he and the Republican Party did nothing but wait out the Great Depression. So, if I had gone into politics, I probably would have begun as a fire-eating, liberal Democrat, identifying with Americans deprived by poverty.

Over the years, I voted both ways. I voted for Truman. I am proud of that. When Eisenhower ran, I cast my first Republican vote, and I never regretted voting for Ike. He was my hero, and I admired him to the point of reverence. Having served under his command in combat, I believe that I earned the right to vote as I thought best for the country, which can be a mixed blessing. Some Republicans still remember that I was out front in my support of my friend Lloyd Bentsen when he ran on the Democratic presidential slate against Republican—and Houstonian—George H. W. Bush in 1988. What a sterling choice of leaders they presented, but what a quandary for the Houston business community. In my opinion, that election produced more ulcers than the plunge to ten dollars per barrel in the price of oil! Even today, if I am participating in a Republican cause, some will ask, "What are you doing here?"

★ CIVIC RESPONSIBILITY—THE FIRST STEPS

I had been active in the Houston chapter of the Young Presidents' Organization since 1957, and I had joined the University of Texas Business School Advisory Council in 1965 when UT recruited George Kozmetsky to be dean of its business school. But my first formal step into civic responsibility, serving the city that had been my passion since my cadet days at Ellington Air Force Base, was taken at River Oaks Bank.

It was a modest step. A good customer of the bank and a great benefactor of Texas Children's Hospital, Mrs. J. S. Abercrombie, was heading a one-million-dollar fund drive for the hospital. I signed up to help, along with several other people my age who were performing civic duties like this for the first time. I organized the contact list so that prospective donors were not solicited by more than one volunteer. We raised the one million dollars, and our reward was the invitation to work on subsequent campaigns.

★ THE M. D. ANDERSON CONNECTION

At Texas Commerce, I continued my community work. One of my first efforts came in 1972 when David Searls died. This managing partner of the Vinson Elkins law firm had been heading the $36 million Houston campaign for the University of Texas M. D. Anderson Cancer Center, and the drive was about 50 percent complete. Dr. R. Lee Clark, the first president of Anderson, asked me to finish the job. I had met Dr. Clark in 1953 when he performed the five-and-one-half-hour cancer operation on Margaret that saved her right arm. She was twenty-six at the time. That began a debt of gratitude that I could never repay—especially for Margaret, who has since survived three other bouts with cancer, but for so many friends as well. I am happy to say that we reached that $36 million goal. This was not to be my last effort, or the last effort of Margaret or our son Jeff, on behalf of this superb institution over the next thirty years.

I began raising money for the hospital on a regular basis in 1973 when Thomas D. Anderson, a nephew of Monroe Dunaway Anderson, the benefactor for whom the hospital was named, invited me to join its board of visitors. At the time, I recall asking my friend Bob Mosbacher, who was already a member, "What is a 'board of visitors'?" Bob explained, "Dr. Clark tells you how much money he needs, and you go visiting." I said, "Oh." I served as chairman in 1978 of the board of visitors of the University of Texas M.. D. Anderson Cancer Center and twenty years later was elected a "Life Member."

In 1991, Dick Johnson was chairman of M. D. Anderson's Board of Visitors. He and Dr. Charles A. "Mickey" LeMaistre, who had taken over the presidency of the Cancer Center from Dr. Clark in 1978, and Patrick Mulvey, the hospital's vice president of development, approached me about heading the hospital's $151 million "Fulfill the Promise" capital campaign. I had persuaded Dick, chairman and publisher of the *Houston Chronicle,* to join the Board of Visitors at Anderson, a time-consuming job, at a point when he was not looking for boards to join. But he agreed. Now came this daunting fundraising undertaking, a five-year, worldwide effort to update the institution's aging hospital complex and increase its endowment. At the time, it was the largest campaign in the history of the hospital, and indeed, of the entire University of Texas system. It was payback time. I had retired from full-time work at Texas Commerce two years earlier, but here was a full-time job I could not turn down. I asked three questions:

"Dick, your term as chairman of the board of visitors lasts just one year. Are you committed to being an integral part of the steering committee for the full five-year drive?" He said, "Yes."

"Mickey, are you sure $151 million is enough money? You won't be coming back for more?" He said, "Yes, it's enough."

"Pat, you're the guy I'll be depending on to administer this project. Do I have your commitment that you will be here for the full five years?" He said, "I'll be here."

Then I discussed it with Margaret. Not only was this to be a huge investment in time and energy for both of us, but we owed her life to M. D. Anderson. Our acceptance was a foregone conclusion. Both Margaret and son Jeff, an attorney and subsequently managing partner of Locke Liddell & Sapp's Houston office, joined the board of visitors during this campaign and continue today serving as members at large.

First, we formed an Office of the Chairman that included Mickey and the committee chairs I recruited to assume responsibility for the three major sources of gifts: individuals, foundations, and corporations. Forrest Hoglund, CEO of Enron Oil & Gas, headed the Individuals Committee; the Foundations Committee was chaired by Goldman, Sachs partner Peter Coneway; and Randy Meyers, the retired CEO of Exxon, was in charge of Corporations. Dr. Stuart Zimmerman ran the committee that solicited contributions from Anderson's faculty and staff. The National Steering Committee included everyone from the Office of the Chairman plus the vice chairmen I recruited to be responsible for six Texas regions.

We ran this campaign by TCB's "Blue Book" rules. In other words, we formulated quantified, easy-to-understand goals; we recruited top-notch regional leaders; and we regularly reported, in a broadly distributed publication, the amount of money each regional chairman had raised versus his assigned budget. For graphic clarity and emphasis, we pictured a version of a United Way thermometer to track financial results in our regularly published reports. I know that graphic symbol was viewed as corny, but it communicated! It immediately depicted how much money we had already raised and how much more we needed, both for each region and in total.

Mickey, Pat, and I traveled all over Texas, recruiting vice chairmen for the various regions. We were fortunate in the people who accepted these assignments. In Fort Worth, Gerald Grinstein, CEO of Burlington Northern Railroad, on whose board I served, headed the drive. In El Paso, Woody Hunt, president of Hunt Building Corporation, accepted a job he "usually didn't do." Both cities came in at more than 200 percent of their assigned goals! In San Antonio, business executive Red McCombs and HEB Grocery CEO Charles Butt served as co–vice chairmen. In Houston, my friend from VPO days, John Duncan, worked with Harry Longwell (Exxon-USA CEO) and Dick Johnson to raise nearly $118 million from two hundred donors. Even Dallas, a tough fund-raising market for a Houston-based hospital, came through under the leadership of Thomas H. Cruikshank, the CEO of Halliburton, and Edwin L. Cox, a prominent oilman. Every member of this steering committee was as generous with their dollars as they were with their time. The Anderson faculty donated $20 million ($10 million toward our campaign and $10 million for various research projects), and 30 percent of Anderson's employees gave $800,000 when the hospital was going through the salary freezes and layoffs that marked that time.

Mickey LeMaistre's contribution to the campaign cannot be overemphasized. This very modest man is an absolute visionary, a quietly motivating leader, and a sincere individual who envisions where his institution should be going. Under his tenure, the words "cancer prevention" were added to the hospital's original mission of cancer research, cancer diagnosis, and cancer treatment. Mickey could present his vision in articulate terms. His reputation, sterling character, and productive longevity lent strength to his requests for contributions—or "investments in the future," as he preferred to say.

"Fulfill the Promise" was scheduled to be a five-year campaign, but we reached the $151 million goal in two and a half years. One of the last gifts came at a donors' luncheon. I had just announced that we needed only $15 million more, when W. A. "Tex" Moncrief of Fort Worth interrupted my appeal to the audience. I responded, in a jocular tone, "I'm making a speech here, Tex." He immediately retorted, "I'll give another million, Ben," after which I told him to interrupt whenever he liked and continued, "We have $14 million to go." Tex later told me that he and his wife, Deborah, took special pleasure in giving to M. D. Anderson. "Besides," he said, "you kept looking at me and looking at me. I had to do something."

Dr. Mickey LeMaistre and his wife Joyce celebrated the culmination of the $151 million "Fulfill the Promise" campaign with Margaret and me at the dedication of M. D. Anderson Hospital's Margaret and Ben Love Clinic on October 26, 1995. (Photo courtesy of the University of Texas M. D. Anderson Cancer Center)

During the campaign, large donors were offered naming opportunities for the actual buildings, new operating rooms, and research labs that our fundraising efforts were to construct. (For example, the new hospital was named for Houston oilman Albert B. Alkek and his wife Margaret. They gave $30 million, our largest single contribution.) Forrest, whose Individuals Committee raised $85 million from three hundred and fifty donors, said one day, "You know, we ought to name one of those buildings for Mickey LeMaistre." I replied, "Well, of course we should," and we contacted Bill Cunningham, chancellor of the University of Texas system. Bill said, "Let me work it through the Board of Regents." The regents met three or four times, and Bill Cunningham wrote three or four times to say that our naming proposal had not made the agenda. Finally, he called and said, "It is on the agenda. I've talked to enough of the regents—I know it will be approved."

On the day the regents met, our family happened to be spending our annual week in Wyoming, at Lost Creek Ranch, about fifteen miles outside of Jackson Hole, in rustic cabins that had no telephones. One evening, I got word to call Mickey LeMaistre in Houston. He said, "I have a surprise." I asked, "What is that, Mickey?" thinking maybe someone had come through with a big gift. He said, "The Board of Regents just approved naming one of the clinics the Margaret and Ben Love Clinic. It was a unanimous decision."

Well, I was stunned. Tex Moncrief and his revered father, Monty Moncrief, once labeled me as "mellifluous," and I acknowledge that I am not often speechless, but that news reduced me to stuttering and stammering. I do not know of an honor that could have been more significant for Margaret and me, or more unexpected. I called Mickey a couple of days later to express my appreciation more coherently and learned that another Anderson clinic had been named for him at the same time.

As I said, M. D. Anderson is a personal, family obligation for Margaret and me. Each year, instead of exchanging Christmas presents, we decorate the reception hall of the Margaret and Ben Love Clinic as our gifts to each other. Margaret also replenishes the clinic's candy bowl year-round.

Actually, community service is a family privilege for all of the Loves. Margaret and Jeff both followed me on the board of the Houston Grand Opera. Jeff has been impressively productive raising money for the Boys and Girls Club of America. Jan Simmons, our older daughter, has been very active with Casa de Esperanza de los Niños for twenty years and now serves on the development board for this group that provides a home-like setting for abused and neglected children until they can be placed in real homes. Margaret has been on the board of the Alley Theatre for more than twenty-five years, and she has been a director of the Houston Youth Symphony & Ballet for nearly that long.

Margaret's passion, however, is the Salvation Army. She joined the board of the Houston Corps in 1984, then was appointed later to the seventeen-state regional board of visitors of its officer training school in Atlanta. In 2002, she was awarded a life board membership in Houston, one of only three life members and the only woman. She believes that community service gives as much to the donor as the recipient, and this is especially true in our family's relationship with the Salvation Army. Although we all enjoy the Army's Harbor Light Choir, our younger daughter, Julie, was an avid fan. Thus, it was especially meaningful in 1991, when she passed away unexpectedly, that they sang at her memorial service. Later that year, when Margaret and I were honored with the Service to Mankind Award by the American Leukemia

After I retired, Margaret and I finally had time to relax from a nearly too-busy life and enjoy our beach house in Galveston. Throughout our marriage—our partnership—Margaret has never complained about a demanding social and business schedule that might have some women throwing up their hands and saying, "No more!" She reared three children, helped build a business, helped TCB open or merge with more than seventy banks, raised money for countless worthy causes, nurtured many arts groups, and participated actively and impressively in the continuous job of making friends for the bank. (Love family archives)

Society of America, we asked the Harbor Light Choir to sing. They aston-
ished us—and brought the house down—with a terrific rendition of "Put a
Little Love in Your Heart."

★ THE HOUSTON GRAND OPERA

Soon after I joined Texas Commerce, Stanford Research conducted a
study of twenty-two cities to find a new home for a large, unnamed New
York–headquartered corporation, which ultimately was revealed to be Shell
Oil Company. In the process, they interviewed a number of Houston's company presidents. I was one of them.

Being an oil and gas center, the city of Houston offered many comparative advantages to a company like Shell, but Stanford Research also pointed
out a deficiency. Culture. Houston had no ballet. Our symphony was fair
(Dallas's was better). Our opera was weak and running in the red, and, unlike
the symphony, it did not have a Miss Ima Hogg, a Gen. Maurice Hirsch, or a
Gus Wortham to write a check each year to make up the deficits. The Stanford Research study said their client liked everything about Houston, except
this "cultural thing." So this "cultural thing" became the catalyst that moved
me to accept the position as chairman of the Chamber of Commerce's new
Cultural Affairs Committee and a position on the board of the Houston
Grand Opera (HGO).

Our committee's first job was to inventory the arts groups in Houston
for a Chamber marketing brochure. Jones Hall had opened with a gala arts
festival week in October 1966, moving the symphony and other performing arts groups out of the old City Auditorium, where they had competed for
rehearsal space for years with the Saturday-night wrestlers. Despite this, the
limited number of Houston arts organizations still supported the Stanford
Research conclusion. Ann Holmes, the *Houston Chronicle's* fine arts editor,
was the Chamber brochure's author and, ever a clever writer, aptly titled it
"Houston and the Arts: A Marriage of Convenience That Became a Love
Affair."

Two years later, Houston Grand Opera director Walter Herbert and his assistant suddenly left for San Diego. Although my musical knowledge was
confined to the opera records my mother required me to listen to out on the
farm when I was eight or nine, I was president of the opera board at the time.

As such, I acquired the challenging assignment of leading the search for a director. And so we began recruiting. We wanted not just *a* body but rather *some*body who could refurbish Houston Grand Opera, removing it from the list of Houston's most glaring cultural shortcomings.

We advertised for an executive director and were inundated with fifty or sixty applicants from throughout the nation. One individual, David Gockley in New York City, stood out. He had studied music at Brown University. He had sung with the Santa Fe Opera. He had earned his MBA from Columbia University. He had a responsible position at Lincoln Center. His wife, Patricia Wise, was a gifted singer at the New York City Opera. He had, in my opinion, the perfect background in business, management, music, and performance for Houston. All he lacked was experience at this level; David was just twenty-seven years old. But my faith in the *right* young people had been forever shaped by my combat experiences flying bombing missions with very young men in World War II.

We interviewed David several times in the heat of Houston's summer, the least attractive time of year to convince anyone to move to the Bayou City. The more we talked, the more I was convinced that David Gockley had everything HGO needed: business acumen, opera experience, and visible energy. Our final effort came one Sunday at lunch with David and Patricia at the River Oaks Country Club. Margaret and I listed all the positive features of Houston as a hometown. We extolled the opportunity he would have—at his age—to build Houston Grand Opera into a world-class organization from both business and artistic sides. His would be the proverbial triple-threat quarterback opportunity here.

David made no commitment during lunch, but as the four of us were driving back to the Warwick Hotel, he quietly dropped his bombshell: "I am going to accept your offer." Well, I jammed my foot down hard on that gas pedal and raced to the hotel to call Ann Holmes, who had been an invaluable source of counsel in filling this position. She was sailing in the Gulf that afternoon, but she had told me to make a shore-to-ship telephone call to deliver the news if David made any decision.

David arrived in September 1970 in full voice. He knew how to market the opera in Houston, how to increase budgets, and how to raise money. He learned who was interested in opera in Houston and to what degree. He laid out a brilliant program for the year. He had an appealing, engaging,

New members of the Houston Grand Opera board joined Gus and Lyndall Wortham's table at the Opera Ball in 1972, soon after the young David Gockley was named general manager. Margaret and I are on the left of the Worthams, with Ted and Ruth Bauer and Joe and Martha Foy filling the table. (Used with permission from the Houston Grand Opera)

enthusiastic personality dressed with the knowledge to attract the finest performers.

At that time, the Houston Grand Opera was running about seventy-five thousand dollars in the red annually on an overall budget of four hundred and fifty thousand dollars. But the opera board now had a talented, visionary manager, and we went to work recruiting prominent Houstonians to join and support this man and his mission. The response was overwhelming— from individuals and corporations (including Shell Oil Company, which *did* move to Houston in 1971 and *did* become an exemplary corporate citizen and a material help in building Houston Grand Opera). Houston's immediate, positive response would not have occurred in many other cities. We gave potential supporters the facts, challenged them to help, and they met the need. Just a few of those joining this effort were Joe Foy, the president of Houston Natural Gas and an opera buff who knew every work ever performed; Gray Wakefield, the regional head of Peat Marwick; Lloyd Fadrique, a major real estate investor and a fabulous fund-raiser; John Heinzerling, a successful oil executive – opera enthusiast; Ed Crum, senior partner of the John L. Wortham Insurance organization; and Ted Bauer, then chief investment officer of Gus Wortham's American General Insurance Company. Today Houston Grand Opera, by any measure, has helped fill Houston's "cultural gap." It is, in fact, one of the five most heavily attended, highest budgeted, internationally acclaimed opera companies in the nation, undergirded by more than $20 million in annual funding.

★ THE GREATER HOUSTON PARTNERSHIP

Soon after Margaret and I moved to Houston, my friend from high school debate tournaments and the University of Texas, attorney John Hill, confided that he aspired to be governor of Texas.[1] Then he asked me, "What do you aspire to be?" Well, my aspiration seemed a few cuts below John's. I responded, "John, my avenue in life is business. Someday I hope to be chairman of the Houston Chamber of Commerce." But at that time, I was working hard to build a successful business and had no time for the Chamber — or virtually anything else outside of my family. The move downtown to Texas Commerce in 1967 put me in touch with the Chamber of Commerce for the first time and, thanks to the Stanford Research study, this relationship began with its new Cultural Affairs Committee.

During my seventeen years as chairman-CEO of Texas Commerce, I was petitioned, on three occasions, to chair the Chamber of Commerce, but I was realistic and knew that "I had sold my soul to the company store." TCB's rapid growth consumed all of my time; thus, I concluded, I should not divert 20 percent of my time from managing the bank. If I accepted Chamber duties, I wanted to perform ably. After all, the Chamber of Commerce had been the unquestioned premier civic-business organization in the city for one hundred and fifty years and being elected chairman was the crowning achievement of many Houston businessmen's careers.

Then conditions changed. In 1981, the price of oil plummeted. Real estate developers took the first hits. Leasing slowed almost instantly; buildings on line were not filled. The more aggressive developers—led by Greenway Plaza's developer, my friend Kenneth Schnitzer—began petitioning the Chamber to market the city, something that had not been necessary before because Houston had been the fastest-growing city in the nation for decades with minimal marketing effort. During the 1970s, *BusinessWeek* magazine referred to Houston as "the new no. 1 city of the Southwest." Years earlier, when Anderson-Clayton, one of the largest cotton brokerages in the world, decided to move the company headquarters to Houston, one of the company's founders said, "Houston is the little end of the funnel that drains all of Texas and the Oklahoma territory,"[2] an apt description of the city's role in the regional economy.

In 1983, Kenneth—together with John Walsh, president of Exxon's Friendswood Development Company, and Bob Onstead, chairman-CEO of Randall's Food Stores—raised $7 million and hired an executive who had achieved success running an economic development council on the East Coast. Then, using the Chamber's Economic Development Department as a nucleus, they set up the Houston Economic Development Council (HEDC) in offices down the hall from the Chamber of Commerce.

The two groups seemed to work well together for several years. However, there were mixed feelings in the business community. Some saw in the Council the future diminishing of the Chamber and its traditions. These feelings were exacerbated in 1986 when, with the city feeling the full impact of the second plunge in oil prices, HEDC solicited a second $7 million, money many corporate and civic leaders believed otherwise would have gone to the Chamber of Commerce. There was a funding conflict. When the Chamber ran deficits in 1987 and 1988, it became obvious that the two groups should not continue operating separately, and several of us who had maintained ties with both organizations—Bob Onstead, John Cater (president of MCorp), Charles Duncan, John Walsh, and I—began discussing the possibility of merging them.

Then that fall, the Chamber's president stepped down. That answered one question about a merged organization: Who would be president? Gerry Griffin, a former astronaut, had performed ably in running the Chamber for three years after he retired as head of NASA. Lee Hogan had been president of the HEDC since 1986, and he also had performed ably in his position. Everyone agreed that economic development should be the first concern of any chamber of commerce, and, logically, agreement emerged that Lee should run the combined organization. That left only questions of committee appointments and finances to be resolved, and we sorted these out in a series of meetings among the five of us at Charles Duncan's home.

Finally, we considered a name. What would we call the new organization? We had been using "Greater Houston Partnership" as a working title, but the

The "founding" chairman of the Greater Houston Partnership turns the gavel over to Robert Onstead, incoming chairman for 1990. (Used with permission from the Greater Houston Partnership)

name "Houston Chamber of Commerce," retained a long, proud tradition dating back to 1840 when a city of two thousand people raised two thousand dollars to buy wagons, shovels, and mules to clear Buffalo Bayou and build a seaport fifty-three miles from the sea.[3] Some favored operating under that respected, historic banner, while others felt just as strongly that the newly combined structure deserved a freshly minted name. Then someone, I believe it was John Cater, suggested, "We're talking here about the Chamber's past 150 years. Shouldn't we be focusing on the next 150 years, instead?" That crystallized our thinking. Our working title became the name for the newly merged organization: "The Greater Houston Partnership." Even so, people still refer to the Partnership as the Chamber of Commerce. Indeed, the Partnership logo carries the names of all three groups that formed it.[4]

On December 31, 1988, Charles Duncan's term as chairman of the Chamber of Commerce expired, as did John Walsh's as chairman of the Houston Economic Development Council. On January 1, 1989, the two groups formally merged to become the Greater Houston Partnership (GHP), and I became its "founding" chairman. Thus was fulfilled my longtime aspiration, on the eve of my retirement from TCB, to serve as "chairman of the Houston Chamber of Commerce."

The business community enthusiastically endorsed the Partnership. Fund-raising went extremely well. We were focused, we eliminated duplicated effort, and we attracted attention and new business to the city. During its first year, the Partnership supported Houston's regional mobility program and gained reaffirmation of major federal financial support for a rail supplement, despite vigorous local debate on the rail issue. Alas, voters rejected the plan in November. The Partnership also backed a $130 million bond issue to widen and deepen the Houston Ship Channel. Happily, voters approved this crucial improvement to the city's lifeline.

There always will be issues that generate heat in a growing city. Whether it is the port, zoning, annexation, rail, or whatever, the Greater Houston Partnership is the vehicle to accelerate the movement of these issues toward constructive resolution. The job-creating sector of Houston is personified in the Partnership. I am a believer. I will always respond when the Partnership bugle blows.

★ LIGHT RAIL ON FANNIN

In fact, the bugle blew one Friday night, when a telephone call from Mayor Lee Brown roused me out of the shower in Galveston. He asked for help with the regional mobility plan that the Partnership had endorsed more than ten years earlier. A standoff was developing between the Metropolitan Transit Authority and the fourteen major institutions in the Texas Medical Center (TMC). This disagreement threatened to halt construction on the light-rail line on Fannin Street from downtown through the Texas Medical Center to the Astrodome and Reliant Stadium—construction that was already straining to meet a tight opening deadline of January 1, 2004. To complicate matters, each institution in the TMC had its individual rail needs, its individual president, and its individual board. Dripping wet, I explained to

Mayor Brown that I was *not* a good choice for this job because the then-chairman of Metro, Robert Miller, was my son Jeff's law partner and I was on the board of the Texas Medical Center. The press could allege that I was biased in one direction or the other.

Mayor Brown said, "Great! That's just what I want. You have balance."

Well, balance or not, my first job was to determine the individual rail concerns of the fourteen largest Texas Medical Center entities. I consulted with each leader of each TMC institution in conjunction with the chairman of Metro, Robert Miller, and the chairman of TMC, David Underwood, in private meetings. Engineers from Metro and the Medical Center attended each meeting, as well as Mayor Brown's appointed traffic consultant from Texas A&M, Brian Bochner. These meetings consumed about eight weeks, and, at the end of that time, we proposed a response to each institution.

Primarily, the hospitals were worried about the impact of rail on the emergency entrances, parking facilities, and physical plants of all forty-two member institutions in the Texas Medical Center—sound, legitimate concerns. Of course, everybody is in favor of less traffic, but the hospitals feared that adding rail to the major traffic artery through the Texas Medical Center would gridlock this already-congested thoroughfare. In other words, they wanted rail, but they wanted the tracks out of the way, on boundary streets. Metro felt just as strongly that tracks on the periphery would make the rail line less useful for the one hundred and eighty thousand employees, students, and visitors who come and go to the TMC every day.

These separate meetings culminated in one formal, final convocation of the presidents of all fourteen major TMC institutions, plus Mayor Brown, County Commissioner El Franco Lee, Metro President Shirley DeLibero, and TMC President Richard Wainerdi. At this meeting, we reviewed our findings, the technical work we had done, and our responses to the various issues, including modifications and enhancements to the original Metro rail plan. We concluded with a memorandum of understanding that was signed by the various officials, thus producing a consensus that allowed Houston's first modern rail rapid transit construction to proceed.

These meetings were cooperative and balanced. Robert Miller and David Underwood and their engineering staffs could not have been more constructive. Andy Icken, senior vice president at Texas Medical Center, Inc., and John Sedlak, vice president of planning, engineering, and construction at

Metro, respected and liked each other and worked effectively together. Brian Bochner was there in case of an impasse, but he did not have to break any deadlocks because all participants worked together to solve the problems identified in our previous fourteen meetings.

The outcome was that Fannin kept two lanes of traffic in each direction but added light rail down the center. We identified new rail boarding areas, recommended skywalks, and commissioned a bus circulator system within the Medical Center to link rail stations on Fannin to the hospitals on the east side of the complex. In my opinion, all of this direct dialogue provided Houston and the TMC with a significantly improved mobility system.

Houston's first light rail line opened on schedule, on January 1, 2004. Its first big job was to transport thousands of Super Bowl XXXVIII visitors between downtown and Reliant Stadium on February 1, 2004. It ran without a hitch.

★ THE REPUBLICAN CONVENTION OF 1992

On April 19, 1989, the Greater Houston Convention and Visitors Bureau, under chairman Robert Sakowitz, formed a committee to explore the possibilities of attracting one, or both, of the 1992 national political conventions to Houston. After I retired from Texas Commerce at the end of 1989, Mayor Kathy Whitmire requested that I head a Houston Host Committee to lead this effort. She noted that Houston had not hosted a national political convention since 1928, when Jesse Jones's offer to build a twenty-five-thousand-seat arena in Houston won the Democratic Convention that nominated New York governor Alfred E. Smith for president.

The Democratic Site Selection Committee arrived first, in February 1990, and we struck out. There is no other way to describe it. The only impact I made on that committee was when one member said, "Of all things, they've got a banker here trying to talk us into Houston." Then she added, "Bankers are anti-labor! You know, we are the party that represents labor!" And she proceeded to give me quite a lecture in that large open meeting.

Nobody other than myself criticized me about our Democratic flop, but I learned much from that experience: first, to be considerably more organized; next, to sell the individual committee members before selling Houston. Fortunately, we had a second chance to apply our newfound wisdom. In

March 1990, we made a preliminary presentation to the Republican Site Selection Committee. This committee visited Houston in August to look over the Astrodome and other facilities and to consider our bid of $10.6 million in cash and services. At that time, they were also looking at Cleveland, New Orleans, and Tampa–St. Petersburg. Tampa–St. Petersburg was in the lead, and Houston was a virtual noncontender.

We determined to roll out the Houston hospitality. First, we delivered a coffee-table picture book, *Houston: A Self-Portrait,* by Douglas Milburn, to introduce the city to each of the committee's ten voting members. Then the committee members—plus a dozen advisors and consultants—were ferried from Cleveland to Houston in two of Enron's corporate jets, entertained en route by a taped recount of the bang-up job Houston had just completed with the 1990 Economic Summit.[5]

Mayor Kathy Whitmire, County Judge Jon Lindsay, and I headed the receiving line that greeted the Republican Site Selection delegates when they landed at a private Houston airport terminal. After refreshments, a police escort led the limousines that had been borrowed from every so-equipped company in town through five o'clock traffic to a red carpet greeting at the Inn on the Park. We staffed the limousines with the "hosts" I had individually assigned to each delegate. These hosts were bright young Houston Republicans from every socioeconomic group who had studied the biography of their assigned Site Selection Committee delegate and knew the facts about Houston, Texas, as well.

That evening, Jeff and Wendy Hines hosted an elegant dinner in their beautiful River Oaks home in honor of the Republican Site Selection delegates. I began to feel that we finally might be making some progress when one delegate, a woman from Vermont, whispered, "I think you really do want us. In St. Petersburg, we ate on tin trays in the employee cafeteria. In Houston, we're served on bone china at a seated dinner in a beautiful private home."

The next day, we toured the Astrodome and the George R. Brown Convention Center; we strolled through the downtown tunnel system; we enjoyed cocktails at the Museum of Fine Arts, cosponsored by Shell Oil Company and The Coastal Corporation; and we dined at the Wyndham Warwick Hotel. On Saturday morning, after reading the *Houston Chronicle*'s "Hey, Look Us Over!" editorial and visiting the Galleria, the committee ended their visit with a fiesta brunch at the Houstonian, President George H. W. Bush's home away from home. When the RNC Site Selection Committee left for the airport, they were positively impressed with both the facilities of Houston and the spirit of its people.

Although the committee preferred the Astrodome over the Brown Convention Center, members were concerned about the adequacy of its lighting and sound systems for television and whether enough setup time would be available during baseball season. The Astros solved this quandary by installing the lighting and sound grid before the season, raising it to the top of the Dome during games and then lowering it for maintenance when the team was on the road. The significant obstacle of Astrodome access was totally eliminated when GOP officials said they were satisfied with the three weeks the Houston Sports Association offered. Astros owner John McMullen had arranged the longest road trip in the Astro team's history, and Bud Adams's Oilers agreed to play three of its four preseason games on the road. Both owners made these accommodations at some financial sacrifice. Thus, the Astrodome "belonged" to the GOP.

In early January 1991, three delegates of the Republican Site Selection Committee returned to Houston. Mayor Whitmire, Judge Lindsay, and I met with them for more than three hours at the River Oaks Country Club to resolve final matters and to increase the cash portion of the city's $10.6 million contribution from $3.5 million to $4.3 million. At the last minute, San Diego had come up as an alternative site with the strong backing of John Sununu, White House chief of staff, and Vice President Dan Quayle. They concluded that the GOP had a lock on the voters in George Bush's home state, whereas a National GOP Convention held in California might help carry that important, but wavering, state. San Diego was proposing to split the convention between two sites, but simply could not guarantee funding beyond their original bid of $8.1 million. On the other hand, we had the Astrodome and $10.6 million committed. We felt good about our chances. In fact, after that meeting, Mayor Whitmire, Judge Lindsay, and I shared a "By Jove, I think we've done it!" moment of exhilaration. Perhaps we were premature, but we had come to the last minute of the game and at least we had not fumbled. We learned later that, despite pressure from party officials to accept San Diego, Jeanie Austin, cochair of the Republican National Committee and chair of the 1992 Site Selection Committee, and her ten voting members stood as one and would not be dissuaded. President George H. W. Bush had told aides that the convention should go to the city that offered the best deal. The GOP Site Selection Committee had done its work thoroughly, city by city, and the delegates had voted. The winner, by unanimous vote, was Houston.

Three days later, after our River Oaks meeting, when word came that Houston had won, Mayor Whitmire and I happened to be at the Greater Houston Partnership's Annual Meeting at the Hyatt Regency with twelve hundred Houston business leaders. Mayor Whitmire insisted that I make the announcement. Well, there are various degrees of spontaneity—mechanical spontaneity and, on rare occasions, electric spontaneity. Those twelve hundred Houstonians leaped to their feet as though each had been hit by simultaneous bolts of lightning! The Radio City Music Hall Rockettes never kicked in more precise unison.

Mayor Whitmire then reported to the GHP assembly that it was no secret that political arguments had been made to encourage the Site Selection Committee to choose San Diego, "but probably more than politics, I think the facilities that we have here, the security, the transportation, the volunteers, the city's enthusiasm, and the ability to host a major event and superbly perform probably won Houston's bid for the Republican convention."

In March, before the convention, I received a call from attorney Bill Harris, the Republican Party's professional convention manager. He and I had become quite close friends. Bill asked to have breakfast with me privately, in Houston, the next morning. He flew from Washington and delivered the news that some GOP officials were uncomfortable with my heading the Houston Host Committee because of my spotty Republican pedigree. They wanted a lifelong Republican. In fact, Bill advised me, they wanted Ken Lay. Well, Ken and I had worked together on the Economic Summit in 1990, and I believed replacing me as chairman of the Houston Host Committee was nothing Ken, personally, had petitioned for with his White House friends. So I quietly stepped aside, and Ken took over as chairman of the Houston Host Committee and cochairman of the Houston Convention Fund. I became cochairman of the Houston Host Committee and chairman of the Houston Convention Fund. We both went to work raising $4.3 million. Happily for the convention and for me, Ken assigned his extraordinarily capable and charming administrative assistant, Nancy Kinder, to this task. Nancy and I worked on all convention planning daily, in complete harmony, aided by the GOP pro, Bill Harris.

Voting for the man versus the party can be a blessing or a curse, but I have always been proud of the job we did for the 1992 Republican Convention.

From every perspective, Houstonians performed well. When it was over, the professionals who are expert in organizing major conventions like this even complimented the extraordinary courtesy of the Houston police force.

★ BACK TO THE AIR FORCE

The many civic projects that had been my duty as CEO of Texas Commerce became a joy after I retired, and in the late 1990s, I took advantage of the opportunity to work on several Air Force projects I particularly enjoyed: the Mighty Eighth Air Force Heritage Museum in Savannah, Georgia; the Texas Aviation Hall of Fame in Galveston; and the American Air Museum in Duxford, England. The Air Force has always been of intense interest to me because of the many close friends I made during three maturing years in the Army Air Force and the lessons I learned during those years.

My association with the Mighty Eighth museum began when I received a questionnaire from retired Maj. Gen. Lewis Lyle. He had mailed it to all Eighth Air Force veterans, asking for biographical data. Naturally, I responded. Gen. Lyle had commanded the 303rd Bomb Group based in England during World War II, about fifty miles from my 351st Bomb Group at Polebrook.

Gen. Lyle surprised me later when he appeared in my office. He told me that he and Lt. Gen. Buck Schuler, the retired commandant of the Eighth Air Force in Vietnam and Desert Storm, were trying to establish a museum commemorating the birth of the magnificent Eighth Air Force that had been organized in Savannah, in January 1942, one month after Pearl Harbor. Chatham County, Georgia, had given the prospective museum a high-visibility site on Highway 95 that carried millions of cars between the East Coast and Florida, but Schuler and Lyle were encountering difficulty getting people in Savannah or Georgia interested enough to raise the money for construction. I could not understand why. Lew's thoughtful, enthusiastic presentation certainly sold me, and the museum offered prospects of powerful economic benefits to the region. It also was in keeping with Savannah's visible dedication to historic events since the Revolutionary War.

I had long served on the board of Cox Enterprises, the large national media corporation headquartered in Atlanta, and offered to set up a meeting with Gen. Lyle and Cox CEO Jim Kennedy the next time I was in Atlanta for a board meeting. Jim Kennedy was immediately responsive and called

James C. Kennedy is chairman and chief executive officer of privately held Cox Enterprises, Inc., one of the nation's leading media companies and providers of automotive services. He is the grandson of former Ohio governor and presidential candidate James M. Cox, who founded the company in 1898. During Kennedy's seventeen-year tenure, Cox Enterprises has increased in size fivefold, growing annual revenues from $1.8 billion in 1988 to more than $11 billion at year-end 2004. Today, Cox is a top ten nationally ranked player, based on revenues, in every major category where it competes. The company has seventy-seven thousand employees located throughout the United States and abroad, and operates three hundred separate businesses. (Photo courtesy of Cox Enterprises, Inc.)

Georgia's Governor Zell Miller. That phone call stirred action! When the state senator from Chatham County heard we were meeting with the governor, he wanted to be there. When the Savannah Chamber of Commerce CEO heard that the senator was to attend the meeting, he wanted to be there. So Lew's and Buck's enthusiasm generated support from the patriotic corporate CEO

Jim Kennedy, the governor, the Chatham County senator, and the Savannah Chamber of Commerce. Soon, the Chatham County Commissioners floated a multimillion-dollar bond issue to finance the museum's construction. And thus, a great museum was built, with displays, art, equipment, exhibits, and interactive videos that would stir the memories of veterans and educate visitors about this chapter of our nation's history. It opened in May 1996 and has attracted more than one hundred thousand visitors every year since. About one-fourth of them are students involved in school projects that build character and kindle interest in our nation's history.

I began work on the Texas Aviation Hall of Fame later that year, when the Seventy-fourth Texas Legislature passed a resolution designating a modest museum that had begun as a private collection of World War II–vintage aircraft as the Texas Aviation Hall of Fame. The collector, Bob Waltrip, CEO of Service Corporation International, tapped me to serve as chairman and recruit a board of directors to combine his sizeable private collection with a new program that would encourage aviation science and recognize Texas's strong ties to the aviation industry. The state had been a breeding ground for aviation since July 14, 1938, when Texan Howard Hughes flew around the world in a record three days, nineteen hours, and seventeen minutes.

Bob Waltrip had a passion for World War II–era airplanes. At first, he displayed his aircraft, which he had designated to the Lone Star Flight Museum four years earlier, in 1986, in a hanger at Houston Hobby Airport. But his expanding vintage plane collection quickly outgrew that space, and Scholes Field in Galveston was selected as its new home. There, for several years, the museum attracted aircraft enthusiasts who were addicted to planes (I am one of those), but it did not attract those who also wanted to know more about the people and events surrounding those planes (I am one of those, too).

Our first job was finding people to help. My natural proclivity is toward strong boards, so I invited five outstanding people with ties to aviation to become founding directors of the Texas Aviation Hall of Fame. All five responded affirmatively and instantly: U.S. Senator Lloyd Bentsen had flown B-24s with the Fifteenth Air Force out of Italy during World War II; Oscar Wyatt, the CEO of Coastal Corporation, flew in the Pacific theater during that war; John Bookout, the retired CEO of Shell Oil Company, and Tom Landry, the legendary coach of the Dallas Cowboys, flew B-17s with the Eighth Air Force out of England; and Malcolm Gillis, the president of Rice University, was an avid aviation buff.

One of this board's jobs was to induct annually into the Hall of Fame select individuals who had Texas roots and who were tied to aviation. Our first inductees, in 1997, included President George H. W. Bush, a naval pilot who was shot down during World War II in the Pacific; Senator Bentsen; Beryl Erickson, lead engineer of the B-58 and a test pilot; and Maj. Gen. Joe Kilgore, a highly decorated Army Air Corps hero from World War II. Subsequently, we inducted the first pilot to fly solo around the world (Wiley Post) and others with records of extraordinary distinction, including combat pilots, astronauts, test pilots, aviation pioneers, aircraft designers, aviation entrepreneurs—and, finally, one football coach and one banker who had flown combat missions over Germany in World War II. Tom Landry and I were honored in 1999.

Today, the Texas Aviation Hall of Fame houses the largest collection of World War II–vintage aircraft in the world, including one of only nine airworthy B-17s that regularly flies. Indeed, the majority of the thirty-eight to forty planes in the collection are in flying condition. The museum attracts more than seventy-five thousand visitors to Galveston each year and thousands more to air shows all over the world.

★ THE IMPORTANCE OF CIVIC LEADERSHIP

I believe civic leadership means doing something that will help a community enhance the quality of its educational, cultural, and economic environment. Why is this important to business? Well, I am reminded of a story related so well in *But Also Good Business,* the centennial history of Texas Commerce Banks, written by Walter Buenger and Joe Pratt:

> In 1931, two Houston banks stood at the brink of failure, but financial contributions from the city's major banks and industrial corporations averted disaster. Jesse Jones, who was chairman of the National Bank of Commerce of Houston and soon to be head of the Reconstruction Finance Corporation under President Franklin D. Roosevelt, orchestrated the rescue effort. When the crisis had passed, Houston's financial institutions remained standing, shaken but sturdy. Panic had been prevented; runs on banks had been stemmed. The regional banking system had survived, largely intact. When asked about these events, Jones observed that the cooperative actions of those who contributed to the rescue effort

were "patriotic acts, but good business as well." His words reflected an attitude toward banking which Jones shared with his counterparts in other Houston banks: What was good for their region was good for their banks.[6]

Call it patriotism, call it enlightened self-interest, call it what you will. I believe strongly that every businessman owes it to his community to do those things on the public stage that improve his region because it is "also good business."

At Texas Commerce, civic obligations were part of my job description as CEO; they were my duty. I enjoyed them. They are still part of my job description as a retired CEO and citizen of Houston, and I still enjoy them. I enjoy applying the lessons I have learned at various stages of my life, hopefully helping the city that has helped me so much. I only wish these lessons had been as simple for me to learn as they sounded when I put them into these twenty-eight words:

"Define a common goal. Organize the work to be done. Pick good people who support that goal and therefore would be motivated to help. Stay focused. Work hard."

That being said, the environment helps, too. Houston provides an environment and a certain challenge where, if the bugle blows, people fall out. If there is a job to do, leadership emerges and the job gets done. I sensed this spirit when I was an Air Force cadet at Ellington Field in 1943, off duty on weekends, riding in the backseat of that car listening to Ralph Schnitzer Sr. and Bob Straus talk about the future of this city. "We *can* do this," they would say. Or, "we *can* do that." They never said, "I *wish* we could do this . . ."

I sensed this same spirit when the opera board recruited David Gockley and raised the money to put Houston Grand Opera on the nation's cultural map. I felt it in the late 1980s, when this community, under the sterling leadership of Bob Cizik, CEO of Cooper Industries, rallied more than thirty-five hundred donors and raised $66 million in private funds to build the Wortham Theatre in the midst of Houston's deep recession. I felt it again when the Houston Host Committee won the bid for the 1992 Republican Convention.

And I feel it today, with an ongoing sense of gratitude to Houston and Houstonians for the opportunity both have provided to a newcomer who was raised during the Great Depression on a farm in Lamar County in Northeast Texas.

NOTES

1. Instead of *the* one top job in Texas, John Hill was to hold three top state jobs: secretary of state, attorney general, and chief justice of the Texas Supreme Court.

2. David G. McComb, *Houston: The Bayou City* (Austin: University of Texas Press, 1969), 77.

3. Marvin Hurley, *Decisive Years for Houston* (Houston: Houston Magazine, 1966), 27.

4. The Houston Chamber of Commerce and the Houston Economic Development Council were joined by Houston World Trade Association, a third area group that promoted trade and development, in July 1989. We debated whether to invite the Greater Houston Convention & Visitors' Bureau and the Downtown Houston organization to join, but decided that the Convention and Visitors' Bureau's use of public funding would change the focus of our privately funded partnership, and Downtown Houston's sharp focus on the central business district was too specific for our Greater Houston–area scope.

5. One strong boost for Houston came that summer as the city's hosting of the 1990 Economic Summit garnered rave reviews. That optimism was tempered, however, by concern that the GOP might send the convention (along with economic benefits estimated at $60 million to $100 million) elsewhere to avoid the appearance of a Houston bias. "Convention '92/Closing the Deal," *Houston Chronicle,* August 16, 1990.

6. Buenger and Pratt, *But Also Good Business,* 3.

More than sixty years after leaving Paris, Texas, for college, I returned there to visit the graves of my parents at the Evergreen Cemetery and my grandparents' graves at the Hopewell Cemetery and to take a look at the farmhouse and the town. The house, so bright and large in the eyes of a child, seemed shrunken in size by my lifetime of experiences. As I toured the area that had marked the boundaries of most of my life during the Great Depression, I could not help but reflect that my values and attitudes had been formed by those years. Much of who I am and what I became reflected the world of that 150-acre farm near Paris, Texas, in the 1930s.

★   LESSONS FROM THE FARM

The demands of the Great Depression shaped the generation that grew up in the 1930s, my generation. Economic security became our dominant concern, but we also came away with eternal empathy for those less fortunate. We understood at a gut level that life could be very hard and that personal sacrifices and the help of others were needed to survive. Nothing was guaranteed. Hard work was a daily fact of life but no guarantee of success. These values proved useful during the extreme demands of World War II and shaped the behavior of most of the Great Depression generation for the rest of our lives. With few exceptions, we "ran scared."

We also came out of these years with a healthy respect for our nation and our democratic system. We had held together as a nation through its greatest economic challenge. We had used democratic institutions to begin to address common problems. The electricity brought to our farm in the late 1930s by the Roosevelt Rural Electrification Administration, for example, fundamentally altered our living conditions and opened many economic and educational horizons.

Closer to home, I saw firsthand that one woman's passion and activism could establish a new school bus route that enabled me, and others, to attend high school. Even in the hardest of times, the American nation still found ways to offer upward mobility to those with a true work ethic, ambition, and promise. A poor farm boy named Benton Love could find a path to college even as his parents continued to struggle to make a go of it on a once-deserted family farm in Hopewell, Texas.

My own journey turned sharply upward when I hitchhiked from home to attend Trinity University on a debate scholarship, duly supplemented by an afternoon sales job at the Cheeves Brothers department store in downtown Waxahachie. Twists and turns in the road later took me far from the farm, to Austin, England, and Houston, but throughout my journey, I carried with me much that I had learned in my years on the farm and in Paris.

Like many others who grew up in the Great Depression, I have continued to embrace many of the lessons I learned in that era. Indeed, when Margaret and I had our own family after World War II, I formed a nightly habit of telling the children—first Jeff, then Jan, then Julie—bedtime stories about my life on the farm. Each story began with "once upon a time" and ended with the implied moral lesson about the value of work, education, determination, and family or the importance of keeping one's commitments. I told the stories in part to try to help my children place in perspective the life of relative prosperity they enjoyed in postwar Houston. But I also told them to remind myself of where I was from and who I was. Years later, at the urging of my children, I repeated the stories to my grandchildren, whose daily reality was far removed from the world I had experienced as a child. One evening, after overhearing me tell one of the stories to my granddaughter, my daughter Jan (affectionately called "The Little General" . . . and not without some justification) convinced me to spend a contemplative retreat at my Galveston beach house and write down these stories for future generations. I must admit the project also gave me pleasure and an overwhelming sense of gratitude to my parents.

The stories stress the importance of a strong work ethic. I learned about hard work first from the daily example of my parents going about the repetitive, physically demanding, stressful drudgery required to keep food on the table and clothes on our backs. The memory of helping clean out the cistern, trying to contribute, still fills me with a sense of sharing. I also recall a less triumphant story of my first day's work for wages. I was employed as a water boy for a crew of a dozen farmers as they baled hay from sunup to sundown. All day, in the hot sun, I hoisted one-hundred-pound blocks of ice into the water barrel, struggling to keep the water free of grass and dirt that swirled in when I opened the lid. At the end of the day, the owner of the baling machine paid me by handing me all the change in his pocket—a grand total of sixteen cents for twelve hours of work! That and such experiences as watching an eager crew of carpenters build our home for a dollar a day reinforced the central lesson of the Great Depression: life was not easy. Hard work was a fundamental part of life.

Another lesson was the need to keep your word and your commitments. My mother's extreme determination to send me off to school on our horse Billy every day, regardless of floods or sleet storms, instilled in me a similar determination to uphold my end of the bargain she had made with the teachers and principal at West Paris Elementary School. Her determination to "make your word as good as a government bond"—her absolute refusal to admit that she and Dad could not deliver the missing farm boy to the class play (as recounted in chapter 1)—made me wonder later in life whether a government bond could be as good as her word! Even the memory of Billy plodding steadfastly forward through a sleet storm on the way to West Paris Elementary School remains a clear symbol in my memory that responsibilities are to be met and commitments are to be kept, especially when conditions are most demanding.

One obligation that my family and others tried to keep, even during the hard times of the 1930s, was responsibility for the less fortunate. Even in the worst of times, when the Love family lived in the old house on the Hopewell farm, my mother made certain that I had a penny to put in the collection plate. Some Sundays, mine was the only coin in the plate, but by training me to give to others, even when we had little for ourselves, Mother taught me the importance of caring for my fellow man and being generous with people in need.

My parents demonstrated the virtue of charity to me even more forcefully one harsh winter on the farm, when they took in an African-American man named Joe, who appeared at the door in dire need during a December storm. The racial divide was the great blind spot of white southerners in these years, but my parents looked past Joe's color to the man in need and gave him food and shelter throughout the winter.

In the same way, others reached out to my family. The help of Aunt Bess and Uncle Oscar Allen changed our lives. Miss Katie Feeser and Dr. Charles "Preacher" Dickey saw something of value in me and went far beyond the call of duty to help me win a college scholarship and increase my opportunities in life. My mother and dad did the same for me throughout our years on the farm. With only three of us there to work, they nonetheless encouraged me to focus first on my education and organized much of their daily life around their quest for their son's improvement.

Above all else, my mother implanted deeply within me the ambition to use education to improve my lot in life. No doubt the poverty of the Great Depression drove me and many others of my generation to strive for success. Poverty is a strong spur to personal ambition, but seeing the wealth of my relatives in Baton Rouge gave me a visible, unforgettable image of a different way of life and further motivated me to seek a bridge out of poverty. My mother's passion for education showed me the tools to build that bridge, and I thank her to this day for the determination and drive she helped place in me through the example of her own behavior. My father was her strong-but-silent partner through this testing journey.

I carried away from this phase of my life an extraordinary respect for the power of education to transform lives. In the years I ran Texas Commerce Banks, I instituted hiring practices that recruited employees from the top 10 percent academically of the best universities in the nation. In my personal philanthropy and community service, I have remained deeply involved in institutions of higher education. Clearly, my early experiences going to school in Paris, riding my horse Billy twelve miles per day, left a lasting mark on me.

Looking back, my own trust in quantitative measures of performance began to take hold during these years. For a poor, insecure farm boy competing for success and acceptance in the "city" schools of Paris, grades were a concrete measure of accomplishment. Mother used my grades and honors such as election to class offices to "keep score." Quantified, top grades became the symbol that our sacrifices and efforts were justified. They allowed me to please my mother and to convince myself that I could succeed, even prosper, in my new, more competitive surroundings. Such numerical standards seemed to offer the fairest, most telling measure of success. Subsequently, in the Army Air Corps, in business, and in banking, I have trusted the sharp explanatory power of well-organized data. I remained convinced of the value of clear quantitative standards in measuring and rewarding comparative performance.

★ ## LESSONS FROM THE ARMY AIR CORPS

My years in the Army Air Corps taught me useful concepts of management. The Eighth Air Force was efficiently run. It had a clear strategy—daylight bombing of key German industries—that proved effective in the long run. To execute such an untried, daring, costly strategic plan required excellent logistics, disciplined organization, imaginative planning, and high morale. Of course, a strong element of "top down" management defined targets and set priorities, but the Eighth Air Force also asked, and received, extraordinary initiative from the young crews who risked their lives daily in implementing this strategy over Germany by bombing Hitler's war-making facilities.

One particular lesson from the 351st Bomb Group, for example, has proved useful to me many times since my Air Force days: "Plan, train, assign duties clearly, keep score—and create a report card. The crew will take care of the rest." For example, a navigator's primary job was to know his plane's location at all times. The pilot's job was to follow the compass headings the navigator gave him. Keeping a detailed log of his plane's ever-changing location was of life-and-death importance because if his plane was shot out of formation, the burden fell to the navigator—no one else—to steer his crew back to safety.

As a lead navigator, I collected logs from the navigators in our 351st Bomb Group after each mission and forwarded them up to 94th Wing Headquarters. Exhortations for better logs would come down periodically, but when the group flew the next mission, the same few navigators turned in the occasional haphazard log entries.

So, in pondering how I could focus these navigators' attention on their duty, I created a graphic "report card." I identified each navigator with a color. In the debriefing room, I installed a huge map of Europe, stretched it across an entire wall, and covered it with a plastic overlay. Then after each mission, I plotted each plane's position along the flight path from its navigator's mission log. I included any extreme variances entered by the "lost" navigators for all the crews to see. Sometimes a navigator's position entry in his log would be fifty miles off his squadron's actual position at a given time.

That map produced swift and improved results. My navigators started posting more position entries in their flight logs. They kept up. Instead of just following the leader, each navigator—in order to avoid post-mission public embarrassment—became intent on knowing where he was throughout each mission and recording that location and time in his logs. I did not have to force them. The facts did that. Each crew let their navigator know, in no uncertain terms, that he better know where their plane was at all times because their lives most probably would depend on knowing that position if their plane was shot out of the formation.[1]

A key to morale was the charismatic, courageous leadership from those above us in the chain of command. The 351st Bomb Group's top command officers concretely demonstrated "leading by example." It mattered to us that our superior officers, long finished with their required tours of duty, would climb back into B-17s and fly with us on important missions. For Colonels Robert Burns and Clint Ball to be putting their lives on the line, again, after they had completed their twenty-five-mission tours reminded us that we all shared a common duty, a common commitment to the overriding goal of defeating the enemy. This bonded us. It helped all crews face the possibility of death each time we flew a mission.

Finally, I knew that I had done my duty in the face of grave and real danger. I felt then, and still experience today, a sense of inner confidence because of this unforgettable chapter in my life. More strongly, I also feel a sense of obligation to those who did not come back. To see comrades die when their B-17 explodes right beside you in the air is to understand the meaning of abstract terms like "courage" and "sacrifice." Having witnessed such sacrifice, most survivors came away committed to making their lives count for something that honored both life itself and the memories of those who did not return.

The war gave me an urgency to live fully, but it also gave me a deep sense of what was real in life. It further prepared me to endure hardship and danger and pressure. It equipped me in later life to be optimistic and to persevere when business conditions seriously deteriorated. It reinforced in me a determination to succeed, to survive, no matter what the odds. Those of us who survived combat over Hitler's Germany were not likely to think of many business problems later as matters of life and death.

The shared experience of young men living together in extreme circumstances tended to create very close ties very quickly. I still value immensely and with deep emotion the friendships I made in this period of my life. I have kept in touch with some of these men and attended various reunions—invariably noting that those who served with me are growing older! We share strong memories of America in an increasingly distant time that younger generations perhaps cannot quite understand. That feeling helps explain my work for the Mighty Eighth Air Force Heritage Center in Savannah, Georgia. I also have helped raise funds for both the American Air Museum in Britain and Holocaust Museum Houston and served as founding chairman of the Texas Aviation Hall of Fame, headquartered in Galveston.

One pleasant memory of a trip back to Polebrook was the day in 1963 that I raced down one of the 351st Bomb Group's abandoned runways in a rented car, trying to demonstrate to the members of my "crew"—my wife Margaret and my children Jeff, Jan, and Julie—what it had felt like to take off in a B-17. They laughed and screamed, fearing I had gone berserk. Pheasants flew wildly in all directions. Farmers stopped their work and gaped at our car speeding along at eighty-five miles per hour over a decaying World War II runway in the middle of a barley field, a relic of a struggle to rid Europe of Hitler's inhumane cruelty from a time almost forgotten. It was a moment of recaptured youth and daring, mixed with traces of madness. And we survived!

The memories of this wartime period of my life center on the satisfaction of being part of a nation that suddenly was confronted with a hard job and came together to get it done. Lloyd Bentsen, who had been a B-24 pilot in the Fifteenth Air Force, bombing Hitler's war machine from Italy, before his successful business career and service as a U.S. senator from Texas and as U.S. secretary of treasury, summed up this sentiment very well in a speech he gave at the Cambridge Memorial Cemetery in 1994. He said: "Those of us who flew had a job—take control of the air, shut down German industries, destroy the fuel supplies and refineries, cut the supply lines, support the landings." Acknowledging the dangerous nature of this job, he noted that fear was put aside by a sense of duty: "Scared? Of course. Anyone who wasn't was either a fool or had no imagination. But they pressed on. It was love of country, and all it stood for, home, family, because it was expected of them. And it was the knowledge that the nation was pulling together, every friend, every farm and factory."[2]

Those of us who fought for the United States emerged from the war with a heightened sense of respect and admiration for our nation and its citizens, and this deep patriotism shaped our lives forever after.

★ THE LESSONS FROM GIFT-RAPS AND GIBSON-CIT

From Gibson and CIT, I absorbed the enhanced lessons of professional financial planning, defined statistical goals, and carefully developed cost controls. Specifically, these involved formal organization charts, written job descriptions, clear-cut definitions of responsibility with appropriate authority, specific marketing plans, expert budgeting, tight financial controls, and open channels of communication. At GIFT-RAPS, I had been a disciple of statistical goals and cost controls, but from Gibson and CIT, I learned that, instead of planning ahead one year, you could accomplish your goals more effectively by forecasting three to five years in the future. Although a company might actually underachieve a five-year plan by 10 percent or so, the exercise, although time-consuming, was still useful because it stretched your mind and your planning into the future.

Also from Gibson and CIT, I learned about the impact of an acquisition and a stock acquisition versus a cash acquisition. A merger effected by an exchange of stock benefits an entrepreneur in several respects. First, it saves taxes. More importantly, it locks him in, gives him "a piece of the rock," and lets him continue to work for his own operation, especially if his earnings "count." For example, if a fellow's company is contributing thirty cents toward the parent company's $3 in earnings, he perceives that his company's efforts may help his own stock appreciate in value. If, however, the parent operation is so large that his unit's contribution is imperceptible, then his incentive may be dulled unless he is kept challenged. In a cash transaction, on the other hand, the entrepreneur becomes a paid employee with a bundle of money. He may enjoy the new arrangement for a while, but eventually, he likely will invest his cash (and his managerial interest) in other enterprises. There are situations where one kind of acquisition works better than the other, but as a general rule, I prefer stock acquisitions—or *mergers,* as I strongly prefer to identify them. Either way, when merging with a company built by an entrepreneur, one of the parent corporation's major challenges is to maintain that original entrepreneur's interest in the ongoing, consolidated concern. These are some of the more valid merger considerations—product, people, profit.

At GIFT-RAPS, I learned the value of negotiating favorable terms and prices on raw materials from suppliers. Persistently pound away until you get what you need, then live up to your commitment to the letter. Pay every bill on time. Do not spend money on overhead, especially to build a structure that eats meaningful cash immediately and generates profits years later. At GIFT-RAPS, such overhead would have meant a large sales organization. At Texas Commerce Bancshares, it would have meant a large holding company staff.

My experience at GIFT-RAPS also taught me that consulting one-on-one with the foremen at our distant supplier mills revealed information (such as placing orders for our raw material in quantities that reduced the supplier mills' production costs) that saved us money and helped capitalize our comparatively small company, even while enabling the supplier mill to increase its profits on our orders. The efficiencies we gained by "going to the guys who produced the product" played strongly into my decision at River Oaks Bank (and later at Texas Commerce Bank) to send lenders, not salesmen, to call on customers. Champion Paper Company's decision to compete against GIFT-RAPS—its own customer—drove home the value of financially supporting certain politicians and maintaining an open, honest relationship with government officials and regulators, a policy that was invaluable as Texas Commerce Bancshares built its statewide organization during the 1970s and 1980s. An astute businessman pays attention to the decisive impact politics can have on his business and learns to participate actively in and manage this often crucial relationship.

Finally, the most exhausting lesson resulted from the effort to meet soaring sales volumes after distributing the GIFT-RAPS sales catalogues to all three hundred in the Gibson sales force at one time. To service the abnormal surge in business, we were forced to run our production three shifts a day and spread our experienced plant supervisors too thin. If confronted with a similar situation again, I would phase in the process, rather than trying to assimilate immediately a tidal wave of new business.

★ THE "LAB" AT RIVER OAKS BANK

Jimmy Lyon allowed me to use his bank as a laboratory. In other words, Jimmy gave me the freedom to apply the lessons I had learned in business and run his bank like a business—which was *not* the way banks were typically run at the time. Traditionally, customers would come into a bank, hat in hand, to ask for service. We turned this concept around, implemented an aggressive marketing plan at River Oaks, and sent bankers out to call on customers and prospects to ask for *their* business. The experiment worked.

We established clear-cut objectives and then structured the organization to achieve those objectives. Simple? On the surface, it might seem so, but we carefully developed these plans and involved tedious detail and discipline. And, of course, River Oaks Bank was a comparatively small test lab. Thanks to Jimmy Lyon, I had complete freedom to implement my ideas. My new program materially helped the bank, and the bank materially helped me. The big financial percentage increases we scored there would be considerably harder to generate in a larger arena, where freedom was more constrained and traditions suited to another era were deeply entrenched.

★ MANAGING TCB'S GROWTH

As an organization grows, so must its management. Unlike a small organization, a large organization cannot be held together with personality and numbers. It is difficult to communicate and exert a constructive presence if you are not present, so you must depend on well-defined goals, on a clear organizational structure, and, most of all, on able, motivated, loyal, informed colleagues.

From my perspective, people were Texas Commerce's most valuable asset, and some of our ablest people managed our Human Resources Department. In 1968, TCB began formalizing job descriptions and establishing salary grades. In short, we began setting up our first professional personnel department. In 1970, we most fortunately recruited Mike Tyson, who had graduated with high honors at UT, from Anderson Clayton to manage TCB's Human Resources. Mike's job grew as Texas Commerce grew. He was such a competent manager that, over time, he assumed additional responsibility for the bank's overall administrative functions and ultimately headed our statewide trust operation. Mike's reward for doing one job well was more work! He wrote his own career ticket.

In 1981, Don Hawk, who had acquired an engineering degree from Ohio State, filled a new position to manage the people assets of TCB's fast-growing holding company. Like Mike, Don did much more. He accepted responsibility for other administrative functions plus the consumer side of the bank, and he coordinated thirteen TCB community banks. I totally trusted and always

One of the ablest executives with whom I have worked, Mike Tyson, joined TCB as head of Human Resources in 1970, then earned responsibility for the full Administration Department. After a hiatus as CFO of the Houston Chronicle, *he returned to Texas Commerce in 1987 as vice chairman responsible for our statewide trust operation. (Photograph © Aker/Zvonkovic Photography, Houston)*

benefited from the counsel of these two men. Then and now, I can imagine no two executives more attuned to others than Mike Tyson and Don Hawk.

I was also blessed by exceptionally hardworking, bright, disciplined administrative assistants who each served approximately two years in that position. These included Jeb Bush, the future governor of Florida; Tom Carter, whose family had ties to the bank for three generations; Jeff Hines, son of Gerry Hines and a future international real estate developer in his own right; and Rice- and Stanford-educated, Phi Beta Kappa, world-class chief of staff Lee Straus. Donna Cowart conscientiously and faithfully processed my voluminous correspondence and handled incoming calls and visitors with intelligent warmth for fourteen of my years as CEO.

A business can be no better than its people. I stated this truism so repetitiously that Ketchum, MacLeod & Grove, our advertising agency, crafted a tagline for TCB's commercials: "It's a people business, and we've got the people." Amen!

Rather than build a separate holding company staff, we made the conscious decision to blur the organization lines between the flagship bank and

Don Hawk managed the human resources function for the holding company; David
Senior oversaw real estate activities involving member bank premises; Beverly McCaskill
coordinated the planning and budgeting activities of Texas Commerce's member banks and
managed investor relations; and Lee Straus was chief of staff and secretary to the board.
(Texas Commerce Bancshares 1984 annual report. Photograph © Aker/Zvonkovic
Photography, Houston.)

the holding company and ask people to work essentially two slots on two different organization charts. Three considerations influenced that decision.

First, we presumed that the ablest people were located at the largest bank
because we paid high salaries for the best people and hired fewer people per
million dollars of loans and deposits than did our four largest Texas bank
competitors. This is a compensation philosophy in which I believe deeply.
I wanted to pay above market because I wanted above-average people.

Second, I was apprehensive about creating a superstructure of people who were not producing business or otherwise contributing directly to earnings per share or asset growth.

My third concern was building a hierarchy of holding company administrators who did not have the foggiest idea about what was really going on in the market. Our basic business is lending money. I wanted information from people who knew about TCB's customers and prospects and about lending money. One time, our directors' Mergers & Acquisitions Committee was considering four identifiable alternatives on a major acquisition. I relied tremendously on Charlie Beall's astute observations of those four organizations because he was senior credit officer of the flagship bank. He wore out his shoe leather every day in the marketplace. If he had been a staff man, perhaps an economist sitting at headquarters, I would have wondered if he really understood the active, real-life market. But when Charlie Beall talked about Houston, or John Adams talked about Dallas, I listened and completely respected their evaluations because they were attuned, knowledgeable officers who were on the firing line, competing against other banks, and therefore understood the market firsthand.

★   ONE MAN VS. TEAM RULE

In addition to Charlie and John, several senior management committees (some formal, some ad hoc) provided considerable input into the day-to-day job of managing Texas Commerce. That this might be unusual never occurred to me until Jack Horner, on the day he retired, dropped by and told me what a culture shock it had been coming from Shell Oil Company to TCB. Jack had worked for Shell in several countries. He was chief financial officer when he retired at age sixty and joined Texas Commerce to run our Commercial Banking Department for five years before he retired for good.

Jack said, "Ben, at Shell, especially in New York, senior managers were graded on how well they executed the orders that came out of the chairman's office. But at TCB, before you make a decision, you call in six or seven of us for input. At first, I thought this was a charade, that you might be doing this to make us feel good, but then I noticed that our input usually showed up in your final decisions. I remember telling my wife, Peggy, this is crazy. It won't work. He'll lose control of the process. But it did work. You incorporated the knowledge and judgment of TCB's best brainpower into virtually every major decision you made. This resulted in better decisions—and there's no doubt about it, you remained in charge. At Texas Commerce, you chose to seek input, then grant autonomy. But you expected results.

"So," he added, "both types of management work."

★ CENTRALIZED VS. DECENTRALIZED MANAGEMENT

When TCB began merging with other Texas banks, we faced the age-old question of centralized management versus decentralized management. Of course, certain functions had to be consolidated—accounting and security investments, for example—and we chose to centralize marketing to a certain extent because all of the member banks wanted to use Texas Commerce's distinctive flag logo and its television and print advertising. We also published a company-wide loan policy. But otherwise, TCB stressed decentralization to keep alive each member bank's pride, motivation, and authority to use their knowledge of their market.

I was determined to retain the spirit of autonomy in each bank, whether it was in Longview or Arlington or El Paso or Brownsville. Some of our CEOs were Texas Commerce–trained and others were not, but each maintained the responsibility and authority to work with his board and originate his own market's loans because lending is the most precious aspect of a banker's job. A member bank might make a bad loan from time to time, but the disadvantage of absorbing an occasional bad loan was offset by the tremendous advantage of keeping that pride, that sense of autonomy, and that creative, productive initiative in each bank.

TCB never dispatched lending officers from Houston to sit on the loan committees of member banks. A Houston-based liaison director, chosen by each TCB member bank CEO from a pool of TCB managers, did attend his or her member bank board meetings to answer any questions about TCB policy, but no liaison director served on any member bank loan committee or presided over any member bank's board meetings. TCB member banks were monitored, yes, but manacled, no.

Occasionally, TCB faced "rebels." The most vocal was my dear old friend Bobby Duffey, down in Brownsville. I invested memorable effort to sell him on certain TCB procedures, but when he was finally sold, he became one of TCB's most enthusiastic supporters. In every way, Bobby reaffirmed a lesson I learned from the master of management in a decentralized structure, Albert D. Sloan, chairman of General Motors in the mid-twentieth century.

Sloan believed in defining goals and policy, then educating managers about their benefits rather than forcing their acquiescence. Sloan's motto for managers was "Sell, don't tell."

We had a troubling time with another member bank's securities investment portfolio until its chairman finally acknowledged that he and his president just had so much *fun* talking to brokers about government securities that they resisted the financial benefits of centralized management offered by TCB's professional securities portfolio managers! We finally sold them on Tom McDade's professional centralized securities system, but that sale also was neither quick nor easy.

Another bank relied on its own petroleum engineer, who, as a consequence of his faulty energy loan analyses and subsequent losses, John Townley and I determined was not qualified to avoid severe energy loan risks. I finally had to instruct that bank to make no more energy loans without approval from Houston. That was one of the rare times any lending restrictions were imposed on a member bank in my seventeen years as chairman-CEO of TCB.

Member banks were keenly aware of their "report cards," the Blue Book's regular numerically quantified gradations of each bank's comparative results and rankings. Overall, however, I believe that each CEO felt his bank was controlled by its own board rather than by an anonymous, autocratic banker or group headquartered in Houston. A blend of autonomy with well-understood performance criteria were the catalysts for the initiative and productivity each TCB member bank experienced in its market with its customers. TCB member banks flew in a single, tight formation, but each bank in the formation relied on its own crew.

★ THE BLUE BOOK

Seventeen years in the manufacturing business gave me a voracious appetite for statistical performance. At GIFT-RAPS, my budgeting was simple but effective, and the highly professional budgeting and planning systems at Gibson and at CIT improved and refined my homegrown ideas tremendously. So I entered banking with a businessman's belief in budgets and quantified goals.

Instead of drowning in a swirling pool of one hundred or one hundred and fifty statistical comparisons, I wanted each bank's CEO to focus on the basics, five simple, clear objectives. For example, banks deal with assets. TCB already had a fine tradition of making quality loans, so assets seemed a logical base for our goals. We quantified each bank's (1) asset growth, (2) asset quality, (3) return on assets, (4) return on equity, and (5) increased earnings per share. Goals should be few in number, easily remembered, and generally accepted as being the most important measures. Our main goals were asset growth, asset quality (as measured by loan charge-offs as a percentage of outstanding loans), and asset profitability (as measured by percentages of return on assets, return on equity, and growth in earnings per share).

I worked with TCB financial planning officer Charles Smith first, and later with CFOs Charles McMahen and Marc Shapiro, to define these goals and establish budgets at Texas Commerce in Houston and then, beginning in 1973, at the newly merged member banks. Marc's industrious, intelligent, trustworthy assistant, Beverly McCaskill, was exceptional at identifying waste and making sure member banks' budgets made sense and fit the overall Bancshares budget plan.[3] The Financial Accounting Group, under our superb controller, Kenneth Tilton, prepared each bank's quarterly performance reports, comparatively ranked each bank in each category, and bound these calculations in blue covers. The "Blue Books," as they became called, were famous at TCB. Each page carried the motto "The whole is the sum of the parts." Each member bank was keenly aware that its part was a visible, important part of that whole.

The Blue Book's numbers measured comparative member bank performance, and it assuredly was a trusted, authentic performance comparison tool and incentive generator for TCB bankers. Some might think it would set off a destructive rivalry among member banks, but I had used the concept of communicating individual responsibility and accountability in 1944–45 when flying combat missions over German-occupied territory and pondering how to focus the attention of each of the thirty-six navigators in the group on his individual duty to know precisely where *his* bomber was at *all* times. Now, as then, I resorted to graphics. But now, instead of posting each plane's post-mission log on a huge map of Europe for all the crews to see during debriefings, we published each bank's "log" in the quarterly Blue Book, where each bank's "navigation skills" were publicly, regularly disseminated for all the TCB banks to see and compare with the other member banks'. Quantified! Peer pressure and individual pride worked in both instances to produce compelling accountability, inescapable responsibility . . . and outstanding results.

★　EXCUSES

There are always excuses for not attaining statistical objectives. For example, by the mid-1980s, 28 percent to 31 percent of our loan portfolio was invested in energy. When the industry turned down, growth in our energy portfolio became muted. That challenge did not change TCB's overall loan growth objectives, however. We simply focused on other industries. After all, TCB had only 10 percent of the Texas market. So if we did *not* have 90 percent of the market, but we *did* have the best bankers, and we *were* geographically well situated throughout the marketplace, then we *did* have abundant opportunity. Our bankers, already working hard, simply had to work ever more productively and imaginatively when oil prices plummeted, real estate values collapsed, and the once-vibrant Texas economy went on "sick call."

TCB was blessed with first-class people. They readily accepted the proposition that they should, therefore, generate first-class results. TCB paid top salaries, too, but the performance of Texas Commerce bankers was not all related to compensation. Much of it related to pride and long-established individual habits of excelling—first in school, now in banking. TCB bankers liked to read in *Forbes* or *Fortune* or *BusinessWeek* or the *Wall Street Journal* that Texas Commerce ranked first in most categories of bank performance among the nation's twenty-five largest banking organizations, and TCB did rank first during this twelve-year period, from 1973 through 1985. TCB bankers—as well as clients and stockholders—relished those business articles.

TCB seldom dismissed people outright because they did not achieve, but the bank did have a reasonable turnover. Some left because of the quantified, publicized individual pressure to achieve their banks' statistical asset goals. Others thrived on it. I grew up on my mother's philosophies: "I think I can, I think I can, I think I can," and "An idle mind is the devil's workshop." Universally, TCB bankers "thought they could, thought they could, thought they could" achieve outstanding results. There was not much of a devil's workshop around Texas Commerce either, because there were not many idle minds.

Sometimes a TCB bank president experienced uncertainty about attaining the quantified goals for the bank because of the limitations of the market, but I would counter that that president did not have *all* of the solid business in that market. In the process, however, no TCB banker was ever encouraged to make marginal loans. Our loan charge-offs generally ran about 60 percent of the banking industry average. TCB's Hank Nelly and his Loan Review Group did not leave that record to chance, either. They audited the member banks' loan portfolios, and I participated actively in quarterly reviews of those audit reports, together with most other senior department heads, seasoned, sound, insightful, shrewd lenders like Lloyd Bolton in real estate, John Townley in energy, Charlie Beall in commercial banking, and Steve Bunten in national accounts. If one bank's loans were heading south, Hank was in that bank every three months, thoughtfully and analytically reviewing that loan portfolio and that bank's lending procedures and consulting with that CEO. This procedure, aided by the superb bankers in each bank, constituted the system of loan quality control that prevented TCB from hemorrhaging uncontrollably during Texas's economic downturn. Member bank loan audits occurred as frequently as every three months or as infrequently as every eighteen months, depending on the appraisal of a member bank's management and Hank's lending systems critique.

★   RECRUITING AND TRAINING

I believe that a successful CEO surrounds himself with the smartest, ablest, most productive people he can recruit so that his decision making, his actions, and his programs are the best that can be produced by five or six minds, rather than by just one. I have long believed in this principle, perhaps realizing that I needed the help!

Soon after the 1964 merger of the National Bank of Commerce and Texas National Bank, John Cater thoughtfully overhauled the bank's training program from a ho-hum, five-year-long, "watch-the-teller-cash-checks" agenda, to an eighteen-month, fast-paced curriculum that began with an instructed, in-depth orientation and ended with a year in the Credit Division, analyzing commercial loan applications. From Credit, a trainee generally moved into one of the lending divisions where he had worked as an analyst—just which division depended on the trainee's area of interest, the division's interest in him, and where there might be an identified need.

At first, young line officers recruited graduates of their alma maters. After I was made president in December 1969, we fine-tuned the criteria and concentrated on prospective recruits who ranked in the top 10 percent of their class. We also looked north of the Red River to business schools from coast to coast—from Harvard to Wharton to Northwestern to Stanford. At my own alma mater, the University of Texas, I used a tool the TCB board had given me, my title, to maximum advantage by speaking to classes in the business school. The fact that TCB's president was working on its recruiting team caused people, inside and outside the bank, to recognize that attracting top-flight talent was a priority at Texas Commerce.

I am a great respecter of grades. Show me a "C" student, I'll show you someone who, nine times out of ten, will give you a "C" performance. But show me an "A" student, and I'll predict, and very seldom be wrong, that if you create the right environment and if that person has determined that banking is really what he or she wants to do in life, he or she will be a solid success and constructive force. Like my mother, I am hard-nosed about grades. I think grades indicate intelligence, of course, but maybe more important, they suggest discipline and the desire to succeed. If a student has performed well in school, I believe he or she will perpetuate that deeply ingrained habit of performance throughout his career. This habit was especially important in the goal-oriented, quantified results environment we were creating within TCB.

Exceptions to the "Top 10 Percent" rule were to be made in only two cases: those who work their way through school and those with extracurricular activities that demonstrate strong leadership. Will Williams is a perfect example of the latter. When Will's Alpha Tau Omega fraternity at the University of Texas experienced serious financial difficulties, he organized a team that instituted a budget, collected delinquent dues, and resurrected the fraternity. He did this and still graduated with a GPA of 3.0 (TCB's mean was 3.4). I am proud to say that Will was hired by TCB in 1975. Today he is the managing director responsible for Houston private banking for the JPMorgan Chase organization.

I also believe in giving young people responsibility. If we hire a student, promise him responsibility, put him through eighteen months of training, and then give him nothing meaningful to do, he is destined to be disillusioned and conclude that the employer is a fraud. But if he is delegated a group of SIC codes, if he is assigned a certain number of customers and prospects, if he is given a specific number of monthly calls and a business production budget, then he owns a defined responsibility and an unencumbered challenge to produce. Some produce results, and some do not. But this is my philosophy of a fair test of productive ability, individually and collectively.

The ambitious banker who coupled sound judgment with the ability to produce was happy working at Texas Commerce. His results were measured; he knew where he stood; he knew that his superiors knew where he stood, too. Performance counted. What did not count was whether the banker was male or female, young or old, black, white, brown, or yellow. Diversity quotas, internal protocols, or social connections did not drive us. We were driven by performance.

The training program populated Texas Commerce's most senior positions in Houston, in our seven international offices, and later, in our member banks throughout the state, with extraordinary, but very young, talent. As TCB began to acquire banks, staffing this explosive growth proved a struggle. Banks often merged with TCB in a quest for management. There was no excess of experienced, seasoned bankers in TCB's inventory at the time. Banking had been a sedentary, poorly paid profession since the Great Depression and thus attracted few talented, dynamic young people. We had to recruit individuals whose academic records could guarantee them a head start, who had demonstrated the IQ and perseverance to solve problems in school, and who, hopefully, were mature beyond their years and could thus assimilate senior management responsibilities quickly. Our training program became a tremendous resource in polishing young talent for us and a great source of opportunity for our trainees. The rosters of bank managers and corporate chief financial officers in Texas today include the names of many former Texas Commerce bankers. Most were recruited by TCB and trained during that eleven-to-twelve-year push to staff our banks.

★ COMMUNICATION

One component of TCB's training program, Tom McDade's one-hour meeting at 8 A.M. on Friday mornings in TCB-Houston's auditorium, grew into a cultural tradition for Texas Commerce Bank and later evolved into the quarterly, daylong Texas Commerce Bancshares Executive Council sessions attended by the CEOs of all member banks.

Each Friday, Tom, who was head of TCB's Investment Department and managed its securities portfolio, devoted thirty minutes to discussions of interest rates, the economy, and financial news of interest to TCB bankers. The meetings were initially for TCB trainees, but those trainees did not stop attending after they graduated into TCB's Banking Department. Soon, word of mouth attracted officers from all over the bank. Tom, a Baylor graduate (with a Harvard MBA), and I would occasionally banter about Baylor and UT football scores, but these were Tom's meetings. They were informative, bolstered by charts, anchored in Fed policy, concise, and to the point. By the 1980s, these meetings were drawing standing-room crowds of three hundred to four hundred Houston TCBers, especially the monthly "debriefings" after board meetings, when new officers were introduced and budget numbers were discussed. Just as in the Eighth Air Force, no TCB banker wanted his department's performance to be off the planned mission route and totally out in the wild blue yonder.

One Friday when TCB's deposits seemed to be gaining fast on First City, I conducted a poll to determine when TCBers thought we would pass the largest bank in Houston. I asked, "One quarter?" and twenty or so hands went up. On it went until finally I asked, "Five quarters?" Richard Esdorn—only poor Richard—raised his hand. Thenceforth, we called these the "Esdorn Polls." But you know, he had the last laugh, because he was right!

With the holding company, we expanded the Friday-morning meeting concept to daylong, much more detailed, quarterly sessions for the member bank CEOs, TCB's Executive Council. The results were the same. Every bank CEO wanted his bank's performance to measure up as the Blue Book comparative statistical performance figures of member banks also were projected onto the large screen. The lively exchange between TCB member bank CEOs kindled feelings of partnership and friendship that helped bind the organization together more tightly and productively.

★ LONG-TERM VS. SHORT-TERM GOALS

The American corporation is often criticized for its emphasis on short-term objectives. It is my opinion that the American system, which involves a necessary combination of both short-term and long-term objectives, is responsible in no small way for the supremacy of the American business structure over that of any other industrialized country in the world. Successful managers are those who have balanced the needs of stockholders in the short term with investments that may somewhat dilute short-term returns but pay off in long-term profits, thereby providing continuity of performance.

If a CEO desires to be head of a company for longer than two or three years, he must invest thought and resources into activities that may not reap profits for the next quarter or even the next year, but five to ten years out. If a CEO thinks about nothing but the upcoming quarter, he is destined to fall over the precipice as quarters become years. He will fall through the trap-door of failure.

I believed that our *de novo* banks, for example, would contribute mean-ingfully to our earnings per share in, maybe, five years, but I also knew that I would be long gone by the time they cumulatively paid off big. I also recog-nized that the investment we made in out-of-state banks consistently diluted earnings. Our return on those long-term strategic investments at that time was about 8.5 percent, whereas TCB's overall return on equity was close to 20 percent. We knew these investments in the future would dilute short-term earnings, but we also anticipated TCB's eventual entry into interstate bank-ing, at which time these strategic "R&D" investments would provide entry points into banks in other states and assure the bank's future. The downtown bank in Dallas would be another example of the conflict between short-term and long-term priorities, but did it ever pay off . . . and not so eventually!

So we did strategically invest in the future at the expense of some short-term earnings, but we kept an eagle eye on quarterly results in the interim. On the opposite side of this equation is the dreamer who never produces any-thing today, but always sacrifices today for tomorrow. In my opinion, that CEO is as inept as the one who thinks of nothing but the next quarter's earn-ings growth.

So if your short-term measures are efficiently profitable, then you have the luxury of plotting long-term strategy and investing some of today's money to assure tomorrow's profits.

★   THE VALUE OF OUTSTANDING BOARDS

Texas Commerce Bancshares had a very large board of directors, forty to forty-five of the best business and political minds in the country and be-yond. I remember talking to Walter Wriston, chairman of Citibank, about the size and quality of our board. With the far-flung, worldwide interests of our directors, he wondered if attendance at board meetings was low. I checked the minutes and found that, during the previous year, TCB had 96 percent attendance! Why? Our directors admired and were challenged mentally by TCB's quantified performance goals and results; further, they were stimulated by one another and by management's encouragement of their material participation and guidance.

Included on TCB's active board of directors were such much-in-demand individuals as former President Gerald Ford; former first lady Mrs. Lyndon Johnson; future secretary of treasury and secretary of state James A. Baker, III; former secretary of energy Charles Duncan; former secretary of commerce Bob Mosbacher; former congresswoman Barbara Jordan; Cox Enterprises CEO Jim Kennedy from Atlanta; Fluor Corporation chairman Bob Fluor from Los Angeles; the world's leading coffee producer, Rudney Atalla, from Brazil; Mexico's largest brewery owner, Eugenio Garza Laguera; and many top Texas corporate CEOs.

I knew if these people left TCB's board meetings as bored as I had been during my early tenure as an outside director at River Oaks Bank & Trust, we would lose them. So I put them to work. Our board was divided into nine committees with specific, written responsibilities and authorities. In general board meetings, approximately 70 percent of the directors might participate actively in discussions, but in the smaller committee meetings, everybody participated energetically. We put propositions to them, they asked questions, and they made decisions. We did not put a spin on ideas so that they simply rubberstamped what management wanted. For example, no merger decision was ever made without honest, thorough consultation with TCB's Long Term Strategy & Merger Committee, which was composed of outside directors. They considered the pros and cons of the transaction, the prospective member bank's earnings history, and how the acquisition might improve returns. This committee gave management the green, or red, light. Highly respected business and political leaders, TCB directors answered questions with thoughtful opinions. We were fortunate to have access to these directors' intellect, experience, and genuine enthusiasm about TCB's performance.

The same conditions prevailed at our member banks. I remember attending the board meetings of TCB banks in Hurst and Fort Worth, and in both meetings, those directors paid close attention, intent on producing quality business and building those banks solidly and profitably. Both banks had internal problems at the time, and the directors materially helped management work through them. I credit the management of TCB's member banks for creating an atmosphere that was conducive to their directors' involvement, and I credit TCB's member bank directors for their spirited participation and substantive contributions to their banks.

I expended considerable time, travel, thought, and energy in working with our member banks' boards. At TCB's peak, we used approximately one thousand outside directors in seventy-three member banks in twenty-eight major Texas markets. We solicited business leaders to serve as local TCB bank directors in every community in which we operated. My travels resulted in my investing one day in every member bank at least once a year. I shook hands and briefly visited with employees, ranging from custodians to chairmen. I believed that TCB's CEO needed to be available, to be visible, and to answer questions and communicate on the site of each member bank. In addition to these scheduled visits, I mailed personalized letters to each director two or three times a year, outlining TCB's goals and performance. The objective of these trips and letters was to communicate, to make each director feel a key part of Texas Commerce—because they were. I hoped this effort might give us one thousand "disciples" who knew that Texas Commerce intended to be responsive to their communities and that their interests were not being traded off to Houston. Further, the fees these directors earned were financially digestible for TCB, especially considering the volume of deposits, loans, and trust business these one thousand disciples generated.

During the 1970s, while the five largest Texas bank holding companies operated under the drastic mobility and size restrictions mandated by Texas law, my counterparts in the other four large bank holding companies consistently advocated branch banking, thereby eliminating member bank boards and consolidating the capital and loan capabilities of member banks. Their premise was that it would be simpler and less expensive to manage one large branched bank than a network of seventy or eighty separate institutions. I countered that branch banking would be politically indefensible in the emotional, independent bank environment of Texas. Further, the bank holding company structure offered discernable advantages, locally attuned boards of directors, and respected titles for senior officers. I firmly believed that a board of San Angelo directors could advise headquarters more about what the San Angelo business community needed than the best economics department operating out of TCB's Houston headquarters.

I liked the bank holding company structure. I thought it was the best way to consolidate Texas banking because we could retain local boards of directors, and our local bank heads could be titled presidents, not branch managers. I still believe that there has been insufficient proof that a bank holding company does not make effective use of its capital or its resources vis-à-vis a branched system. A local board of directors for every bank offers many advantages. All wisdom is not concentrated in one man, or one small group, or one often-distant office. A local board gives a bank CEO one more check, one more source of information, and one more direct contact with customers in his market, all to keep the organization heading in the right direction.

Dissenters warned that member bank boards could go off in separate directions, resulting in seventy-three different policies. I reasoned that if that happened, I would have done a hideously poor job of selling TCB's objectives to these member bank boards and winning their enthusiastic, loyal support.

A thoroughly informed board can also help keep a member bank CEO attuned to meeting his bank's quantified objectives. If directors are enthusiastic about their bank, saying, "Look, I am part of this progressive effort to build Texas and this bank. and just look at how well we're doing compared to those distant, large money center banks," then those directors probably would feel involved enough and responsible enough to ask their bank's CEO, "Now, is our bank making its proportionate contribution?" Every month, in every director's board manual, we comparatively ranked each bank in five distinct categories. If a bank ranked fiftieth or sixtieth, that CEO was not doing a very good job, and he might be embarrassed to bring up the subject at his board meetings. His directors, however, would bring it up, because they had the report right there in their individual manuals. Every one of those member bank directors was a winner, and each wanted their bank to be a winner, too. If a bank ranked fifth or tenth or even twentieth, that CEO would savor discussing his bank's quantified performance, compared to his TCB bank peers. This process bred pride, effort, and positive results.

★ DID OUR SYSTEM PERFORM?

Our system was simple. We set clear objectives; we installed autonomous, decentralized management; we prepared quarterly performance reports for all to see; we paid above market for top-rate people; we controlled expenses; and we worked hard.

The system worked extremely well for our customers, for our shareholders, and for our employees. Statistically, TCB zoomed from the fifty-seventh to the twenty-first-largest bank in the nation between 1969 and 1984. In every quarter for sixty-five consecutive quarters, Texas Commerce increased its earnings per share from the prior year, a record matched by no other large U.S. bank and exceeded by only 5 of the 1,510 companies then listed on the New York Stock Exchange. As a consequence of this consistent earnings performance, Texas Commerce ranked first in profitability among the nation's twenty-five largest banking organizations for the 1974–84 decade in compound annual growth in earnings per share (15 percent), in average return on assets (1 percent), and in average return on equity (18 percent). During that same period, Texas Commerce's loan losses ranked as the second lowest as a percentage of average outstanding loans among the twenty-five largest U.S. banking organizations. So these young TCB bankers did perform.[4]

There is no question that our system worked. Whether it would work for others, I do not know, but it worked for us. People often ask me, "If Texas banks were beginning to consolidate fast enough to keep up with the economy they were financing, then why, despite the downturn in oil, did so many Texas banks fail? Why does the state with two or three of the largest cities in the country today have no banks that rank above eighty-fourth in size?

In contemplating the answers to these questions, I am reminded of Reconstruction. Just as the North shoved the South back after the Civil War, I believe that Texas banks were excessively "reconstructed" by northern-influenced OCC federal regulators during the energy downturn. In the 1980s, when the price of oil collapsed, real estate, manufacturing, retail sales—everything—were affected adversely in Texas. However, many New York banks were in worse shape due to their Latin American loans versus our Texas real estate loans. Yet, remember the response of Bill Taylor, chief of staff at the Federal Reserve, when I flew to Washington in 1986 to feel his pulse about merging Texas Commerce with Chase or Chemical. He said: "As an element of government policy, the Federal Reserve will not let them [the ten largest banks in the nation] fail. That's the way it is. But I will tell you one other thing: If we think it is proper, we *will* let any Texas bank fail, because not one Texas bank is among the ten largest banks in the nation." So Bill Taylor's advice about merging Texas Commerce with Chemical or Chase was, in nine words: "You get out of here and get that done." That was a pivotal moment in the history of Texas Commerce and, in fact, in Texas banking.

The Federal Reserve, the Office of the Comptroller of the Currency, and the Federal Deposit Insurance Corporation would not let the New York banks fail, even with their "bushel baskets" overflowing with high-risk Latin American loans, but they would let Texas banks fail, even though, with a little time, the Texas economy recovered and many of the Texas real estate loans would have again become good loans.

The regulators must have assumed that New York, Chicago, and West Coast banks were superior to Texas banks in terms of management and in their ability to steer through problems, even though Standard & Poor's seemed to hold a different view when, in 1983, it named Texas Commerce as one of only two banks in the United States holding its top AAA credit rating.[5]

Bankers, too, seemed to hold a different view. During my years at Texas Commerce, the Financial Services Roundtable (then known as the Reserve City Bankers Association) was unquestionably the most prestigious banking organization in the country, with a membership restricted to four hundred of the most senior officers of the nation's largest banks. Any government official who was invited to speak to this prestigious banking organization invariably accepted, ranging from the chairman of the Federal Reserve, to the secretary of the treasury, to the comptroller of the currency. Its annual meetings were considered to be so important that I cannot recall any member ever missing one. Four Texas bankers had been elected president of Reserve City Bankers since its inception in 1912. When I was elected to this office in 1981, I received a call from Vinson Elkins senior attorney Marvin Collie, who had been president of the National Bank of Commerce in 1958 under Bob Doherty. Marvin commented that the four hundred bankers who cast ballots to elect me made up, in fact, a jury of my peers. I have often wondered if a jury of peers might have thought differently than a jury of regulators during the Texas downturn in judging the ability of Texas bank management to steer Texas banks through this troubled period.

I do know that Texas had modest political clout in Washington at that time. There was no one like Lyndon Johnson or Sam Rayburn who would say to the OCC regulators, "You are not going to do that." Senator Lloyd Bentsen's was the lone, powerful Texas voice on Capitol Hill. One day at the airport, I took a call from Ben Cohen, who ran TCB's money desk. He said, "The Federal Home Loan Bank just called to say they were going to pull out all of their deposits from Texas Commerce—$300 million." Well, not only did that represent a lot of money, it also signified that a major, influential government agency was publicizing its concern about the stability of the bank. I called Lloyd Bentsen immediately, and he advised, "Your timing is perfect, Ben. Ed Gray [chairman of the FHLB board] is due in my office in a few minutes. We'll discuss this." Later, I had two phone calls. First, Lloyd called to report, "You're okay. The FHLB is not going to pull out anything." That afternoon, however, Ben Cohen advised me, "A moment ago, the FHLB pulled everything out of our bank."

The tragedy for the state, though, is that Texas could have been one of the three financial centers in the country. I do not mean that destiny was always in the cards for Texas. It *was* always in the cards for New York, California, and perhaps even Illinois. But it was *not* always in the cards for Texas. However, beginning in 1970, with bank holding companies, the rules changed. The five largest Texas banks were consolidating the state's fragmented banking system, providing us with a currency (stock price and stock liquidity) that would enable us to expand into other states, if only the Texas legislature had allowed it. Instead, oil prices collapsed and the Texas economy took a very rough bump, forcing Texas banks to merge with or be acquired by large out-of-state banks after failing and having federal bailout money injected. Of the top five Texas banks in the 1980s, only Texas Commerce avoided this last fate.

I envisioned that Texas Commerce could become an international banking force. That was my dream. It did not materialize. But I remember one of our TCB-Austin directors telling his fellow directors that TCB had received about thirty-six dollars per share for our stockholders in the Chemical merger, contrasted to First City shareholders, who had received about twenty-two cents. He knew, because he owned a substantial amount of stock in each bank. Then Roy Butler, a supremely successful businessman and former mayor of Austin, spoke up. He was the second-largest stockholder in the Austin bank that had merged with First City. Within the hearing of every director in the room, he declared, "You're wrong. I know, because I owned a lot of First City stock. I didn't get one penny for it!" So, in trying to balance the scales, I guess I would have to take into account Roy Butler's comparison.

The historical tragedy of this era was that every large Texas bank was lost.[6] Only TCB and Allied Bancshares managed to save its shareholders and employees. The OCC examiners judged the majority of Texas borrowers and Texas lenders to be inept and the State of Texas as undeserving of any large banks that could possibly finance the state's economy, much less compete against the distant money center banks. The insufferable arrogance of the OCC examiners (none of whom we would have hired to be TCB bankers) ruled the day.

Another tragedy for the state, and I say tragedy in the sense of leadership, is that Texas had the chance to be one of the three major financial centers in the country today—that is, *if* we could have marshaled that interstate banking bill through the Texas legislature a few years earlier and diversified our markets, and *if* we could have experienced five more years of healthy economic growth. In our own case, TCB's long-term, 4.9 percent investments in banks throughout the mid-America Energy Belt strategically equipped us with a stake so that, if Texas interstate banking laws had been enacted as, for example, they were in North Carolina, TCB would have had the inside track to merge with these select, large, Energy Belt, out-of-state banks quickly, diversify our markets, and increase our size rapidly. Merging with those banks would have catapulted Texas Commerce onto the list of the ten largest banks in the United States. Instead, after merging with Chemical, TCB's interests in those seven out-of-state banks were sold for a $23 million profit, a pittance for today derived at the expense of a much larger profit and opportunity for tomorrow, liquidating our since-proven-sound strategic plan for our future. Today, not one of the nation's top fifty banks is headquartered in Texas. Cullen Frost Bank, with headquarters in San Antonio, is the largest, with just over $10 billion in assets. Nationally, it ranks eighty-eighth.[7]

Whether it really means anything that out-of-staters own all the big banks in Texas depends on the wisdom of the controlling bank. The nature of the banking business is that each banker must work his own market, so one could contend that out-of-state control has made little difference. But what happens if this nation encounters another real credit crunch and that out-of-state bank CEO must decide who gets the scarce credit, that corporation next door or that business down in Texas? In the merger with Walter Shipley's bank, I believed that Texas would always be treated fairly and equitably, and we were.

★ THE IMPORTANCE OF LEADERSHIP

In summing up the importance of productive leadership in any business, I am reminded of Robert Frost's depiction of the man who was neither a leader nor had productive leadership to follow. In his poem "The Death of the Hired Hand," Frost notes that this distraught man had "nothing to look backward to with pride, and nothing to look forward to with hope."[8]

Business managers assuredly have as their primary responsibility the obligation and the exhilaration to provide leadership that motivates and generates opportunities for everyone in the organization, from custodians to stockholders. The "hired hands" at every level must have something "to look backward to with pride" and something "to look forward to with hope." President Harry Truman identified who was responsible for discharging that leadership job when he stated, "The buck stops here!"

With these predicates, I invite you to roll up your mental sleeves and explore my perceptions, after more than fifty years in business, banking, and investing, of the five basic attributes I believe are necessary for successful leadership. They are: competence, a desire to excel propelled by optimism, high energy, a strong work ethic, and integrity.

First, competence. There is conclusive evidence that the successful leader must use disciplined brain power, which is the catalyst for competence. We live in a world where knowledge is doubling every ten years. This explosion of information constantly introduces and accelerates structural change in American business. This structural change creates tremendous opportunities for fresh new leaders. Your ability to think and your competence are tested daily. That inescapable reality is consistent with the philosopher's observation that "every morning puts a man on trial, and each evening passes judgment."

Next, a desire to excel, propelled by optimism. For productive leaders, these terms are synonymous. When skeptics ridiculed Henry Ford's revolutionary automobile assembly line, he responded: "If you *think* you can—or can't—you're right."

Strong leadership flows from the individual who has a clear, informed, *positive attitude* in *setting quantified goals* for the organization and its people—and then *achieving* those goals. Ponder for a moment one cliché, the basic wisdom of which has withstood the test of time: "If you don't know where you are going, any road will take you there." A productive leader's short-term and long-term objectives are not for the faint of heart.

Productive, inspirational leaders are universally optimists. I am reminded of Senator Lloyd Bentsen's father, who, at the young age of ninety-four, was vigorously farming several thousand acres in the Rio Grande Valley. The area had been suffering from a terrible drought and, home from Washington on a visit, Senator Bentsen noted the parched land, brown grass, and dying vegetation. He quietly empathized with his father and asked, "Dad, do you think it will *ever* rain again?" The elder Bentsen immediately exclaimed: "You're mighty right it will! And Lloyd, I'll tell you another thing. At sundown this evening, we'll be one day closer to it!" Now, that's optimism!

The third ingredient is a high energy level. Jack Welch of GE or Roberto

Goizueta of Coca-Cola would tell you: "Talent and ability are not enough. Those traits are important, but they will produce nothing without endurance." Leaders possess a competitive spirit and a joy of achievement that springs from a well filled with high-velocity energy.

Fourth, successful leadership requires a strong work ethic. I do not suggest that a strong work ethic is confined to those who are physically strong. After all, the strongest man in the world probably works in a circus. I am talking about a leader who continually seeks, and will work extremely hard, to develop opportunities in this changing environment. That leader is happy to pay the proverbial price to realize his and his organization's top-priority goals. For this leader, work is akin to an athletic contest: after the action, what counts is the score. Productive leaders identify with the comic strip character Charlie Brown when he declares: "It doesn't matter whether you win or lose—unless you lose."

Finally, the essential ingredient for successful leadership is integrity. Without exception, a leader's integrity is the one quality all others depend on. It is the element that convinces people to trust you, to do business with you, and to follow you.

Britain's famous prime minister Benjamin Disraeli once observed, "The secret to success in life is for a man to be ready for his opportunity when it comes." With these five traits—competence, a desire to excel propelled by optimism, high energy, a strong work ethic, and integrity—you will find abundant rewards in a business world yearning for productive leaders.

NOTES

1. One careless navigator illustrates the reason why accurate position logs were so important. One day this man's B-17 was shot out of formation, badly damaged. He had no idea where he was, so he simply headed west in hope of finding the English Channel and landing at some base on the English coast. In doing so, he navigated his plane right over German-occupied Ostend, and two of his crew were killed . . . absolutely needlessly. Ostend was colored in red on the maps supplied to all of us before the mission. Red meant "WARNING! Heavy flak installations." Translation: Do not fly over Ostend unless you are bombing it.

2. U.S. Treasury Secretary Lloyd Bentsen (remarks, Cambridge American Cemetery and Memorial, Cambridge, England, June 4, 1994).

3. Later, as executive vice president and secretary of the board, Beverly McCaskill applied to the board minutes the keen mind and sharp attention to detail that she had dis-

played in member bank budgeting. We never had to worry about whether those minutes were complete and accurate. They were!

4. *Texas Commerce Bancshares 1984 annual report.*

5. Elizabeth Bramwell, "The Conservative Investor," *Bottom Line Tomorrow,* November 2003, 6. Today, Wells Fargo is the only AAA-rated U.S. bank.

6. "With the interstate consolidation of banking in Texas, which began in 1986, the eight largest banking organizations were reduced to four: NationsBank absorbed NBC and First Republic (which had previously absorbed InterFirst); Bank One Corporation acquired MCorp and Team Bank (formerly TAB); Chemical bought Texas Commerce, which subsequently purchased the major assets of First City; and First Interstate acquired Allied." Joseph M. Grant, *The Great Texas Banking Crash: An Insider's Account* (Austin: University of Texas Press), 250.

7. Cullen Frost ranking on December 31, 2004, *American Banker,* "Banking and Thrift Holding Companies with Most Assets," April 27, 2005.

8. Ben Love (speech, Rice University Jesse H. Jones Graduate School Alumni Association, Houston, Texas, March 13, 1997).

INDEX

Italic page numbers indicate material in tables or figures. Page numbers followed by "n" indicate notes.

Abercrombie, Mrs. J. S., 257–58
acquisitions, stock *versus* cash, 289
Adams, Bud, 94, 95, 274
Adams, John, 199–200, *221,* 240, 294
Adams, Nancy, 94
Ada (Okla.), 33–34
Airline National Bank, 159, *159,* 163
Air Medal, 58
Air Medal Oak Leaf Cluster, 64, 67, 72
Aker, Joe, *211*
Alkek, Albert B., 261
Alkek, Margaret, 261
Allen, Asa Benton, 14, 15–16
Allen, Bess
    family, 3
    financial help from, 7–8, 12, 285
    invites Ben Love for visit, 14, 15
    sells farm, 28
Allen, Herbert, 154–55
Allen, Oscar (O. K.), 3, 7, 8, 12, 285
Allen, Oscar (O. K.), Jr., 28
Alley Theatre, 262
Allied Bancshares, 227, 309, 313n6
Allison, Bill, 148
Allright Auto Parks, 208–9
American Air Museum, 276, 288
American Consulting Engineers Council, 216
American Express, 189, 202
American General Corporation, *231*
American General Insurance Company, 135–36, 137–38, 141n6, 165, 251n6. *See also* Wortham, Gus
American Leukemia Society of America, 262, 264

American National Bank, 163–64, 165
Anawaty, Margrette, 128, 130
Anderson, Dillon, 121–22
Anderson, Monroe Dunaway, 258. *See also* University of Texas M. D. Anderson Cancer Center
Anderson, Thomas D. (M. D. Anderson Cancer Center Board of Visitors), 258
Anderson, Tom (pediatrician), 111
Anklam (Germany), 57
Aramco, 155
Arlington Bank & Trust, 195
Army Air Corps, 31–42
    assignment to Kearney (Neb.), 38–39
    enlistment in, 31
    joins Eighth Air Force in England, 40–42
    lessons learned from, 286–88
    navigation school, 35–38
    training in Ada (Okla.), 33–34
    training in Wichita Falls, 32–33
    training on B-17, 39–40
Arnold, Dan, 139
Arnold, Hap, 41
Association of Reserve City Bankers, 189, 308
Astrodome, 273, 274
Atalla, Rudney, 242, 304
Aubrey, Victor, 26
Austin, Jeanie, 274
Austin Bancshares, 188
Austin National Bank, 187

B-17 bombers, 39–40, 51–53, *52,* 60–62, *62,* 79n3
B-24 bombers, 43n3

B-29 bombers, 77
Bahrain, 155
Baker, James A., III, 304
Ball, Clint, 72–73, 287
Bankers Trust, 232
Bank Holding Company Act, 137, 158–59,
    162, 165
banking industry
    changes in 1980s, 218–19
    effect of Great Depression on, 105–6, 107
    Houston, 106–7
    "sedation and segmentation," 105–6
    Texas law, 178, 186, 226–29, 254, 256
Bank of America, 182
Bank of England, 157
Bank of Pasadena, 204
Bank of the Southwest, 123, 125, 126–27
Bank One Corporation, 313n6
Barnhart, Allen, 39, 55–57
Bass, Hutch, 32
Bass, Perry, 193
Bauer, Ruth, 266
Bauer, Ted, 266–67, 266
Bayliss, Jim, 98
Beall, Charlie, 143–44, 172, 190, 294, 299
Beaumont State Bank, 164
Behrendt, Allen, 57–58
Beissner, Henry, 109
Bemrose, John, 223
Bentley, Henrietta, 9–10, 22
Bentsen, Lloyd
    father, 311
    military service, 288
    in Senate, 95, 181, 252–54, 253, 257,
        308–9
    and Texas Aviation Hall of Fame, 278,
        279
    and Young Presidents' Organization,
        94, 95
Berlin (Germany), 57–58
Berry, Jim, 190
Bexar County National Bank, 188
Big Three Industries, 151

Billy (pony), 18–19, 29, 284, 285
Bishop, Bob, 225
Blaffer, John, 133
Block 67 (Houston), 208–9
Block 68 (Houston), 207–9
Blue Books, 130, 259, 296–97
Bluhdorn, Charles, 114
board of directors, value of, 303–6
Bochner, Brian, 271, 272
Bogart, Bill, 247–48
Bolton, Lloyd, 144, 146, 206, 220–21, 221,
    299
bombing missions
    general routine, 50–55
    specific missions, 55–74
    See also specific targets
Bond, Lewis, 192, 93
Bonn (Germany), 70–71
Bookout, John, 278
Boyd, Bill, 57
Boyd, Howard, 210
Boyd, William Paxton, 81
Boys and Girls Club of America, 262
Brady, Nicholas, 202
Bragdon, Cal, 56
branch banking, 226–27, 228–29, 248, 251n5,
    305–6
Brazil, 155
Brest (France), 58
Bright, Bum, 189, 190
Britain, Al, 232
Brown, Bill, 235
Brown, Cleve, 208
Brown, Lee, 270–71
Brown, Lew, 143–44
Brown Convention Center, 273, 274
Browning, Sterling, 96
Buck, E. O., 133, 144
Buenger, Walter, 279–80
Bulge, Battle of the, 70–71, 78
Bunten, Steve, 299
Burlington Northern Railroad, 260
Burns, Arthur, 141n6, 187

Burns, Robert
briefings, 50, 58, 65, 66, 69, 73
lessons learned from, 287
Ben Love's promotion to captain, 73
missions flown with Ben Love, 57–58, 66–67
Burr, Lt., 73–74
Burston, Howard DeWalden & Co., Ltd., 152–53. *See also* Burston & Texas Commerce Bank, Ltd.
Burston, Neville, 152–53, 156–57
Burston & Texas Commerce Bank, Ltd., 152–53, 154, 156–57, 160. *See also* Texas Commerce Bank
Bush, George H. W., 254, 257, 273–74, 279
Bush, Jeb, 155, 292
But Also Good Business (Buenger and Pratt), 279–80
Butcher, Bill, 232, 236–37
Butler, Roy, 309
Butt, Charles, 260
Byus, Grant, 144

Callaway, Pat, 196
Campaign Battle Star, 56
Caraway, Col., 76
Carnes, Webb, 83
Carothers, Durell, 209
Carter, Tom, 292
Casa de Esperanza de los Niños, *98*, 262
Cater, John, 268, 269, 299
CBM Engineers, 216
certificates of deposits (CDs), 111, 116n2
Champion Paper Company, 88, 91, 96, 253, 290
Chase Manhattan, 151, 182, 232, 236–37, 251n7, 307
Chateaudun Airport (France), 56
Chatham County (Ga.), 276–78
Cheeves Brothers department store, 24, 26, 283
Chemical Bank, 159, *159*, 193, 199, 203, 251n7. *See also* Shipley, Walter; Texas Commerce Bancshares, Inc.–Chemical Bank merger
Churchill, Winston, 41, 256
Cisneros, Henry, 188
CIT Financial Corporation, 100–102, *101*. *See also* Gibson-CIT
Citibank, 231
Citizens First National Bank of Tyler, 187
Cizik, Bob, 280
Clarke, Edward, 155
Clemens, R. E. (Buddy), 208, 209
Cohen, Ben, 308, 309
Colaco Engineers, Inc., 211
College Training Detachment, 33–34
Collie, Marvin, 308
Cologne (Germany), 66
Commerce Company, 158
communication, 301–2
competence, as leadership attribute, 311
Comptroller of the Currency, 189, 205n2, 232–33. *See also* Office of the Comptroller of the Currency (OCC)
Coneway, Peter, 259
Conover, Todd, 189, 232–33
Continental Illinois, 232–33
Cook, Lt., 68–69
Corcoran, Andrew, *177*
correspondent banking, 227
cotton industry, 5–6, 12–13, 219
Cowart, Donna, 292
Cox, Berry, 197
Cox, Edwin L., 260
Cox, James M., *277*
Cox, Martin, 198, 200
Cox, Tommy, 195, 225
Cox Enterprises, 276, *277*
Craig, Lt., 59–62, 62
Creeden, Carole, 225
Creekmore, Howard, 158, 242
Crow, Harlan, 197, *198*
Cruikshank, Thomas H., 260
Crum, Ed, 266–67
Crutcher, Bill, 86, 88, 89

Cullen Frost Bank, 194, 310
Cunningham, Bill, 261

Davies, Maj., 67
Davis, Bill (head of Montgomery Ward),
    110, 111
Davis, W. N. (Bill) (chemical engineer),
    144
"Death of the Hired Hand, The" (Frost), 310
Decherd, Robert, 200
DeLibero, Shirley, 271
Delta Kappa Epsilon, 29–30, 49, 80, 81, 84
Democratic Site Selection Committee,
    272–73
Dennis, Capt., 68–69, 70–71, 73–74
Deputy Lead, 53–54
Dickey, Charles (Preacher), 24, 27, 285
Disraeli, Benjamin, 312
Distinguished Flying Cross, 72–73, 79n6
Doherty, Robert P. (Bob), 118, 119, 122, 136–
    37, 308
Douglas Amendment, 189
Dowell, Cam, 195
Downtown Houston (organization), 281n4
Doyal, John, 225
Duffey, Bobby, 176, 295
Duncan, Charles
    Greater Houston Partnership, 268, 270
    Long-Term Strategy & Merger Commit-
        tee, 230, 242, 251n6
    photograph, 230
    as Texas Commerce board member, 190,
        304
    Young Presidents' Organization, 94, 95
Duncan, Howard, 155
Duncan, John, 94, 95, 114–15, 139, 196, 260
Dunn, John, 146, 147
Dyersburg (Tenn.), 39–40

Eaker, Ira, 41
Eaves, Barbara, 196
Ebanks, George, 144, 153
Echeverria, Luis, 154

Economic Summit (1990), 273, 275, 281n5
Eickhoff, Capt., 66–67
Eighth Air Force
    combat crew deaths, 42, 63–64
    lessons from, 286–88
    mission formations, 50–53, 66
    organization, 45
    in World War II, 40–42, 44–77
    See also Mighty Eighth Air Force Heri-
        tage Museum
Eisenhower, Dwight D., 78, 257
electricity, 27, 42n1, 282
Elkins, Jim, 139
Ellington Field (Tex.), 35–38
Ellsworth, Ralph, 81
El Paso Natural Gas Company, 164, 210
Empire State Building, 212, 217
energy, as leadership attribute, 311–12
Engleman, Gene, 194
Erickson, Beryl, 279
Esdorn, Richard, 302
Eurodollars, 151, 154, 160, 167n4
European Theater Campaign Ribbon, 56
Eyles, David, 246

Fadrique, Lloyd, 266
Fannin Bank, 203
Farben Chemical Works, 60, 62
Farrar, R. M., 121
Federal Deposit Insurance Corporation
    (FDIC), 229, 307–8
Federal Home Loan Bank, 308–9
Federal Reserve
    American General Insurance Company
        and Texas Commerce Bank relation-
        ship, 137–38, 141n6
    American National–Texas Commerce
        merger, 164, 165
    bank failures, 307–8
    Bank Holding Company Act, 158–59
    Beaumont State Bank–Texas Commerce
        merger, 164
    certificates of deposits, 161

Cullen Frost–First City merger denied, 194

MacGregor Park National Bank–Texas Commerce merger, 164, 165

merger policy, 187–90

money supply in late 1960s, 159–60

reserve requirements, 160

Texas Commerce–Austin National Bank merger denied, 187

Texas Commerce Bancshares approved, 162

Texas Commerce–Bexar County National Bank merger denied, 188

Texas Commerce possible merger with Chemical Bank or Chase Manhattan discussed, 232, 235–36, 246, 307

Federal Reserve Advisory Council, 187

Federal Reserve Bank of Dallas, 149–50, 183

Feeser, Katie, 22, 24, 285

Field, Steve, 220–21, 240

Financial Services Roundtable, 308

First City National Bank
assets acquired by Chemical, 309, 313n6
deposits, 123, 302
drop in earnings (1983), 218
and John Duncan, 114–15
as largest bank in Houston, 112, 125
merger with Cullen Frost, 194
real estate lending, 145, 222
recruits Ben Love for president, 139

First Interstate Bank, 313n6

First National Bank (Dallas), 191, 198

First National Bank of Boston, 146, 147

First National Bank of Hurst, 194

First National Bank of Seattle, 232

First National Bank of Stafford, 159, 159

First National City Bank, 106, 116n2, 182

First Republic Bank, 199, 220, 313n6

First United Bancorporation, 192

Fishburn, Maj., 59–62, 62

flak, as danger in B-17, 53, 54

Flamson, Dick, 230

Fluor, Bob, 254–55, 255, 304

Foley's department store, 89

Follis, Jim, 154

Ford, Gerald, 215

Ford, Henry, 311

Foy, Joe, 266, 266

Foy, Martha, 266

Frankfurt (Germany), 67–68

French prisoners of war, 74–75, 75

Freshfields, 157

Fronterhouse, Jerry, 190

Frost, Robert, 310

Frost, Tom, 194

Fuller, William, 194

Gaetz, Mike, 153

Galleria, 145, 146, 147

Galloway, Carl, 128

Gammage, Bob, 179

Garza Laguera, Eugenio, 304

George R. Brown Convention Center, 273, 274

Germany, 53–54, 59, 59, 74

Gerrard, Bob, 138–39, 144, 153

Gibbons, Jim (Hoot), 46, 47, 66, 67–73, 78n2

Gibson-CIT, 100–102, 104, 105, 289. See also Gibson Greeting Cards

Gibson Greeting Cards, 90, 98, 100–102. See also Gibson-CIT

GIFT-RAPS, Inc., 86–94
competition from Champion Paper Company, 96
customers, 89, 91, 92, 93–94
growth, 89–94
lessons learned from, 289–90
merger with Gibson Greeting Cards, 90, 98, 100
potential merger partners, 97–98
start-up, 86–89
suppliers, 88, 90–93, 96
Young Presidents' Organization tour, 95

Giles, Bob, 239

Gillis, Malcolm, 278

goals, long-term *versus* short-term, 302–3
Gockley, David, 265–66, 280
Goering, Hermann, 71
Goizueta, Roberto, 311–12
Golden, Sam, 233–34, 235
Goodson, Jim, *172*, 197, 198, *198,* 199, 200
Gorham, James, 66, 67–68
grades, importance of, 285, 300
Grand Conceptor Award for Engineering
    Excellence, 216
Grant, Jody, 163, 165, 170, 171, *171*
Grant, Joseph M., 205n2
Gray, Ed, 308–9
Great Bend (Kans.), 77
Great Depression, 6–13, 105–6, 107, 257
Greater Houston Convention & Visitors'
    Bureau, 272, 281n4
Greater Houston Partnership, 268–70, *269,*
    275, 281n4
Griffin, Gerry, 268
Grinstein, Gerald, 260
Gulf Building, 112, *113–14,* 117–18, 206–7
Gulnac, Lt., 59–62, *62*
Gunter, Terry, 225
Gutfreund, John, 230

Hanover (Germany), 66–67, 69–70
Harris, Bill, 275
Harris, Charley, 13
Harris, Jack, 110
Hawk, Don, 291–92, *293*
Heinzerling, John, 266–67
Herbert, Walter, 264
Hercules Concrete Pumping Service, Inc.,
    217
Herring, Robert (Bob), 95, 96, *134,* 135
Hibbert, Jim, 225
Hickson, Richard, *240*
Highland Park State Bank, 188, 247
Hill, John, 267, 281n1
Hillebrand, Capt., 63–64, *65*–66
Hines, Gerald (Gerry)
    financing, 145–46, 147

GIFT-RAPS plant, 98, 101
    Pennzoil Place, 207
    Personage and Birds sculpture, *213,* 216
    relationship with Texas Commerce, 209–
        10, 220
    Texas Commerce Tower, 210, 211, 212
Hines, Jeff, 273, 292
Hines, Wendy, 273
Hiroshima bombing, 77–78
Hirsch, Maurice, 264
Hobby, Bill, 228
Hocher, Herbert, 89
Hogan, Lee, 268
Hogg, Ima, 264
Hoglund, Forrest, 196, 259, 261
Holder, Lewis, 81
Holmes, Ann, 216, 264, 265
Holmes, Walter, 100–102, *101,* 105
Holt, Joe, 225
Hong Kong, 155
Hook, Harold, 141n6, *231,* 244, 251n6
Hoover, Herbert, 118, 257
Hopewell School, 13–14, 17
Hopewell (Tex.), 8–14
Horne, Howard, 207–8, 209
Horner, Jack, 156, 294–95
Hoskins, Jack, 39, 47, 55–57
Houck, Harvey, 111
Houston
    banking industry, 106–7
    housing situation after World War II,
        85–86
    Ben Love's early exposure to, 36–37
    oil industry, 143, 144
    after World War II, 82–83
Houston Advertising Club, 148, 167n1
Houston Astros, 274
Houston Chamber of Commerce, 264, 267–
    70, 281n4. *See also* Greater Houston
    Partnership
Houston Chronicle, 244
Houston Convention Fund, 275
Houston Economic Development Council,

268, 269, 270, 281n4. *See also* Greater Houston Partnership
Houston Endowment, 136–37, 158–59, 165, 166, 167n5, 242
Houston Grand Opera, 262, 264–67, *266*, 280
Houston Host Committee, 272–75, 280
Houston Oilers, 274
Houston Sports Association, 274
Houston World Trade Association, 281n4
Houston Youth Symphony & Ballet, 262
Hrdlicka, Charlie, 228
Hughes, Howard, 278
Hunt, Woody, 260
Hunter, Robert
  due diligence, 246
  international banking, 153, 154–55, 158
  loan administration, 223–24, *224*, 228

I. G. Farben Chemical Works, 60, *62*
Icken, Andy, 271–72
Independent Bankers Association, 179, 228
integrity, as leadership attribute, 312
InterFirst Corporation
  acquisition of banks in Tyler and Houston, 204
  acquisition of Citizens First National Bank denied, 187
  loses money in 1983, 218
  merger with Austin Bancshares, 188
  merger with First United Bancorporation, 192
  merger with Republic, 199
  Texas Commerce explores possible merger with, 190, 229
interstate banking, 200–202, 226–32
Irving Bank & Trust, 195
Ivy, David, 239

Japan, bombing of, 77–78
Japhet, Bill, 241
Joe (man befriended by Ben Love's parents), 284

John Hancock Building, 217
Johnson, David, 201
Johnson, Dick, 258, 259, 260
Johnson, Hugh, 25
Johnson, Lady Bird, 155–56, 193, *215*, 304
Johnson, Lyndon, 308
Johnson, Oren, 29–30
Johnson, Philip, 207
Jones, Jesse
  Block 68 property, 207
  business philosophy, 252, 279–80
  customer leads, 127
  Gulf Building, 112, *113*, 114, 117–18, 206
  and Houston Endowment, 121, 136, 166
  as inspiration to Ben Love, 125
  legacy, 121
  management loyalty to, 123
  portrait, *119*
  real estate lending, 145
  suburban banking, 158
  and Gus Wortham, 135–36
Jones Hall, 207, 209, *214*, 217, 264
Jordan, Barbara, 204, 244, *254*, 254–56, 304
Jordan, Don, 242, 244
J. P. Morgan (firm), 203, 222, 231, 251n7
Justiss, Thomas, 38

Kadourie, Lawrence, 155
Kamin, Jake, 146, 147
Kassel (Germany), 64, 65
Kearney (Neb.), 38–39
Keller, Capt., 58–59, 64
Kelley's Oyster Bar, 208
Kennedy, James C. (Jim), 276–78, *277*, 304
Keough, Jim, 157
Ketchum, MacLeod & Grove, 148, 292
Kilgore, Joe, 279
Kinder, Nancy, 275
Knox, John Jay, 205n2
Kozmetsky, George, 170, 257
Kress store, 93–94

LaBoon, Bruce, 228, 237, 246, *247*
Lacey, Brig. Gen., 73

Landry, Tom, 32, 34, 81, 278, 279
Lane, Bill, 95–96, 111, 115, 133, *134*, 134–35
LaRue, Dick, 84
Las Colinas (Tex.), 197
Lavine, Ken, 237
Lawrence, Harold
  GIFT-RAPS founding, 86
  GIFT-RAPS operations, 88, 89, 93, 96
  retirement, 98, 100
Lay, Ken, 275
Layden, A. J. (Jay), 208–9
Lea, Steve, 225
Lead Crew, 45, *46*, 47, 52–54, 74
leadership, importance of, 310–12
Lee, El Franco, 271
Lee, Lawrence, 145, 146
LeMaistre, Charles A. (Mickey), 258, 259–
  60, 261, *261*, 262
LeMaistre, Joyce, *261*
lessons learned
  from Army Air Corps, 286–88
  from the farm, 282–85
  from GIFT-RAPS and Gibson-CIT,
    289–90
  from Texas Commerce, 291–310
Levit, Maurice, 209
Levit's Jewelers, 209
Liddell, Sapp, Zivley & Brown, 159
Liddell, Sapp, Zivley & LaBoon, 228
light rail line, on Fannin Street, 270–72
Lindsay, Jon, 273, 274
Linz (Austria), 74–75, *75*
loan limits, 149, 154, 167n2, 178, 232–33
Lockwood National Bank, 159, *159*
London, 48–49, 152–53, 154–55, 156–57
Long, Huey, 7, 15
Longwell, Harry, 260
Love, Benton Fooshee, Jr.
  in Army Air Corps, 31–78, *38, 46, 62*,
    286–88
  in banking, 104–250, 291–310
  birth, 1
  in business, 83–102

children, 89, 103n10
college education, 25–26, 29–31, 80–
  81, 84
combat decorations, 56, 58, 64, 67, 72–73,
  79n6
combat tour, 44–76
community service, 257–81, *261, 266, 269*
debate participation and scholarship,
  22–24
early ambitions, 13–14
early life, 5–6
elementary education, 13–14, 17–21
farm life, 8–13, 282–85
Great Depression, 6–8, 282–86
high school education, 21–24
Louisiana visit with Allen relatives, 14–17
marriage, 78n2, *85*
move to Austin, 28–29
move to Houston, 85–86
political interests, 252–57
promotion to 1st Lieutenant, 65
promotion to captain, 73, 76
promotion to chairman and CEO of
  Texas Commerce Bancshares, 166
promotion to Lead Crew, 45, *46*, 47
promotion to president of Texas Commerce Bank, 139, *140*, 141
retirement, 249
return to U.S. after VE Day, 76–77
speech lessons, 9–10, 22
Texas Bankers Association speech,
  179–85
transportation to school, 18–19, 20–22
See also specific organizations
Love, Benton Fooshee, Jr. photographs, *ii*
  Army Air Corps, *38, 46, 62*
  Greater Houston Partnership, *269*
  Houston Grand Opera, *266*
  with Lloyd Bentsen, *253*
  with Margaret Love, *85, 261, 263*
  M. D. Anderson Cancer Center, *261*
  Texas Commerce, *172, 177, 247*
  with Walter Shipley, *243, 253*

Love, Benton Fooshee, Sr.
  as cotton dealer, 5–6, 219
  as Democrat, 257
  early life, 2–4
  family, 1
  illness and death, 27–28
  job loss during Great Depression, 6–7
  lessons learned from, 283, 284, 285
  life on farm, 9–13
  move to farm, 7–9
  photograph, 3
  transportation, 18–19, 20–21
Love, Benton (grandson of Ben Love), 79n3
Love, Henry Benton, 1–2, 3
Love, Jan. See Simmons, Jan
Love, Jeffrey Benton
  and Ben Love, 94, 283, 288
  birth, 89, 103n10
  community service, 262
  education and work life, 97, 103n10, 271
  and M. D. Anderson Cancer Center, 258, 259
  photograph, 97
Love, Julie, 99, 103n10, 262, 283, 288
Love, Louisa Fielding, 2
Love, Margaret
  and Ben Love, 78n2, 84–85, 85, 288
  cancer bouts, 258
  children, 89, 103n10
  community service, 262, 264, 265
  GIFT-RAPS work, 88–89
  and Hamilton, Ohio, 96
  and Houston Grand Opera, 266
  and M. D. Anderson Cancer Center, 258, 259, 261, 262
  and Nancy Adams, 94
  photographs, 85, 261, 263, 266
  and Ralph Yarborough, 103n8
Love, Mollie Fooshee, 2
Love, Nell Scott
  correspondence with Ben Love during World War II, 48–49
  death of husband, 27–28

as Democrat, 257
early life, 4–5
during Great Depression, 6
importance of education, 13–14, 17–19, 21–22
lessons learned from, 282–83, 284, 285, 298
life on farm, 7–13
move to Austin, 28–29
move to San Antonio, 30
photograph, 4, 38
standards, 20–21
work at GIFT-RAPS, 89
Ludwigshafen (Germany), 60–62, 62
Lyle, Lewis, 276, 277–78
Lyon, Jimmy, 104, 108, 112, 115, 176, 290–91
Lyttle, Capt., 66–67

MacGregor Park National Bank, 163, 164, 165
Maclin, Todd, 225
Magdeburg (Germany), 64
Magnolia Paper Company, 83–84, 86
Maignot Line, 68, 74–75, 75
Main Street National Bank, 195
Maltby, Capt., 66–67
management, decentralized versus centralized, 184, 295–96
management committees, 294–95
Mann, Bill, 127–28, 129
Manufacturers Hanover Corp., 232, 251n7
Margaret and Ben Love Clinic, 261, 262. See also University of Texas M. D. Anderson Cancer Center
Mary (maid in Louisiana governor's mansion), 15–16
Mason, Elvis, 203
Mason, Paul, 192
Mauthausen concentration camp, 75–76
McCall, George, 81
McCashan, Harris, 121
McCashan, S. M., 121
McCaskill, Beverly, 293, 297, 312n3

McClelland Engineers, Inc., 216
McClure, Sam, 22, 23, 38
McClusky, Capt., 59–62, *62*
McCombs, Red, 260
McConnell, Ched, 178
McDade, Tom
   centralized securities system, 296
   communication, 301–2
   holding company, 162–63
   international banking, 153
   mergers, 164, 170, 171, 195
   photograph, *172*
   "puts and calls," 157
   regulatory politics, 186–187
McFadden Act, 189
McGillicuddy, John, 232
McKean, Lonnie, 134
McKean, Margaret. *See* Love, Margaret
McKinney, Joe, 240, *240*
McLean, J. W. (Bill), 121–23
McLean, Scott, 176, 197, *198*, 200
McMahen, Charles, 132, 163, 195, 228, 297
McMullen, Jon, 274
McNair, Lesley J., 69
MCorp, 199, 313n6
M. D. Anderson Cancer Center, 258–62, *261*
Mecom, John, 136–37, 167n5
Mercantile National Bank, 205n3
Mercantile Texas Corporation, 189, 191, 198
mergers, lessons learned from, 289. *See also*
   Texas Commerce Bancshares, Inc.–
   Chemical Bank merger; Texas Com-
   merce Bancshares, Inc. mergers and
   acquisitions
Merseberg (Germany), 55–56, 63–64
Metropolitan Transit Authority of Harris
   County, Texas, 270–72
Metz Fortress (France), 68–69
Mexico City, 154
Meyers, Randy, 259
Mighty Eighth Air Force Heritage Museum,
   276–78, 288. *See also* Eighth Air Force
Milburn, Douglas, 273

Milby, Charles, 208
Milby Hotel, 208
Miller, Robert, 271
Miller, Zell, 276–78
Miró, Joan, 213, *213, 214,* 216
Mischer, Walter, 227, 228
Mitchell, George, 94–95
Moncrief, Deborah, 260
Moncrief, Monty, 262
Moncrief, W. A. (Tex), 260, 262
money center banks, 149–50, 151
Montgomery County Bank, 229
Montgomery Ward, 100, 108, 110, 207–8
Moriniere, Jack, 154
Morrie (navigator), 44
Morton, Merriman, 205
Mosbacher, Bob, 133, 304
Mulvey, Patrick, 258, 259–60
Munster (Germany), 67, 71–72
Murchison, Robert, 197
Murphree, Gene, 111
Musolino, Joe, 190

Nagasaki bombing, 77–78
Namur (Belgium), 59, *59*
Nassau, 154, 157, 160, 161
National Bank of Commerce
   acquired by NationsBank, 313n6
   deposits, 106–7, *123*
   and Houston Endowment, 167n5
   merger with Texas National Bank, *118,*
     122–24
   pre-merger history, 117–18, 121, 125
   real estate lending, 145
   See also Texas Commerce Bank
National Loan Bank, 239, 246
NationsBank, 313n6
Nelly, Hank, 299
New Deal banking legislation, 218
Newton, Jon, 244
New York Stock Exchange, 166, *177*
nightmares, about combat missions, 45, 55
Nixon, Richard, 162, 163

Noel, Bill, 164–65, 178
Nolen, Norman, 154
Norden Bombsites, 53, 54, 70
Northern France Campaign Battle Star, 58
North Freeway State Bank, 163
Nuremberg (Germany), 65–66

O'Brien, Mr., 20, 21
Office of the Comptroller of the Currency
    (OCC)
    anti-Texas bias, 232, 233, 309
    bank failures, 307–8
    examinations of Texas Commerce, 222–
        23, 233–35
    reading mood of, 186
    See also Comptroller of the Currency
oil industry, 143, 144, 218, 219, 220, 221–22
Oldfield, Keith, 225
Olivi, Fred J., 77
Olsen, Capt., 57–58
One Shell Plaza, 145
Onstead, Robert (Bob), 268, 269
optimism, as leadership attribute, 311
Ostend (Belgium), 312n1

Pan American Bank, 176
Paramount Pictures, 196
Paris High School (Tex.), 21–24
Paris (Tex.), 8–13
patriotism, 287–88
Patterson, Bill, 232–33
Patton, George, 68, 69
Pei, Eileen, 213
Pei, I. M., 210–12, 213, 214, 215, 216, 217
Pelli, Cesar, 210
Penn Square Bank, 232–33
Pennzoil Place, 207, 209
Peoples Bank, 203
Personage and Birds (Miró), 213, 213, 214, 215,
    216
Phillips, Bill, 163, 164
Pistor, Charlie, 190
Pitzer, Benny, 229

Plaza of the Americas, 195, 199
Polebrook, East Anglia (England), 44–45,
    47–48
Port Neches (Tex.), 188
position logs, 286–87, 312n1
Post, Wiley, 279
Poston, Capt., 73–74
practice missions, 47
Pratt, Joe, 279–80
Presley, Dewey, 190
Preston, Lew, 231
prime rate, 160, 167n6
prisoners of war, French, 74–75, 75
Procter & Gamble, 81–82
Prudential Bache, 189
Pugh, Bill, 126, 129
Purcell, Jim, 65
"puts and calls," 156–57

Quayle, Dan, 254, 274

Ralph, Fred (Fritz)
    military service, 46, 47, 50, 66, 67, 68–73
    Texas Commerce Tower project, 212–13
Rayburn, Sam, 308
Reagan, Ronald, 232
Reagan State Bank, 158, 159, 159, 163
Reconstruction Finance Corporation, 118,
    279
recruiting and training, 299–301
Reed, Alan, 63–66
Reed, John, 231
Rehrauer, Pete, 129, 133, 146
Republican Convention (1992), 272–76, 280
Republican Site Selection Committee, 272–
    75, 281n5
Republic Bancorporation, 190, 191, 198, 199,
    218, 229
Republic Bancshares, 188
Revere Copper & Brass Company, 88, 92
River Oaks Bank & Trust Company
    advertising, 110–11
    board of directors, 110–11

River Oaks Bank & Trust Company
(*continued*)
budget, 109–10
call program, 109, 131
certificates of deposits, 111
charity work, 257–58
deposits, 109, 111–12, *112*
history, 116n1
inventory financing, 90
lessons learned from, 290–91
Ben Love as outside director, 104, 105
Ben Love as president and CEO, 104–5,
107–12, 115
size, 106–7
Roberts, M. L., 93–94
Robertson, Ruben, 96
Robicheaux, Sgt., 70
Rodman, E. G. (Rod), 164–65, 178
Roff, Hugh, 210, *213*, 216
Rogers, Warner, 144, 147
Roosevelt, Franklin Delano, 41, 118, 279, 282
Roper, Leonard, 69–70
Rose, Jesse, 29
Royal Air Force, 41
Rural Electrification Administration, 42n1,
282

Saarbrucken (Germany), 57
Sakowitz, Robert, 272
Salvation Army, 262, 264
San Antonio, 188
San Diego, 274, 275
Sapp, Charlie, 137, 159, 162
Savage, Jim, 220–21
Savannah Chamber of Commerce, 277–78
Saxon, James J., 122
Schnitzer, Kenneth, 37, 146, 147, 220, 267,
268
Schnitzer, Max, 83
Schnitzer, Ralph, Jr., 32, 37, 83
Schnitzer, Ralph, Sr., 37, 83, 280
Schuler, Buck, 276, 277–78
Scott, William, 4, 21

Searls, David, 114, 139, 258
Sears, 89, 91, 100, 108, 189, 202
Seay, Greg, 226
Securities and Exchange Commission
(SEC), 234–35, 246
Security Pacific Bank, 230
Sedlak, John, 271–72
"sell not tell" philosophy, 129, 296
Senior, David, *293*
Service to Mankind Award, 262, 264
S. H. Kress store, 93–94
Shapiro, Marc, 190, 237, 297
Shell Oil Company, 264, 266, 273, 294
Sheppard Field, 32–33
Shilcutt, Bruce, 223
Shipley, Walter
explores merger with Texas Commerce,
232, 237–38
fair treatment of Texas Commerce after
merger, 310
Ben Love's gratitude toward, 250
meets with Texas Commerce stakehold-
ers, 242, 244, 246–48
photographs, *243, 253*
promises Texas Commerce autonomy
after merger, 244, 249
Texas Commerce–Chemical merger
announced, 245–46
See also Chemical Bank; Texas Com-
merce Bancshares, Inc.–Chemical
Bank merger
Shirley, Terry, 125–26
Shivers, Allan, 187
Shryock, Larry, 225, *240*
Silverman, Sam, 241
Simmons, Jan, *98*, 103n10, 262, 283, 288
Simmons, Tom, *98*
Simpson, A. D. (Dee), 118, *119*, 124, 127
Slaughter, Enos (Country), 34
Sloan, Albert D., 295–96
Smith, Alfred E., 272
Smith, Charles, 131–32, 297
Smith, Harry K., 133, 151, 189, 190, 239

Smith, Lowell A. (Stretch), 228

Smith, Truett, 185

Smith, William F. (pilot), 212

Smith, William French (U.S. Attorney General), 189

Soest (Germany), 72–73

Southern Bank & Trust, 195

Southland Financial Corporation, 197

South Texas National Bank, 121, 150. *See also* Texas National Bank

Southwest Bancshares, 189

St. Germain, Fernand, 233

Standard Industrial Classification codes, 128–29

Standard Metropolitan Statistical Area plan, 170, *171*

Standard & Poor's, 308

Stanford Research, 264, 267

Steinhart, Ron, 195

Steitz, Warren, 67–68

Stewart, Bobby, 190

Stewart, Col., 71–72

Stirring Life of William Penn, The, 19–20

Straus, Bob, 37, 280

Straus, Lee, 195, 292, *293*

Strauss, Richard, 195

Strickland, Bob, 231

Stuttgart Airfield (Germany), 58–59

Sun Banks, 202

Sununu, Jon, 274

superstitions, and rituals before bombing missions, 50

suppliers, lessons learned from, 289–9c

Tacquard, Eleanor, 28

Tacquard, Fred, 28, 29

Tacquard, Jane, 28

Tacquard, Mackie, 28

Tandy, Charles, 194

Tandy, William, 125

Taub, Sam, 118, 137

Taylor, Bill, 232, 235–36, 307

Taylor, T. O., 145, 146

Team Bank, 313n6

Texas American Bank, 192–94, 205n2

Texas Aviation Hall of Fame, 276, 278–79, 288

Texas Bankers Association, 179, 179–85, 186, 228

Texas banking law, 149–50, 226–28

Texas banks
challenges in 1970s, 180–86
consolidation, 309–10, 313n6
deposits, 149–50
loan limits, 149, 154, 167n2
regulation, 185
See also specific banks

Texas Children's Hospital, 257–58

Texas Commerce Bancshares, Inc.
and American General Insurance Company, 165
analysis of performance, 306–10
board of directors, 196–200, 303–6
branch banking, 228–29, 248
call program, 198, 199, 226, 248
communication, 301–2
correspondent banking, 227
in Dallas–Fort Worth Metroplex, 191–200
decentralization, 184, 295–96
de novo banks, 171, 172, 303
earnings per share, 168, *169*, 178, 218–19
energy loans, 220, 298
Executive Council, 301–2
financial performance, 168–69, *169*, 178, 203–5
in Florida, 202
formation, 162–65
goals, 298–99, 302–3
growth, 168–70
interstate banking, 200–202, 229–32
loan limit, 178
loans, 220–26, *221, 224*, 250n3, 298–99
Long-Term Strategy & Merger Committee, 171–72, 229, *230, 231*, 242, 251n6, 304

Texas Commerce Bancshares, Inc.
(*continued*)
Ben Love promoted to chairman and
CEO, 166
management committees, 294–95
member banks, *173–75*
and Mid-America Energy Belt, 200–202,
310
New York Stock Exchange listing, 166,
177, *177*
Office of the Comptroller of the Currency examinations, 222–23, 233–35
OnePlus, 249
organization, 292–94, 305–6
personnel recruitment, 172
priorities in 1983, 202–4
real estate loans, 220–21, 222–23
recruiting and training, 299–301
regulatory challenges, 187–91
return on assets, *169*, 203
return on equity, *169*
television advertising, 196, 248–49
in Wyoming, 201
See also Texas Commerce Bank
Texas Commerce Bancshares, Inc.–
Chemical Bank merger
announced, *245*, 245–46
approval by Federal Reserve and SEC,
246
approval by Texas Commerce and Chemical stockholders, 248
approval by Texas Commerce board, 242,
244
compatibility of partners, 239–41
Dallas office, 199–200
discussion with Federal Reserve, 232,
235–36, 307
discussion with stockholders, 241–42
due diligence, 246–48
exploration of, 232
financial performance after, 249
in *Houston Chronicle*, 244
nonperforming loans, 239, 246

as part of Texas banking consolidation,
313n6
pending, 229
photograph of Walter Shipley and Ben
Love, *243*
results, 248–50, 310
terms, 237–39
Texas Commerce Bancshares, Inc. mergers
and acquisitions
Airline National Bank, 163
American National Bank, 163–64, 165
Arlington Bank & Trust, 195
Austin National Bank merger explored,
187–88
Bankers Trust merger explored, 232
Beaumont State Bank, 164
Bexar County National Bank merger ex-
plored, 188
Chase Manhattan merger explored, 232,
236–37
First United Bancorporation merger
explored, 192
InterFirst merger explored, 190, 229
Irving Bank & Trust, 195
J. P. Morgan merger explored, 231
MacGregor Park National Bank, 163, 164,
165
Main Street National Bank, 195
merger strategy, 170–72, 176–86
North Freeway State Bank, 163
Pan American Bank, 176
Reagan State Bank, 163
Republic Bancorporation merger ex-
plored, 189–90, 229
Security Pacific Bank merger explored,
230
Southern Bank & Trust, 195
Texas American Bank merger explored,
192–94
Trust Company of Georgia merger ex-
plored, 231
Union Bank of Fort Worth, 194
West Texas banks, 164–65

Texas Commerce Bank
  advertising, 147, 148, *148*, 167n1, 292
  and American General Insurance Company, 137–38, 141n6
  Bahrain operations, 155
  Ben Love's promotion to president, 139, 141
  and Big Three Industries, 151
  Blue Books, 130, 259, 296–97
  board of directors, 133, *134*
  Brazil operations, 155
  budget, 131–32
  and Burston, Howard DeWalden & Co., Ltd., 152–53
  and Burston & Texas Commerce Bank, Ltd., 152–53, 154, 156–57, 160
  call program, 127–31
  certificates of deposits, 160
  deposits, *123*, 161
  earnings per share, *161*
  Family Banking Center, 147–48, 160–61, 167n1
  family tree, *120*
  gifts to depositors, 160–61
  growth management, 291–94
  Hong Kong operations, 155
  and Houston Endowment, 158–59
  international banking, 150–57, *152*, 309
  liquidity, 176–78
  logo, 148, *148*, 167n1
  London operations, 152–53, 154–55, 156–57
  Mexico City operations, 154
  and money center banks, 151
  name change, 141n1, 148, *148*
  Nassau operations, 154, 157, 160, 161
  officers, 143–44, 149
  organization chart lacking, 125–26
  "puts and calls," 156–57
  reaction to change, 132–33
  real estate lending, 144–47
  recruits Ben Love for senior vice president, 115–16

  reputation, 112, 114, 115
  retirement policy, 138
  status when Ben Love arrived, 124–25
  Tokyo operations, 154
  Venezuela operations, 155–56
  and Gus Wortham, 137–38
  See also Texas Commerce Bancshares, Inc.; Texas Commerce Shareholders Company
Texas Commerce Bank–Brownsville, 241
Texas Commerce Bank–Dallas, 195–96, 197, 198–200
Texas Commerce Bank–Fort Worth, 194
Texas Commerce Bank–Greenway Plaza, 197
Texas Commerce Bank–Houston, 199, 233–34
Texas Commerce Bank–Katy Freeway, 171
Texas Commerce Bank–River Oaks, 239
Texas Commerce Bank–The Woodlands, 229
Texas Commerce Center, 206–7
Texas Commerce Shareholders Company, 159, *159*, 160, 161, 162
Texas Commerce Tower
  assembling the land, 207–10
  construction, 199, 216–17
  deciding to build, 198–99, 206–7
  dedication, *215*, 216
  designing the building, 210–13
  model, *198, 211*
  sculpture, 213, *213, 214, 215*, 216
Texas Crude Oil & Gas Corp., 196
Texas legislature, 179, 186, 226–29, 254, 256
Texas Medical Center, 270–72
Texas National Bank
  deposits, *123*
  formation, 150
  merger with National Bank of Commerce, 115, *118*, 122–24
  pre-merger history, 121–22
  real estate lending, 145
  See also Texas Commerce Bank

Texas National Bank of Commerce of Houston. *See* Texas Commerce Bank
Thalaneus, Margie, 84
Thornton, Bob, 199, 205n3
Thornton, R. L., 205n3
3D/International, 210–11
351st Bomb Group, 44–76, 286–89
Tilton, Kenneth, 297
Toggery, The, 29–30, 80
Tokyo, 154
Tomforde, Mike, 111
Torres, Tony, 223
Townley, John, 144, 220, *221*, 296, 299
Trammell Crow, *198*, 199, 220
Trinity University, 24, 25–26, 29
Truman, Harry, 77–78, 257, 311
Trust Company of Georgia, 231
Turner Construction Co., 217
243rd Army Air Force, 77
Tyler Doctrine, 187
Tyson, Mike, 291–92, *292*

Underwood, David, 271
Union Bank of Fort Worth, 194
Union National Bank, 121, 150. *See also* Texas National Bank
United Energy Resources, 210
University of Texas, 29–30, 49, 80–81, 84, 257, 300
University of Texas M. D. Anderson Cancer Center, 258–62, *261*
Upton, King, 146

Valenti, Jack, 32–33
VE Day, 74
Venezuela, 155–56
Vernon (Tex.), 1, 5–8
Von Rundstedt, Gerd, 70–71

Wainerdi, Richard, 271
Wakefield, Gray, 266
Walsh, John, 268, 270
Waltrip, Bob, 278

Wasserstrum, Harriet, 224–25
Wear, Dr., 24, 27
Weaver, Max, 98, 100, 105
Webb, Hall, 225
Welch, Jack, 311–12
West Paris Elementary School (Tex.), 17–21, 284, 285
White, Mark, 228
Whitmire, Kathy, 272, 273, 274, 275
Whitmore, John
  and Lloyd Bolton, 146
  family banking, 147
  and Gus Wortham, 137, 139
  international banking, 153
  land assemblage, 207–8
  and Ben Love, 115–16, 132–33, 134, 166–67
  London operations, 157
  mortgage warehousing, 145
  personnel appointments, 115–16, 144, 198
  philosophy, 129, 132–33
  retirement, 166
  stock share sales, 176–78
  and Texas Commerce Bancshares, 162
  as Texas Commerce Bank chairman and CEO, 139, *140*
  as Texas Commerce Bank president, 123–24, 126, 137
  and Texas Commerce Shareholders Company, 159
Wichita Falls (Tex.), 32–33
Wick, Merle, *177*
Williams, Will, 300
Willome, Jack, 247
Wilson, John, 179
Wilson, Terry, 197, *198*
Wise, Patricia, 265
Wodje, Alex, 39, 55–56
Wooden, Ray, 89
Woodson, Ben, 95, 137–38, 139
Woolworth's, 89
work ethic, 283–84, 312

Workman, Rusty, 197
World Presidents' Organization, 102n7
World War II
    attack on Pearl Harbor, 26
    combat tour, 44–76
    following progress of, 27, 30–31
Wortham, Gus
    as American General Insurance founder,
        95, 118, 121
    financial support of arts, 264, 266
    and Jesse Jones, 135–36
    and John Whitmore, 137
    as mentor, 133–38, 135, 139
    and Texas Commerce Bank, 137–38
Wortham, Lyndall, 266

Wortham Theatre, 280
Wright, Gary, 240, 240
Wriston, Walter, 303
Wyatt, Oscar, 278
Wyatt Boiler Works, 127–28
Wyoming Bancorporation, 201

Yarborough, Ralph, 86, 103n8, 252–54
Young, Greg, 198
Young, Harold, 151
Young Presidents' Organization, 94–96,
    102n7, 252–53, 257

Zeiss Optical Instrument factory, 73–74
Zimmerman, Stuart, 259

ISBN 1-58544-489-8

DATE DUE

			Printed in USA

HIGHSMITH #45230